Golden Verses:
Poetry of the Augustan Age

THE FOCUS CLASSICAL LIBRARY

Golden Verses:
Poetry of the Augustan Age

PAUL T. ALESSI

Previously published by Focus Publishing/R. Pullins Company

Focus an imprint of
Hackett Publishing Company

P.O. Box 44937
Indianapolis, Indiana 46244-0937
www.hackettpublishing.com

ISBN 13: 978-1-58510-064-4

Cover: Tellus, Goddess of the Earth. Panel from the Ara Pacis. 13-9 BCE. Copyright Nimatallah /Art Resource, N.Y. Museum of the Ara Pacis, Rome, Italy.

18 17 16 15   3 4 5 6 7 8 9

CONTENTS

PREFACE

This book is designed for the general reading public and for students and teachers in courses on the literature of the Augustan Age. Almost all courses on Augustan Age literature include the *Aeneid* of Vergil and Ovid's *Metamorphoses*. To cover the broad range of other works and authors of the period teachers and students must buy numerous other books from which normally only a quarter of the poems (at best) are read and discussed, or teachers are reduced to distributing massive amounts of photocopies simply to provide modest samplings from the great poets of the period. It is my hope that this volume will be useful in the classroom and be appealing to the public in its own right.

I have tried to offer translations that are accurate, vigorous, fresh, and rhythmic. In making this anthology, I have followed a few simple principles. With the exception of two passages from the second book of the *Georgics*, I have translated complete poems and books. The two passages referred to are so well-known and appreciated that I did not think it was possible to omit them in any selection from the *Georgics*, and, besides, they are self-containing and powerful enough to be read and valued on their own. I have not included any selections from the *Aeneid* or the *Metamorphoses*. Their inclusion in their entirety would produce a prodigious and unwieldy tome and it would be difficult to make any one selection. I refer the reader and teacher to the number of available and inexpensive translations of both texts

I have preserved the general shape and have retained the structure, line-division, and couplet and stanza form of the originals. The translations are not so literal as to be stilted nor too free to puzzle and frustrate the reader of Latin. Since it is impossible to reproduce the sounds of the Latin in an English translation, I have concentrated on attempting to capture the tone and diction. When the original language is elevated or vulgar, so too is that of the translation. I hope that the modern reader of these translations can hear the living voices of those poets who delighted an audience of two thousand years ago.

I wish to thank profusely Ms. Theresa Lu Koch for her generous assistance in editing this volume. Because of her unflagging work, her constant encouragement, and, most importantly, her friendship, I dedicate this book to her.

INTRODUCTION

On 12 May, 2 BCE Caesar Augustus formally dedicated the temple
to Mars Ultor (Mars the Avenger) which he had vowed decades before
on the eve of the Battle of Philippi in 42 BCE. The temple rose at the
end of a magnificent colonnaded courtyard that made up the Forum of
Augustus. This complex of forum and temple was the culmination of a
vast building program of Octavian/Augustus, was extremely admired
in antiquity, and was included in Pliny's (HN 36.102) list of the three
most beautiful buildings in the city of Rome. The functions and activi-
ties held in this complex attest to its importance. Provincial governors
began their office from here; here the senate deliberated declarations of
war and awarded triumphs to victorious generals who then dedicated
to the god their crowns and scepters and the captured standards of
enemies; the feasts of the Salii were held here; here boys assumed the
toga of manhood; and, most significantly, a kind of foreign office was
established from which the provinces were administered. The design,
architecture, and art also lent to the complex's propagandistic value, its
polysemic statement of Augustan ideals, and its synthesis of multipli-
cate political views in Roman history. In addition, the "Hall of Fame"
of prominent men in Roman life, sculpted and placed in the colonnade
of the Forum, indicates Augustus' desire to be included among his Ro-
man predecessors and to place before the eyes of the Roman people his
political achievements, adaptations, and innovations. In many ways the
polysemous virtues suggested by the Forum of Augustus parallel the
values, principles, and positions expressed and intimated in the literature
of the age, a period roughly chronological with the vowing of the temple
to Mars Ultor (42 BCE) and its dedication in 2 BCE.

The poetry of the Augustan Age has many references and levels.
Far from being monolithic and narrowly restricted to a political pro-
gram favored by Octavian/Augustus or anti-Augustan in its stance

and ideology, the literature of the period shows a complex degree of sophistication, evolution, experimentation, and creativity. The poets of the age, like their Latin predecessors, relied on and adapted Greek genres. For example, Horace experimented with the meters, tenor, and themes of Archilochus, Sappho, and Alcaeus among others. Propertius claimed to be the Roman Callimachus, a model also for Vergil who expanded the bucolic genre, and combined references to Roman history and politics and to contemporary literary concerns and issues. Following in the footsteps of Cornelius Gallus, Propertius revitalized elegy, and Ovid manipulated myth, religion, and elegiac conventions in his varied works. As a religious calendar the *Fasti* far outstrips Hesiod's *Works and Days*; the *Metamorphoses* is epic in its scope, and in poetic treatment unique; and the *Heroides* in elegiac couplets fictionalizes well-known women of myth and epic. The audience of the Augustan poets expected and appreciated the complex and creative adaptations of the literary tradition. Readers and listeners were treated to bold imagery, deft characterizations, and sometimes poignant and profound views on life and circumstances interspersed with historical, social, and political comment on contemporary events and mores. The poets, too, were as diverse as their treatments, genres, and approaches to their poetic art and practice. Some of the differences can be attributed to the chronological gap in age. Propertius, Tibullus, and Ovid were young during the years of the power struggle between Antony and Octavius. It is the civil war between these two rival dynasts that engages them. Few references and little attention are directed toward the political struggles of Julius Caesar, his death, or the throes of a dying Republic. For Horace and Vergil, however, the turmoil of the late republic and the dictatorship of Julius Caesar shaped their view of historical imperatives and bolstered their yearning for a day of peace, a stable society, and restored values. The older poets of the age reflected on moral and political issues and ideals; the younger generation enjoyed the benefits of the Pax Augusta. With their emphasis on the transcendental power of love they avoided direct engagement with the Augustan state yet filled their poems with themes shared by all the poets of the period.

Recent scholarship on Augustan literature has discarded the idea of anti-Augustan or pro-Augustan attitudes and intimations from the poets and has de-emphasized the tendency to speak of a "public" and a "private" voice operative in the individual works. Instead, more scholarly attention has been directed to the ambiguities, multiple associations, and contradictory references embedded in the poems and expressed by the individual poets. Scholars are detailing the intricacies of the varied associations and contradictions, elaborating upon the many levels of references, meanings, and interpretation. These features are prominent in all the poetry of the age and contribute to the lasting appeal of the authors and their works. The interaction of innovation and adaptation by the poets parallels the similar development and essence of Augustan art, architecture, religion, politics, and government.

VERGIL

Publius Vergilius Maro was born 15 October, 70 BCE in a village near Mantua. His family status is unclear, but Vergil possessed some ancestral land in the area of his birth and upbringing. He received a good education, first in the Po valley at Cremona and Milan, and, then, as a youth, in Rome and Naples. We surmise that before 42 BCE Vergil spent some time in Rome and Naples studying and writing, although the poems in the *Appendix Vergiliana* are most likely not his. For us Vergil enters the literary world with the ten pastoral poems that comprise the *Eclogues* published in 39-38 BCE. Intricately arranged and juxtaposed, the poems blend contemporary concerns in a make-believe world of rustics who sing highly sophisticated songs with shifting meanings and nuances. In the *Eclogues* Vergil adapts and reworks the bucolic poetry of Theocritus, but he adds many Roman elements charged with moral overtones and literary matter. For example, the first Eclogue blends the melancholic state of the freeborn citizen Meliboeus with the happiness of the resourceful slave Tityrus who has won his freedom (*libertas*). No contemporary could have failed to appreciate the feeling for political freedom. Moreover, the ideals of the pastoral world complement the intrusive nature of history, seen in the character of Gallus (*Eclogue* 10) and the figure of Daphnis (*Eclogue* 5) whose deification recalls that of Julius Caesar. The ease and contentment of the vague, pastoral Arcadia contrast with the venality and ingratitude of the city. This dichotomy may be the result of Vergil's own thinking of his Italian experience: early life in Cisalpine Gaul, the years of his youth spent around the Bay of Naples, and his maturity associated with the political nexus of Octavius/Augustus and Rome. After the publication of the *Eclogues* Vergil became a member of Maecenas' literary coterie. At the request of Maecenas he began to compose the *Georgics*. This work, finished in 29 BCE, was dedicated to Maecenas. Ostensibly a didactic work on agriculture, the *Georgics* was modeled on and adapted from numerous Greek and Roman poems and treatises on the subject. Frequently, direct didacticism is broken by reflective and/or descriptive passages that digress from the nominal topic. Notable in this regard is the "epyllion" of Aristaeus and Orpheus. It is mainly in the so-called digressions where thematic contrasts, oppositions, and multilayered references occur. For example, Book I ends with a description of the turmoil in Italy after the assassination of Julius Caesar. Book IV contains an implicit contrast and comparison of the society of bees with the state of Rome. In fact the entire *Georgics* reverberates with the theme of the vicissitudes of life, the constant fluctuation of success and failure. The end of the *Georgics* engenders two feelings. As readers we laud the success of Aristaeus' religious piety and hard work, but we regret the failure and loss of Orpheus. Despite his artistic abilities to change and control nature, Orpheus ultimately fails because of love. Similarly, in Eclogue 10 because of frenzied love Gallus cannot thrive in the pastoral environment of Arcadia.

After the success of the *Georgics* Vergil turned to writing the *Aeneid*, his recognized masterpiece. Propertius heralded the "work in progress" and prophesied its greatness (2.34.66). Tradition also maintains that Vergil read several books to Augustus and his family. At his death in 19 BCE he considered the work incomplete. In that year Vergil had left Rome on a trip to Greece and the Middle East ostensibly to correct and edit the poem. After meeting Augustus in Athens and contracting a fever, Vergil decided to return to Italy. In very ill health he died on 20 September at Brundisium. The "unfinished" *Aeneid* was edited and published posthumously by Vergil's friends Varius Rufus and Plotius Tucca. At the heart of the epic is a profound look into the Roman experience, both spiritual and moral. Like the other works of the period the *Aeneid* shows many dichotomies, ambivalences, and ambiguous references to the Roman character and state. Scholars continue to debate Vergil's true intent. Yet, we can truly assert that the *Aeneid* has strongly marked the European poetic tradition.

HORACE

On 8 December, 65 BCE Quintus Horatius Flaccus was born at Venusia, a town on the border of Lucania and Apulia. Horace's father had been a freedman, most likely a man enslaved as a result of the Social War of 91-88 BCE during which Venusia had joined the losing side of the allies who revolted against Rome. After the war and his subsequent manumission Horace's father became an agent of auctioneers from which job he earned enough money to provide the young Horace with an excellent education in Rome and later in Athens. Modern scholars argue that Horace was fairly wealthy and in his youth had important social and political contacts in Rome. Horace's supposed servile background and impoverished state were programmed parts of a carefully constructed image in order to exalt Maecenas and to establish the merits of his own character. It was while Horace was studying in Athens that he was recruited by Iunius Brutus to join the armed forces led by Brutus and Cassius, the men who were most responsible for the conspiracy and assassination of Julius Caesar. The young Horace was commissioned with the high rank of *tribunus militum*. After the conspirators' defeat and deaths in 42 at the battle of Philippi, Horace returned to Rome where he purchased a clerical and semi-administrative post as *scriba quaestorius* (scribe of the quaestor), an official who assisted elected magistrates in maintaining accounts and payrolls. During this period of his life Horace began writing poetry. By 35 BCE the first book of *Satires* appeared and soon afterwards Horace was welcomed into the circle of Maecenas and provided by his patron with a farm in Sabine territory near Tibur (Tivoli). This grant gave Horace equestrian status and afforded him the opportunity and leisure to devote himself exclusively to poetry. By the end of the 30s Horace had produced the complete *Satires* and the contemporaneous *Epodes*, a collection of poems written in iambic meter. By 29 BCE Horace was at work on his collection of lyric poems (*Odes*) which he published in three books in 23. The first book of the *Epistles* appeared in 19. In 17 the *Centennial Hymn* (*Carmen Saeculare*) was commissioned to celebrate the centennial festival inaugurated by Augustus to proclaim Rome's (and his) achievements. The second book of *Epistles* and a fourth book of *Odes* came out in 13. They were to be Horace's last published work. He died on 27 November, 8 BCE, two months after the death of Maecenas. Although Horace had been on very close terms with his patron Maecenas and in later years Augustus courted his friendship and attention, he maintained an independent stance. He seemed to have kept a friendly relationship with all of his intimates and fellow members of Maecenas' coterie.

With such variety in genres of literature not surprisingly one finds differences in tone, style, and treatment between and among the individual works. Beneath the colloquial tone of the *Satires* Horace gently moralizes. In the *Epistles* a more unified and serious tone is maintained throughout as Horace concentrates on moral and literary issues. The *Odes*, on the other hand, display suggestive and significant changes in tone, expression, and content, sometimes within the same poem. Shifts in mood, subjects, and language are most often unified by a type of ring composition. The poems are often complex with subtle transitions, with rich resonances of sound and sense, and with an elaborate structure in fixed meters. More than any other of his works it is the *Odes* that have established Horace's reputation.

PROPERTIUS

Sextus Propertius was born around 50 BCE at Assisi from equestrian parents. His father died early in Propertius' life: perhaps he was one of those executed by Octavius after his capture of Perugia in 41 BCE. The family property suffered from the Perusine confiscations executed by Octavius. The war of Perugia and the subsequent confiscations deeply affected the young Propertius. He alludes to these matters several times and in 1.21 and 1.22 he seems to identify and ally himself with the losing side, an independent political stance that he seems to maintain throughout his poetry. Despite the diminution of his family's estate enough resources remained that Propertius' mother managed to have him educated in Rome. Early on he turned to writing poetry and by 29 BCE he published the first of four books of elegies. The last book of poems is dated to 16 BCE. The poems of the first book of elegies, called the *Monobiblos*, constitute an organized sequence and concentrate on the figure of Cynthia whom Propertius posits as his absorbing love interest. Her name is a clear reference to the mythic character of Artemis and of Apollo, patron of the arts. Her poetic character is developed from Catullus' Lesbia, a dominating mistress, sophisticated, probably married, but sexually liberated. Her persona appears in subsequent books, but less frequently than in the first. We need not interpret the Cynthia-Propertius affair as a reworking of an autobiographical history. Even the famous "farewell" to Cynthia of 3.24 and 3.25 most likely is a literary conceit whereby Propertius cleverly swears off writing about Cynthia with the intent of concentrating on other themes. Joining Horace and Vergil, Propertius became a member of Maecenas' literary circle soon after the release of Book I. In his programmatic first poem of Book II, Propertius dedicates the book to his new patron Maecenas, but humorously presents Cynthia as his muse.

Propertius' style is intricate and complex: he associates abundantly; he strains transitions with psychological jumps; he innovates in his grammar; and confounds his readers with his knowledge and allusive use of myth and lore. He demands his audience follow his recondite allusions, his psychological transitions, and his difficult forms of expression. Many have attributed his overall complexity to the wretched nature of the manuscript tradition, but most likely this difficulty is the result of his often convoluted style and clever adaptations. Some Romans disagreed with Quintilian's assessment that Tibullus was the most polished and elegant of the Roman elegists. Instead, they preferred the more demanding and complex style—as many moderns do—of Propertius. Although he may not have been an open supporter of the Augustan regime, he is not overtly hostile to Augustan themes. Political references pepper his oeuvre. Sometimes they are defiant or seemingly unpatriotic; often the political associations are muted by the innovative reworking of Callimachean poetic principles and techniques.

TIBULLUS

It is likely that Albius Tibullus' first book of elegies was published after the *Monobiblos* of Propertius, but before Propertius' second book. Yet, the tradition states that Tibullus was older than Propertius and, therefore, most scholars place his date of birth around 55 BCE. He, like his contemporary, was of the equestrian class, and from poem 1.1 he intimates that some of his family's estate may also have been confiscated. The manuscripts of Tibullus contain two books of elegies attributed to him and a third to other poets. He cultivated the friendship and had the patronage of Marcus Valerius Messalla Corvinus. Contemporaries of the poet have noted his person and his work, as both Ovid and Horace expressed a heartfelt admiration. In Tibullus' honor Ovid wrote a very favorable elegy (*Amores* 3.9) at his death. In the elegy Ovid envisions the presence and participation of Delia and Nemesis, the women in

Tibullus' poetic life, at his funeral pyre and heralds their immortality in literature. Horace, too, if the Albius of *Odes* 1.33 and *Epistles* 1.4 is indeed Tibullus, praised him and revealed an intimate association and appreciation of the elegist.

Tibullus' poetry, like that of Propertius, fosters the notion of the transcendental power of love. In his sixteen poems Tibullus addresses three separate lovers: a Delia and a Nemesis, two women, and a male youth, Marathus. In contrast with Propertius, Tibullus' style is simple and polished; mythological references are few. Although admitting that some preferred Propertius, Quintilian judged Tibullus to be the most polished and elegant (*tersus atque elegans*) of the Roman elegists. His simplicity and direct expressions, however, are deceiving because of the subtlety of his transitions and the frequent weaving in and out of multiple themes and conventions. In many of his poems Tibullus fashions as his persona a lower-class rustic. Most of the poems have a rural setting and embody values consistent with the pastoral world. Tibullus' persona longs for peace and has a deep affection for the simplicity of the countryside. With his emphasis on the countryside in an essentially urban genre (viz. the elegiac woman [*domina* or *puella*] is always imagined and depicted as urban), Tibullus experiments by combining elegiac conventions and themes with a pastoral setting and rural values. In this way Tibullus adapts for his purposes some of the virtues associated with the ethos and program of Augustus.

SULPICIA

The manuscripts of the Tibullan corpus also contain six poems written by Sulpicia, the daughter of Servius Sulpicius Rufus and niece of M. Valerius Messalla Corvinus. The poems of Sulpicia are the only works of a female poet to survive from classical Latin. The six poems are elegiac epigrams that record her love for a youth she calls Cerinthus. Sulpicia's style is somewhat contorted but the poems reveal some original thought, language, and treatment. Because of the paucity of material, judgment of quality or significance must remain suspended.

OVID

Born on 20 March, 43 BCE in Sulmo, Publius Ovidius Naso came from an equestrian family. Too young to have participated in the war between Antony and Octavius, Ovid benefited from the Pax Augusta established by the emperor after his defeat of Antony. In his youth Ovid received an excellent education in rhetoric at Rome and abroad in Greece and began a political career. After serving on some boards in a minor capacity, Ovid quit public life and devoted himself to writing poetry. He enjoyed the early patronage of M. Valerius Messalla Corvinus during which time he composed and edited the *Amores*, elegies which he later published in three books. We can say with certainty that in the late

Augustan Age Ovid became the most prominent of poets, a position he relished until his sudden exile in 8 CE. Relegated by Augustus to Tomis on the Black Sea because of the offense caused by the *Art of Love* and some mistake or indiscretion, as Ovid himself often admits, he died in exile in 17 CE, frustrated by his failure to appease first Augustus, then Tiberius for his recall.

Ovid was very prolific. Of his surviving works, except for the *Metamorphoses*, all the poems are written in elegiac couplets. With Ovid Augustan poetry reached the acme of refinement and elegance. Not only does he adapt the rich models of the Hellenistic world, especially Callimachus and Nicander, but he also alludes to and reworks the Latin tradition, frequently responding to and recasting his older contemporaries. His explorations into various genres and subjects, executed in facile elegiacs, and his tendency to test the limits and extremes of the genre or work are hallmarks of his composition and expression. Ovid so exploits the conventions and characters of elegy that the genre disappeared for a time because he seemingly had exhausted the supply of invention and execution. To him elegy was one elaborate game, his lover a composite of all elegiac lovers, and his poetic language a manipulation in service to his wit, sophistication, and creativity. Ovid's versatile exploitation of the elegiac couplet is underscored by his experimentation and innovative approaches in subject and theme. For example, the fictitious letters of the *Heroides* fully develop an experiment of Propertius (4.3) and owe much to the tenor and characterization found in epic and tragedy. In the *Fasti* Ovid explores and adapts elegiacs to a didactic and aetiological genre influenced by the Hellenistic poets Aratus and Callimachus and by the Roman Varro. In the *Art of Love* Ovid continues and develops many of the themes, situations, and conventions of the *Amores*. Ovid assumes the role of the preceptor to oversee the reader's approach to erotic intrigue and seduction. The work is often irreverent; it mocks and parodies serious didactic poetry. When Ovid directly involved the reader in a text that was somewhat salacious to begin with and that humorously flaunted an open sexual freedom, it is difficult to doubt that some would object and criticize the content of the message as well as the messenger. Even though the poet could claim he was being ironically satirical and facetious in tone and treatment of the subject, he ran the risk of incurring antagonism and smoldering resentment. As history was to show, Ovid's irreverent attitude in the *Art of Love* helped cause his banishment. In the works from exile, the *Tristia* and *Epistulae ex Ponto*, Ovid displays his versatile and skillful ability to adapt the elegiac couplet to a new medium and genre. In a sense, the poems from exile are true elegies in that they are laments that overlay the touching appeals and harsh travails, both physical and emotional, that the poet in heart-wrenching detail depicts. The poems present a poignant characterization of the anguish and obsessions of an urban poet separated from his natural milieu. Ovid relieved the ennui and tedium of his sorrowful laments by including much geographical and ethnographical material that no doubt interested and engaged his audience. It is both ironic and tragic that the last great poet and purest product of the Augustan Age and Peace ended his life in exile far from home and the Rome he loved so well.

As these brief sketches of the major Augustan poets show, the literary expectations and pressures of contemporary society promote a great variety of approaches to the literature. Imposing any homogeneity upon the poets either collectively or individually would be difficult indeed. Disparities in age, social antecedents, place of birth, and political background preclude any simplistic characterization of the nature of their poetry and their response to the political realities of Rome under a young dynast. On the whole, the poets of the period deflect both the presence of and pressure from the new regime. And many contradictions and ambiguities fill the works of even those poets who owed so much directly to Octavius and his party and who appreciated the bringing of peace to a war-torn and war-weary world. For example, both the *Eclogues* and the *Georgics* of Vergil register wistful melancholy and a nostalgic tone that are embedded in the depiction of an idyllic society and Golden Age. Each in its way poignantly portrays regret, failure, and loss. Yet all the poets share a common trait: they believed in the elegance and sophistication of their poetry that reflected the refinement of the age. Each acknowledged his debt to Greek and Latin precedents in form, but each also reworked the literary tradition to produce fresh works, either in pastoral, didactic, lyric, elegiac, or epic verse. In every work the poet emerges at the center, an authorial voice—sometimes narrative, other times moral—that repeatedly challenges the reader to explore numerous connotations and levels of interpretation. Concepts and notions like *virtus* (manly courage, moral excellence), *otium* (ease, tranquility), *furor* (madness, extremism) take on special suggestive meanings and broad metaphorical range. The poets elevate themes shared in the period and bring enduring perspectives to them. Direct propaganda or ideology are generally absent or muted in the poetry, although the art of the period directs more attention to their symbolic representations. Like the literature, the art, too, displays a sophisticated and creative energy in its numerous images. Many of the values envisioned by Octavius/Augustus are represented in both art and literature. The poets, however, exercised an independence from their imperial ruler, producing a body of work complex in associations and of multileveled meanings and interpretative possibilities, poetry that transcends its time and place.

CHRONOLOGY

753 BCE	Traditional date of the founding of Rome
753-509	Monarchy; the seven kings of Rome
509	Expulsion of Tarquin the Proud, Lucius Iunius Brutus and Lucius Tarquinius Collatinus first elected consuls
509-27	Republic
451-449	The Twelve Tables, Rome's first law code
396-394	Veii besieged, captured and destroyed by Marcus Furius Camillus
387	Sack of Rome by Gauls
343-341	First war with Samnites
327-304	Second war with Samnites
298-290	Third war with Samnites
280-275	War with Pyrrhus of Epirus who invaded Italy
264-241	First Punic War with Carthage
240-207	Livius Andronicus, founder of Latin Literature, active
218-201	Second Punic War with Carthage
213-211	Roman siege of Syracuse; victories of Marcus Claudius Marcellus
212-205	First Macedonian War with Philip V
202	Publius Cornelius Scipio defeats Hannibal at Zama
200-197	Second Macedonian War with Philip V
191-188	War with Antiochus III, Hellenistic king of Syria
184	Cato the Elder is censor
171-167	Third Macedonian War with Perses
149-146	Third Punic War; P. Cornelius Scipio (Aemilianus) destroys Carthage
148-146	Fourth Macedonian War; Corinth destroyed; Macedonia becomes a Roman province

133-121	The Gracchi brothers active in Rome
112-105	War with Jugurtha of Numidia
107-100	Gaius Marius consul six times
91-88	War with Italian allies
88-82	Rome's first Civil War between "Marians" and "Sullans"
82-78	Sulla dictator; death of Sulla
73-71	Slave revolt of Spartacus
70	Consulship of Marcus Licinius Crassus and Gnaeus Pompeius (Pompey); birth of Vergil
65	Birth of Horace
63	Consulship of Cicero; Julius Caesar elected pontifex maximus; birth of Gaius Octavius (Augustus)
60	Formation of the First Triumvirate of Caesar, Pompey, and Crassus
49	Caesar crosses Rubicon; Civil War between Pompey and Caesar begins
48	Pompey defeated at Pharsalus and killed in Egypt
48-44	Caesar victorious over remaining opponents. Caesar's dictatorship
44	Assassination of Caesar on 15 March; Gaius Octavius designated Julius Caesar's heir
43	Battle of Mutina and the deaths of the consuls Hirtius and Pansa; Mark Antony, Gaius Octavius, and Marcus Aemilius Lepidus form the Second Triumvirate; birth of Ovid
42	Brutus and Cassius defeated at Philippi; the settlement of soldiers on confiscated land
41	The siege of Perugia by Octavius
41-30	Mark Antony's relationship with Cleopatra
40	Mark Antony marries Octavia, Octavius' sister
39/38	Publication of the *Eclogues*
38	Octavius marries Livia
38/37	Horace's journey; Triumvirate renewed at Tarentum
35	Book I of Horace's *Satires* published
31	Battle of Actium
30	Mark Antony and Cleopatra commit suicide; Book II of Horace's *Satires* and the *Epodes* published
29	Publication of Book I of Propertius' *Elegies*; the *Georgics* of Vergil published
28	Dedication of the Temple of Apollo on the Palatine
27	Octavius receives the name of Augustus; beginning of the Empire; Agrippa builds the first Pantheon
27/26	Book II of Propertius' *Elegies* and Tibullus' *Elegies* published

26	Disgrace and suicide of Gaius Cornelius Gallus
23	Publication of Books I-III of Horace's *Odes* and Book III of Propertius' *Elegies*
20	The return of Roman standards by the Parthians lost by Crassus in 53
19	Book I of Horace's *Epistles* published; deaths of Vergil and Tibullus
17	Horace composes the *Centennial Hymn*
16/15	Publication of Book IV of Propertius' *Elegies*
15/14	The *Amores* and *Heroides* of Ovid published
14/13	Publication of Book II of the *Epistles* of Horace
13	Book IV of Horace's *Odes* published
12	Death of Agrippa
8	Deaths of Maecenas and Horace
2	Exiling of Julia, Augustus's daughter
	Dedication of the Temple of Mars Ultor
1 BCE/1 CE	Publication of Ovid's *The Art of Love*
1/2 CE	*The Remedies of Love* of Ovid published
4	Augustus adopts Tiberius Claudius Nero, the son of Livia
6-8	Publication of Ovid's *Metamorphoses* and the *Fasti*
8	Exile of Ovid to Tomis on the coast of the Black Sea
8-17	The composition and the publication of Ovid's *Tristia* and *Letters from Pontus*
14	Death of Augustus; Tiberius becomes Emperor
17/18	Death of Ovid

Central Italy

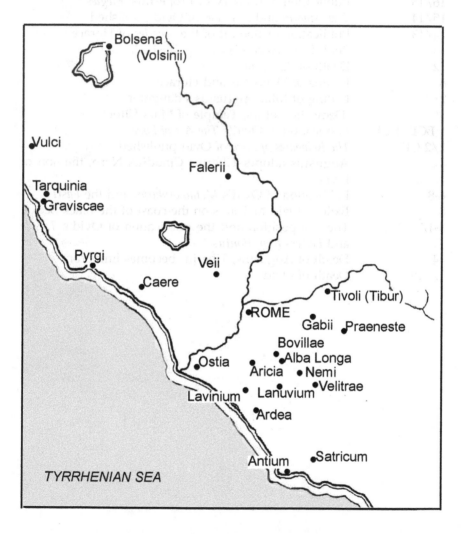

Bolsena (Volsinii)

Vulci

Falerii

Tarquinia
Graviscae

Pyrgi

Veii

Caere

Tivoli (Tibur)

ROME

Gabii   Praeneste

Bovillae

Ostia   Alba Longa

Aricia   Nemi

Velitrae

Lavinium   Lanuvium

Ardea

Antium   Satricum

TYRRHENIAN SEA

Italy

Greece
and Aegean Sea

MACEDONIA

Philippi

SAMOTHRACE

HELLESPONT

CHALCIDICE

Apollonia

Abytus

Acroceraunia

Oricos

Troy

Mount
Olympus

LEMNOS

EPIRUS

LESBOS

Dodona

THESSALY

AEGEAN SEA

EUBOEA

Actium

CHIOS

AETOLIA

BOEOTIA Chalcis

Delphi

Thebes

Eretria

Eleusis

SAMOS

Megara

ACHAEA Sicyon

Athens

Corinth

DELOS

ARCADIA

Argos

Olympia

CYCLADES

NAXOS

PELOPONNESUS

Sparta

IONIAN SEA

LACONIA

MELOS

THERA

Asia Minor during the Roman Empire

VERGIL

ECLOGUES

The publication of the *Eclogues* established Vergil's reputation as a master poet. The ten poems that make up the collection are a blend of traditions, themes, and treatments. Drawing from Theocritus' *Idylls*, they contain bucolic, rustic features mixed with urban elements and incorporate references to contemporary issues, both political and literary. The *Eclogues* became the standard and a reverent model for pastoral poetry of the Renaissance. Even today the resonances of the tensions between the rustic world of song and the realities of a political present intrigue and appeal.

1°

MELIBOEUS: Tityrus, you lie beneath the spreading shade of a beech,
And are rehearsing the woodland music on a slender reed,
But we are leaving the borders of our father's land, those sweet fields,
We, forced to flee the fatherland; you, O Tityrus, lingering in the
    shade,
Are teaching the woods to echo the beautiful Amaryllis.   5

1.1: the dramatic date of this eclogue is 42-41 when Octavius confiscated land for the resettlement of veterans who fought in the Brutus-Cassius campaign. Tityrus, an aging slave, secured both his freedom and land by visiting Rome to petition the young Octavius. Meliboeus, on the other hand, is evicted from his ancestral land and forced into exile.

1

TITYRUS: O, Meliboeus, he is a god who has brought to us these
   leisured times.
And yes, always to me he will be a god; his altar
Often a tender lamb from our fold will stain.
He, as you see, has granted me the right for my cattle to roam
And for me myself to play on rustic pipe whatever I please.   10

MELIBOEUS: Well, I do not grudge it; no, but I am amazed: for in all
The fields abounds trouble on trouble. Look, on and on, sick
I drive my little goats: this one here, Tityrus, I barely manage.
Right here in the thick hazel thicket, ah, upon a bare flint
She has abandoned the twins just now delivered after long labor, the
   hope of our flock.
This disaster for us, if only my mind had not been so dull, often   16
I remember its foretelling from oaks struck from the sky.
But yet, O Tityrus, tell us about that god—who he is.

TITYRUS: The city they call Rome, Meliboeus, I was foolish to believe
Was like our town, where it is the practice of us shepherds   20
To wean the tender lambs from the flocks.
Thus I learned how similar puppies are to dogs, kids to mother goats,
And thus I used to compare the large with the small.
But this city towers her head above the others
As the cypresses soar among the willowy wayfaring shrubs.   25

MELIBOEUS: And what great reason had you to view Rome?

TITYRUS: Freedom, though late, looked back on me, a sluggard,
When a whitish beard was already falling to the barber.
Yet it looked back on me and after a lengthy time came,
Now that Amaryllis has a hold on us and after Galatea left.   30
Well, I confess it, yes, while Galatea had a grip on me,
I had no hope of freedom, no chance for saving money;
Though many a victim came from my enclosures
And I pressed fat cheese for an ungrateful city,
In my right hand I never once came home loaded with coins.   35

MELIBOEUS: I used to wonder why, Amaryllis, in grief you called
   upon the gods,
Why you allowed the fruits to hang upon their trees;
Tityrus was not here. These very pines, Tityrus,
These very springs, these very orchards called you.

TITYRUS: What was I to do? I could not find a way out
   of slavery   40

And nowhere else could I discern deities so favoring.
Here I saw that young man, Meliboeus, for whom, year in, year out,
My altars will smoke for twelve days.
Here I petitioned; he responded right away:
"Pasture your cattle, boys, as before; breed your bulls."   45

MELIBOEUS: Fortunate old man! So the fields will remain yours,
And large enough for you, although a bare rock
Or marsh of muddy rushes covers all the pastures.
No unfamiliar fodder will afflict the pregnant ewes,
No damning disease from a neighbor's herd will harm them.   50
O fortunate old man! Here among your known streams
And sacred springs you'll seek out the cool of the shade.
Here by your neighbor's path, as always, your hedge of willows,
Whose blossom Hyblaean° bees have sipped,
Will often whisper lulling you to gentle sleep.   55
Here beneath a steep crag a pruner will sing to pastoral breezes
As the throaty woodland pigeons, your special delight,
And the turtledove will coo on and on from the lofty elms.

TITYRUS: Sooner shall nimble deer graze on thinning air
And seas leave fish washed naked on shore,   60
Sooner too the Parthian will drink from the Saone or the German
The Tigris, each a migrant who has traveled the other's land,
Than his face would fade from our heart.

MELIBOEUS: But for us, some will leave from here bound for the
      thirsty Africans,
Some to Scythia, some to arrive at the Oaxes churning up chalk,   65
Others still to peoples of Britain cut off from the whole world.
Oh, will I ever see and marvel, after too long a time, at ancestral lands,
The roof of my impoverished hut topped with turf,
And then the wheat ears, my kingdom?
These fields so well cultivated a godless soldier will possess,   70
A foreigner these crops. Ah, what kind of misery for citizens
Discord has produced; for these types we have sown the fields!
Now, Meliboeus, graft your pears and row your vines.
Go, my little goats, go, my once-happy flock.
I, stretched out in some grassy hollow, no more   75
Will see you almost dangling from some far-off bushy slope;
No more will I sing pastorals, my little goats, no more will I shepherd
As you nibble on blossoming clover and bitter willows.

1.54: Hyblaean refers to a Greek city in Sicily near Syracuse founded by Megara
   in the eighth century.

TITYRUS: Yet here you could rest this night with me
On green foliage; we have mellow fruits,   80
Soft chestnuts and an ample store of cheese;
Off in the distance now smoke the chimneys of farmhouses
And from the mountain heights fall growing shadows.

4

Muses of Sicily,° let us sing of loftier themes.
Shrubs and lowly tamarisk do not please everyone;
If we sing of woods, let those woods be worthy of a consul.
The last age of Cumaean song has now come;
The great cycle of centuries is born anew.   5
Now too Virgin Justice returns, the kingdoms of Saturn return,°
Now a new race is being sent down from heaven on high.
You now, O chaste Lucina, shed favor on the boy being born
Through whom the iron age will begin to cease and a golden race
Will arise in the whole world; now reigns your Apollo.   10
Your consulship, O Pollio, *yours* will thus initiate
This glorious era, and the splendid months will begin to march;
With you as leader, if any traces of our sin remain,
Obliterated, they will free the lands from constant fear.
He will gain the life of the gods and will see heroes associating   15
With the divine, and they will view him,
And he will rule a world made peaceful by the virtues of his father.
But for you, child, the earth uncultivated will
Pour forth its first little gifts, ivy meandering everywhere,
Primrose plants, and beanstalks entwined with smiling acanthus.   20
Goats on their own will bring home udders swollen full
With milk, and the herds will not fear mighty lions;
Of its own accord your cradle will pour forth flowers to charm you.
The serpent too will die, and the deceptive poisonous herb
Will fade away; Assyrian balsam will spring up everywhere.   25
But once you are able to read of the renown won by heroes and the
     deeds
Of your father, and to learn what manliness is,
Little by little a flat field will grow yellow with soft wheat,

---

4.1: Vergil alludes to his predecessors in pastoral poetry, Theocritus and Bion,
     who were from Sicily.
4.6: the virgin goddess Astraea, patron of justice, abandoned the earth and
     became the constellation Virgo. Her return envisions the inception of a re-
     stored Golden Age. Saturn was identified with Cronus who reigned in the
     Golden Age.

The blushing grape will hang from untended brambles,
And hard oaks will exude dewy honey.   30
Yet a few traces of our ancient sin will surface,
Bidding us to test the sea in vessels, to fortify towns
With surrounding walls and to split furrows in the earth.
Then there will be a second Tiphys, a second Argo to carry
Chosen heroes; a second round of wars will come   35
And once again a mighty Achilles be sent to Troy.
Later, after the passage of time strengthens and makes you a man,
The traveler will abandon the sea and the sailing pine will
Not exchange goods: every land will produce everything.
The ground will not suffer hoes nor vines the sickle;   40
Then too the sturdy plowman will unyoke the collars from his oxen;
And wool will not learn the various tricks of colors,
For the ram himself in the pastures will dye his fleece,
Now to a sweetly blushing purple, now to a saffron hue;
Spontaneously crimson will clothe the pasturing lambs.   45
'Ages like these, run on,' the Fates, agreeing
On the fixed will of destiny, in unison exclaimed to their spindles.
Enter upon your illustrious honors (the time will soon come), O
    dearest
Offspring of the gods, mighty descendant of Jove.
Look! The world teeters on all its rounded mass,   50
The lands, the expanse of the sea, and the deep heaven;
Behold how all things exult in the age to come.
May, then, the final curtain of a long life remain for me
And a sufficient breath to herald your deeds.
Neither Orpheus of Thrace nor Linus will surpass me in song,   55
Though mother Calliope may support Orpheus
And father Apollo, the handsome, assist Linus.
Were even Pan° to compete with me and Arcadia judge us,
Even Pan would declare, were Arcadia judge, his defeat.
Begin, little boy, with a smile to recognize your mother;   60
(Your mother endured ten long months of impatient waiting).
Begin, little boy: those who have not smiled for a parent,
A god has never honored with his table, or a goddess with her bed.

5

MENALCAS: Since we have met here, Mopsus, both of us skilled,
You at piping on the light reeds, I at singing lyrics,
Why aren't we seated among the elms entwined with hazel?

4.58: Pan, the woodland god of pastoral music, inhabits Arcadia.

MOPSUS: You are the elder; it is proper for me to defer to you,
    Menalcas,
Whether we go close under the shade shimmering from the westerly
    breezes   5
Or better yet to a hollow in the rocks. Look there, a hollow
Where scattered clusters over a wild vine interlace.

MENALCAS: In our hills only Amyntas challenges you.

MOPSUS: Yes, he would be the one vying to out-sing Apollo.

MENALCAS: Begin first then, Mopsus, if in your repertoire you have
    in memory   10
"The Passion of Phyllis," "The Praiseworthy Fame of Alcon," or
    "Codrus' Taunts."°
Begin: Tityrus here will tend to the pasturing kids.

MOPSUS: Fine, just let me try this song which recently I wrote
On a green trunk of beech and as I played through the melody
    inscribed it.
So you, then, tell Amyntas to challenge this.   15

MENALCAS: As the pliant willow bows to the pale olive,
As the lowly yellow nard bows to the purple roses,
So, in our judgment Amyntas yields to you.
But no more talk from you, boy; we have come under the rock-
    hollow.

MOPSUS: Daphnis was dead;° nymphs were mourning his cruel
    death—   20
You hazels and streams were witnesses to their lament—
Clasping the pitiable corpse of her own son
His mother invoked gods and stars, calling them cruel.
Throughout those days no one drove your pastured bulls,
Daphnis, to cooling streams, no animal sipped from a river   25
Or tasted a blade of pasture-grass.
Daphnis, the wild mountains and woods proclaim
That even African lions groaned your passing.
Daphnis taught the yoking of Armenian tigers to a chariot;

5.11: common titles or themes in the repertoire of pastoral singers.
5.20: Mopsus begins his song on the death of Daphnis. Daphnis belongs to an
    earlier mythology. The putative son of Hermes and a nymph, he was raised
    by Sicilian herdsmen whose pastoral lifestyle he adapted.

Daphnis introduced the ecstatic companies sacred to Bacchus   30
And began the intertwining of pliant spears with delicate leaves.
As the vine graces trees, as grapes grace the vines,
As bulls the herd, as wheat crops the fertile fields,
So you are a perfect jewel for your people. When the fates took you,
Pales herself and Apollo, too, abandoned the lands.   35
From the furrows in which we often entrusted fat grains of barley
Up spring worthless darnel and sterile wild oats;
In place of soft violet and purple narcissus
There rise thistle and prickly thorns.
Strew the ground with leafy flowers, shepherds, shade the springs   40
(Daphnis wills such things on his behalf),
And build a tomb, and upon the mound write this verse:
'I am Daphnis, renowned in forests and now known all the way to the
     stars,
A keeper of a beautiful flock, even handsomer than I.'

MENALCAS: To us, divinely inspired poet, your song is like   45
A sleep on grass for tired souls, as sweet as water
From a bubbly brook in the heat of summer quenching thirst.
You are the master's equal in reed playing and singing voice:
O fortunate lad, you now will succeed him.
But we somehow will sing this song in response to you   50
And will extol your Daphnis to the stars;
We will raise Daphnis to the stars, for he loved us, too.

MOPSUS: Oh, can there be any greater gift for us than this?
For that youth has earned the elegies, and we have already
Heard Stimichon praise your songs about him.   55

MENALCAS: He shines and marvels at the uncommon threshold of
     Olympus,°
Daphnis beneath his feet sees clouds and constellations.
So, joy on swift wing grips the forests and the countrysides,
And Pan and Dryad girls, and shepherds.
Neither the wolf plots against the flock nor nets   60
Intend to trick the deer: the good Daphnis loves peace.
Virgin mountains hurl their voices in joy to the heavens,
Spontaneously the rocks echo songs, spontaneously the orchard trees
Resound in song: 'A god, a god he is, Menalcas.'
Be propitious, be prosperous for your people; Look! Four altars,   65

5.56: Menalcas begins his song on the deification of Daphnis.

Two for you, Daphnis, and two altars for Apollo.
For you every year I will stand two cups brimming with fresh milk,
And two bowls of plump olives.
Above all else I'll revel, feasting with ample wine before the fireplace
In the bitter cold of winter, in the shade during summer.   70
From magnum bottles I'll pour Chian varietals—fresh nectar.
Damoetas and Aegon from Crete will sing for me;
Alphesiboeus will imitate the dance of frenzied satyrs.
These will ever be your rites whenever we honor our solemn vows
To the nymphs, whenever we bless our fields.   75
As long as the boar loves the mountain heights, or the fish
    the streams,
As long as bees feed on thyme, or cicadas sip on dew,
Respect, fame, and glory will always be yours.
As to Bacchus and to Ceres, so to you each and every year
The farmers will make vows: you, too, will bind them to these
    vows.   80

MOPSUS: What present, what gift could I render you for such a song?
Neither the whisper of the rising south wind
Nor the drumming of waves upon the shore, nor the flow
Of water rushing through rocky glens pleases me so much.

MENALCAS: We will offer you first this gift of fragile pipe;   85
This very flute taught us: "Corydon blazed for handsome Alexis,"
And likewise: "Whose flock is it? Meliboeus'?"°

MOPSUS: And take this crook that Antigenes, although he asked me
    for it
Several times—and he deserved love then—did not win;
Beautiful it is, evenly notched and bronze studded, Menalcas.   90

6°

First in the pastoral rhythms of Syracuse our Muse, Thalia, deigned
To play; she did not blush to haunt woodland homes.
But when I started to sing of kings and battles, Apollo
Tweaked my ear, advising me: "Tityrus, a herdsman should feed
His sheep fat, but sing poetry well-spun."   5
As there will be poets in plenty to extol your glorious exploits,
Varus, and to celebrate sorrowful wars,
I now pledge myself to harmonize on a slender reed a rural Muse.

5.86-87: the opening lines of *Eclogue* 2 and 3 respectively.
6.1: the poem is addressed to Publius Alfenus Varus.

Not unasked the songs I sing. If anyone, if only a single person,
Captivated by love, reads them, you, yes, you, these our tamarisks, 10
Our entire grove will praise in song; not a single page
Pleases Apollo more than the one that has inscribed the name of
  Varus.
Begin, O muses! The boys, Chromis and Mnasyllus,
Spied Silenus lying asleep in a cave,
His veins bloated as always with yesterday's wine;   15
Garlands were lying at a distance, fallen from his head,
A heavy bowl was dangling by its well-worn handle.
Coming close—for the old fellow often teased them both
In the hope of a song—they wrap him in bonds made from his
  garland.
Aegle, most beautiful of nymphs, collaborated, coming to abet   20
The pair as they hesitated in fear; she tinged his brow and temples
With black mulberry juice, as he, awake, looked on.
With a smile acknowledging the prank, "Why do you tie me in
  fetters?"
He asked; "Let me loose, lads; enough, you've had an eyeful.
Learn getting the songs you desire; for you poetry,   25
But for her there'll be some other reward." Without delay he begins.
Truly you could have seen the fauns and wild animals gamboling
In time to the rhythm, and the tops of firm oak trees swaying;
Not so much do Rhodope and Ismarus marvel at Orpheus.
Yes, he sang on and on—about the seeds   30
Of earth and air and sea and liquid fire
That had been fused together by necessity through vast void;
About all the created things arising from these first principles;
And how the young world cohered into a ball;
Then how little by little the earth began to harden, to cut off Nereus 35
In sea space, and to assume the shapes of matter.
Next he sang about the lands dazzled by the sudden shine of a new
  sun
From higher up and how rain showers fall from the separated cloud
  banks.
Then for the first time forests arise, then
A few animals here and there wander through hills virgin to them. 40
He recalls the stones tossed by Pyrrha, the reign of Saturn,
The eagles at the Caucasus, the theft of Prometheus.
He adds the story of Hylas° left at a fountain where the Argonauts
Shouted till the whole shore echoed: "Hylas, Hylas"—
And of Pasiphae, fortunate had herds of cattle never lived;   45

6.43: alludes to a minor episode of the voyage of the Argonauts. Hercules lost
  his minion Hylas to river-nymphs of the Propontis.

He comforts her hurt for the snow-white bull.
Oh, unfortunate girl, what madness possessed you!
Proetus' daughters filled the fields with counterfeit bellowings,
But as heifers none pursued unions so shameless,
For each shrank from a plow yoked to the neck   50
And often had searched for horns on her smooth forehead.
Ah, unfortunate girl, now you roam the mountain sides,
While he, that bull, propping his snowy white flank on soft hyacinths
Beneath a dark live oak, chews cud on fading grass,
Or is out chasing one of the numerous heifers among the herd.
    "Close off,   55
O Nymphs, you nymphs of Dicte, close off the defiles of the woods,
In case by chance somewhere the labyrinthine footprints
Of my bull meet my eyes; perhaps that bull of mine,
Enchanted by green grass or in chase of the herd,
Some other cows may entice to the stables at Gortyn."   60
Next he sings of the girl Atalanta lured by the apples of the
    Hesperides;
Then he surrounds the sisters of Phaethon with the moss of bitter bark
And raises them high, straight up from the soil, as alders.
He sings now how one of the sister Muses meeting Gallus,
As he was wandering by the streams of Permessus, led him into the
    Aonian hills   65
Where the entire chorus of Apollo stood up in tribute to a man;
And how Linus, the shepherd with the divine gift of song,
His locks wreathed in flowers and bitter parsley,
Said to him: "These pipes the Muses present to you—accept them;
They were once plied by the old man of Ascra;   70
With them he sang songs that charmed down sturdy ash trees from
    mountains.
Use them to sing the genesis of the woods of Gryneia
That not any grove be more a boast from Apollo."
What need I say about Scylla, Nisus' girl? The story followed her
That she was beautiful; but she lived to harass Odysseus' ships,   75
Her loins girded by barking monsters, and in the deep whirlpool
To rip apart with her raging sea-dogs the sailors, ah, so fearful.
Or his story of Tereus' transformed limbs,
The feast Philomela prepared for him, the gifts she presented him,
Her course of flight, the haunts she sought out,   80
On which wings the ill-fated man hovered above his roof?
All the songs which once the favored Eurotas heard
When Apollo rehearsed and ordered his laurels to learn,
Silenus sang: the stunned valleys reverberate them to the stars.
At last the Evening Star ordered them to gather in the sheep   85
And to count up their number again, and then rose reluctant in the
    sky.

8°

We shall sing the music of shepherds Damon and Alphesiboeus,
A heifer forgot her grass to listen in wonder,
Lynxes were dumbfounded at their contest in song,
And rivers stopped, then changed their course of flow;
Yes, we will sing the pastoral muse of Damon and Alphesiboeus.   5
If you are shooting the rocky rapids of great Timavus
Or taking in the shoreline of the Adriatic, oh, will that day
Ever be when I'll be allowed to sing your exploits?
Or will the day come when I may herald throughout the world
Your poetry that rivals the tragic buskin of Sophocles?   10
From you my source, with you I'll conclude. Accept then
These songs begun with your encouragement and allow this ivy
To snake around your temples threaded with victorious laurel leaves.
The chilly shade of night had just faded from the sky,
When dew on tender grass was most pleasing to the herd.   15
Lying against an olive's smooth trunk Damon began:

DAMON: O morning star, come early and bring forth the fostering
     day;
Deceived by the unworthy love of Nysa, my woman,
I have gained nothing from deities, these witnesses of my complaints;
Yet, I address them in the death-throes of my final hour.   20
     Come, my flute, begin with me the Arcadian song.
Mount Maenalus is known for its whistling forest of whispering pines;
It always hears the love-pangs of shepherds,
And heeds Pan who first did not allow reeds to stand idle.
     Come, my flute, begin with me the Arcadian song.   25
Nysa is pledged to Mopsus: for us lovers what hope is there not?
Soon gryphons will mate with mares, and in the coming age
Timid does will meet hounds at drinking bowls.
     Come, my flute, begin with me the Arcadian song.
Mopsus, cut fresh bridal torches; you lead home a wife.   30
Scatter walnuts, bridegroom; for you the Evening Star abandons Oeta.
     Come, my flute, begin with me the Arcadian song.
You have wed a *worthy* man, you who despise all others
And find my panpipes loathsome, my little goats,
My shaggy brow and unkempt beard offensive,   35
And have no faith that any god concerns himself with mortal matters.
     Come, my flute, begin with me the Arcadian song.
In our hedged orchards I saw you, still a child, with your mother—
I was your guide—picking apples dripping with the morning dew.

8.1: the poem is addressed to Gaius Asinius Pollio.

I was just twelve at the time,   40
But from the ground could reach the fragile boughs:
When I saw you, I perished—such a frenzied misjudgment.
   Come, my flute, begin with me the Arcadian song.
Now I know what Love is: on hard rocks either Tmaros
Or Rhodope or farthest Africa gave him birth,   45
A boy, not of the human race or of human blood like us.
   Come, my flute, begin with me the Arcadian song.
Savage Love drove a mother to stain her hands with the blood
Of her children; you, his mother, are cruel too!
But who is more cruel, the mother or that depraved boy?   50
As that boy is depraved, so you, his mother, are savage.
   Come, my flute, begin with me the Arcadian song.
Now may the wolf shun the sheep; may hard oaks
Bear golden apples; may the alder blossom narcissus,
And may thick drops of amber exude from the tamarisk bark.   55
Let screech owls challenge swans; let Tityrus be Orpheus,
Be Orpheus in the woods, but Arion among dolphins.
   Come, my flute, begin with me the Arcadian song.
Let everything become sea, mid-sea. Farewell, my woods.
Headlong into the waters from a lookout on a lofty peak   60
I'll hurl myself; this last gift of a dying man take.
   Stop, my flute, cease now the Arcadian song.
Thus Damon: now, O Muses, sing for us what Alphesiboeus
Responded; not all things can all of us do.

ALPHESIBOEUS: Bring water and wreathe these altars with soft
   woolen fillets;
Burn thick verbena and masculine incense;   66
I'll try by magic rites to alter the healthy senses
Of my man; I lack nothing except spells.
   Draw him home from the city, my spells, draw home Daphnis.
Spells can eclipse the moon from the sky,   70
With magic spells Circe transformed Ulysses' men,
By magic chants the cold snake in meadows snaps.
   Draw him home from the city, my spells, draw home Daphnis.
First I bind upon your image triple laces of triple colors,
Then around this altar I carry your effigy   75
Three times—the god likes an odd number.°
   Draw him home from the city, my spells, draw home Daphnis.
Plait in triplicate knots, Amaryllis, three colors,
Wind them now, Amaryllis, and chant: 'I wind the chains of Venus.'

8.74-76: three and its multiples have a significant role in magic and ritual.

Draw him home from the city, my spells, draw home Daphnis.   80
Like this clay hardening and like this wax melting
From the same fire, so Daphnis hardens and melts from our love.
Sprinkle the meal and fire up the laurel leaves crackling with pitch:
That bastard Daphnis sets me ablaze, so on Daphnis I'll burn this
   laurel.
Draw him home from the city, my spells, draw home Daphnis.   85
May a longing grip Daphnis like that of a heifer weary
In search for her bullock-mate through woods and deep into groves
Sinking down on green sedge by a stream,
Desperate and forgetting to move in surrender to late night;
Yes, may such a desire take Daphnis, and may I not have a care to
   heal him.   90
Draw him home from the city, my spells, draw home Daphnis.
These keepsakes the liar sloughed off and left for me,
Precious pledges of his being, I now consign to you, O earth,
At my threshold; they guarantee Daphnis' payment due.
Draw him home from the city, my spells, draw home Daphnis.   95
These herbs, these drugs culled just for me from the Black Sea,
Moeris himself furnished—the Pontus grows them in abundance—
With them I have seen Moeris, more than once, turn into a wolf and
   lurk
In woods, seen him raise spirits from the deepest tombs,
And seen him transfer sown crops to another field.   100
Draw him home from the city, my spells, draw home Daphnis.
Bring ashes outside, Amaryllis; throw them in a flowing brook
Over your head, and don't look back. In this way I'll get
Daphnis. He cares not for gods; he cares not for witchcraft.
Draw him home from the city, my spells, draw home Daphnis.   105
Look! Spontaneous flickering of flames, the altar catches fire, live
   ashes,
While I was dilly-dallying to dispense them. Glory be!
Something is up; Hylax is barking at the doorway.
Are we to trust it? Or are they just the dreams of lovers?
Cease, yes, cease the spells, from the city comes Daphnis.   110

10

Grant me, Arethusa, to fulfill this final task:
A brief song for my Gallus such as Lycoris° herself may read
I must sing: who would begrudge songs to Gallus?
So for you, when you glide beneath the waves off Sicily,

10.2: Lycoris is Gallus' pseudonym for Volumnia, a freedwoman who became
   a celebrated actress with the stage name "Cytheris."

May the bitter sea not mingle its waters with yours,   5
Begin: let us sing the stormy loves of Gallus,
While snub-nosed little goats crop tender boughs.
We do not sing to the deaf; the woods re-echo all.
What groves, what ravines detained you, young
Naiads, when Gallus was dying from unrequited love?   10
Neither the heights of Parnassus nor of Pindus
Delayed you, nor Aganippe in Aonie.
For him even the laurel trees, even the tamarisks wept,
For him, as he lay beneath a lonely cliff, even
Maenalus and its pines wept, and the rocks of icy Lycaeus.   15
The sheep are standing about; (they are not ashamed of us,
And you, divine poet, shouldn't be ashamed of the flock;
The handsome Adonis, too, pastured sheep near streams;)
And the shepherd and the weary swineherds came;
Menalcas, dripping wet from steeping winter acorns in water, came. 20
All of them ask: "Where does this love of yours come from?" Then
  Apollo came;
He asks: "Gallus, what, are you insane? Your loved one, Lycoris,
Has followed another man through snow and horrid camps of war."°
Then came Silvanus, too, his head wreathed with the pride of the
  countryside,
Waving flowering fennel and large lilies.   25
Pan, the god of Arcadia, came; we ourselves saw him
Stained blood-red from elderberries and cinnabar.
"Will there be no limit?" he said; "Love cares not for such things,
And cruel Love is not sated by tears, nor grasses by streams,
Nor bees by clover, nor goats by foliage."   30
But he replied sadly, "Still, Arcadians, you will sing°
This song to your mountains; you alone are skilled to sing,
Arcadians. O how gently my bones would rest then,
If your reed hereafter would proclaim my love.
Oh, how I wish I had been one of you and had been   35
Either the guardian of your flock or the dresser of your ripening
  grapes.
Surely, whether Phyllis were mine or Amyntas,°
Or some other madness, (so what if Amyntas is dark?

10.22-23: familiar elegiac theme of the rich military rival. See Propertius 1.8
    & 2.16.
10.31: begins Gallus' lament which underscores the difficult, if not impossible,
    dilemma of the elegiac poet thriving in the pastoral world of Arcadia.
10.37: Gallus accepts the bisexuality of Arcadia.

Violets, too, are dark, and dark are hyacinths),
With me among the willows beneath a pliant vine they would lie;   40
Phyllis would gather wreaths for me, Amyntas would sing to me.
Here are icy springs, here, Lycoris, are soft meadows,
Here a grove; here I could have wasted away an age with you.
But now an insane love for relentless war detains me
In arms amid weapons, face to face with a foe.   45
You, far from the fatherland (I just can't believe it's so),
Without me gaze alone at the snows of the Alps, O hard-hearted one,
And the freezes of the Rhine; ah, may those chills not harm you,
And I hope the jagged ice does not cut your tender feet.
I shall go, and in the verse of Euphorion of Chalcis on the reed   50
Of a Sicilian shepherd modulate the songs I have composed.
I am resolved to prefer to endure it in the forests among the caves
Of wild animals and to carve my love songs on the bark
Of tender trees; they will grow; and you, my love poems, will grow
     with them.
Meanwhile, among the nymphs I'll haunt Maenalus   55
Or I'll go hunting for fierce wild boars. No frosts will stop me
From surrounding the glades of the Virgin Mountain° with dogs.
Already I see myself passing over cliffs and the echoing woodlands,
Happy to be shooting Cretan arrows from a Parthian bow
Horn-made, as if this were a cure for my frenzy,   60
Or as if that god could soften at the pains of men.
Ah, no, neither the nymphs of the woods, nor even songs
Delight me; you woods, be off again.
Our efforts cannot change him,
Not even if we were to drink from the middle of icy Hebrus,   65
Or to undergo the snows and rainy winter of Thrace,
Nor even if, when the bark dries and dies high on the elms,
We were to drive sheep in Aethiopia beneath the sign of the Crab.
Love conquers all; we too should yield to Love."
That will be enough for your poet to sing, goddesses,   70
While he sits and weaves a small basket of slender hibiscus,
Muses of Pieria; you will make even this precious to Gallus,
Yes, to Gallus; for him my love grows hour by hour,
As much as a green alder spiring in early spring.
Let us rise: shade is usually grievous upon singers;   75
Shade is grievous for the juniper; shade hurts the crops.
Go home, you are filled; the Evening Star comes; go home, little goats.

10.57: 'Virgin Mountain' translates *Parthenius*, a reference also to the poet
   Parthenius. See Propertius 1.1.11.

GEORGICS

The richness of the *Georgics*, the so-called 'poem of the earth,' far exceeds the didactic function promised by its title. Many have admired its poetic language, the moral fervor of the presentation, and the dramatic polar pairing of hard work and loss, of success and failure, and of direct instruction and recondite lore. Included in descriptions of the labors of the farm are passages that are cosmic in scope: myths of gods and heroes, human and divine wars, the rise of heavenly bodies, names of lakes, important commercial districts, and references to famous families. It is impossible to read the *Georgics* without sensing the pathos of various depictions and the dignity imbued in its lines and books.

BOOK I

What makes the crops fruitful, what star
It's best to plow the soil by, Maecenas, and to wed the vines
To elms, what is the proper care of cattle, what treatment
For breeding a herd, how much experience is needed for the
    cultivation of thrifty bees,°
Such is the song I now commence. You, most glorious lights of the
    world   5
Conducting the year gliding through heaven,
And as surely as by your gifts, father Liber° and nourishing Ceres,
    earth
Exchanged the Choanian acorn for the teeming wheat stalk,
And mixed draughts of river water with the juice of discovered
    grapes;
And you Fauns, deities present for farmers,   10
Step forward in rhythm, O Fauns, and you, too, young Dryads:
I sing of your gifts; you, too, at whose command the earth
Struck by your mighty trident brought forth the first horse neighing,
Neptune; and you, patron of groves,° whose lush thickets in Ceos
Three hundred snow-white bulls crop;   15
And you yourself leave your father's woods and Lycaean glens,
Pan, protector of sheep, out of the love for your Maenalus
Stand by me in grace, O god of Tegea,° and you, Minerva,
Maker of the olive, and you, child, founder of the curved plow,°

1.1-4: the opening lines herald the major themes of the four individual books
    of the work.
1.7: Father Liber is Bacchus.
1.14: the reference is to Aristaeus, deified for his benefits to mankind, and looks
    forward to Book 4.317-558.
1.18: the reference to Tegea emphasizes Pan's close connection with Arcadia.
1.19: Triptolemus, consort of Demeter, and teacher of agriculture to humans.

And you, Silvanus, carrying the cypress with its roots,   20
And all you gods and goddesses who wish to protect the fields,
And who make grow new fruit plants from seeds unsown,
And who send from the sky soaking rain to feed the planted crops,
And above all, you, for it is not yet set what society of gods°
Will soon possess you, Caesar, should you wish to grace cities,   25
To make the lands your care, and should the mighty globe
Welcome you as the grower of fruits and powerful controller of
    seasons,
And garland its temples with the myrtle of your mother;
Your arrival will be as god of the unmeasured sea and to your
    divinity alone
Sailors will pay tribute, and farthest Thule will serve you,   30
And all the waves of Tethys will buy and dower you as her son-in-
    law;
Or should you rise as a new constellation in the lingering months
Where a region between Erigone and the claws of Scorpio in pursuit
    of her
Lies open (look, already fiery Scorpio on his own draws in his arms
And has left for you a share of heaven more than just),   35
Whatever you will be—the realms of Tartarus, lest we forget, have no
    hope
To make you their king and no ambitious desire to reign there would
Move you, although Greece herself glorifies those Elysian fields
And Proserpina, long searched for to return above, refuses to follow
    her mother—
Grant me a smooth course and approve with a nod my bold
    endeavors,   40
And in pity of farmers ignorant of the way
Step forward and even now attune yourself to entreaties and prayers.
In early spring, when the icy moisture from snowy-white mountains°
Begins to melt and clods thaw and crumble from the balmy Zephyrus,
Right then my ox begins to groan over the plow pressed into the
    earth   45
And the blade glistens, rubbed smooth in the furrow.
Only that cropland which has twice felt the sun,
Twice the wintry cold, answers the prayers of the greedy farmer.
From it boundless harvests burst the barns.
Yet, before we split open the virgin soil untouched by the iron
    plow,   50

1.24-42: these lines are the climax of the prayer to the gods, reserving a special
    address and place for Octavius who awaits deification and future dominion
    over everything except the underworld.

Let us take care to learn the winds, the ever-changing nature of
    climate,
The hereditary cultivation and character of the places,
Whatever each region bears and what each refuses to yield.
In one place crops, in another grapes, grow in greater bounty;
Elsewhere the young growth of trees and spontaneous grains flourish
    green.   55
You note how the Tmolus exports scented saffron,
India ivory, and the effeminate Sabaeans their own incense,
The naked Chalybes steel, the Pontus strong perfumes,
And Epirus the palms won by Olympic thoroughbreds.
Nature has imposed these uninterrupted laws and eternal
    covenant   60
Upon determined locales straightway from the time
Deucalion threw the first stones upon the empty world
Whence humans sprang, a hearty race. So, come, make
The strong oxen turn the rich soil of the earth right away
In the early months of the year, as the dusty heat of summer bakes 65
Under ripening rays the clods exposed to the sun.
However, if the earth fails to produce beneath the rising
Of Arcturus, plow a shallow furrow, grazing the ground just enough.
Thus, weeds will not choke the luxuriant plants in the rainy climes,
Nor in the dry areas a little moisture escape the sterile, sandy soil.   70
You will best allow in alternate years the lands to lie fallow after
    harvest,°
And the sluggish fields to harden from moldy disuse;
Beneath another star plant yellow grain there
Where earlier you plucked up the bean, burgeoning in its splitting
    pod,
Or peas growing on a slender stalk, or where you removed   75
The brittle tangle and rustling undergrowth of the bitter lupine.
A crop of flax exhausts the field, and oats exhaust the soil,
So too poppies steeped in the sleep of forgetfulness use up the
    ground.
Yet by rotating crops easy is the work, if you are not embarrassed
To moisturize the dry soil with enriching manure   80
And to spread dirty compost over effete fields.
So when crops are rotated, the soil finds rest,
And even then for land unplowed there is bounty.
Often too it has proved useful to set the barren fields afire,

---

1.43-70: entertain the proper time and place for plowing determined by varied
    geography and climate.

And to burn the light stubble in crackling flames: 85
Then because of the fire the earth assumes hidden strength
And rich nourishments, or its every fault is cooked out
And useless moisture evaporates
Or the heat opens up more passages and unlocks
Blocked pores by which sap reaches the young plants,   90
Or it hardens and tightens the gaping veins,
So that steady rains or the searing heat of the powerful sun
Or the piercing cold of the north wind not burn up the earth.
So he who breaks up the lifeless clods with rakes
And drags harrows of wicker over them greatly enriches the fields, 95
Nor from lofty Olympus does golden-haired Ceres view him without
      reward,
And likewise he who splits the surface and then breaks up the piled
      ridges,
Turning his plow across the furrowed plain,
Over and over to train the earth and to issue orders to the fields.
Farmers, pray for wet summers and mild winters;   100
In the dust of winter most fruitful are the grain crops,
Productive the field: so without any tillage Mysia with pride
Boasts and Gargara too marvels at its own harvests.
What shall I sing of him who, once the seed is sown, attacks
Hand to hand the fields and smashes mounds of unfertile sand,   105
And then brings to the crops a channel and streams flowing with
      water,
And, when the field is parched and teems with heat burning up the
      dying plants,—
Look!—he charms down a wave of water over the ridge of a steep
      sluice,
As it cascades over smoothed rocks and raises a raucous roar
And gushes to temper the burning plowland?   110
What of him who to keep the stalks from drooping beneath the
      weight of their ears
Clips the growth of the field crops while the blade is young,
As soon as the plants equal the furrow's top? And him who
Drains off with thirsty sand the moisture gathered in a swamp?
Mostly in the unstable months a river gushes, overflows,   115
And far and wide coats and mires everything in mud,
And causes hollow ponds to steam with warm vapor.

1.71-99: instructions on the care and preparation of the soil and irrigation.

Yet despite the toiling of both men and beasts,°
Skilled in tilling the land, the gluttonous goose
And Strymonian cranes and chicory with its bitter fibers   120
Hinder the work; shade too harms it. The father himself
Ordained that the road of agriculture not be easy, and was first
With a system to cultivate the fields, sharpening mortal minds with
    worries;
He did not suffer his realms to grow dull from sluggish disuse:
Before Jupiter no farmers subdued the fields;   125
To mark off and divide a field with a boundary stone
Was taboo: their gains were for the common stock, and the earth
Brought forth all things too freely and without command.
But he imbued foul snakes with poisonous venom
And ordained wolves to prey, the sea to swell;   130
He shook honey from the leaves, removed fire,
And prevented wine from flowing everywhere in streams
So that experience and reflection little by little would hammer out
    various skills,
And would cull the blade of grain from plowed furrows;
And forge fire hidden in the veins of flint.   135
Then for the first time rivers felt hollowed alders,
The sailor numbered and named the stars,
The Pleiades, Hyades, and Arctos,° radiant daughter of Lycaon;
Then men discovered how to catch wild animals in traps and snare
    them
With birdlime and to surround large glades with hounds;   140
One beats a broad river with a casting net
Seeking its bottom, another trawls his dripping line from the sea;
Then came the hardness of iron, the sharp blade of a shrill saw,
(For the men of old used to split wood open with wedges),
Then all kinds of skills. Unrelenting toil overcame all things   145
As did the pressure of want in the harsh realities of their lives.
Ceres first taught mortals to plow the earth with iron
When the sacred forests were failing in acorns and berries
And Dodona was denying food.
Soon to the wheat crops trouble came so that   150
Ruinous mildew consumed the stalks, and the lazy thistle
Bristled in fields; the crops die, up springs ragged growth,
Burrs and thorns; amid the glistening cultivated plants

1.118-159: Vergil here details the transition from the Golden Age of Saturn to
    the Age of Iron imposed by Jupiter, bringing harm and damage to crops and
    the necessity of hard work (*labor*) and constant vigilance against ruin.
1.138: constellations important in sailing.

The unproductive darnel and sterile wild oats overpower the field.
So, unless you attack weeds with constant hoeing   155
And scare away birds with noise, and with a pruning hook lop off
The shading branches darkening a field, and invoke rain in prayers,
Oh, in vain you will eye the huge pile of another,
And in the woods shake an oak to relieve hunger.
Now I must sing of the weapons of hard farmers:°   160
Without them crops could not be planted or raised,
First the plowshare and the weighty frame of the curved plow,
Then the slow-rolling wagon of Eleusis' mother,°
The threshing sledge and drags, the hoes of cruel weight,
And too the cheap wicker ware of Celeus,   165
The wooden baskets and mystic winnowing fan of Iacchus.
Remember to provide and store all these things well in advance,
If worthy is the promised glory of the divine countryside awaiting
   you.
First with great effort bend a forest elm, skillfully work the wood°
To shape it into the curve of a plowshare.   170
Fasten to the top of the stock a pole eight feet long;
Fit on two molded flaps, and share beams with double ridge.
For a yoke cut a light linden, and a tall beech
For the handle, which from the rear you guide the moving chariot
   below,
And all of this hang over the hearth for smoke to temper its
   strength.   175
I can relate to you many precepts of the ancients,°
Unless you shrink back, loathing to learn such mundane chores.
First, the threshing floor must be made level by a huge roller,
Then worked by hand and hardened by binding clay
To prevent weeds cropping up, the floor cracking and crumbling
   into dust,   180
And numerous pests from mocking you: often a small mouse
Beneath the ground has built his homes and raised his barns,
Or moles, robbed of eyes, have dug out chambers;
In holes a toad can be found and all manner of beasties

1.160-175: list the weapons of the farmer with a detailed description of the plow,
   the primary implement in man's battle with the soil.
1.163-165: Eleusis' mother is Ceres; Celeus and Iacchus are connected to the
   cult of Ceres (Demeter) at Eleusis. See Glossary: CELEUS.
1.169-175: the description of the plow reworks Hesiod. In general the plow is
   depicted as a chariot, making it a military-like 'weapon.'
1.176-203: Vergil provides examples of the frustrations and forces plied by na-
   ture against the struggles and efforts of the farmer. Extra work is needed to
   counter nature's inevitable tendency toward degeneration.

The earth breeds; the weevil lays waste a huge heap   185
Of grain as does the ant that fears a destitute old age.
Ponder, too, when the walnut tree richly clothes
Itself in blossoms and bends its fragrant limbs,
If the fruits thrive, so in equal measure will grain crops follow,
And a great threshing will arrive with the intense heat;   190
But if shade abounds from the excess growth of foliage,
The threshing floor will fail, grinding up stalks rich only in chaff.
I have witnessed many planters steep their seeds
And soak them in soda and dark oil-lees before sowing
So that from the deceptive pods might come larger produce,   195
And the seeds, however slight the fire, might become soaked.
I have seen seeds, long-picked and watched laboriously,
Degenerate nonetheless, unless with effort every year human hands
Pick all the largest. Thus all things are fated
To fall into a worse condition and, retrograde, slip backwards,   200
Just like one who with difficulty and against the current
Plies his boat with oars; if by chance he relaxes his arms,
Headlong the channel hurls him and boat downstream.
We farmers must also observe the constellations: Arcturus,°
The ascendant days of Haedus, and gleaming Draco,   205
As do they who, sailing over windy seas to their countryland,
Tempt the Pontus and the straits of Abydus rich in oysters.
When Libra has equaled the hours of the day and sleep
And has divided the earth in two, half in light, half in darkness,
Be men, work the oxen, sow barley in the fields   210
Until the unmanageable winter's storm ends work;
Then, too, it is time to bury in the ground the crop of flax
And Ceres' poppies, and high time to bend over the plows,
While dry soil permits and clouds hang high.
In spring sow beans; at that time, too, the crumbling furrows   215
Welcome clover; millet receives annual care,
When bright Taurus with gilded horns opens
The year and the Dog-star sets, giving way to Taurus, the facing
    constellation.
But if you work the soil for a crop of wheat
And the hardy spelt, and make ears of grain your one aim,   220
First let the Pleiades sink from sight in the dawn
And the Cretan star of blazing Corona° set

1.204-258: Vergil treats the time to plow and sow with reference to astronomical
    and climatological patterns and conceptions.
1.222: when Dionysus rescued Ariadne of Crete from Naxos and made her his
    divine wife, he catasterized (i.e., made into a constellation) her crown as the
    constellation Corona.

Before you commit seeds, owed to the furrows, and hasten
To entrust to the unwilling soil the hope of the year.
Many have begun before the setting of Maia;   225
But the expected crop frustrated them with sterile wild oats.
But if you sow vetch and the vulgar kidney bean
And do not spurn the cultivation of Egyptian lentil,
Bootes descendant will send unmistakable signs:
Begin and extend your sowing into the frosts of deepest winter.   230
To that end the golden sun directs its circuit measured
By set divisions through the world's twelve constellations of the
    zodiac.
Five zones occupy heaven; one of these
Is always ablaze from the glowing sun, always from the scorching
    fire;
Around it on the right and the left two extend very far out,   235
Dark and clogged with ice and black storms;
Between them and the one in the middle two zones were ordained for
    feeble mortals,
A gift assigned from the gods; and a path was cut through both
Along which the series of constellations at a slant revolved.
The world rises high to Scythia and the peaks of Rhipae,   240
Then sinks sloping towards Libya's south winds.
One pole is ever high over us, the other
Dark Styx and the infernal shades buried deep beneath our feet see.
Here in his sinuous coils glides mighty Draco
Like a river around and through the two Bears,°   245
The Bears that shrink in fear from dipping into Ocean's expanse.
There, some maintain, either is the dead silence of unseasonable night,
And there dark gloom always spreads and thickens the pall of night,
Or else Dawn returns from us and restores to them the day.
When the rising sun with its panting horses has breathed upon
    us,   250
There the Evening Star kindles red its late rays.
Hence we are able to forecast the patterns of weather even in
    a changeable sky,
The day and time to sow and harvest,
The best time to drive upon the distrustful sea in oared ships,
To launch fleets fitted for war,   255
Or in season to fell the pine.
Not in vain do we scout out the risings and settings of signs
And the year uniform in its four different seasons.

1.245: the Two Bears are the Big and Little Dipper.

Whenever a cold shower keeps the farmer contained indoors,°
He can use the chance to ready all the many projects that
    otherwise   260
Under a clear sky would be hurried: the plowman hammers out
The hard share of the blunted plow, hollows out vats from a tree,
Or brands his herd and labels his heaps of grain;
Others sharpen stakes and two-pronged forks
And get ready willow ties from Ameria° for the pliant vine.   265
So in this period weave a pliable basket from red twigs,
Now roast the grains by fire, now grind them on stone.
Yes, even on holidays religion and laws allow
Some activities: no religious ban is there
On irrigating with rivulets, fencing in a crop,   270
Setting traps for birds, firing thorny briar bushes,
And dipping a flock of sheep in a healthy stream.
Often the driver loads the sides of a stubborn ass
With oil or cheap fruits, and returns from the city
Bringing back a rough-dressed millstone or a mass of black pitch. 275
The moon has arranged various days in varied grades
Favorable for work: avoid the fifth, on this day pale Orcus
And the Furies were born; also from an unspeakable birth
Earth bore Coeus, Iapetus, savage Typhoeus,
And those brothers Aloidae who conspired to tear down heaven: 280
Three times they strove to pile Mt. Ossa on Pelion,
And, yes, to roll leafy Olympus onto Ossa;
Three times the father with a thunderbolt split the stacked mountains.
The seventeenth is lucky for planting the vine,
For breaking and yoking bulls and for looping threads
    on the warp.   285
The ninth is the best day for a runaway, not so good for a thief.
Many tasks present themselves better in the chill of the night,
Or at sunrise as the Morning Star besprinkles the lands with dew.
Night is a better time to cut the light stubble, to row the parched
    meadows;
For moisture that softens the stalks permeates night.   290
And there is a man who by the blaze of a winter fire
Stays awake late to hone torches with a sharp knife,
While his wife relieves her long toil with singing
As she runs the shrill comb through the loom's webs
Or boils down the sweet juice of must over a fire,   295

1.259-310: the useful work to be performed during spells of bad weather, in
    winter, at night, and on holy days.
1.265: Ameria: a town in Umbria about 55 miles north of Rome.

And with leaves skims off the foamy water from a bubbling bronze
  cauldron.
But in the heat of noon cut down Ceres ripening red-brown;
In the heat of noon the threshing floor grinds the toasted grains.
In the nude plow, in the nude sow. For a farmer winter is a lazy time;
In cold seasons farmers enjoy their produce most of all,   300
Happily they celebrate feasts shared among them.
Festive winter invites cheer and dissolves cares,
As when ships stuffed full with cargo have reached harbor
And happily sailors have garlanded the decks;
But that is the time to strip acorns from oaks,   305
The laurel berries, olive, and blood-red myrtle;
The time to set traps for cranes and nets for deer,
To pursue long-eared hares; the time to shoot does,
Hurling the hempen thongs of a Balearic sling,
When snow lies deep, when rivers pack ice.   310
Now I shall sing of the storms and stars of autumn,°
And what signs men should watch when now the day
Is shorter and the summer milder, or when spring comes down in
  rain,
Or when the harvest of wheat spikes has already bristled over the
  plains,
And on the green stalk the grain swells with milky moisture.   315
I have witnessed often, when the farmer has brought the reaper
To his yellowing fields and has stripped the brittle stalk of barley,
All the battles of the winds rush together
To uproot violently and far and wide the pregnant crop
And to upheave it on high; so, too, in a black whirlwind   320
The winter storms carry off the light straw and flitting stubble.
Yes, often I have eye-witnessed the coming of a vast column of water
  from the sky,
Cloud banks gathered from on high cluster and whip up a foul storm
Of dark downpours; the lofty heavens collapse,
And from the deluge the rain sweeps away the fruitful crop   325
And the labors of oxen; ditches fill up, rivers with hollowed channels
  swell
And roar; and the sea and its inlets boil and heave.
The father himself in a midnight of stormy clouds
Wields lightning in his flashing right hand; it shakes, shocks,

---

1.311-350: the unpredictable and unseasonable storms that can bring ruin de-
  spite all the labor of the diligent farmer. Vergil maintains that only constant
  vigilance and piety can hope to minimize the destruction. The sudden storm
  metaphorically presages the political devastation described at the end of the
  book.

And makes the mightiest earth tremble; beasts flee and cowering
   terror   330
Throughout nations lays low mortal hearts: with blazing bolt
He dislodges Mt. Athos, or Rhodope, or lofty Ceraunia;
The south winds double up and the rain becomes thick upon thick:
Now groves, now shores they blast.
In dread of this mark the months and stars of heaven,   335
Where Saturn's cold star retires,
What orbits in heaven fiery Mercury wanders.
Foremost, worship the gods, duly pay annual sacrifices
To great Ceres, sacrificing on burgeoning grass
At the setting of winter's end, as soon as it becomes mild spring. 340
Then fat are the lambs, at that time most mellow the vines,
Then sweet are sleeps, and dense are the shadows on mountains.
Make sure all your rustic youth worship Ceres;
Mix honey with milk and mild wine,
Let an auspicious victim three times circle the young crops,   345
And all the chorus of friends accompany it in celebrating,
And with loud cries welcome Ceres in their homes; let no one
Wield his pruning hook upon the ripening grain
Before he binds his temples with a crown of oak for Ceres,
And dances impromptu and sings hymns to her.   350
So that we could learn these things by reliable signs,°
Intervals of heat, rain, and winds that bring the driving cold,
The father himself decreed what warning the monthly moon was to
   reveal,
Under what sign the south winds were to descend, at what frequent
   sight
Farmers were to keep their herds nearer to their stalls.   355
Right away with rising winds the straits of the sea
Begin to swell and churn and from lofty mountains
A dry clash is heard, or shores ring out a confused echo
From afar and a murmur grows loud in groves.
Then too the wave of the sea scarcely restrains its attack on curved
   keels   360
As swift gulls fly from the mid-sea,
Screeching toward the shores as marine coots
Sport upon the dry land, and the heron deserts
Its familiar marshes, then soars high above a cloud.

1.351-463: the need for vigilance outlined in the previous section leads to the
   necessity of frequent observances of weather signs that forecast bad and fair
   weather. Particularly important are prognostic signs given by the moon and
   sun.

Often too, while a wind threatens, you will see stars   365
Shoot headlong from the sky, and behind them throughout
     the darkness
Of night long trails of flame glowing white;
Often light chaff and falling leaves flit about
Or on the surface of the water feathers float and play.
But when lightning strikes from the region of the savage north   370
And from the home of the east and west winds, all the countryside
Floods from overflowing channels and every sailor on the sea
Furls dripping sails. Never has a rain storm overtaken
Anyone unawares: either in depths of valleys airy cranes
Flee the gathering storm or a heifer, looking up   375
To the heaven, spreads its nostril and sniffs the air;
Or a shrill swallow skims over the ponds
And frogs in the mud croak, harmonizing an old elegy.
Often too an ant wears a narrow path in bringing out
Her eggs from her innermost cells; a huge rainbow drinks
     the flood,   380
And an army of ravens quit their pasture and in a long column,
Crowded wing to wing, they caw on and on.
All kinds of sea-birds are evident, and those swans that root about
In their favorite lakes, the Asian meadows of the Cayster;
They rival each other in pouring abundant spray upon their
     shoulders;   385
You may see them dipping a head in the waters, now skipping into
     the waves,
And aimlessly reveling in their zeal for a bath.
Then the unscrupulous crow croaks and clamors for rain
And struts alone with himself on the dry sandy beach.
Even night-spinning girls as they pluck wool have not failed   390
To mark a winter's storm, when they see the oil in a blazing lamp
Sputter, and moldy fungus grow on the wick.
You can also discern bright suns after a shower and clear, calm
     weather,
And recognize them by reliable signs.
For then the stars' brilliant edge is seen undimmed,   395
And the Moon rises unobliged to her brother's rays;
No fleecy thin clouds pass over the sky;
No halcyons dear to Thetis spread their wings on the shore
Toward the balmy sun; no filthy pigs have mind to use their snouts
To toss bundled straw into pieces.   400
But misty clouds steal to the valleys and hang above the plain;
The owl observes the setting of the sun from a roof top
And plies its useless hooting in late song.
High in the clear air appears Nisus

And Scylla who pays the penalty for clipping the purple lock
    of hair: 405
Wherever she flies, cutting through the light ether on wing,
Look! Through the breezes, relentless and savage, whirrs
Nisus in pursuit; wherever Nisus soars through the air,
She speeds in escape, splitting the light ether on wing.
Then the ravens from muffled throat three or four times   410
Multiply their piercing sounds, and often from high nests,
Overjoyed with some delight, they caw
With one another among the leaves: pleased that the showers have
    stopped,
They are glad to see once more their young and sweet nests.
No, I do not believe that it is because they possess a nature   415
Endowed by god or a greater foresight granted by fate;
But when the weather and the changeable humidity
Have altered the temper of the sky, and rainy Jupiter, aided by the
    south wind,
Condenses what was thin before and rarefies what was dense,
The phases of their spirits change and their breasts conceive   420
Impulses, now one, now another, different from those they felt while
    the wind
Was chasing away the clouds: for this reason the gathering of birds
    takes place
In the field, the flocks gambol, and the ravens caw happy gutturals.
But if you look to the scorching sun and the phases of the moon that
    follow
In due order, never will tomorrow's hour deceive you,   425
Nor will you be ensnared by the clear night.
As soon as the moon amasses its cyclical fires,
If she embraces black air in her darkening crescent,
A most powerful rain shower awaits farmers and the sea;
But if she suffuses on her face a virginal blush,   430
There will be wind; wind always makes golden Phoebe blush.
If on the fourth rising—for that is our surest proof—
She passes pure through the sky and without blunted horns,
All that day and those that arise from it
To the end of the month will be without rain and heavy winds,   435
And rescued sailors will pay their vows upon the shore
To Glaucus, Panopea, and Melicertes,° son of Ino.
The sun, too, both rising and when it sinks into the waves,
Will portend the weather; most reliable are the signs that attend the
    sun,

1.437: all sea gods; Melicertes was metamorphosed along with his mother.

Both those it brings in the morning and those as the stars arise;   440
When, buried in a cloud, it changes, rising with spots,
And shrinks back in the center of its orb,
You should expect showers; for then from the deep sweeps the south
     wind,
Bad omen for orchards, crops, and herd.
When the dawn's rays part and break out   445
Amid dense clouds, or when paling Aurora
Rises leaving the saffron bed of Tithonus,
Oh, oh, then the vine-leaf will poorly protect the mild grapes;
A heavy and bristling hail rattles and dances on roofs.
When the sun has traversed Olympus and departs,   450
You will profit to remember this too, for often we observe
Different hues spread over its face:
A dark blue portends rain, a fiery one east winds;
But if spots appear mixed with a glittering fire,
Then you will see everything seethe with wind and storm
     clouds alike.   455
Not on such a night will I follow anyone's advice to test the deep
Or pull the mooring cable from the land.
Yet when the sun reconstitutes the day and closes the day restored,
And if clear will be its disk, you will have no cause to fear the rain
     clouds
And you will detect a clear north wind stirring the forests.   460
So whatever the late evening brings, from what direction the wind
Drives the serene clouds, what the rainy south wind plots,
The sun will give you signs. Who would dare to say
The sun plays us false? It often warns that the disturbances even
     unseen°
Are at hand, that cancerous treachery and secret wars fester.   465
Yes, after Caesar was extinguished, the sun took pity on Rome
When it covered its shining head with a dull rust,
And the impious ages feared eternal night.
Yet in those days the earth, too, and the surface of the sea,
And damned dogs and ominous birds   470
Kept providing signs. How many times we saw the Cyclopean°
Furnace of Aetna erupt, pour a boiling flood into the fields,
Whirl balls of fire and streaming molten lava.

1.464-514: the prognostic signs also portend ruinous wars and political turmoil.
     Vergil specifically details the warnings attending the assassination of Julius
     Caesar and the subsequent civil wars.
1.471: the Cyclopes serve as blacksmiths and forge Jupiter's thunderbolts in
     Aetna.

Germany heard the noisy clash of arms through all the sky,
The Alps trembled from unusual commotions.   475
In silent sacred groves a voice was heard by many—
A mighty voice—ghosts of the dead, pale in wondrous ways,
Were seen at the darkening of night; and beasts spoke
(Unspeakable!); rivers halt, lands gape wide open,
And in temples the ivory statues weep in mourning and
     the bronzes sweat.   480
The Po, king of rivers, overflowed, twisting and hurling
     in its maelstrom
Whole forests, and throughout all the plains
Carried herds and their stables. During that same time
From grim sacrificial entrails threatening fibers appeared,
And blood flowed from wells, and lofty cities   485
Echoed throughout the night with howls of wolves.
At no other time did more lightning fall from a clear sky
Nor so often dire comets blaze.
So, once more Philippi witnessed Roman battle lines
Clash with one another, armed with like weapons;   490
The gods above did not deem it monstrous that Emathia
And the broad plains of Haemus be fattened on our blood.
No doubt some day will come when a farmer
Tilling the soil with his curved plow in those lands
Will find spears corroded with scaly rust,   495
Or will strike with his heavy hoes empty helmets;
Then he will marvel at the huge bones dug up from their graves.
O you ancestral gods, native heroes of our people, you, Romulus, and
     you,°
Mother Vesta, who preserve the Tuscan Tiber and protect the Palatine
     of Rome,
Do not prevent the youth at least from bringing aid to a topsy-turvy
     age.   500
Long enough we have paid with our blood
For Laomedon's perjuries at Troy;
Long enough, Caesar, the royal palace of heaven has begrudged
You to us and has complained of your concern for mortal triumphs;
For here right has become wrong and wrong right: so many wars   505
Throughout the world, so many shapes of crimes; the plow
Lacks honor, the fields robbed of their farmers lie in waste,
And pruning hooks are forged into a steely sword.
Here the Euphrates, there Germany foments war;

1.498-511: included in Vergil's prayers is an appeal to Octavius to rescue the
     world.

Neighboring cities break the treaties between them   510
And take up arms; unholy Mars rages over the entire globe:°
Just as chariots break and stream from the starting gates,
They speed on lap after lap, and the driver, helplessly gripping
The reins, is swept along by the horses; the chariot pays no heed to
   his controls.

BOOK II. 136-176

Neither the forests of Persia, a most wealthy land,°
Nor the beautiful Ganges, nor the Hermus river muddied with gold
Can compare with Italy's glories, not Bactra nor India
Nor all of Panchaia, a place rich in incense-bearing sands.
The lands here in Italy no bulls breathing fire from their nostrils   140
Have plowed, nor have been sown with the teeth of a huge dragon;
Not here a field crop has bristled thick with warriors' helmets and
   spears,
But pregnant produce and Bacchic drink from Campania's Mt.
   Massicus
Have filled them; olives and fruitful herds occupy them.
From here the war horse marches tall and proud over the plain;   145
From here herds of white bulls, noblest victims at sacrifice,
Often anointed from your holy spring, Clitumnus,
Have led Roman triumphs to the shrines of the gods.
Here there is continual spring and summer in months not its own.
Twice per year the flocks breed, twice the orchard benefits with
   fruits.   150
Absent are wild tigers, the savage breed
Of lions, no aconite to deceive unlucky gatherers,
No scaly snake slithers its monstrous coils along the ground
Or winds itself into a huge trailing spire.
And note too the many glorious cities, the products of so much
   effort,   155
And the many towns erected by toiling hands on precipices of sheer
   rock,
And rivers that glide beneath ancient walls.
Shall I recall the Adriatic Sea and the Tyrrhenian,
Or our lakes, so many: you, mighty Como, and you, Garda,

1.511-514: for the image of the chariot and charioteer out of control see Horace,
   Satires 1.114-116.
2.136-176: the so-called 'praises of Italy.' Italy is blessed with natural resources
   and advantages far surpassing those of other storied locales. The human ef-
   fort resulting from the agricultural ethos brought civilized life and numerous
   human achievements.

Surging with waves and with the roar of a sea?   160
Or shall I recall in song the ports, the moles strengthening Lake
    Lucrino,°
And the sea, indignant, crashing loud against the barriers
Where the Julian waters reverberate far off as the sea is hurled back
And the teeming tide from the Tyrrhenian pours into the straits of
    Avernus?
This same land has brought to light rivers of silver, and in veins   165
Ores for bronze, and in abundance has flowed with streams of gold.
She has engendered a fierce race of warriors, the Marsi, the Sabine
    stock,
Ligurians inured to hardship, and Volsci, expert spearmen;
She has produced the Decii, Marii, the great Camilli,
Scipios, hardened by war, and you, mightiest Caesar,   170
Who, already victorious on the farthest borders of Asia,
Turn aside the unwarlike Indian° from the citadels of Rome.
Hail, great mother of field crops, land of Saturn,
Great parent of heroes; for you I embark on the themes and skills
Of ancient lore, daring to unlock the sacred springs;   175
And now I sing through Roman towns the song of Ascra.

BOOK II .458-540°

O how fortunate are farmers if they ever come to know their own
    wealth.
For them the earth itself, far from the weapons of civil wars,
Sprouts an easy livelihood from the soil, an earth most just.   460
For them no lofty house with haughty doors spews out from all its
    rooms
A huge tide of morning clients;
They do not gape in awe at doorposts inlaid with beautiful
    tortoiseshell,
Or at robes tricked with gold and at Corinthian bronzes;°

2.162: Lake Lucrino is a lagoon near Puteoli (Pozzuoli) across the Bay of Baiae
    where in 37 Agrippa built a causeway. See Propertius 1.11.
2.172: a reference to the Eastern allies of Antony and Cleopatra.
2.458-540: are praises of rustic life. The involvement of farmers with the de-
    piction of the country evokes the Golden Age of Saturn. Vergil argues his
    personal preference for the lifestyle of the country over that of the urban
    Iron Age.
2.464: bronzes made from Ephyra (Corinth) were highly prized by the Ro-
    mans.

Nor do they look upon white wool that is stained with Assyrian
    dye°   465
Or the use of clear olive oil corrupted by scent of cinnamon.
For farmers secure is their rest and a life that knows no fraud,
Rich in many resources, a life of leisure on broad farm lands:
Caves, natural lakes, cool valleys,
The lowing of cattle, and gentle sleep beneath a tree—   470
These, too, are present for them. They find glades there and haunts of
    wild animals,
Also youth hardened to work and accustomed to little,
Reverence for the holy rites of gods and for respected ancestors;
    among them
Justice, as she abandoned the lands, planted her last footsteps.
But as for me, above all else may the sweet Muses,   475
Whose sacred objects, enthused with deep love I bear,
Welcome me and show me the paths of heaven and the stars,
The varied eclipses of the sun, and the labors of the moon;
From them derive tremors of the earth, the power to make deep seas
    swell high,
Break retaining moles, and then on their own subside again;   480
Teach me the reason that winter suns so quickly speed to dip into the
    Ocean,
Or some delay obstructs the sluggish winter nights.
But if I am unable to reach these realms of nature
Because cold blood surrounds and obstructs my heart,
May the countryside and refreshing streams in valleys delight me; 485
Let me live inglorious by falling in love with rivers and forests. Be
    mine, O fields,
O Spercheus river, O woods of Taygetos, where Spartan maidens
    perform Bacchic rites.
Let someone plant me in the cold valleys of Haemus
And shelter me under the expansive shade of branches.
Happy the man who has been able to learn the causes of things, 490
And has trampled beneath his feet all fears, inexorable fate,
And the howl of greedy Acheron.
And fortunate too is he who knows the gods of the countryside,
Pan, old Silvanus, and the sister nymphs.
Him the honors from the people, or the purple of kings   495

2.465: Assyrian is used here loosely for Syrian or Phoenician, referring to the
    famous dye.

Have not perturbed, or the discord that drives brothers to distrust,
Or the Dacians who conspire to descend from the Danube,
Or the politics at Rome, or the foreign kingdoms soon to perish;
No, he has not felt the pain of pity for the poor nor has envied the
  rich;
He has plucked the fruits which branches, which the fields   500
Of their own free will have produced; and he has not witnessed
Iron laws, the insane forum, or the public archives.
Some churn unknown straits with oars, some rush
To the sword, and others penetrate the courts and thresholds of kings.
One wreaks destruction upon a city and its pitiable homes   505
To drink from a jewel-incrusted goblet and to sleep on Tyrian purple;
Another hoards his wealth and broods over his buried gold;
One is dazed and spellbound by the rostra; another, all agape,
The applause of commoners and nobles alike that redoubles
  throughout the seats
Fascinates; and some are elated to steep themselves in their brothers'
  blood,   510
Or to exchange their homes and sweet thresholds for exile,
And seek a country that lies under a different sun.
Meantime, the farmer cleaves the soil with his curved plow:
Here is the year's labor; by it he nourishes his ancestral home and
  young grandchildren;
By it he sustains his herds of cattle and deserving bullocks.   515
There is no respite: the year teems either with the fruit
Or the offspring of the sheep or the sheaf of Ceres' grain;
The harvest loads the furrowed rows with its yield and bursts the
  barns.
Winter has come: The Sicyonian° olive is crushed in the presses,
Pigs return fat from acorns, the forests produce the wild strawberry
  bushes,   520
And autumn serves up its various fruits, and high
On sunlit rocks basks the mellow vintage.
Meanwhile, the farmer's sweet children hang on his kisses,
His pure housewife preserves her chastity; the udders of his cows
  hang full
Of milk, and fat young goats on rich grass   525
Horn to horn grapple with each other,
He himself whiles away his holidays, spread out on grass,
As his companions around a fire wreathe bowls;
To you, Lenaean Bacchus,° he pours libations and invokes in prayer;
  for the shepherds

2.519: Sicyon on the Gulf of Corinth was known for its olives.
2.529: Lenaean refers to the famous winter festival of Dionysus in Athens.

Of the flock he sets up targets on an elm for a contest of speeding
    javelins;   530
They bare their toughened bodies for rustic wrestling.
Once the Sabines of old cultivated this style of life,
This life Remus and his brother lived; from such a way of life Etruria
    grew sturdy,
And, beyond doubt, Rome became the most beautiful city of the
    world,
And as one surrounded her seven citadels with a wall.   535
Long before the scepter of king Jupiter, god of Mt. Dicte,
And before an impious race feasted on slaughtered bullocks,
Golden Saturn once lived this style of life on the earth;
Not yet were heard the blasts of war trumpets, not yet
The clang of swords hammered on hard anvils.   540

BOOK IV°

Now I shall treat honey, the heavenly gift from the sky.
Look upon this section too, Maecenas, with favor.
You will marvel at the pageant of a small world,
And I will relate in due order the courageous leaders of an entire race,
Its mores, pursuits, peoples, and battles.   5
My toil is on a slight theme, but not slight is the glory,
If hostile divine powers allow and Apollo listens to my prayer.
First, seek a home and settlement for the bees,°
A place where no winds have access—for winds prevent
Them carrying home their food—where no sheep and frisky young
    goats   10
May gambol on flowers, or a stray heifer may brush off the dew
From the meadow and bruise the growing blades,
Where spotted lizards with scaly backs avoid
The rich hives, where bee-eaters, and other birds such as Procne,
The swallow, with her breast marked by her bloody hands, may be
    kept away.   15
For they wreak complete havoc on the bees, and they carry them
On the wing in their mouths to be the sweet feast for their pitiless
    nestlings.
But let there be nearby flowing springs and pools green with moss,
And a trickling stream winding through the grass;
Let a palm tree or a huge wild-olive shade the porch   20

4.1-7: the theme of Book IV: the cultivation of bees. The approach to the subject is
    ethnographical. Throughout the presentation Vergil emphasizes the parallels
    and differences between the community of bees and human society.
4.8-50: treat the geography and nature of the hives.

So that, when the new kings° lead the early swarms
In the spring dear to them, and the young frolic, released from the
   combs,
A nearby bank may tempt them to retire from the heat,
And a tree in their path may provide them the hospitable shade of
   leaves.
In the middle, where the water lies still in a pool or flows in
   a stream,   25
Toss willows across and hurl large stones
So they may have bridges to make frequent stops on and to spread
Their wings to the summer sun, if by chance, as they linger,
The southwest wind has doused or plunged them in water.
About all let green cassia, very fragrant thyme,   30
And copious bunches of strong-smelling savory
Bloom, and let violet beds drink of the trickling spring.
Now as to the hives, whether you have one sewn from hollow bark
Or woven of pliant osier,
They should have narrow entrances; for wintry cold   35
Hardens honey, and heat liquefies it;
Each force is to be equally feared for the sake of the bees; and not
Without success in their homes do they eagerly smear with wax
The small pores and fill up chinks with bee-paste from flowers;
For these very purposes they gather and store up   40
The glue, stickier than birdlime, and pitch from Phrygian Ida.
Often in tunneled hideaways, if the report is true,
They cherish their Lar underground, and they have been found deep
In hollow pumice and a cavern eaten out of a tree.
Yet, you, devote yourself to their care; smear the chinks of their
   chambers   45
With smooth clay and throw on a few leafy twigs.
Do not allow the yew too near, nor roast
Red crabs on the hearth; and do not put trust in a deep marsh
Or anywhere there is the strong stench of muck or where hollow rocks
Ring out when struck and the sound echoes from the shock.   50
For the rest, when the golden sun has routed and driven the winter°
Under the earth and has unlocked the sky with the light of summer,
Right away they range over glades and forests,
They crop the purple flowers and hover to sip
The surface of streams. Thus, they take joy and marvelous delight,   55
And rear their young, their nestlings; so, skillfully
They forge fresh wax and mold the sticky honey.

4.21: the ancients thought that the queen bee was male.
4.51-66: the work of bees beginning at winter's end parallels the activity of the
   farmer outlined in 1.43-70.

When you look up to see a squadron, just let loose from the hive,
Soar through the clear summer air towards the stars of the sky,
And when you marvel at the dark cloud trailing in the wind,   60
Mark it with care; they are always in search for sweet waters
And leafy shelters. Here scatter the prescribed scents,
Crushed balm and the lowly honeywort herb;
Ring bells and shake the cymbals of the Great Mother° all about:
The bees themselves will occupy the scented settlements   65
And by their rule will bury themselves in their innermost cradles.
But if they should go out to battle, for often°
Two kings become embroiled in discord and there is a terrible tumult,
Straightaway from afar you can sense the passions of the mob
And hearts pounding for war; for that warlike blast from a raucous 70
Bronze trumpet shames the loiterers, and a sound is heard
Very much like the broken blasts of trumpets;
Then excited they come together, their wings flash,
They sharpen their sting with their beaks, and make ready their arms;
Around the king and at his royal quarters they swarm   75
In a thick mass and challenge the enemy with loud cries;
So when they have obtained a clear day in spring and open skies,
They erupt from the gates; there is a clash, in the high sky
A din; they mingle together and mass into a great ball,
And fall headlong; no more thickly from the air rains hail   80
Nor so many acorns from a shaken oak tree.
Through the middle of the ranks the kings with conspicuous wings
Ply mighty spirit in tiny breasts,
In battle unyielding until the pressing victor has forced
The other side to turn its back and flee.   85
These disturbances, passions, and the rivalries so intense,
Are quelled and quieted by the tossing of a little dust.
But when you recover both leaders from the battle field,
Kill the one who seems inferior lest he be a wasteful parasite;
Let the better one reign supreme in his court;   90
This winner will be ablaze, mottled with golden specks.
For there are breeds of kings: the superior one is distinguished in
    looks
And has brilliant auburn scales, but the other is unkempt
From sloth and drags an inglorious broad belly.
As the kings have two different appearances, so do the bodies of their
    subjects.   95

4.64: the Great Mother is the Phrygian goddess Cybele.
4.67-102: these lines describe swarming, the battle of rivaling kings, and the
    process and selection of the stronger rival. The presentation approximates
    civil discord and war in human society .

Some are ugly and shaggy, just like a parched traveler
Coming from a dusty road spits dirt from his mouth;
Others shine and flash with blazing splendor,
Their bodies symmetrically covered with gold spangles.
This strain is more powerful; from it in due season   100
You will strain sweet honey—yet not so sweet as clear
And fit to mellow the harsh flavor of wine.
But when the swarms fly aimlessly about, play in the sky,°
And scorn the honeycombs and leave their homes cold,
You will put a stop to such idle sport, constraining their giddy
    spirit.   105
Nor is it a hard task to stop them; just rip the wings
Off the kings; as they perforce hesitate, not one bee
Will take to the lofty air or seize banners from camp.
Attract them by inviting gardens that breathe the fragrance of saffron
    flowers;
Set up the protector against thieves and birds,   110
The guardian, Priapus of the Hellespont, watchman god with the
    willow hook.
The beekeeper who has such concerns will bring thyme and the wild
    laurels
From high on the mountains and plant them all around the shelters.
He himself will blister his hand from hard work; he will be the one
To set fertile cuttings in the soil and water them with friendly
    rains.   115
And were I not truly already at the very end of my labors,
About to furl my sails and in a hurry to turn the prow toward land,
Perhaps I would sing of rich gardens, what careful cultivation
Adorns them, and would sing of the rose gardens of Paestum that
    blossom
Twice a year, how endives love the streams they drink,   120
How the lush banks delight in parsley, and the cucumber snakes
Through the grass bulging into a belly; and I would have heralded
The narcissus blooming late or the stalk of the twining acanthus,
Pale ivy and myrtle that love the shores.
For I remember beneath the towers of Tarentum's citadel,   125
Where the dark Galaesus river waters its yellow fields,
Seeing an old man from Corycus who had a few acres

4.103-148: prescribe methods of keeping the bees near the hive, ending with
    a directive to plant a garden which leads to a transition on the subject of
    gardens—a famous *praeteritio*, a device that ostensibly "passes by" an issue,
    but that emphasizes it. Vergil then characterizes an old man of Tarentum
    who succeeds in his rustic environment.

Of abandoned countryside, neither rich for oxen,
Nor fodder suitable for livestock nor favorable for the grapevine.
Yet he planted among the bushes the odd vegetable and
    roundabout   130
White lilies, vervain, and the slender poppy;
In his spirit he equaled the riches of kings, and when he returned
Home late at night, he piled his tables with feasts unbought.
He was the first to pluck a rose in spring and fruits in autumn;
When grim winter was still breaking rocks   135
With its cold and was curbing the flow of water with ice,
He was already pruning the leafage of the soft hyacinth,
Cursing summer for being late and the west winds for lagging.
So this same man was first to be enriched with mother-bees and a
    teeming hive,
And the first to gather fermenting honey from the pressed combs; 140
Luxuriant were his lindens and pine
And all the fruits with which in early bloom his productive tree had
    dressed itself,
So in autumn it kept them all ripened.
He even planted elms in rows when it seemed too late to plant,
The pear already hardened and the blackthorns already bearing
    plums,   145
And the sycamore already serving shade for drinkers.
But I for my own part, barred by unfair constraints of space,
Pass over and leave them to others after me to recall.
Come now, I will unfold the natural qualities of bees, the ones which
    Jupiter°
Himself gave them. They paid for this gift: as they followed   150
The ringing sounds and clashing bronze of the Curetes,
They fed the god, king of heaven, in the shelter of a cave on Mt. Dicte.
Bees are the only creatures to have their children in common, to hold
In partnership the dwellings of their city and regulate their lives
    under a strong code
Of laws; they alone know an unchanging fatherland and household
    gods.   155
Mindful of the winter to come, in summer they engage in hard work
To store up their gains for common use.
Some watch over the collecting of food and by a fixed contract
Labor in the fields; others within the confines of their homes
Lay narcissus tears for the first foundations of the combs   160
And the gluey propolis from tree-bark, then hang high

4.149-202: detail the communal society of bees, their ethos, achievements, and
    reproductive habits.

The sticky wax; others lead out the young, already full-grown,
And the hope of the tribe; others pack the purest
Honey and swell the cells with liquid nectar of honey.
There are some who are allotted the watch at the gates,   165
Taking turns to spy for rains and the clouds of the sky,
Or take the loads of incomers, or, formed into ranks,
Keep the drones, that lazy bunch, from the confines.
Seething is the work: the fragrant honey teems with thyme.
And just as the Cyclopes busy themselves in forging the lightning
    bolts°   170
From malleable ore, some from bull-like bellows
Take in and then expel the blasts of air, others dip
Hissing bronze in a vat; Aetna groans beneath the pounded anvils;
With mighty power they lift their arms together swinging
In rhythm, and then turn with gripping forceps the tempered iron: 175
No differently, if I may compare small matters with the great,
The innate passion for gain drives Athenian bees,°
Each in his own sphere of work. The venerated aged bees have charge
Of the towns to build strengthened hives and to fashion intricate cells.
But far into the night the younger ones weary themselves
    in bringing back   180
Their legs loaded full of thyme; they feed on arbutus trees all about,
On gray willows, on wild cinnamon, on the blushing crocus,
The rich linden and dark hyacinths.
For all of them there is one time of rest from the work, one time of
    work for all:
In the morning they burst from the gates, no loitering anywhere; 185
When the evening sky has warned them to leave their pastures in the
    fields,
Only then they seek their homes, only then they refresh their bodies;
A din arises and around the entrances and thresholds they hum.
Later, when they have composed themselves in their chambers,
    there is silence
Into the night, and one by one slumber seizes their weary limbs; 190
And when rain threatens, they do not move very far from their cells,
Nor trust the sky when east winds approach;
But all around beneath the walls of their security they fetch water
And venture brief sallies, and, as unstable boats,
Tossed on waves, take on ballast of sand, they often   195
Carry pebbles; with these they balance themselves through the
    insubstantial clouds.

4.170-175: see note to 1.471.
4.177: the honey of Mt. Hymettos in Athens was treasured.

You will marvel that the bees choose the following practice:
They do not indulge in conjugal visits or relax their idle bodies
In love or bear young with labor;
But without males they gather in their mouths their children born
    from leaves   200
And sweet herbs; on their own they furnish the kings and tiny
    citizens,
Remodel the courts and kingdoms of wax.
Often too, as they stray on rugged rocks, they bruise°
Their wings and willingly surrender their lives under their burden.
Such is their love for flowers and the glory of making honey.   205
So, however short the life span that awaits the individual bees—
For it never extends beyond the seventh summer—
Still their race remains immortal; for many years
The fortune of their house stands fast, and they count grandfathers of
    grandfathers.
Moreover, as for the king, no Egyptian, not mighty Lydia,   210
Not the peoples of Parthia nor the Hydaspes of the Medes
So pay homage to their king. All are of one mind to keep the king safe;
When he is lost, they break faith; on their own they loot
The honey combs they have assembled and destroy their wicker-cells.
The king is guardian of their work, he is the one everyone
    admires;   215
They all mob him and throng about him in a dense roar.
Often they lift him on their shoulders; for him they expose their bodies
In war and through wounds meet a beautiful death.
From these signs and influenced by these epic paradigms
Some have asserted that bees share in divine intelligence   220
And drink of heaven's ether; for they say a god pervades all the lands,
The expanses of the sea, and the deep space of the sky.
From him, flocks, herds, men, every species of wild beasts,
From him, each one of these, as it comes to birth, derives the slender
    threads of life.
They maintain that everything broken down is restored and
    brought back   225
To him; there is no room for death, but all beings alive fly
To the ranks of the stars and ascend to lofty heaven.
When you unseal the stately dwellings and the honey hoarded°

4.203-227: treat life expectancy of bees and their renewal, particularly relevant
    for their reverent protection of the king.
4.228-280: Vergil describes the methods of collecting honey and notes the pests
    and disease that afflict the hive. The poet's treatment of disease leads naturally
    to the next theme: the loss (death) and regeneration of the hive through the
    process of *bougonia*.

In the treasure-cells, first with a swig of water sprinkle
And rinse your mouth, and in your hand directly in front of you use
  searching smoke.
Twice per year beekeepers gather the heavy yield; two seasons for
  a harvest: 231
First, as soon as Taygete, the Pleiad, has shown her noble face,
And has scorned and spurned to touch with her foot the streams of
  Ocean,
And next, when that same star flees the sign of watery Pisces
And sinks sadly from heaven into the waves of winter.   235
Their rage is beyond measure and when they are wounded they
  breathe
Poison in their bites; leeching on veins, they leave
Their unseen stings and lay down their lives in the wound.
But if you fear a harsh winter coming on, and have tender feelings
  for their future,
And pity their crushed spirits and broken fortunes,   240
Do not hesitate to fumigate them with thyme and cut away
The useless wax. For often the newt, unnoticed, gnaws the
  honeycombs,
And rooms are found stuffed full of skulking beetles,
Or the drone that does not contribute sitting at a meal belonging to
  others.
Under ill-matched arms the fierce hornet engages the bees,   245
Or the grub, a pestilent race, or the spider, hateful to Minerva,
Hangs on the doorway its flimsy webs.
The more drained their stock, all the more fiercely they all
Press on to repair the ruin of their fallen race:
They fill up the rows of the cells and weave their barns with flower
  wax;   250
Since life has also brought to the bees our ills,
If their bodies droop, succumbing to grievous disease—
This you can recognize by unmistakable signs:
When they become ill, their color changes at once; a shaggy
  scrawniness
Deforms their look; soon afterwards they carry from the cells   255
The bodies of the dead and in mourning lead funerals for them,
Or else joined foot to foot they hang at the doorways
Or they all linger in locked chambers,
Slothful from hunger or lazy from the pinching cold;
Then is heard a duller sound, and they utter a long drawn-out
  buzz,   260

As at times the chilly south wind rustles in the murmuring forests,
As the sea in turmoil whistles when waves surge back,
And as consuming fire seethes in closed kilns.
At that point I will advise you to burn incense of Syrian balm
And introduce in hollow stalks honey, as you freely   265
Urge and call them, though weary, to their familiar food.
It will help too to blend the flavor of pounded oak-gall
And dried rose-petals or must enriched from strong boiling,
Or a raisin-wine pressed from the Psithian vine
With Attic thyme and strong-smelling centaury.   270
There is also a flower in the meadows which farmers have given
The name "starwort," a plant easy for searchers to find;
From a single clump of fibers it produces a great bush;
Its center is golden in color, but its petals that stream
Profusely around have a red sheen beneath dark violet;   275
Often in woven garlands it decorates the altars of the gods;
Bitter to the taste, shepherds cull it in meadows cropped by their
     flocks
And near winding streams of the Mella river.°
Boil its roots in scented wine,
And at bees' doors in full baskets set this out for nourishing food.   280
But if a keeper suddenly loses the entire stock
And does not know how to restore the race in a new line,
Then it is time to reveal the marvelous remedy of the Arcadian
     master,°°
How the rotting gore from a slain bullock
Has often engendered bees. Tracing it back from its first source,   285
     I shall unfold the entire story in a loftier mode.
For, where the fortunate race of Macedonian Canopus
Cultivates swampy waters of the flooded Nile,
And sails around their countryside in painted boats,
And, where the borderland of quiver-bearing Persia presses nearby, 290
The river branches out into seven separate mouths
And fertilizes lush Egypt with black loam—
The Nile that flows down from the colored Indians—
All the region lays its sure salvation on this device.
First, they select a place, small and confined   295
For this special purpose: this area they shut in with a narrow roof

---

4.278: the Mella is a small tributary of the Po in northern Italy flowing by
     Brescia.
4.283: a reference to Aristaeus whose story soon follows.
4.283-314: are mostly concerned with the lore of the *bougonia* and serve as a
     transition to the story of Aristaeus.

Of tiles and tight walls; they add four windows
Set away from the four winds to provide light from the sides;
Then they look for a bullock whose horns are just curving
On his two-year-old forehead; despite his many struggles, they
    gag   300
His two nostrils and block the breath from his mouth;
Then he is beaten to death; his carcass is pounded to a pulp through
    the intact hide;
They leave him in this condition in the enclosure, and they put
Under his ribs broken twigs, thyme, and fresh cinnamon bark.
This is done as soon as the west winds begin to stir the waves,   305
Before the meadows blush with new hues, before
The chattering swallow suspends its nest from the rafters.
Meanwhile, the moisture in the soft bones has warmed
And ferments, and living creatures of remarkable forms,
At first without feet, but soon whirring with wings,   310
Swarm; and ever more and more they take to the thin air,
Until, like a rain shower pouring from summer storm clouds,
They burst forth, or like arrows from a twanging bowstring
Whenever light-armed Parthians begin combat.
What god, O Muses, who has forged this device for us?°   315
From where did the new human experience take its first steps?
The shepherd Aristaeus was fleeing Tempe by the Peneus,—
The story is that he had lost his bees from disease and famine—
When sadly he stopped near the sacred source of the river's end
And made many laments; he then addressed his mother in these
    words: 320
"Mother, my mother, Cyrene, you who occupy the depths
Of this pool, why did you give birth from the famous stock
Of the gods—that is, if my father is truly Apollo of Thymbra, as you
    assert—
Me hated by fate? Or where has your love for me
Been banished? Why did you bid me to hope for heaven?   325
Look, even this very hour of mortal life
Which I scarcely forge for myself by the skillful tending of crops
And flocks, trying every device, I resign, even though you are my
    mother.
So come, with your own hand level my fruitful orchards,
Set ruinous fire to my stables, destroy my crops,   330
Burn the plants and wield a stout ax upon my vines,
If such disdain for my reputation has possessed you."

4.315: from this point until near the end of the work three separate stories are
    involved: Aristaeus, Proteus, and Orpheus.

His mother caught the sound in her chamber beneath the depths
   of the river.
Around her nymphs were plucking Milesian wool°
That had been dyed a rich, glassy green: 335
Drymo, Xantho, Ligea, Phyllodoce,°
[Nesaee, Spio, Thalia, and Cymodoce]
Their shining curls streaming over their white necks;
And Cydippe and blond Lycorias, one a virgin,
The other having for the first time experienced the pangs of
   childbirth;   340
And Clio, and her sister Beroe, both daughters of Ocean,
Both in gold, both wearing belts of dappled skins;
And Ephyre, Opis, Deiopea of Asia;
And finally swift Arethusa who had set aside her arrows.
Among them Clymene was recalling Vulcan's useless precautions, 345
The deceits of Mars and his sweet subterfuges.°
She also recounted in song the numerous divine love affairs
   beginning from Chaos.
Captivated by this song, the nymphs were unraveling their soft
   measures
Of wool from their spindles, when again the lament of Aristaeus
Penetrated the ears of his mother; all of them in their glassy seats 350
Were shocked; first, of all her sisters Arethusa
Looked out over the surface of the water, lifted her golden-haired
   head,
And from far off cried, "O my sister Cyrene, not without cause has
   been your fright
At such deep groaning; your Aristacus, yes, your main care
Stands in sorrow, crying at the river of the sire Peneus,   355
And is calling you a cruel mother."
To her the mother whose mind was stricken with a sudden, strange
   terror
Said: "Come, bring him, bring him to us; it is right for him to touch
The thresholds of gods." At once she commands the deep streams
To separate far apart so the young man could enter. The water   360
Curved around him in the shape of a mountain,
Received him in its huge fold and hurled him beneath the current.
And now, marveling at his mother's home and her watery realm,

---

4.334: Miletus is said to produce the finest wool.
4.336-344: the catalogue of nymphs has epic connections with Homer, *Iliad*
   18.34-147.
4.346: refers to the famous story of the affair between Ares and Aphrodite told
   in Homer, *Odyssey* 8.266-366.

The lakes locked in caves, and the echoing groves,
He proceeded on; stunned by the mighty rush of waters,   365
He gazed at all the different rivers flowing beneath the great earth
To separate lands, the Phasis, the Lycus,°
And the source from where the deep Enipeus first gushes forth,
From where father Tiber, Anio's flowing waters,
The Bug roaring over rocks, the Caicus of Lydia,   370
And the Po, whose twin horns are gilded on its bull's brow;
No other river flows through rich croplands
To the purple sea more violently.
When he arrived into her grotto beneath the hanging ceiling of
    pumice,
Cyrene learned of her son's empty laments.   375
Her sisters in due order offer fresh water for the hands
And bring napkins of shorn wool;
Some load the tables with exquisite foods, and set up and replenish
The goblets; the altars blaze high with Arabian incense,
And his mother says: "Take up tankards of Maeonian° wine;   380
Let us pour a libation to Ocean." At once she prays
To Ocean, the father of the world and to her sister nymphs
Who watch over a hundred forests and who watch over a hundred
    rivers.
Three times she poured liquid nectar on the blazing hearth;
Three times a flame shot up to the top of the roof and each time
    flashed bright.   385
With her mind buoyed by this omen, she says the following:
"In Neptune's Carpathian Sea there is a prophet,
Sea-blue Proteus, who traverses the wide sea with his fishes
And a yoked team of two-footed horses.
He is now on a visit to Thessaly's ports and his native   390
Pallene; to him we nymphs do homage, as does the aged
Nereus himself; for he is a prophet who knows all the things
That are, the things that were, and the things that the future brings:
Surely, this is Neptune's will, whose enormous herds
Of ugly seals he pastures under the waves.   395
Son, you must first capture and chain him that he may make
Clear to you the reason for the disease and may bless the issue.
For without force he will offer you no precepts, nor will you
Move him with prayers; apply brute force and chain him for his
    capture;   399

4.367-371: a catalogue of rivers that parallels the catalogue of nymphs. The
    Phasis and Lycus are rivers in Colchis; the Enipeus is a tributary of the Pe-
    neus in Thessaly.
4.380: Lydia was often called Maeonia.

Against these obstacles alone his deceptive tricks will be useless
    and shatter apart.
As soon as the sun has kindled its midday heat,
When grasses thirst and shade is very welcomed by the flock,
I myself will lead you there to the old man's haunts where,
Weary from the waves, he retires, so you may approach him as
    he lies in sleep.
But after you have caught him with your hands and have him in
    chains,   405
Then his varied shapes and appearances of wild animals will
    confuse you.
For suddenly he'll take the form of a bristling boar, a deadly tiger,
A scaly snake, and a lion with a tawny mane;
Or he will impart the sharp crack of fire and seek to elude his bonds,
Or melting into parting waters be gone.   410
The more he changes into all kinds of shapes,
So, you, my son, draw the clinging bonds tighter,
Until after his physical transformations he will be the same as
You saw him when he closed his eyes as he fell asleep."
So she spoke: she poured the clear perfume of ambrosia,   415
Coating her son's body with it; a sweet scent
Breathed upon his coiffured hair
And a supple vigor suffused into his limbs. There is a huge cave
Hollowed in the side of a mountain; here many waves
Are wind driven and split into recessed bays;   420
From time to time it has been a most safe haven for sailors caught
    in a storm;
With a huge boulder Proteus barricades himself inside it.
It is here the nymph stations the youth in ambush, away from the
    light,
While she, veiled in mist, stands a little off.
The consuming Dog-Star that scorches the thirsty Indians   425
Was ablaze in the sky; the fiery sun had used up half
Its course; grass was withering; the sun's rays were cooking
The hollow rivers and their parched channels were baked down
    to the mud,
When Proteus came out of the waves in quest of his grottoes,
His usual haunts; around him the watery clan of the vast sea   430
Gamboled, scattering the salty sea-spray.
Spread here and there along the shore the seals lay in sleep;
And he, like a herdsman in the mountains at times,
When the evening star brings calves back from pasture to their stalls
And lambs whet wolves' hunger with the sound of their bleating,   435
Sits on a look-out rock among them and recounts their number.
Aristaeus took this offered opportunity to seize him,

Hardly letting the old man settle his weary limbs;
With a loud shout he pounced; he surprised him,
Shackling him as he lay. But the old man did not forget his skill: 440
He transformed himself into all kinds of miraculous things,
Fire, a horrible beast, a flowing stream.
Yet none of his usual tricks earned him escape; beaten,
He returned to his own form and with the lips of a human spoke:
"You most presumptuous young man, who, I ask,   445
Has ordered you to enter my home? What are you after here?"
    But he replied,
"You know, Proteus, you know full well; no trick can escape you:
So don't try to pretend. I have followed the dictates of the gods
And have come here to seek oracles for my weary fortunes."
Only this he said. Finally, the prophet under compulsion   450
Rolled his eyes blazing with blue-gray light upon him,
And grimly gnashing his teeth, opened his lips of destiny:
"Divine anger, nothing else hounds you;°
You are paying for the sins you have committed; against you pitiable
    Orpheus
Evokes punishment—not at all undeserved, but the fates oppose
    him—   455
He rages wildly because his wife has been stolen from him.
While she was trying to escape you, running at top speed along a
    river,
Merely a girl, but doomed to die, she did not see at her feet a huge
    snake
Which was hugging the banks in the tall grass.
Her band of companion dryads filled the mountain tops   460
With shouting: there wept Rhodope's heights,
Lofty Pangaea, the war-like land of Thracian Rhesus,
The Getae people, the river Hebrus, and Orithyia of Attica.
And he played his hollow lyre to soothe his pain and love;   464
And over and over he sang of you, his sweet wife, yes, of you, alone
    with himself

4.453-529: Proteus tells the story of Orpheus and Eurydice. Aristaeus learns that
the cause for the disease that killed his bees was his own fault. Because he
had caused the death of Eurydice, divine vengeance from the nymphs was
now visiting him The myth of Orpheus and Eurydice can stand on its own,
but it is intimately connected with Aristaeus and the moral implications of the
entire work. The story serves as a divine warning: that Aristaeus, in order to
redeem himself and his bees, must follow without fail all divine directives.
Orpheus' failure provides a lesson of what Aristaeus must avoid.

On a deserted shore, of you at the approach of day, of you at day's
   end.
He entered the maw of Taenarus, deep to the doorway of Dis
And his murky grove which was shrouded in black terror;
He approached the dead shades, and even the awesome king,
And hearts that know not how to soften to human prayers.   470
But stirred by his song, from the deepest recesses of Erebus
Came the insubstantial shades, images of those denied light;
As many as the thousands of birds that shelter themselves among
   leaves
When the evening star or a winter storm from the mountains drives
   them:
Mothers, husbands, the bodies of courageous heroes   475
Devoid of life, young boys and unmarried girls,
And young men who had been placed on funeral pyres before their
   parents' eyes.
All around, the black mud and ugly weeds of Cocytus,
The slow, winding stream of that hateful swamp, the river Styx,
Bind them; the Styx that flows around them in nine circles herds
   them together.   480
Yes, the very halls of hell were moved, truly stunned, innermost
   Tartarus,
Seat of death, and even the Furies in whose hair dark blue snakes
Intertwined; and Cerberus held agape his three mouths,
And the wheel that Ixion spun stopped turning in the wind.
And he had avoided every trap as he was retracing his steps: 485
Eurydice, restored to him, was on the verge of reaching the breezes
   above
As she followed behind him—for Proserpina had given this very
   directive—
Suddenly, a mad impulse seized the incautious lover,
Forgivable, if the shades knew how to forgive.   489
He halted; oh, he forgot! His senses befuddled, and just about in the
   light himself,
He looked back at his own dear Eurydice. In that moment
All his effort was spent; the conditions of the ruthless tyrant
Were broken; three times was heard a crash of thunder over the pools
   of Avernus.
She cried out: 'Who has destroyed us, me, so pitiable, and you,
Orpheus? What madness so intense? Look, once more the cruel
   fates   495
Call me back, and for a second time sleep covers my swimming eyes;
And now goodbye; I am being swept off, surrounded by immense
   night,
As I stretch out my feeble hands to you, I, oh, yours no longer.'

She spoke: right away, like smoke that wisps and joins the thin air,
Far from his sight she vanished; she did not see him   500
Desperately grasping at shadows and wanting to say
Something more; and Orcus' ferryman did not permit
Him to cross again the barrier of the marsh.
What was he to do? Where was he to turn now that his wife had been
    robbed from him
A second time? How could his lamenting and weeping move
    the dead shades,   505
How his cries the infernal divinities? Already she was afloat
    on Styx' boat.
They say that for seven whole months one after another
Beneath an airy crag at deserted Strymon's waters
He wept and unfolded this lament beneath icy grottoes,
Soothing tigers and moving oak trees with his song.   510
Just as a nightingale mourns beneath a poplar's shade
And complains of the loss of her young nestlings which a hard-
    hearted
Plowman has spotted and hauled down unfledged from their nest,
    all night long
She weeps and perched on a branch renews her plaintive song
And fills far and wide the countryside with her mournful elegies. 515
No passion for love, no wedding hymn bent his soul;
Alone he wandered the glaciers of Hyperborea, the snowy Don,
And the fields of Rhipae never widowed from frost;
All the while he complained of Eurydice stolen and of the useless gifts
Of Dis. Matrons of Thrace felt scorned by his devotion
    to the dead;   520
During the sacred worship and nightly orgies of Bacchus
They tore the young man apart and scattered him over the wide
    fields.
Then the head that had been ripped from its marble neck
Was swept and rolled in mid current by the Hebrus, Oeagrus' river;
Only his voice and his cold tongue   525
Kept calling out, as his breath faded, 'Eurydice, O lost Eurydice,'
All along the river the banks echoed back 'Eurydice'."
When Proteus had uttered this, he hurled himself into the deep sea
And where he leapt, he made the water whirl and eddy with foam.
But Cyrene straightway said this to the startled youth;   530
"Son, you may put these grim concerns out of your mind.°
This is the whole cause for the disease; the nymphs who have danced

---

4.531-548: Cyrene's second set of instructions regarding the correct religious
    formula of the *bougonia* from which the bees will be regenerated.

Deep in the groves with Eurydice have sent miserable ruin
On your bees. You now supplicate them, offer propitiatory gifts,
Seek out peace from them, venerate the woodland nymphs easy to
    appease.   535
They will forgive, if you pray, and will surrender their anger.
But as to the manner and proper order of prayer I will instruct you:
Select four excellent bulls of outstanding bodies
Which you now have pasturing on the hills of green Lycaeus,
And an equal number of heifers whose necks have yet to feel
    the yoke;   540
For them set up four altars at the lofty shrines of the goddesses,
Draw the sacred blood from their throats,
And leave the bodies of the steers within the leafy grove.
Later, when the ninth dawn has beamed her appearance
Send poppies as death offerings to Orpheus,   545
Slay a black ewe, and return to the grove:
Honor Eurydice with a slain calf to appease her."
No delay: right away he follows his mother's directives;
He goes to the shrines, as instructed, he erects the altars,
And brings four excellent bulls of outstanding bodies   550
And an equal number of heifers whose necks have yet to feel the
    yoke.
Afterward, when the ninth dawn had beamed her appearance,
He sends the death-offerings to Orpheus and returns to the grove.
Here suddenly and marvelous to tell they see
A portent; throughout the liquefied entrails of the cows   555
Bees buzz everywhere in their wombs and from their sides
They burst forth, swarm, and trail huge clouds; now at the top
Of a tree they flow together and hang in a cluster from bending
    branches.
These strains I have been singing about the cultivation of fields°
And about the tending of flocks and trees, while mighty Caesar
    thunders in war   560
Near the deep Euphrates and as victor apportions laws
To willing peoples and strives to make his way to Olympus.
In those days sweet Parthenope was nourishing me,
Vergil, as I flourished in the pursuits of inglorious leisure,
Yes, me, who in my audacious youth dallied in shepherds' songs   565
And sang of you, Tityrus, under the shade of a spreading beech.

4.559-566: Vergil ends the work with a personal signature with alludes also to
    the *Eclogues*.

HORACE

SATIRES

Horace refers to his *Satires* as *sermones*, "conversations," an appropriate term for the colloquial nature of the poems. He eschews the bitter and pugnacious style of his predecessor Lucilius in favor of a gentler tenor of criticism. As he himself claims, he strives to tell the truth through a smile. The objects of his attacks are more stereotypical or generic in character than personal. Quite frequently Horace lodges some self-effacing criticism in his attempt to expose vice and correct moral misgivings and errors.

1.1

Why is it, Maecenas, that no one lives happy
With the lot either his own rational choice has given him or pure
    chance
Has hurled in his way, but in envy praises those who do something
    else?
"Now traders are well off," says the soldier
Burdened with years of service, his limbs broken by hard
    campaigns;   5
On the other hand, says the trader as the South winds are rattling
    his ship,
"Military life is better. You know why? There is the shock of battle
And in a moment death comes quick or victory brings sweet success."
The skilled lawyer praises the farmer
When some client comes pounding on his door just before
    the cock-crow;   10
While the farmer, dragged into town from his fields to post bail,
Loudly exclaims that only city-folks are happy.

Other examples of this kind—and there are many—could even
Tire out that gossip Fabius.° Not to detain you; just listen
To my spin on the matter. Suppose some god would say: "Hey!   15
I'll make you whatever you want to be; you, there, a soldier,
Be a merchant; and you, the lawyer, be a sod-buster: off with you both,
Change your roles in life.—Well!
What are you standing around for?" They'd refuse, even though it
    means they could be
Happy. Why is that? Why wouldn't Jupiter rightly get angry,   20
Puff up both of his cheeks, and swear he would never again
Lend a receptive ear to human prayers?
I won't indulge in a comic routine,
But what's wrong with speaking the truth
With a laugh? Think of teachers who coax their young students   25
With cookies to make them learn their ABCs.
But putting the jokes aside, let me turn serious:
The farmer busting hard sods with a steel plow,
The cheating innkeeper, the soldier, the merchant boldly
Charting every sea, say that they endure   30
Their labor with this idea: to retire as old men in secure ease.
When they have heaped up a store of rations, they take
As a model the tiny ant who works mightily
Dragging in her mouth whatever she can and storing it
In a pile constructed bit by bit, fully aware and conscious
    of the future.   35
As soon as January casts a gloom over the year beginning anew,
She crawls out no more, but wisely indulges herself from the stock
Stored up before. But, as for you, not blistering heat,
Not winter, fire, sea, or sword would sway you from the pursuit of
    profit;
Nothing stands in your way; no one is going to be richer than you. 40
What good does it do you to dig up the ground? Furtively and in
    terror
To bury an immense fortune in silver and gold?
"Well, if you nibble at it, all that's left is a measly dime."
But if you don't do it, what good is a pile piled on a pile?
Your threshing floor has ground a hundred thousand bushels: 45
Yet, your belly still holds no more than mine; so, if along with some
    slaves
You should happen to carry on your weary shoulders a sack of bread,
You wouldn't receive any more than the slave
Who carried nothing. Say, what difference would it make

1.1.14: Fabius Maximus, a tedious Stoic writer from Narbonne.

For one living within nature's bounds whether he plows
    a hundred   50
Or a thousand acres? "Ah, but it is nice to draw from a big savings
    account."
Fine, since you grant that I can take as much from a small pile,
Then why do you praise your granaries over our small bins?
As if you needed no more than a pitcher or cup full of water,
You were to say: "I'd prefer to quaff the same amount   55
From a large river than from this little stream." So it happens
That those who enjoy a greater amount than is moderate,
The wild Aufidus sweeps away, bank and all.
But he who needs only so much as needed, neither drinks
Water churned with mud nor loses his life in the waves.   60
Much of mankind, misled by false desire,
Says, "There is no such thing as 'enough,' because you're worth
    only as much
As you have." What do you do with such a person? Why, you'd bid
    him to be miserable,
Since he chooses to do it: he's like the filthy rich man in Athens°
Who they say despised the people's remarks about him   65
And used to say, "The people may hiss at me, but I applaud
Myself at home as soon as I fix my gaze on the coins in my safe."
Thirsty Tantalus gapes for waters that recede from his lips—
Why do you laugh? Just change the name
And the myth is about you: you gloat, falling asleep   70
On the money bags amassed from everywhere, and you are forced
To treat them as sacred or enjoy them as if they were paintings.
Don't you know the value of money? What's its purpose?
It buys bread, vegetables, a carafe of wine,
And whatever else humans would naturally suffer from were it
    withheld.   75
Sleepless nights, half-dead from fear, night and day
In terror of depraved thieves, fires, slaves,
Who would fleece you good and hightail it—you like this?
I'd opt for being the poorest soul among such blessings.
For if your body is wracked by a painful chill   80
Or some other affliction has consigned you to bed, do you have
Someone to sit by your side, to ready bandages, to call a doctor
In order to revive you and restore you to children and dear relatives?
Your wife does not want you back alive nor your son; all the
    neighbors,

1.1.64-67: Some believe that Horace is referring to the infamous Timon.

Acquaintances, boys, and girls hate you.   85
Are you surprised when you put money before everything else
That no one shows you love which you did not earn?
Or should you want to hold and keep dear relatives whom nature
Gave you with no thanks to you,
Would you waste your labor fruitlessly like a guy trying   90
To teach a donkey to respond to reins and to race on the Campus
   Martius?
So end your grasp for money; since you have more than most,
Fear poverty less, and begin to finish up your work;
As you have gotten all you have been wanting, don't end up
Like Ummidius did. It is not a long story: he was so filthy rich 95
He measured out his money, and so stingy he never
Dressed better than a slave; right up to his final days
He was in fear of a lack of food
Overwhelming him. But a freedwoman, like Tyndareus'
Gutsiest daughter,° split him in two with an ax.   100
"So, what are you advising me? To live like a Naevius?
Or a Nomentanus?"° You are proceeding to match
Opposites head to head. No, I veto your being a miser;
And I'm not ordering you to become a bum or reckless spendthrift:
There is a difference between the eunuch Tanais and Visellius'
   father-in-law.   105
There is a mean in things and set boundaries, firmly fixed,
Which 'right' cannot find a footing on one side or the other.
I return where I started: that no greedy man
Approves of himself, but out of envy praises those who do
   something else.
And should someone else's goat bear a bigger udder,   110
He wastes away. He won't compare himself to the huge throng
Of poor people, but strains to surpass one man after another.
So someone wealthier always blocks his driving,
As, when bolting from the starting blocks, thoroughbreds speed
   on the chariot,
The charioteer drives his horses to catch those beating him,   115
And despises the one he has passed and left in the rear.
That's the reason we can rarely discover someone
Who says he has lived a happy life, and, when his time has come,
Leaves his life content like a guest satisfied by his dinner.
OK, that's it. You may start thinking that I have fleeced   120

1.1.100: Tyndareus' daughter is Clytemnestra, sister of Helen and the Gemini.
1.1.101-102: Naevius and Nomentanus are typical spendthrifts.

The bookshelves of Crispinus, the sore-eyed.° I utter not a single
  word more.

1.2

The unions of strippers, quacks, beggars,
Off-Broadway actors, stand-up comics, all that ilk
Is in mourning and depressed at the death of the singer Tigellius.
Yes, he was really nice and generous. Conversely, someone else fears
  being called
A spendthrift and refuses a loan to a destitute friend   5
So he may ward off a cold and banish bitter hunger.
If you ask a third why he would out of malice strip his grandfather's
Or father's splendid estate for his ungrateful gullet,
Buying up all kinds of delicacies on borrowed money,
He'd answer: because he wouldn't like to be labeled as stingy   10
And mean-spirited. For this he is praised by some, criticized
  by others.
Fufidius fears the reputation of being a bum or spendthrift,
Even though he's loaded in farmlands and rich from interest-bearing
  loans.
He takes his cut of five times normal interest from the principal
And whoever is in serious arrears, he duns more intensely;   15
He tracks the names of young men who have just assumed the toga
Of manhood and are under the control of strict fathers. Who does
  not exclaim:
"Right on, by Jupiter!" when he has heard this? And, "Does he spend
  money
On himself with that income?" Hardly. You'll find this hard
  to believe:
He is not even a friend to himself; he's like the father Terence   20
Portrays in his play who banished his son and suffered a life of
  misery;°
Why, he didn't inflict upon himself worse tortures than Fufidius° did.
Now if anyone asks: "What's the point of all this?" Just this:
In avoiding some vices, fools run into their opposites.
Maltinus walks about in baggy pants and another guy   25

1.1.121: Plotius Crispinus was a tiresome Stoic writer. Horace alludes to the
  eyestrain from excessive reading.
1.2.20-21: The Terentian play alluded to is the *Heautontimoumenos* (*The Self-
  Tormentor*).
1.2.22: like Malthinus (25), Rufillus and Gorgonius (27), Cupiennus (36), Mar-
  saeus (55), Cerinthus (81), Hypsaea (91), and Catia (95), Fufidius is otherwise
  unknown.

With his tunic tucked up to his raunchy crotch; that stylish dandy
Rufillus reeks of candy and Gorgonius of a smelly goat.
There is no middle ground. Some men refuse to touch any woman
Except those whose matronly ankles a flounce of a hemmed gown
    covers;
Another man pursues only a whore standing in a foul brothel.   30
When a man he knew once exited from a whore house, Cato
Said in his revered style: "Well done, my good man!
When poisonous lust swells their veins, young bucks
Are right to deign coming here instead of grinding down the wives
Of other men." "I wouldn't like that kind of praise,"   35
Says Cupiennus, the admirer of white married pussy.
It's worth hearing if you don't like adulterers
To get away with it: how they have to work really hard,
Their pleasure ruined and racked by a lot of pain,
And it rarely befalls them considering the dangerous risks
    they take.   40
One leapt from a roof, head first; another was whipped
To death; and then one man fled only to fall into the clutches
Of a gang of tough muggers; another guy ransomed his life for cash,
And one was pissed on by the hired help; there was also a case
In which a man got his balls and horny prick lopped off   45
By a sword. Everybody says: "And serves him right!" But not Galba.°
So much safer is the merchandise in second class,
I mean freedwomen—Sallust° goes crazy
Over them as hotly as the adulterer chases wives. But if a man,
So far as his circumstances and reason guide him and as far as   50
His liberal generosity allows, wanted to be kind and right,
He would give what is enough and not so much as to go bankrupt
And cause a scandal. But, proud of this one fact,
He hugs, loves, and congratulates himself: "I don't touch a married
    woman."
Just as Marsaeus, notorious lover of Origo, the porn star,   55
Who lavished on her his ancestral estate and home, once said:
"Not for me any fooling around with other men's wives."
But he plays around with porn actresses and with whores, which
    drags
His reputation into the mud, a more dangerous crisis than the loss of
    his property.
Is it enough for you to avoid the role of adulterer but not the
    consequent harm   60

1.2.46: Galba is often identified as a prominent jurist.
1.2.48: the Sallust mentioned is not the famous historian Gaius Sallustius Cris-
pus.

From it? The loss of a good reputation, the squandering and messing
   up
Of your father's estate is bad form anywhere, anytime. What is the
   difference
Whether you screw up with a married woman or a slave-girl?
Poor Villius, ersatz son-in-law of Sulla, was deceived by Fausta's° one
   asset:
Her name. He suffered enough punishment, yes, more   65
Than enough, hacked by fists, slashed by a sword,
And even excluded from the door of his house while Longarenus was
   inside.
Suppose in his mind the words of his prick that saw all these troubles
Said: "Just what do you want? Did I ever ask you,
Even when my passion was boiling fire, for a cunt   70
Descended from a powerful consul and dressed in matronly gown?"
What would he respond? "She's a girl born of a famous father."
But Nature, rich in her resources, advises much better courses,
Different from those of yours, if you really want
To deal yourself a good hand in life and renege on mixing the
   desirable   75
With the objectionable. Do you think it makes no difference
If it's your fault or those of circumstance that cause you distress?
Don't be sorry: stop chasing married women; you swallow more
   serious
Trouble from it than you pluck delicious fruit.
The lady in emeralds and pearls, contrary to your belief,   80
Cerinthus, rarely has a softer thigh or nicer leg
Than the hooker who is very often better endowed.
Besides, she openly displays her merchandise without disguise,
Plainly revealing what she has for sale, and, if she has some beauty,
She does not flaunt and keep it out in the open to conceal
   other faults.   85
Rich people have this custom: when they are buying horses, they
   inspect
Them covered over so that a beautiful shape disguising
A tender hoof, as often is the case, will not trick a buyer
Admiring handsome haunches, a short head, and a stately neck.
And rightly, too. So, don't study with the eyes of Lynceus° the best
   parts   90

1.2.64-67: the scandalous Fausta, the daughter of Sulla and wife of Titus Annius
   Milo, had numerous lovers, among whom were Villius and Longarenus.
1.2.90: Lynceus was one of the Argonauts, known for his keen vision.

Of a body and yet be blinder than Hypsaea scanning those
That are flawed. "O what a leg, what arms;" But she has
A tight ass, a big nose, short waist, and clodhoppers for feet.
You can't see anything of a married woman except her face;
She hides everything else, unless she is Catia, with a long dress.   95
If you seek the forbidden, so well barricaded—this, of course,
Drives you crazy—many obstacles get in your way:
Attendants, litter with bearers, hairdressers, hanger-ons,
A dress hanging down to the ankles, and a cloak wrapping
     all around her,
So many things that begrudge you a clear view.   100
As for the other woman, no obstacles: you can almost see her nude
In her Coan negligee, checking for a bad leg or ugly foot;
You can measure her figure with the eye. Or would you prefer
To be tricked, your money snatched from you
Before you can see the merchandise? The lover sings   105
About the hunter who tracks a hare in deep snow, but refuses
To touch it once it is caught, and adds this ditty: "My love is like
The hunter; it flies by prey sitting there for all but chases that on the
     wing."°
With poetic cliches like these do you hope to be able to banish
     pangs,
Passions, and depressing worries from your heart?   110
What limit nature sets upon your desires,
What she requires for herself, what brings her pain, if denied,
It would really profit you to ask and help you to distinguish shadow
     from substance.
When your throat is parched and burning with thirst, do you look for
Cups of gold? And when you are hungry, do you despise all food 115
Except peacock and turbot? When your prick swells
And a servant girl or a household boy is nearby ready
To indulge your impulse, do you choose to explode with all your
     come?
Not me. I like my sex accessible and easy to get.
The lady with her "a little later," "more money," "if my husband
     is out of town,"   120
She is for eunuch priests. Philodemus claims for himself the woman
Who neither costs an eye nor hesitates to come when called.
For me a blond, tall and straight, elegantly made up so that
She cares not to appear taller or more attractive than nature provides;
When she lays the left side of her body beneath my right,   125
She is Ilia and Egeria combined. I give her any name I like.

1.2.107-108: these lines are a Latin reworking of a famous epigram by Cal-
     limachus.

Nor do I have to fear, while I'm fucking her, a husband running back
   from the forum,
A door being flattened, a dog barking, the house pounded,
Rebounding in a massive crash and uproar, a wife pale as a ghost
Leaping from a bed, her maid and accomplice screaming
   she's done for,   130
Terrified of her legs being broken, her mistress caught red-handed
   fearing for her dowry,
And me in fear for myself, barefoot, having to run for it with my tunic
   undone,
Losing my money, my ass, or my good name.
It's awful getting caught. I'd win that argument even if Fabius were
   the judge.   134

1.3

All singers have this fault: requested to sing among friends,
They never make up their minds to do it;
But unasked they never stop. The Sardinian, Tigellius,
Was just like that. Caesar, who could have compelled him,
Would get absolutely nowhere, asking on behalf of his father's
   friendship   5
And his own; but if Tigellius got it in his head, he would roar
From eggs to apples, "Yo Bacchus," sometimes at the top of his lungs,
Other times in a low pitch responding to the notes of the four strings
   of the lyre.
That man lacked consistency: at times he ran off like a soldier fleeing
From an enemy and very often stopped like a priest carrying   10
The sacred emblems of Juno. Sometimes he kept two hundred slaves,
At other times only ten; one moment he'd be yakking about kings and
   princes,
Everything grand, then say, "Let me have a three-legged table,
Plain salt in a sea-shell, and a toga however coarse
To ward off the cold." Yet if you gave this frugal guy,   15
So content with a little, a cool million sestertii, within five days
There'd be nothing left in his wallet. He used to stay up
Until morning, then snore the whole day through; there was
   never a man
So inconsistent. Now someone might ask me, "What about you?
Don't you have any faults?" Sure, other kinds and, I hope, more
   trivial.   20
While Maenius was criticizing Novius° who was out of earshot,
   somebody

1.3.21: Maenius and Novius in this line, Hagna and Balbinus (40), and Ruso (86)
   are all nondescript individuals whose excessive conduct Horace decries.

Said, "Hey, you, don't you know yourself? You think we don't
   know you?
Trying to put one over us?" "I excuse myself," replied Maenius.
This is stupid and depraved self-love, and deserves censure:
Whereas you look upon your own misgivings cross-eyed and
   blurred with grease,   25
Why do you study the faults of your friends with eyes as sharp
As an eagle's or those of the holy snake at Epidaurus? For it could
Turn out against you: those friends may begin prying into your faults.
A friend is a little bit too hot-tempered, not very sophisticated
For the discriminating noses of men nowadays; he gets a big laugh 30
With his old-fashioned hick haircut, the way his baggy toga hangs,
   the clopping
Of his shoes loose on his feet. But he's a fine man, none better;
He is your friend whose uncouth exterior hides
Profound talent. So shake yourself
To see whether nature has planted any seeds   35
Of vices in you or some bad habits; for if fields are neglected,
You have to burn out the weeds flourishing there.
Let's take a close look at this: the ugly defects of a girlfriend can
   deceive
The blind lover, yet also please him,
Like Hagna's wart that delighted Balbinus.   40
I wish that we made the same mistake in the name of friendship
And that our ethics would have bestowed an honorable name upon
   that error.
As a father indulges his son's, so we ought not scorn
The faults of a friend if there be any. A father
Calls his cross-eyed son "Wink," and "Chick" stands for   45
A runt of a boy, like that old dwarf
Sisyphus;° if he has bow-legs, he's "Bandy;" if he wobbles supported
On weak ankles, the father babbles in baby-talk: "Hoofy."
If he is somewhat stingy, call him 'frugal;' for someone who is silly,
Shows off a little too much, he only wants to appear   50
An adequate comic to his friends; if he is too rude
And outspoken, then call him 'honest' and 'sincere.'
He's got a hot-temper? Count him 'spirited.' I think
This practice draws friends together and keeps them cemented.
But we turn their virtues upside down,   55
And are crazy enough to smear a clean bowl. To an honest fellow
Who lives among us, yet very reserved, we give
The sobriquet "slow," "fat-headed." Another avoids traps

1.3.47: Sisyphus, a dwarf kept by Mark Antony who gave him the name from
   Greek myth.

Of all kinds and never exposes his person to any evil,
Since we involve ourselves in a life of this kind wherein bitter envy 60
And slanders thrive: instead of "sensible"
And "cautious" we call him a phony and sly fox.
The man who is too direct, like me, Maecenas, when I often
Interrupt you, perhaps jarring and annoying you
As you read or are in contemplative mood, for some chat or other, 65
"What a bore! Utterly devoid of common sense and tact," we say.
Yes, look how thoughtlessly we enact an unjust law against ourselves.
For none of us is born without faults. The best man is he
Who carries the smallest load of them. He is truly a dear friend,
     as is fair,
Who weighs my virtues against my faults, and tips the scale,   70
If my virtues are actually more, in favor of the good points.
If he wants me to love him, I will weigh his on the same scale.
The man who expects not to see his friend repelled by his own acne
Will forgive his friend's warts. It is only right
That one asking pardon for his misgivings should grant it in
     return.   75
And, since anger can't be wholly cut out
And all the other failings that cling to fools, why not
Use reason in weighing and measuring and make
The punishment fit the particular crime?
If anyone nailed to a cross a slave who sopped up   80
Some leftover fish and licked lukewarm sauce from a platter
He had been ordered to remove, sensible people would call
Him crazier than Labeo.° A much more insane
And more serious offence is this example: a friend has committed
Some peccadillo, you'd be assailed as insensitive and mean not to
     overlook it.   85
But you hate and avoid him like a debtor steering clear of Ruso,
A debtor aware that, when the grim first of the month comes around,
If he doesn't scrape together interest and principal from some source
     or other,
He has to stretch out his neck like a prisoner of war to listen to some
     dreary histories.
A drunken friend has peed on the couch or has knocked off
     the table   90
An antique saucer worn smooth by Evander's hand: for this reason
Or because in his hunger he snatched some chicken from my side of
     the plate,
Would he be less of a friend or dear to me?

1.3.83: Labeo boldly criticized Octavius/Augustus.

What would I do if he stole something or if he betrayed
A trust or reneged on a pledge?   95
Those who hold that all faults are about equal get into a lot of trouble°
When they face reality: human feelings and customs work against
   them,
As does experience, the mother, so to speak, of justice and right.
When creatures first crawled forth on the earth,
A mute and ugly herd, they fought over acorns and lairs   100
With fists and nails, then with clubs, and in due course
With weapons forged by experience.
Then they discovered words, language, to express
Their ideas and feelings; after that they began
To abstain from war, to build towns, and to enact laws   105
Against theft, against banditry, and against adultery.
Cunt was the most revolting cause for war
Long before Helen. They perished unknown deaths,
Those who took, as beasts do, wanton sex,
Until a stronger man, like the bull of the herd, killed them.   110
You must admit that fear of injustice created laws,
If you care to read the history and records of the world.
Nature herself cannot discern right from wrong
As she distinguishes good things from bad, the desirable from the
   undesirable;
Nor can philosophic reason prove that he sins in the same kind
   and degree   115
Who breaks off young cabbage heads in another's garden,
As he who steals at night the sacred emblems of the gods.
There should be a rule to balance the punishments with the crimes,
So you don't flay someone with a horrifying notched whip when a
   deserving smooth
Strap will do. I'm not afraid that you will tap someone with
   a ruler who deserves   120
To suffer a heavy beating, when you say that crimes are equal:
That petty thefts are equal to piracy, and when you threaten to prune
   away
With the same sickle the large and small—if men endow you
A kingdom. But if the wise man is also wealthy,
A good cobbler, and the only hunk, and is a king too,   125
Why do you wish what you already have? "You don't understand,"
He quips, "What Chrysippus our father says: the wise man never
Makes his own shoes and sandals; but a wise man is a cobbler."
   How's that?

1.3.96-142: Horace answers Stoic critics who maintain that all sins are equal.

"Even when Hermogenes is silent, he is still the best singer
And musician as crafty Alfenus° even with all the tools   130
Of his trade thrown away and his shop closed
Was still a cobbler: in the same way the wise man is the best workman
Of every trade; therefore, he alone is king." Boys in play
Pluck at your bread; if you don't drive them off with a stick,
They will crowd around you, push and taunt you, until in misery 135
You'll split open barking, O greatest King of Kings.
I'll make it brief: while you're off , O King, to the baths—for a fee
Of a quarter—with no attendant to escort you
Except that idiot Crispinus, my sweet friends
Will forgive me for any stupid mistake I make,   140
Just as I'll cheerfully put up with any of their faults.
As a private citizen I'll live a happier life than you, king that you are.

1.5

I left lofty Rome,° welcomed first in Aricia
At a modest little inn: Heliodorus, the professor by far
Most learned of the Greeks, was my companion. Then to Forum Appii
Stuffed with sailors and crooked innkeepers.
For this stage of the journey we lazy ones used two days; for those
    faster   5
Travelers: one day. The Appian Way is less rough for slowpokes.
Here, because the water was unspeakably foul, I declared war
On my stomach, waiting in a terrible mood for my companions
To eat their dinner. Soon night was preparing
To spread shadows upon the earth and scatter her stars in the sky: 10
Then our slaves began heaping insults upon some boatmen,
The boatmen upon the slaves, "Dock here," "You're reboarding three
    hundred,"
"Hey, enough already." Paying up the money and hitching up the
    mule
Wasted a whole hour. Mosquitoes and swamp frogs
Prevent sleep. Drunk on cheap wine, a boatman   15
Sings in competition with a passenger about his absent girlfriend.
Finally, the traveler drops off to sleep
And a lazy stevedore ties the mule's rope to a rock,
Letting it feed itself; he then lies back and snores away.
Come daybreak and we observe our boat hasn't moved at all;   20

1.3.130: Alfenus Varus early in life was a cobbler from Cremona. See Glossary
    under VARUS.
1.5.1: In 38 or 37 Horace was part of an entourage traveling to Brundisium to
    broker a peace between Octavius and Antony.

Some hot-head leaps ashore and with a cut switch
Begins flogging the back and butts of mule and boatman;
We barely are at port by mid-morning.
We wash our faces and hands, Feronia,° in your spring.
After brunch we creep along three miles, and then   25
We arrive beneath Anxur loftily poised far off on cliffs gleaming
    white.
Here distinguished Maecenas was scheduled to arrive,
And Cocceius, both ambassadors sent to negotiate
Affairs of state, each skilled at reconciling estranged allies.
I smear my inflamed eyes with black salve;   30
Soon Maecenas arrives and also Cocceius,
Along with Fonteius Capito, a man's man down to his fingernail,
A friend, as no other, of Antony's.
At Fundi we gladly leave behind the mayor,
Aufidius Luscus, laughing at the medals of this insane clerk,°   35
The broad-stripped toga and charcoal burner.
Exhausted we rested in Formiae, the Mamurrae's town,
Hosted at Murena's° villa, dining at Capito's.
The next day dawned most pleasing. For at Sinuessa
Plotius, Varius, and Vergil meet us,   40
Nobler souls than these the earth does not possess,
And no one is more indebted to them than am I.
How often we embraced; how great the rejoicing!
In my right mind I would compare nothing to a delightful friend.
Next, a small farm house near a Campanian bridge provides us
    shelter,   45
And local officials give us fuel and food;
At Capua even the mules put their saddle bags down early.
Maecenas goes to gamble, Vergil and I to sleep;
Playing ball is unfriendly sport to the red-eyed and to those with a
    delicate stomach.
From here Cocceius' well-stocked farm receives us,   50
Right next to the taverns of Caudium. Now, Muse,°
I'd like to recall briefly the battle between that buffoon, Sarmentus,
    and Messius,

1.5.24: Feronia was named after an Italic goddess often identified with Juno.
1.5.35: Horace satirizes Aufidius Luscus' pretensions to the dress of a high-rank-
    ing Roman magistrate. He carries the charcoal burner for burning incense
    to honor Maecenas.
1.5.38: Murena may be Lucius Licinius Murena, who was to become the brother-
    in-law of Maecenas. See Horace, *Odes* 2.10.
1.5.51-70: in mock-epic style Horace pokes fun at the dramatic confrontation
    between the rustics Sarmentanus and Messius.

AKA Cocky; what origin belonged to each combatant of the dispute:
Messius is of distinguished blood—Oscan;
Sarmentus belongs to his owner, still living; from such ancestors   55
Our heroes entered the fray. First Sarmentus: "You're like a wild
   horse,
I do declare." We laugh, Messius too;
He jerks his head: "Right on!" Then Sarmentus adds: "If your brow
Still had its horn uncut, you'd be a fright,
Since even cut off you are a terror," for an ugly scar   60
Disfigured the left side of his bristly forehead.
Sarmentus continued to crack jokes about the "Campanian disease,"
  referring to his face,
And he asked several times if he danced the shepherd's jig,
Guffawing that Messius didn't need a tragic mask or boots.
Cocky responded in kind: that Sarmentus should dedicate
  his chains°   65
To the Lares; although he was a clerk,
Still his mistress had property rights. He ended by asking
Why he had run away in the first place, that a single pound
Of flour would suffice him since he was so little and skinny.
With fun like this we prolong that dinner.   70
Next stop: Beneventum. Here our busy host
Almost burned down his place while basting some bony thrushes.
The flame from a fallen fireplace log nonchalantly slipped out
Around the old kitchen, made a dart to lick the roof beams.
You should have seen the starving guests and terrified slaves   75
Grab the food and try to put out the fire too.
From here on my native Apulia starts
To show her wind-parched mountains
Familiar to me; we would have never wriggled our way through
If a farm near Trevicum hadn't welcomed us with teary smoke   80
From wet branches and leaves, smoldering in the fireplace.
Here, utter moron that I am, I lie awake until midnight
Waiting for a liar of a girl who never showed up; finally sleep
Robs me of a sexual fantasy, naughty dreams so real
That I make a mess on my pajamas and on my belly.   85
Next, for twenty-four miles we're whisked in carriages,
Staying in a village whose name just won't scan,
But hints make it easy to know: They sell the cheapest thing there:
  water;
But the bread is the very best

1.5.65-66: the lines facetiously suggests a runaway slave's dedication of his chain that parallels the offering to Lares made by freeborn young men upon entering manhood.

And the smart tourist loads up with it.   90
Now at Canusium, a spot long ago founded by valiant Diomedes,
It's gritty, and there is not a jug more water.
Here Varius leaves, upsetting his friends;
Then really bushed, we arrived in Rubi,
Completing a long stretch made muddier by rain.   95
The next day the weather was better but the road worse
All the way to the walls of Bari, famous for sea food. Then Gnathia,°
A town built when nymphs were on strike, provided us with some
    jokes and good laughs;
They wanted us to believe that incense melts on temple steps
Without fire. Let Apella the Jew believe it—°   100
I won't. For I have learned that the gods live a tranquil life
And, if nature produces a miracle, the gods
Do not surrender their care-free time to send it down from high
    heaven.
Brundisium marked the end of the long trip and my writing paper.

1.6

Maecenas, not one of the Lydians who settled Etruscan°
Territory was nobler than your ancestors;
In time past your grandfathers, both paternal and maternal,
Commanded huge armies.
But you do not, as many do, turn up a bent nose   5
At nobodies like me, born the son of a freedman father.
As you refuse to count as important a man's parentage,
Freeborn or not, you seem truly convinced
That before the rule of Servius Tullius, that commoner,
Many times many men with nobodies for ancestors   10
Lived exemplary lives and won high offices;
On the other hand, someone like Laevinus from the clan of Valèrius,
Who drove out Tarquin the Proud, is not worth
More than a penny because of his parents. At least it was so
In the eyes of the people and you know what kind of judges
    they are, often stupid   15
Enough to elect to office the undeserving and to be slaves to fame,
Stupefied by titles and family images. What should we people,
Who are far, far removed from the public eye, do?

1.5.98: Gnathia, like Canusium (91) and the unnamed town of lines 87-88, had
    a shortage of water.
1.5.100: the Romans believed that the Jews were unduly superstitious.
1.6.1: Herodotus claimed that colonists from Lydia in western Asia Minor settled
    in central Italy and were the progenitors of the Etruscans.

Let's suppose that the crowd conferred office upon Laevinus
Rather than Decius, the new man, and the censor Appius°   20
Impeached me because I was not born from a freeborn father:
And rightly so, if I refused to accept the skin I was born with.
But in her shining chariot Ambition pulls
In chains both high and lowborn. What else, Tillius,°
Drove you to regain your lost stripe and become a tribune?   25
Envy increased which would be less for you as a private citizen.
For as soon as some nut has wound black laces
Half-way up his leg and donned the broad stripe, he hears
Right away: "Who is he? Who was his father?"
It's as if he had Burrus' disease, craving to be considered
     handsome,   30
And, wherever he goes, inspire the girls
To study his features one by one—
His face, calves, feet, teeth, hair.
Thus, when a politician promises citizens he'll take care of the city,
The empire, Italy, and the shrines of the gods,   35
His father's background or maybe his low birth from an unknown
     mother
Causes everybody to become concerned and to ask questions:
"You, the son of Syrus, or Dama, or Dionysius (all slaves), dare
Execute citizens, hurling them from the rock, or hand them over
     to the hangman?"
'But my colleague in office, Novius, sits one seat behind me;   40
He is now what my father was.' "So you think that you are
Paulus or Messalla? Well, if two hundred carriages
And three funerals met in the forum, blowing horns and trumpets,
Novius would out-volume this noise; at least he grabs our attention."
Now I come back to myself, the son of a freedman,   45
Everybody's back-biting target for being the son of a freedman,
For being associated with you, Maecenas, and once
For being the military tribune commanding a Roman legion.°
The first charge differs from the last, because anyone could
     legitimately
Envy me my office, but not the fact that you are also a friend   50
Who is especially careful to choose only worthy men

1.6.20: Appius Claudius Pulcher, censor in 50, exercised his office severely and
     with some bias. He censored the historian Sallust and the sons of many
     freedmen.
1.6.24: Tillius regained his senatorial rank which permitted him to wear the
     distinctive toga with the broad purple stripe.
1.6.48: Horace refers to his stint in the army of Brutus.

Free of warped ambition. To call me "lucky"
I cannot accept; not by chance I "lucked" into your friendship.
No, it wasn't chance that threw you in my way. First that excellent
    Vergil
And next Varius told you who I was.   55
When I came into your presence for the first time, I managed a few
    awkward words;
Tongue-tied bashfulness kept me from uttering more.
I did not claim my father was noble or that I loved riding
Around my native estate on my nag.
But what I was I state. You respond, as usual,   60
In a few words; I go. About nine months later you call me back and
    invite me
To join your circle of friends. I hold this a great honor,
To have pleased you, who distinguish the honorable from the base
Not by a father's fame but by conduct in life and moral character.
Now if my faults are few and modest and my character   65
A little flawed, but generally decent, rather like
The occasional warts you fault on a beautiful body;
If no one can justly accuse me
Of greed or vulgarity or debauchery;
If, to praise myself, I be pure and conscientious and well-liked by
    friends,   70
Then the cause is my father, a poor possessor of a tiny farm.
He refused to send me to Flavius' school,
Where came the big sons of big centurions,
Carrying satchels and slates slung across the left shoulder
And paying eight bits tuition every fifteenth;   75
Instead, he had the nerve to bring his boy to Rome to learn
The 'liberal arts' that any Equestrian or Senator wants his own sons
To learn. If anyone noticed my clothes, the retinue of slaves
In the midst of the crowd, he would believe
Such expenses derived from inherited wealth.   80
My father was himself my guardian, incorruptible,
Near me in the presence of all my teachers. Why say more?
He adhered to the primary virtue; he kept me decent, free from every
    vice,
And free from ugly scandal. He did not fear anyone finding fault in
    him,
If someday I earned low wages   85
As an auctioneer or tax collector, as he was;
I would not have complained. But as things turned out,
I owe him greater praise and greater thanks.
In my right mind I could never be ashamed of such a father.
Unlike the majority who would claim that they can't be blamed   90

Because they lack freeborn and famous parents,
I will not aver it; that's not my defense; my way of thinking and
    speaking
Is far distant from theirs. For instance, if a law of nature destined
    each of us,
After a specific number of years, to start life over
And to choose the parents who suited our individual fancy,   95
I'd be happy with my own, refusing to select
Persons famed by *fasces*° and curule chair.
The mob would, no doubt, judge me crazy, but perhaps I'd be sane
In your eyes because I was unwilling to shoulder a heavy load that
    I'm not used to.
Otherwise, right away I'd need to look for greater resources,   100
To greet more visitors, and to have one friend or other accompany
    me
So that I'd never be alone in the country or abroad.
I'd have to feed many horses and grooms
And to use wagons everywhere. Now I can ride
On a small mule to Tarentum, if I want,   105
Although a knapsack and the weight of the rider may blister
    his loins and flanks.
No one will charge me with being cheap as you are called,
    Judge Tillius,
Whenever on the road to Tivoli you lead a mere five boys
Following behind and carrying a chamber-pot and wine jug.
In this and a thousand other ways I live a better life than you,   110
Famous senator. Wherever it is my pleasure,
I go, alone; I ask the price of vegetables and flour;
In the early evening I often wander over to the crooked circus
And forum; I stop to take in the fortune tellers, then I mosey on home
To a plate of pancakes à la leeks and chickpeas;   115
Supper is served by three slaves; on my white stone table
Stand two cups and a ladle, a cheap flask,
An oil jar and saucer, Campanian ware.
Then I go to sleep unworried about arising
Early the next morning to meet Marsyas   120
Who claims he cannot bear the sight of Novius Junior.
I lie in bed up to ten o'clock, then I take a stroll or I read
Or write something I privately may like, have a rub-down,
Not with the stuff that dirty old Natta stole from lamps.
When the sun growing ever hotter reminds me, I go, all tired out,   125
To the baths, being careful to avoid the Campus Martius and
    pick-up game.

1.6.97: the *fasces* are the bundled axes that symbolized power.

I have a light lunch, just enough not to pass the day
On an empty stomach. I mill about the house. This is my lifestyle,
That of people free from the weight and misery of ambition;
With these things I comfort myself ever knowing that I live more
    sweetly than   130
If my grandfather, my father, and my uncle had been quaestors.°

1.8

Once I was the trunk of a wild fig tree, a useless log;
A carpenter was not sure whether to make a stool or Priapus;
He chose the god. So I am a god, scaring the hell out
Of thieves and birds. You see, a sickle in my hand and a red pole
Sticking straight up from my lewd crotch threaten thieves,   5
And a reed fixed on my head frightens away meddling birds
And prevents them from lighting in these new gardens.
In former times a fellow slave paid for corpses,
Removed from their narrow rooms, to be brought here in a cheap
    coffin.
Here used to be the common burial site for poor people,   10
For Pantolabus, the scrounge, and that spendthrift Nomentanus.
A pillar reads: '1,000 feet across and three hundred deep,
This plot and monument do not descend to the heirs.'
Nowadays, anybody can live here in the healthful Esquiline area°
And stroll on the sunlit embankments where not long ago
    mourners   15
Grimly used to look upon the ghastly field adrift with whitening
    bones.
As for me, I am not as worried and troubled by the thieves
And wild animals that usually haunt this place
As I am by the witches who go to work with spells and potions
On human souls: I cannot find a way to get rid of them,   20
Nor, as soon as the wandering moon shows her
Lovely face, prevent them from gathering bones and poisonous herbs.
I, yes I myself, have seen Canidia, tucked up in a black cloak,
Scurrying, her feet bare, her hair disheveled, howling
Like a wolf, and accompanied by Sagana, an even older witch.
    The pale   25
Upon their faces made the pair a ghastly sight. They began to tear up
The earth with their nails and with their teeth rip apart a black lamb;

1.6.131: the quaestorship was the lowest of the political offices that permitted
    admission to the senate.
1.8.14: an area on the Esquiline was being converted by Maecenas from a watery
    cemetery to a housing development.

Then they poured the blood in a ditch to summon up the shades
  of the dead
To give responses to questions of the future.
They had two doll-like images, one fashioned of wax, and a larger
  one of wool;   30
The woolen one was apparently made to punish the smaller wax one;
It stood groveling, set up like a slave
About to die. One witch called upon Hecate, the other
Invoked savage Tisiphone, the fury. You'd have seen snakes,
Stray hellhounds, and the blushing moon,   35
Who hid behind the large tomb-monuments, ashamed to be a witness
  of these events.
Now if any word I'm saying is a lie, may white crow shit splatter
My head and I be pissed and crapped on when Julius
And that fairy Pediatia and that thief Voranus come by.
Now I could mention every detail: how the ghosts took turns to speak
  in response
To Sagana, squeaking out shrill and mournful hums;   41
How they buried a wolf's beard secretly in the ground,
And a single tooth of a spotted viper; how they raised a blazing fire
With the waxen doll, and how I shuddered witnessing
  the hocus-pocus
And going-ons of those two furies. But I got my revenge: 45
As loud as an exploding bladder I farted,
When my fig-ass split; they then made a bee line to the city;
Canidia's false teeth fell out, and Sagana lost her thick wig.
They also dropped their herbs and magic bracelets from their arms.
It was a grand farce, a hilarious scene; you'd have had
  a belly-whopping laugh.   50

1.9°

I happened to be walking down the Sacred Way, as was my custom,
Thinking over some trifling verses that had me totally absorbed.
There ran up a man I knew only by name,
And seized my hand: "How are you, you sweet old thing?"
"Nicely, as matters go for now," I answered, "and I hope you're
  doing fine."   5
When he kept on following near me, I anticipate: "Nothing you
  want, no?"
But he said: "Oh yes! Get to know us; we are erudite." Here I replied,
"How impressive." Pathetically, I kept seeking a way to shake him,

---

1.9.1. It is seriously doubted that the social-climbing poet/con-man depicted in
  this poem is Propertius, as is claimed by some.

Sometimes picking up the pace, sometimes stopping in my tracks
To say something in my boy's ear, as the sweat streamed down   10
To the bottom of my ankles. "Lucky you, Bolanus, for your short
    temper,"
I muttered to myself. Meanwhile he blabbered on
About anything and everything, gaga over the neighborhood streets,
    and the city.
When I made no response to him, "You're awfully anxious to get
    away," he said,
"I've noticed it for some time now; it's no use. I'm sticking with
    you;   15
I'll just tag along wherever you are off to." "No reason for you
To go all about. I want to visit someone you don't know,
Way across the Tiber by Caesar's gardens; he's in bed sick."
"I have nothing to do and I'm not lazy, so I'll follow you."
My poor ears droop like a donkey resentful   20
When too heavy a load mounts his back. He starts up:
"If I know myself, you'll be making me a better friend than Varius or
    Fuscus;
For who can write more verses than I,
Or write them faster? Who can shake his limbs in more delicate
    dance?
Why even Hermogenes would envy my singing."   25
This was the spot for cutting in: "You have a mother?
Relatives who rely upon you staying healthy?" "Nary a single one;
I have laid them all to rest." "Lucky them, now only I'm left;
So finish me off. Now that sorry fate impends foretold to me in my
    youth
By that old Sabine fortune teller who shook lots in an urn: 30
'Not dire poison, not an enemy's sword, not pleurisy,
Not pneumonia, and not lingering gout will finish him.
Someday a yakking jackass will be his ruin.
He'll be wise to avoid, when he comes of age, Big Mouths.' "
Half the morning was already gone by the time we reached Vesta's
    temple;   35
By pure chance he was overdue in court,
If he failed to respond, he'd lose his case.
"Please," he said, "stay and lend a hand." "I'll be damned
If I have the strength to stand around; and I know nothing about
    the law
And, besides, I'm in a hurry to go you know where."
    "I'm undecided." he stated,   40
Should I leave you or drop the case." "O, please, me!" He answers,
"Nope, no can do,"
And proceeds to go ahead; and I—well you can't beat a winner—

Follow along. "How are things going with you and Maecenas?"
He picks up from here. "He's a man of few friends and sound
    judgment."
"No one has used good fortune more adroitly. You'd have someone 45
Who would be able to play a great supporting role,
If you would just introduce him to me: damn it all,
You'd outdo all the others!" "We don't live quite
The way you think; there is no home more honest than his,
No place freer from intrigue; it doesn't bother me," I said,   50
"If someone else is richer or better educated; there, to each person
His own niche." "What a tall story, hard to believe."
"But it's true." "You make me hotter than ever to get near him."
"Just keep wishing: you'll storm him with your heroic qualities,
I'm sure; he's an easy conquest,   55
So he makes first encounters difficult." "I won't fail:
I'll bribe his servants; and if today
I am shut out, I will not quit. I'll pick my times,
Bump into him on the streets, join his escort. In life nothing
Has come to mortals without hard work!" While this was going on,
    suddenly   60
There came on the scene Aristius Fuscus,° my dear friend,
Who knew perfectly well that character. We stopped: "Where you
    coming from?
Where you going?" the usual amenities of questions and answers.
    I began to pluck,
To pull his unbending arms, nodding my head,
Winking at him to *please* save me. But that smart-ass   65
Chuckles and pretends to misunderstand. My liver burned with
    raging bile.
"Eh, Fuscus, you said you wanted to discuss something
Confidential with me." "Ah, yes, I remember it well,
But I'll speak to you at a better time. Today is the thirtieth Sabbath;
You don't want me to offend the circumcised Jews, no?" "But I'm not
    very religious."
I chimed—"Ah, but I am: you see, I am just one of the many,   71
A bit more weak. Please excuse me, we'll talk soon." Oh, that a sun
So black rose over me! That bastard ran off and left the knife
Under my throat. But then, the plaintiff, his adversary,
Chanced to come by. He yelled: "You scallywag, where do you think
    you're off to?"
And to me: "Sir, will you testify?" I offer   76

1.9.61: Fuscus is a very good friend of Horace. See *Odes* 1.22 and *Epistles*
    1.10.

My ear—gladly. He hauls him off to court; on both sides there is
   shouting,
On all sides confusion. Thus Apollo° saved me.

1.10

Yes, I did say that Lucilius put together verses that run
On clumsy feet. Now what admirer of Lucilius is so gauche as
Not to confess that? At the same time on the very same page
I praised him for rubbing down the city with plenty of salt.
I'll grant him that, yet I couldn't possibly praise him in all else;
   otherwise,   5
I'd have to admire Laberius' mimes as beautiful poetry.
So, it is not enough to spread a grin on the audience's
Face; yet there is some merit in that, too.
A work should be concise for the thought to flow and to keep it free
From the entanglement of words that tire and burden the ears.   10
The diction should sometimes be serious, sometimes comic,
Playing the part of the orator or poet,
Now and then of the polished wit who spares his strength and on
   purpose
Tones it down. Humor is often more powerful and better able
To cut through big issues than something serious.   15
The old masters of Old Comedy succeed in this;
And they deserve to be our models; that Romeo
Hermogenes never reads them and that ape man
Trained himself to sing nothing but Calvus and Catullus.
"But Lucilius accomplished something good by mixing Greek   20
In his Latin." You late-bloomers, do you think that
That is difficult or remarkable? Even Pitholeon of Rhodes
Managed that. "But satire that combines both languages
Is mellower, just as a Falernian varietal when blended with
   a Chian."
Now I ask you, only when you compose poetry or also   25
When you have to plead Petillius' tough case?
Whereas Pedius Poplicola and Corvinus sweat over preparing their
   briefs,
You forget your fatherland and father Latin
Choosing, like a bilingual Canusian, to blend lingo
Borrowed from abroad with native words.   30
I too, born on the Italian side of the Ionian Sea, had in mind

---

1.9.78: Apollo is referred to, most likely because he is the patron god and divine
   protector of poetry and poets.

Composing some Greek ditties, when Quirinus appeared to me
A little past midnight, the time of true dreams, and stopped me with
   this warning:
"You'd be as crazy to carry wood to a forest as
To plan to swell the throngs of Greeks."   35
While that bombastic Alpine bore murders Memnon and botches°
The muddied source of the Rhine, I amuse myself with these satires,
Which do not echo in a temple nor compete for Tarpa's verdict there,
Nor return again and again to be viewed in the theaters.
Only you among our contemporaries, Fundanius, can charm us   40
With chatty comedies wherein the sassy mistress and clever slave
   Davus
Trick the old man Chremes. Pollio sings of the deeds
Of kings in tragic trimeters, and Varius has the power and might to
   spin
The strands of epic like no one else. The muses of the pastoral world
Are delighted: they have nodded approval of Vergil's tender and
   graceful oeuvre.   45
For me there was left this, the genre which Varro of Atax, and others
   too,
Who tried but failed, whom I surpassed in better writing,
Yet still falling short of Lucilius, its inventor; from him I'd never dare
To remove the crown that clings to his head and wreathes him in
   glory.
But I did say that his poetic stream flowed muddy, often sweeping
   along   50
More debris to be cleared out than left floating in. Come now, I ask
   you,
Professor of Lit., don't you ever find something in Homer, the great
   one,
To criticize? And doesn't your genial Lucilius find something to
   change
In Accius' tragedies and laugh at Ennius' verses that lack dignity,
Meanwhile claiming to be inferior to those he himself criticized?   55
Why can't we read Lucilius' works and stop to ask
Whether his own rugged nature or that of his themes
Denied him more finished verses, more smoothly flowing?
Than he would compose quite content with this one practice: to frame
His every idea in hexameters and pride himself on writing two
   hundred lines   60

1.10.36-37: the lines refer to the bombastic Marcus Furius Bibaculus who wrote
   an epic on the Gallic Wars and an *Aethiopis*.

Before eating and just as many after dinner? Such was
The talent of Cassius, the Etruscan, more impetuous than a flooding
   river.
They say he was cremated from the fire of his own books
And bookcases. Suppose, as I maintain, Lucilius
Was genial and witty, and was also more polished   65
Than some amateur, an author of a new genre untouched by Greeks,
And then, too, by the throng of earlier, senior poets. And yet,
If fate had prolonged his life and dropped him into the lap of our
   time,
He would erase much and prune away every excess which spread
Beyond perfect growth; and, while he was composing his verse,   70
He would often scratch his head and bite his nails to the quick.
You've got to use and reuse the eraser, if you hope to write something
Worth reading twice; don't work to delight the crowd,
But content yourself with a few readers. You're not so crazy as
To want your poems dictated in second-rate schools.   75
I certainly don't. I'm happy enough to win the applause of the
   knights in the front rows
As gutsy Arbuscula, when she was being hissed from the stage, in
   scorn of all the others
Said. You think that I'd let that louse Pantilius provoke me,
Or Demetrius torment me by his carping slanders behind my back,
Or that idiot Fannius, as a guest at Tigellius Hermogenes' dinner,
   injure me?   80
Plotius and Varius, Maecenas and Vergil,
Valgius and Fuscus, and excellent Octavius,° their approval I seek,
And the praises of the Visci brothers;
Putting aside flattery, I can name you,
Pollio, you, Messalla, and your brother, as well as you,   85
Bibulus and Servius, together with you, unbiased Furnius.°
Many others, some scholars and friends,
I purposely leave out: I'd like to please them, for them to smile
At these verses, such as they are; and I would regret it, if they fail
To bring less joy than I hope for. But you, Demetrius,   90
And you too, Tigellius, I bid to whine on among the chairs of your
   female students.
Go, boy, be quick, and add these lines in my little book.

1.10.82: the Octavius mentioned is not Octavius/Augustus but one Octavius
   Musa, a poet and historian whose works do not survive.
1.10.86: Bibulus is Lucius Calpurnius Bibulus, a fellow-student and fellow-sol-
   dier of Horace. Servius Calpurnius Rufus was a celebrated jurist and Gaius
   Furnius became consul in 17.

2.6

This was in my prayers: a piece of land not very big,
A garden with a fresh-flowing spring near the house,
And a wood just above it. Greater the gods have done
For me and better. It's perfect. I ask for nothing more,
Except, son of Maia,° that you make these gifts mine forever.   5
Whereas I have not enlarged my property by shady deals,
Nor will I reduce it through waste and neglect;
Whereas I am not fool enough to make any of the following prayers:
"Oh, if only I could add that corner, adjacent to my strip,
    that disfigures it,"
Or, "May good luck show me a pot of silver as that field-hand   10
Who bought the very field with money there where
He used to plow for hire, rich thanks to his buddy Hercules;"
Whereas I'm content with what I have, I offer you this prayer:
Fatten my flock and everything else except my brain,
And be, as usual, my special guardian.   15
So now that I have removed myself from the city to my mountain
    retreat,
What first shall I celebrate in my satires and with my pedestrian
    muse?
Here no mean-spirited ambition corrupts me, no leaden sirocco,
And no fatal autumn, a gain for the gloomy funeral goddess.
Father of Morning, or Janus, if you prefer it,   20
To whom men dedicate the early labors of their daily tasks—
As the gods have destined—be the start of my song.
At Rome you rush me off to court to vouch for someone.
"Hey, get a move on, or someone else will respond to his duty more
    quickly than you!"
I have to go, whether the North wind scrapes the earth   25
Or winter in ever narrower curve drags a snowy day.
After speaking out loud and clear something that may incriminate me,
I must struggle with the crowd, bumping slowpokes.
"What are you up to, you crazy man? What's your problem?" Some
    jerk assails me
In anger and with curses, "You're knocking over everything in your
    path,   30
With your mind, obviously, intent on racing back to Maecenas."
All this is as pleasing as honey, I will not lie. But as soon as
I arrive to the dreary Esquiline,° a hundred tasks
That don't concern me leap around my head and side: "By seven

2.6.5: the son of Maia is Mercury, the god of luck and wealth.
2.6.33-34: Maecenas had a huge garden on the Esquiline Hill.

Roscius kindly requests that you meet him tomorrow at the Puteal;" 35
Or, "Because of an important matter, something new and of mutual
  interest,
The scribes,° Quintus, respectfully ask that you remember to return
  today;"
Or, "See to it that Maecenas stamps these forms."
Should I say, "I'll try," he adds and then insists: "You can do it, if you
  want to."
The seventh year, more like the eighth, has passed   40
Since Maecenas added me in the number of his company;
Inasmuch as he wanted to take someone along
In his carriage on one of his trips to whom he could entrust such
  small talk
As this: "What time is it? Is the Thracian Bantam a match for the
  Syrian?°
The morning frost really bites you, if you don't bundle up enough." 45
These gossipy subjects are perfectly safe to deposit in my ear.
Throughout all this time our man, yours truly, is ever, hour by hour,
  day by day,
The subject of envy. He watched the games with Him;
He played some ball on the Campus with Him: all chime, "Fortune's
  son, that's you."
A chilly rumor rolls from the rostra through the streets,   50
And whoever meets me seeks my advice, "O good sir—
For you should know, since you can almost touch the gods—
What have you heard about the Dacians?" "Nothing at all."
"You're always the comedian." "May the gods torment me, if I know
  anything."
"What about the veterans' rewards that Caesar promised,   55
In Sicily? Or will he offer them on Italian soil?"
When I swear that I know absolutely nothing, they marvel at me
As the sole human being able to keep a deep and remarkable silence.
All my daylight is wasted in such matters, forcing me to pray:
When will I see again my country farm and when will it be
  possible   60
For me to indulge my sweet hours oblivious to life's worries,
Sometimes in the books of the ancients, in sleep, and sometimes in
  laziness?
Oh, when will beans,° Pythagoras' relatives,

2.6.37: Horace had been a scribe and was still a member of the guild.
2.6.44: the reference is to matched pairs of gladiators so named from their ar-
  mor.
2.6.63: Horace humorously suggests that the Pythagorean doctrine included
  dietary restrictions against the eating of beans.

And greens dripping oily with bacon dressing be served me?
Oh, what divine nights of dining when I and mine before our own
    sacred hearth   65
Feast and provide from our plates to our sassy servants
The choice morsels; as each guest so desires,
Free from crazy rules, he drinks dry goblets of various sizes,
One boldly quaffing strong drinks,
Another merrily getting soused on moderate portions.   70
Conversation ensues, not about the villas and homes of others,
Nor about the style of Lepos' latest performance in dance; but we
    discuss
What we consider apposite and unseemly not to know, such as:
Does wealth or virtue make men happy?
What makes men friends, self-interest or rectitude?   75
What is the nature of the good? What is the ultimate good?
My neighbor Cervius often spins old wives' tales with a point,
For example, if someone praises Arellius' wealth,
Unknowing the trouble that it brings, he starts off:
"Once upon a time a country mouse welcomed a city mouse   80
Into his poor hole of a house, both host and guest being old friends.
The country mouse roughed it, keeping an attentive eye on his larder,
    yet he relaxed
His frugal disposition for his friend's entertainment. What else to say?
He did not begrudge choice chickpeas that he had stored away, and
    long-grain oats.
Carrying them in his mouth he vainly offered him a dried grape   85
And half-nibbled pieces of bacon, eager to conquer the disdain of one
Who with haughty tooth barely touched the individual courses of the
    two-course meal.
The master of the house, stretched out on straw and chaff,
Ate stubble and cocklebur, leaving the better stuff for his guest.
Finally, the city mouse spoke up: 'My friend, what's the fun   90
Living here, eking it out on the edge of a precipitous forest?
Surely you prefer humans and the city to these wild woods.
Seize the road! Trust me, your pal, for earthly creatures
In life have drawn the lots of mortal souls and there is no escape
From death for large and small. Therefore, old chap,   95
While you can, live well in surroundings you can enjoy;
Live mindful of how short is your life.' These words inspired
The hick; he eagerly bounced out of the home.
Together they set out on the charted way in eager desire
To creep beneath the walls of the city by night. As night was
    poised   100
In mid course of the sky, each mouse
Sets footprints in a rich house where covers

Dyed deep red, blazed, draped over ivory couches;
And many food trays, left over
From the night's banquet, were piled high in baskets.   105
So, once he has his rural guest relaxed, stretched out on a purple
    cloth,
The host scurries about like an officious waiter with tucked-up tux,
And serves up course after course, performing his duties
In true slave style, foretasting every dish that he brings.
The other lies back and takes in with glee the change of fate and
    the good food.   110
While he was playing the joyful role of dinner guest, a sudden loud
    rattling
Of doors shook them from their couches.
Over the entire room they scampered in fear,
And became more terrified and terrorized when the lofty halls
    redounded
With the barking of huge dogs. Then the country mouse:
    'This kind of life   115
I don't need one bit. Goodbye and good riddance,' he said, adding:
    'The forest
And my hole with its thin hay will console and keep me safe from
    snares.' "

2.8

(*Horace*) How did you enjoy the dinner at Nasidienus', that rich man?
I was looking for you to be my guest yesterday, but I heard that
You were drinking from noon on. (*Fundanius*) Yes, and I never had
A better time in my life. (*H*) O.K., if it's not too much trouble, tell me
What first course settled your growling stomach.   5
(*F*) First up, a boar from Lucania, caught when a gentle south wind
Was blowing, so said the father of the feast: around it
Tart turnips, lettuces, radishes, the kind of stuff
That whet a jaded belly: caraway, fish-brine, wine lees from Cos.
When they were removed, a slave boy in a waiter's tux wiped   10
The maple wood table clean with a purple towel and another
Swept up the scraps lying about and anything else
That could annoy the dinner guests. Then like an Attic maiden
Bearing the sacred emblems of Ceres, dark-skinned Hydaspes°
    solemnly marched
Forward carrying Caecuban wine, and Alcon brought in brine-free
    Chian.   15

2.8.14: from the name, Hydaspes presumably is a slave from India, a very rare
    possession indeed.

Here the host said: "Maecenas, if Alban or Falernian appeals to
   your palate
More than those that have been served, we have both."
(H) Those poor rich people! Who were your fellow diners,
Fundanius? What kind of fun did you have? I am eager to know.
(F) I was at the head couch, next to me was Viscus from Thurii,
   and by him,   20
As I remember, was Varius. Then present were Servilius Balatro
And Vibidius whom Maecenas brought along as uninvited "shades."°
Nomentanus was next to the host and so was Porcius,°
A joker who made us laugh by gulping down cakes whole.
Nomentanus' presence was to point out with his index finger   25
Lest we miss anything. The rest of us, I mean the entire mob of us,
Dined on fowl, oysters, fish—everything
Concealing a sauce unlike any we had ever tasted.
That became evident as soon as he handed me
Livers of flounder and turbot which I had never tasted before.   30
Next he lectured me saying that his honeyed apples were picked
In the light of a waning moon. What difference that makes,
You'll have to hear from him. Then Vibidius spoke to Balatro:
"Let's get drunk and ruin this guy, otherwise we'll die without
   revenge."
So he asked for larger goblets. A pallor descended over the face   35
Of our caterer who dreaded nothing so much as hard drinkers,
Either because they talk too "dirty" and curse openly,
Or because wines that heat the drinkers dull a sensitive palate.
Everybody followed Vibidius and Balatro in upending
Whole carafes into Samnite beakers; however, the diners   40
At the end of the table did no damage to their flagons.
For the next course a lamprey eel is brought in stretched out
On a platter with shrimp swimming around it. The master explained
   it: "It was netted
Pregnant with roe; after spawning its flesh would be less tasty.
The sauce combines the following: olive oil from Venafrum,   45
Extra-virgin of the first pressing; juicy roe from Spanish mackerel;
Wine aged five years, barreled from the Italian side of the Ionian Sea,
Blended during the cooking—once cooked, Chian is added,
   which suits it better
Than any other varietal; then white pepper and a little vinegar
Fermented from clusters of grapes from Methymna in Lesbos.   50

2.8.22: "shades" or "ghosts" are the uninvited friends accompanying an invited
   guest.
2.8.23-24: there is a pun on the name Porcius. It means "pig."

Now as I first demonstrated, green arugula and bitter chicory are
    folded in
During the cooking; Curtillus discovered that unwashed sea urchins
Produce a better brine from the shell's salty sea liquid."
Just then the awnings hanging overhead collapsed with a heavy
    thud
On the platter, bringing with them more dark dust   55
Than the north wind stirs up on the plains in Campania.
We were in fear of further disaster, but when we sensed that the
    danger
Had passed, we recovered; Rufus Nasidienus put his head down
    and wept
As if his son had died a premature death. I wondered how it would
    have
Ended, if that sage Nomentanus had not given his friend a lift with
    these words: 60
"Oh, Fortune, what god is more cruel to us
Than you? You always enjoy playing with human life."
Varius could scarcely muffle laughter
With his napkin; Balatro who thumbs his nose at everything
Said: "Such is life; your reputation   65
Never will correspond to your hard work.
So that I may be entertained royally, you are wracked, tormented
By every angst-driven problem, fearing that the bread be burnt,
The sauce be served badly seasoned, all the slave boys
Not be dressed just right, neatly combed, proper for serving.   70
Add such accidents as these, the collapse of the awning
As happened just now, or a clumsy slave who trips and breaks a
    platter.
But a party-giver's abilities, like those of a general, adverse
    circumstances
Usually reveal in the raw, while favorable events keep them hidden."
Nasidienus responded like this: "May the gods grant to you   75
Everything you pray for. You are a good man and kind guest."
He called for his sandals; then you could just see the buzz
Of whispers on the couches passed from secret ear to ear.
(H) There is not a single play I'd rather see. But please,
Continue, tell me what made you laugh next. (F) While Vibidius   80
Was asking a slave boy if the carafe had been broken too,
Since the cups he called for were not handed him, and while
We were laughing at the jokes contributed by Balatro for the occasion,
Nasidienus, you returned, with a cheerful look on your face, as if
Determined to correct bad luck with your art. Slave boys followed   85
Bringing on a large board a crane cut up into pieces,
Sprinkled with salt and coated with flour;

The liver of a white goose, fed on fat figs, and hare legs
Torn from the body—much tastier eating that way
Than if connected to the loins. The next course we saw   90
Was broiled blackbird breast and assless pigeons,
Neat stuff, if our master had not been discoursing on their causes
And natures. We hightailed it out of there, taking our revenge on him
By not tasting any of that food, as if Canidia
Had breathed upon it a breath worse than vipers from Africa.   95

ODES

The Greek models for the *Odes* were numerous. Horace himself touts his adaptation of Sappho and Alcaeus, but other lyric poets such as Anacreon and Pindar have a definite influence. The themes and the tones of the collection vary greatly from the high and philosophical to the light and humorous. Among poems that are erotic, hymnal, or sympotic Horaces includes and groups many poems with political themes and social concerns. In fact, Horace's reputation depends to a great degree upon his developing lyrics of a political and social character.

1.1

Maecenas, descendant of ancient kings,
protective stay and sweet luster of my life,
there are men who delight in collecting the dust
of Olympia, their chariot wheels hot
as they graze the turning post, the palm of victory ennobling
    them   5
as masters of the earth, lofted among the gods.
One man enjoys the high of winning
public offices by the whim of the mob;
Another delights to cram full his silo
all the grain swept from the threshing floor of Libya.   10
Him, happy to split clods with a hoe
on his ancestral lands, not even the legacies of Attalus
would ever move to plow the Aegean sea
as a shivering sailor on a Greek freighter.
The trader, scared by the south wind that wrestles ocean waves, 15
sings the praises of the peaceful countryside of his home town:
soon he refits the battered fleet of ships,
untaught to endure hard times.
Another man does not spurn cups of an aged varietal,
nor to pause on a business day, stretching out   20
his limbs sometimes beneath a green arbutus,
sometimes by the soothing fount of a sacred stream.

Many enjoy the camp, the blast of bugle
and trumpet, the battles so abominable to mothers.
Under the cold of heaven   25
the hunter waits unmindful of his young wife,
if his faithful dogs have sighted a deer,
or a wild boar has smashed through his finely-meshed nets.
For me, the ivy crowns, reward for poets,
make me one among the gods above; the cool grove   30
and the nimble dances of nymphs with satyrs
distance me from the masses, as long as Euterpe
does not deny me her flute and Polyhymnia
refuse to tune the lyre of Lesbos.°
Should you rank me among the lyric poets,   35
my head will strike the stars aloft.

1.2

Already enough snow and portentous hail has the Father°
hurled upon the earth and with his glowing right hand
smashed the sacred citadels; he has
    terrorized the city,

He has terrorized peoples fearing that there may come again   5
the era of Pyrrha pregnant with complaints of strange portents,
when Proteus drove his entire herd
    to visit mountain peaks,

When species of fish clung to elm-tops
which once had been the well-known roost   10
for doves, and when in flooding waters
    swam trembling does.

We have seen the yellow Tiber with waves
hurled back in violence from the Etruscan shore
advance to dash to ruin the monuments of king Numa   15
    and the shrines of Vesta,°

Boasting himself to be the avenger of Ilia
who protests too much, and flowing pell-mell
over the left bank without Jove's approval,
    uxorious river.   20

1.1.34: Horace alludes to Sappho and Alcaeus, two of his principal Greek models,
    both from the island of Lesbos.
1.2.1: the "Father" is Jupiter, called the father of gods and men.
1.2.15: the line refers to the *regia*, official headquarters of the Pontifex Maximus
    and the nearby shrine of Vesta that was tended to by the Vestal Virgins.

How citizens sharpened steel against citizens, swords
by which dreadful Persians might have perished,
of battles fought, they will hear, our young,
    thinned out by parents' sins.

What god should the people call to the affairs   25
of a collapsing empire? With what prayer
will the sacred Virgins importune Vesta,
    oblivious to their hymns?

Whom will Jupiter cast in the role of expiator
of crime? We pray that you come at last,   30
your gleaming shoulders clothed in a cloud,
    mantic Apollo;

Or you, if you choose, smiling Venus of Eryx, as Play and Desire
flutter about you; or you, if you care for
a neglected race and your descendants,   35
    our founder,

Glutted too long on the game,
pleased by the fierce shouts, the smooth helmets,
the looks of the Marsian infantry
    against a bloodied foe;   40

Or you, winged son of nourishing Maia,°
if you assume a young man's shape
on earth, ready to be called
    the avenger of Caesar,

May you return late to the sky   45
and for a long time be happy to be among the people
of Quirinus, and may no breeze, too swift, lift you away,
    offended by our sins;

Here rather may you relish mighty triumphs,
here be greeted as father and prince, and permit not   50
the Medes to ride unpunished,
    under you, our leader, Caesar.

1.2.41: Horace is referring to the god Mercury and intimating in the stanza that
    Octavius is an earthly manifestation of the god. Horace emphasizes Mercury
    by placing him last in his hymnal addresses to the gods.

1.3

May the powerful goddess of Cyprus,°
may the gleaming constellation, twin brothers of Helen,°
   and the father of winds° confining all others
except the northwesterly guide you,

  O ship, transporting our Vergil   5
entrusted to you: deposit him safe and sound
   upon the shores of Attica, I pray,
and preserve him who is half of my own soul.

  Oak and layers of bronze in triplicate surround
the heart of that man who was the first   10
   to entrust a frail ship to a rough sea,
unafraid of the southwesterly squalls

  In battle with the blasts from the north;
nor does he fear stars portending rain or the rage of Southwind
   who is the supreme master of the Adriatic,   15
either churning or calming the waves at his will.

  What kind of near-death did he fear
who with dry eyes looked upon monsters of the deep,
   who witnessed the stormy sea
and Acroceraunia's infamous cliffs?   20

  In vain god in his wisdom has
divided the lands by the estranging
   sea, if unholy ships, nonetheless,
dash across straits that he ordained not to be ventured.

  The human race, daring to endure   25
anything, rushes into prohibited wrong.
   The reckless son of Iapetus°
with malice and guile brought fire to humanity.

  After the theft of fire from its home in heaven
famine and new strains   30
   of fevers fell upon the earth,
and the doom of death formerly slow and distant

1.3.1: Cyprus is the mythological and cultic home of Venus.
1.3.2: the twin brothers of Helen are the Gemini (Castor and Pollux) who are
    special patron gods of sailing.
1.3.3: the "father of winds" is Aeolus.
1.3.27: a reference to Prometheus, son of Iapetus.

Quickened its pace.
Daedalus tested the empty air
    on wings denied to men;   35
in one of his labors Hercules smashed through Acheron.

    There is no path too steep for mortals:
we are stupid to stake a claim to heaven itself
    and because of our crime we don't allow
Jove to store away his angry thunderbolts.   40

1.5

What slender boy amid many roses,
soaked with moist scents, is pressing
    you, Pyrrha, in a pleasing grotto?
    For whom do you bind your blond hair,

So simply elegant? Ah, how often he'll sob   5
over your promises and the shifting gods,
    shocked at the seas rough with black winds,
    the innocent

Who now enjoys you, trusting your golden glow,
who ever expects you always to be free for him,   10
    always to be desirous for love, unaware of the
    deceiving breeze. Poor wretched souls for whom

You glitter untried; for me, a votive plaque
on the sacred wall of the temple serves notice:
    I have hung up my sopping clothes   15
    to the powerful god of the sea.

1.6°

Brave and as conqueror of enemies you will be depicted
by Varius, the swan of epic song, whatever the exploit
the soldier, daring on ships or horseback, has managed
    with you as general;

1.5.13: the plaque marks Horace's gratitude to Neptune for saving him from
    the dangerous sea of Pyrrha, i.e. his liaison with her.

1.6.1: This type of poem is called a *recusatio*. The poet declines to write about
    the glorious feats of a powerful person and suggests another poet to take up
    the epic themes required for the task. Horace can compliment the subject(s)
    of the poem (here, Agrippa and Octavius—cf. "noble Caesar" in line 11) and
    the poet Varius. See Propertius 2.1.

Agrippa, to relate such grand themes as these   5
or the peevish spleen of Achilles who knew not how
to yield or the twists across the sea of clever Ulysses
    or the savage house of Pelops,

We slight poets do not try, since propriety and the powerful
Muse of the non-belligerent lyre forbid me to detract   10
from the praises of noble Caesar and from your own glory
    by my want of talent.

What poet is worthy to write of Mars clad in his
adamantine mail or of Meriones black with Trojan dust
or of Diomedes, aided by Athena, an equal   15
    match for the gods above?

I, whether afire or fancy-free, sing of banquets;
I sing of the fingernail-battles of virgins valiant
in their manicured attacks upon boys,
    I, ever the flippant one.   20

1.8

Speak, Lydia, by all
    the gods I ask, why by your love-making
do you speed Sybaris on to ruin?° Why does he loathe
    the sunny field, inured to dust and heat?

Why does he neither maneuver on horseback   5
    among his fellow-cadets nor rein in his Gallic mount
with mouth-bits like the teeth of wolves?
    Why does he fear a dip in the yellow Tiber? Why does

He shun the wary rubbing oil more than
    the blood of a viper? Why does he not show off arms   10
bruised by arms, who time after time proved his prowess
    with a discus and javelin throw way beyond the record?

Why does he lie low like the son of sea-born°
    Thetis during the deaths of Troy,
afraid that the clothes of a man would rush him   15
    against Lycian troops and to slaughter?

1.8.3: Horace suggests that the young Sybaris has gone soft and become licen-
    tious because of his name that is associated with the Greek city of Sybaris in
    southern Italy, known for its luxurious and extravagant living.
1.8.13: Achilles' mother, the Nereid Thetis, tried to prevent his going to Troy by
    hiding him on an island (Scyros) dressed as a girl.

1.9

See how deep with snow bright
Soracte° looms and no longer trees bear
    the strain and burden, and streams
    stand fast from the fierce freeze.

Melt the cold, piling plenty of logs   5
on the fireplace, and bring out generous
    wine, your four-year varietal, from
    a Sabine jar, Thaliarchus.°
Leave all else to the gods; for once
they have quelled the winds warring with   10
    the raging tide, neither cypress
    nor ancient ash trees shake.

Avoid asking what the morrow may be;
ante as credit whatever day
    chance deals; spurn not sweet loves   15
    and dances while young

And the green of youth blossoms before whining white hair
intrudes. Now is the time for playing fields and piazzas
    to extort soft whispers under cover
    of darkness at the trysting hour;   20

Now for the welcomed giggle betraying
a girl hiding in some nook
    and the pledge snatched from her shoulders
    or from a finger that—not quite—resists.

1.11°

Do not ask, for it is not right to know, what end for me,
what for you, Leuconoe, the gods have assigned; do not test out
Babylonian higher math. How much better to endure come what may.
Whether Jupiter allots us many more winters or this that now
    exhausts
the Tuscan Sea beating on pumice cliffs   5
is the last: be smart, strain the wines, and in your short life-span
prune long-term hope. As we talk,
spiteful time has fled: seize the day! Trust little the morrow.

1.9.2: Soracte is a mountain north of Rome on the border with Sabine territory.
1.9.8: in Greek "Thaliarchus" means something like "master of festivities."
    Horace may be so designating a slave boy of his.
1.11.1 Horace's dramatic monologue of the *"carpe diem"* theme already evoked
    in 1.9.

1.12

What man or hero do you choose to celebrate
on your lyre and plaintive flute, Clio?
What god? Whose name will the teasing
    echo resound

On the shady slopes of Mount Helicon,   5
on the peak of Pindus or chilly Haemus,
whose trees blindly followed
    Orpheus singing,

Who using his mother's skill checked
the cascades of rapid rivers and swift winds,   10
and charmed the oaks to respond to the strains
    of his tuneful lyre?

First I shall honor in song the Father,
controller of the affairs of men and gods,
who guides the sea and earth and universe   15
    in all its seasons.

From him generates nothing that surpasses him,
and nothing thrives his equal or like.
But yet the honors nearest his, Athena
    has secured,   20

Brave in battle; I will not fail to sing
of you, Bacchus, nor of the virgin Diana, mistress
of the beasts, nor of you, Phoebus, feared for your
    unerring arrow.

I shall sing of Hercules, and Leda's sons,°   25
one a famous master of horses and one
excelling with fists; when their bright constellation has
    shone for sailors,

Turbulent water streams down rocks,
winds quell, storm clouds turn tail   30
and the menacing wave, at their command, falls
    to relax on the sea.

Only then shall I sing of Romulus first,
Pompilius' reign of peace, then the arrogant
power of fascist Tarquin, lastly the noble   35
    death of Cato.

1.12.25: Leda's sons are the Gemini, Castor and Pollux.

Regulus, the Scauri, and Paulus°
who gave up his life when Hannibal was winning,
these I shall thank and honor in distinguished song,
    and Fabricius too.   40

Him and Curius of untrimmed hair
and Camillus, these men beastly poverty
trained for warfare, as did life on the family farm
    in a religious house.

There grows like a tree as time sneaks by   45
the fame of Marcellus; the Julian star glows
among all the others like the moon
    among fainter lights.

Father and guardian of the human race,
son of Saturn, to you Fates have destined   50
the care of mighty Caesar; may you rule with Caesar
    as second in command.

Whether he conducts in just triumph
conquered Parthians, threats to Latium,
or from the Eastern borders the Seres   55
    and the Indians brought low,

After you he will rule with justice the wide earth;
you will shake Olympus with your heavy chariot,
you will launch hostile thunderbolts
    against polluted groves.   60

1.13

Lydia, when you rave on about Telephus'
    rosy neck, Telephus'
smooth arms, oh, my liver°
    swells with boiling black bile.

Then neither my mind nor my complexion   5
    remain moored, a teardrop upon my cheeks
sneaks and slides down convicting me
    of how deep within longing consumes me.

1.12.37-48: a list of Roman military heroes who serve as paradigms of mo-
    rality.
1.13.3: the liver was considered the seat of passion.

I burn up when drunken donnybrooks
    leave bruised your white shoulders   10
or a boy out of control with his teeth
    has planted a memento on your lips.

No, if you would listen to me,
    you would not expect him to be forever true,
a crude violator of sweet kisses that Venus   15
    imbued with the quintessence of her own nectar.

They are happy three times over
    who are held by an unbroken link,
whose love ugly quarrels have failed to divide
    and which outlasts their final day.   20

1.14

O ship, new waves again will carry you out to sea.
O what are you to do? Try valiantly
    to embrace a port. Do you not see
    how your side is naked of oars,

How the mast, shattered by a gale off Africa,   5
and the yardarms moan, and without ropes
    the hulls can scarely survive
    the ever imperious

Sea? You have no sails still whole,
nor gods to summon when again beset by debacle.   10
    Though you are made from Pontus' pine,
    offspring of a noble forest,

And you can boast of your class and name—useless—
the cautious sailor puts no faith in painted poops.
    That you not be destined a plaything   15
    of winds, be careful.

A while back, I became weary, disillusioned;
now, I have a longing and care, not trifling, for you:
    steer clear of the waters that rush
    between the gleaming Cyclades.°   20

1.14.20: the Cyclades are a group of islands in the Aegean east of the mainland.
    Some see a reference to a full-flowing gown, the fancy dress of a prostitute.

1.18

Plant no tree, Varus, before inserting the sacred vine
in the pregnant soil around Tibur and Catilus'° walls;
for god has ordained all things hard for teetotalers;
without wine biting worries linger on.
After a little wine who harps on the hell of military life or his lack
    of money?   5
Anyone would rather rattle on about you, Bacchus, and you, comely
    Venus.
Let no one transgress the gifts of moderate Bacchus, the Liberator;
The drunken brawl bitterly fought out between Centaurs and Lapiths
serves as warning, as does the severe treatment of Bacchus toward
    Thracians,
when in their greed they distinguish right from wrong, narrowly
    defined   10
by their lust. Radiant Bassareus,° I'll not be the one
to arouse you against your will, nor bring to daylight your emblems
covered with all kinds of leaves. Temper the wild drums and frenzied
    Phrygian horn
that accompany blind love of self,
Boasting which lifts its empty head too high,   15
and Trust, betrayer of secrets, more transparent than glass.

1.20

Cheap generic Sabine you will drink from plain
tankards which I myself sealed and stored in a Greek jar
on that day the theater was filled
    with applause for you,

Maecenas, honored equestrian, so that the banks of the Tiber,   5
your native river, and the Vatican hill°
rebounded in playful echo
    praises of you.

You can sip Caecuban and the grape from Cales'°
press; neither Falernian vines nor the hills   10
of Formiae flavor
    my goblets.

1.18.2: Catilus was one of the mythical founders of Tibur.
1.18.11: Bassareus means "fox-skin."
1.20.6: the Vatican Hill across the Tiber was so called because it was associated
    with prophesy (*vaticinium*) and where a shrine to Cybele was later erected.
1.20.9-11: Horace lists several varietals from south of Rome which, according to
    Pliny the Elder, were among the finest in Italy.

1.22

If upright in life and free of crime,
he needs not Moroccan spears nor bow
nor quiver laden with poisoned
    arrows, Fuscus,

Whether he be about to make his way through the blazing sand   5
of Africa or across the inhospitable Caucasus
or over the regions that the storied
    Hydaspes lap.

For once in Sabine woods while I was singing
of my Lalage, straying carefree beyond my farm's   10
boundary, there ran from me,
    unarmed, a wolf;

What a monster he was! Such as neither soldiering
Apulia in its vast scrub-oak forests nourishes
nor the land of Juba, barren   15
    nurse of lions.

Station me in limp fields, where no tree
renews its leaves in the breezes of summer,
a piece of the world which clouds and inclement
    sky oppress,   20

Station me under the chariot of the too-near sun,
in a land denied to homes,
still will I love Lalage sweetly laughing,
    sweetly prattling.

1.23

You shy from me, Chloe, like a fawn
seeking her frightened mother on pathless hills
    in groundless fear of the breezes
    and the woods.

If the coming of spring has made the light leaves   5
quiver, or if green lizards have
    twitched a bramble, her heart
    and knees tremble.

Now I am not a savage tiger, nor an African
lion out to track you and maul you: 10
    So then, stop following your mother;
    you are ripe for a man.

1.25

Less often now the good-time boys pitch stones
that rattle your closed shutters;
they don't deprive you of sleep and your door
    makes love to its threshold

That once swung all night so easily   5
on its hinges. Less and less you hear now:
"While I spend long nights dying for you,
    do you, Lydia, sleep?"

Your turn comes: a crone in a lonely alley,
you will wail at your arrogant screwers,   10
while the rising Thracian wind like a bacchant rages
    on a moonless night.

Then the burning of love and lust
that maddens mares will drive
your gnawing liver wild; then you   15
    will lament that

The rowdy guys now find their fun
with the green ivy and dark myrtle,
dedicating sere leaves to the east wind,
    winter's companion.   20

1.30

O Venus, queen of Cnidos and Paphos,°
spurn your beloved Cyprus and appear
at the charming shrine of Glycera who summons you
    with much incense.

May your boy, on fire, and the Graces,   5
their belts undone, and the Nymphs hurry with you,
and Youth who lacks grace without you,
    and Mercury° too.

1.30.1: Cnidos in Caria, southern Asia Minor, and Paphos, the capital of Cyprus,
    are two centers of cult worship of Venus.
1.30.8: the reference to Mercury has many associations. He stands for eloquence,
    inventor of the lyre, merriment, civilized living, and commerce. The last at-
    tribute gives a humorous touch to the poem.

1.31

What does a poet ask Apollo just dedicated?°
What does he pray, as he pours new wine
    from the shallow libation bowl? Not for the rich
    crops of fertile Sardinia,

Not for the herds welcomed in steamy Calabria,   5
not for gold, nor ivory from India.
    not for fields which the swelling river Liris
    nibbles with its quiet waters.

Let them, to whom fortune has granted it, with pruning hook
lop the vine of Cales, so that the wealthy   10
    trader may drain dry from golden goblets wines
    bartered with Syrian goods;

He is dear to the gods, for three or four times
yearly he returns to the Atlantic Ocean,
    safe and sound. As for me, olives are my feasts,   15
    endive and low-cal mallows.

To enjoy in good health what I have got, O son of Leto,
grant to me I pray, and with sound mind
    may I pass an old age neither in disgrace
    nor in want of a lyre.   20

1.37°

Now is the time for drinking, now the freedom
for foot-stomping of the ground, now, friends,
    would be the time to adorn the dining couches of the gods
    with Salian delicacies.

Before today it was wrong to bring up Caecuban   5
from ancestral cellars, while a crazy queen
    was plotting mad ruin for the Capitoline
    and death to an empire

1.31.1: In 36 after the defeat of Sextus Pompey, Octavius vowed a temple to
    Apollo. Subsequent political events delayed its construction and it was not
    until the defeat of Antony and Cleopatra in 31 that the temple was revowed.
    It opened with a formal dedication on 9 October, 28. The temple had a portico
    and two libraries. See Propertius 2.31.
1.37.1: this ode heralds the news of Cleopatra's death.

With her polluted crew of diseased and foul
men, uncontrolled in her hope of   10
  some success and drunk on sweet luck.
  She sobered up her madness,

When scarely a single ship survived fire
and her mind, deluded on Egyptian wine,
  Caesar shocked to the stern reality of fear   15
  with his galleys in hot pursuit of her as she

Fled from Italy, like a hawk
gentle doves or a quick hunter a hare
  in the fields of snowy Haemonia,
  so that he might surrender to chains   20

That doomed monster: she sought
a noble way of death; she did not tremble,
  like a woman, at the sword
  nor with her swift fleet hie to secret shores;

She had the courage to tour with calm countenance   25
her palace in ruins, and bravely handle
  the scaly snakes, her body drinking
  their black poison,

More determined in premeditated death.
Scorning to be led on board hostile ships as a private   30
  citizen and to be paraded in an arrogant triumph,
  she was no humble woman.

2.1°

The civil unrest since Metellus was consul,
causes, crimes and phases of war,
  Fortune's sport, the burdensome
  coalitions of dynasts, and weapons

Smeared with gore still not expiated,   5
a work full of risky dice,
  these are your themes; and you are walking across fires
  concealed beneath deceptive ashes.

2.1.1: this poem honors C. Asinius Pollio's history of the civil war between
  Julius Caesar and Pompey, of which Pollio was a significant part. Quintus
  Caecilius Metellus Celer was consul of 60, the date of the formation of the
  First Triumvirate of Caesar, Pompey, and Crassus.

May the solemn tragic muse, only for a while,
be missing from the theaters. Soon, once you have   10
 composed your political history, you will assume
 again the grand vocation of Athenian drama,

You, famous protector of troubled clients,
of the Senate's counsel, Pollio; for you
 the triumphal victory in Dalmatia°   15
 earned eternal glory.

Now with the threatening blast of horns
you batter our ears, now the trumpets' blare,
 now the flash of arms and the faces of riders
 terrify nervous horses.   20

Now I seem to hear the great generals,
defiled with dirt that is no disgrace,
 and all the world conquered,
 except the fierce heart of Cato.°

Juno and some other gods, more partial   25
to Africans who left the land, powerless
 to avenge it, offer the victors' grandsons
 as victims to Jugurtha's grave.

Is there a plain not fertile with Italian blood
that does not bear witness with its tombs   30
 to unholy battles and to the sound of the crash
 of the West heard by the Parthians?

Are there gorges or rivers untouched by mournful war?
What sea have Apulian slaughters
 not discolored? Is there   35
 a coast that lacks our gore?

But don't, O muse, become reckless, forsaking play,
and attempt again the role of the Cean dirge;°
 come with me into Venus' grotto
 to look for music of a lighter style.   40

2.1.15: Pollio won a triumph against the Parthini in 39. See Vergil, *Eclogue* 8.
2.1.24-28: refer to the Battle of Thapsus in 46 in which Julius Caesar fought the
 remnants of the Republican army led by Cato the Younger.
2.1.38: the "Cean dirge" refers to the solemn style of Simonides of Ceos.

2.3

Remember to maintain a level head in difficult
matters, the same in good times,
    restrained from hubristic euphoria,
    as you will die, Dellius,°
Whether you live in gloom all your hours   5
or make yourself happy on festival days
    stretched out on a remote grassy knoll
    with a classic varietal wine.

Why do the towering pine and white poplar
love to intertwine branches weaving   10
    a welcoming shade? Why does the rushing water
    hurry to shimmer along its winding river?

Order them to bring wines, perfumes, and the blossoms—
too brief—of the sweet rose, here,
    while resources, youth, and the dark   15
    thread of the three sisters° allow.

You will say good-bye to the woodlands you bought,
to the home, and to the villa bathed by the yellow Tiber,
    good-bye, too, to the riches piled up high
    that an heir will possess.   20

Rich man descended from ancient Inachus,
or poor man from the lowest class,
    it makes no difference; you linger in the clear day
    a victim of Orcus who pities no thing.

All of us are herded there, for everyone's   25
lot is tossed in an urn: sooner, later,
    out it will come and reserve our passage
    on the boat for eternal exile.

2.7

Often serving with me in dire straits°
under Brutus, general of the army,

2.3.4: Quintus Dellius was a known *bon vivant* who frequently changed sides
    in the various military engagements from 43 to 31.
2.3.16: the three sisters are the Fates who are envisioned as spinning out the
    threads of human lives.
2.7.1: After the battle of Philippi, Octavius pardoned many of Brutus' supporters,
    including, as it seems, Horace. This Pompeius continued to resist Octavius,
    perhaps fighting with Sextus Pompeius, as his name implies.

who has restored you to civil rights,
to ancestral gods and Italian skies,

Pompeius? Foremost of my friends,   5
many a dragging day I broke
    with you, with wine, and with hair
    garlanded and glistening with Syrian ointment.

With you I suffered Philippi, panic, flight,
and a shield ingloriously abandoned,   10
    when valor was smashed and menacing hosts
    befouled their chins on dirt.

But me, scared stiff, Mercury in a thick mist
quickly lifted through enemy lines;
    the undertow sucked you   15
    back into war on teeming tides.

So render to Jove the feast you vowed,
rest your body exhausted from long service
    beneath my laurel, and do not scrimp
    on the jugs of wine set aside just for you.   20

Fill the polished, leafy cup with Massic,
a vintage that helps us forget; pour ointments
    from generous shells. Who will hurry
    to weave us garlands of fresh parsley

Or myrtle? Whom will the Venus throw   25
declare the master of the cups? I will riot
    more wildly than Thracians; a friend is restored,
    a sweet time for me to go crazy.

2.8

If you had ever suffered just once,
Berine, for your perjured vows,
if your beauty had become spoiled by a single black
    tooth or fingernail,

I'd trust you. But every time you have warranted   5
your perjured head on vows, you glow more brightly,
lovelier than ever, and advertise
    a public problem for boys.

It helps you to play false your mother's
buried ashes, night's silent stars,   10
and the whole sky and the gods, exempt
    from icy death.

And Venus herself, I say, laughs at this, also
laugh the innocent nymphs and Cupid uncivilized
who is always sharpening burning arrows   15
    on a bloodied whetstone.

A whole crop of boys is growing up for you,
a new gang of slaves is maturing, but the former ones
do not leave the home of their immoral mistress,
    despite frequent threats.   20

Mothers fear you for their young bullocks,
and stingy old men, and worried brides, recent
virgins, suspect that your aura will whisk
    away their husbands.

2.9

Not forever do showers cloud the soggy
fields or storms harass
    and chop the Caspian Sea
      or on the frontiers of Armenia,

Friend Valgius, the ice stands fixed   5
every month, or Mount Garganus'
    oak groves strain from blue northers
      and ash trees stand stripped of leaves:

You forever persist in mournful melodies
on the loss of Mystes, nor desist   10
    your love songs from Morning to Evening
      Star in flight from the racing run.

Not even old Nestor, who survived three generations,
wept for his dear Antilochus
    all his life, nor did the Trojan parents   15
      and sisters for young Troilus

Cry forever. Stop these
effeminate elegies; but rather let us manfully
    sing the new trophies of Augustus
      Caesar, ice-hard Mt. Nyphates,   20

The Euphrates, a river added to the list of conquered
peoples, swirling with smaller eddies,
    and the Geloni restricted to riding
      within prescribed plains.

2.10

Better live, Licinius,° not always
pressing upon the deep, and not, when cautious
fear of storms makes you shiver, hugging too close
    to the dangerous coast.

A man who values golden moderation   5
avoids in safety the filth of the slum
and prudently stays clear of a palace
    others would envy.

The giant pine is more often shaken by the wind
and the loftiest towers collapse   10
with a heavier fall and bolts of lightning strike
    the tops of mountains.

Hopeful in bad, fearful in good times,
he has readied his heart for the turn
of events: Jupiter brings back foul   15
    winters; he also

Takes them away. If things are bad now, not always
will they so be; sometimes Apollo
awakes the silent muse with his lyre; not always does
    he flex the bow.   20

In difficult straits show spirit
and bravery; but also be wise
to tack sails swelling in a wind
    not too favorable.

2.13

On a black day he planted you,
whoever he was, and with sacrilegious hand
    nurtured you as a tree to destroy
        descendants and to disgrace the village;

I would think him a man who would break   5
his own father's neck and at night splatter
    the hearth of a home with the blood
        of a guest; he dealt in Medean

2.10.1: If this Licinius is Licinius Murena, the brother-in-law of Maecenas, then
    ironically, he failed to heed Horace's call for moderation and his warning
    about the disadvantages of position and power. In 23 or 22 he was accused
    of conspiracy against Augustus.

Poisons and every conceivable kind
of wrong, who staked you out on my farm,
    you sadistic stump, to fall on the head
        of your undeserving owner.

                                                  10

What to avoid, hour by hour, no one is ever
cautious enough; the Punic sailor utterly
    quakes at the Bosporus, but has
        no fear of blind fate elsewhere;

                                                  15

The soldier is petrified of Parthian tactics°
of shoot and run, the Parthian fears Italy's
    chains and rugged strength; but unforeseen the power
        of death has swept and will sweep over peoples.   20

How close I came to seeing the realm
of dark Proserpina, the judge Aeacus,
    the abodes set apart for the devout,
        Sappho lamenting on Aeolian

                                                25

Lyre about the girls among her folk,
and you, Alcaeus, resounding golden in stronger strain
    the arduous life at sea, the bitter
        ills of exile, the hard times of war.

                                              30

The shades marvel at each singing poems
worthy of sacred silence; but it's the battles
    and tyrants ousted that the horde, crowded
        together shoulder-tight, drinks in more.

Is it a wonder when those songs enchant
the hundred-headed beast° until its black
    ears droop, and lull the snakes to rest
        from writhing in the hair of the Furies?

                                              35

Even Prometheus and Pelops' parent°
find delusive respite from the torment in sweet sound,
    and Orion does not bother to track
        lions nor cautious lynxes.

                                              40

2.13.17: "Parthian tactics" refers to a maneuver of Parthian mounted archers
    who rode close up to an enemy's infantry, wheeled, and discharged their
    arrows in apparent flight.
2.13.34: Cerberus, the watch dog of hell, is intended.
2.13.37: Pelops' parent is Tantalus who cut up and served his son to the gods.

2.14

How they speed, Postumus, Postumus,
how the years slip by; and piety
    will not delay wrinkles and the threat
        of age and death, ever unbeaten,

No, my friend, even if day after day   5
you tried with three hundred bulls to please
    Pluto, the unweeping, who jails
        the three-bodied Geryon and Tityus on the murky

Stream whose ferry is a must for all
who feed on the bounty of the earth,   10
    whether we be kings
        or dirt-poor farmers.

In vain we escape bloody Mars,
the smashing waves of the raucous Adriatic,
    in vain we quiver at the autumnal   15
        sirocco so harmful to our bodies.

We must confront the slow winding stream
of dark Cocytus, and the infamous tribe
    of Danaus, and Sisyphus, son of Aeolus,
        condemned to long labor;   20

We must leave behind earth and home and dear
wife, and all those trees you now tend,
    not any, except the hated cypress,
        will follow you, their short-term master.

An heir, more deserving, will guzzle the Caecuban   25
you stored away with a hundred keys, and he will soak
    the floor with a superb varietal finer than
        the wines served at the festival banquets of priests.

2.16

For peace of mind he asks the gods, when caught unexpectedly°
on the open Aegean after a dark storm-cloud has
buried the moon and the stars cease shining
    sure for sailors;

For peace prays Thrace raging in war;   5
for peace the Medes distinguished by their quiver.

2.16.1: Pompeius Grosphus owned farms in Sicily. See *Epistles* 1.12.

It is not to be bought, Grosphus, by jewels, purple
   raiments, or by gold.

No, it is not royal treasuries nor the bodyguard
of a consul that shoves aside the mental turbulence and the pitiful   10
mob of worries that flit around
   paneled ceilings.

He lives well with a little whose ancestral
salt shaker gleams on his frugal table
and whose soft sleeps neither fear nor filthy   15
   greed steals.

Why in our brief lives do we strive so valiantly
for so much? Why do we opt for other lands boiling
under a different sun? What exile from his fatherland also
   has escaped himself ?   20

That disease, Worry, boards even bronze-prowed
ships and overtakes squadrons of horsemen
swifter than deer and swifter than the east wind that
   drives the rain clouds.

May the mind be tranquil in the present and despise   25
any concern for what is beyond, and with a resigned smile
temper bitterness. Nothing in every respect is
   pure happiness.

Sudden death robbed us of glorious Achilles,
protracted old age reduced Tithonus,   30
and to me perhaps this hour will extend what
   it denies to you.

Around you a hundred herds of Sicilian cows
low; for you your mare trained for the chariot race
lifts a whinny; wools twice dipped   35
   in African purple dye

Clothe you: to me Fate that doesn't cheat
has given a few acres of land, disdain
for the spiteful crowd, and the slender spirit
   of Greek poetry.   40

2.17

Why do you keep killing me with your complaints?
Neither I nor the gods will it that before me
   you pass away, Maecenas, my great
     honor and the pillar of my estate.

Ah, if an untimely power snatches you, a part   5
of my very soul, why would the rest of me linger on,
    less dear to myself and, if I survive you,
      a whole man? No, that day will bring

Doom for us both. I have not uttered
a false oath: we will go, yes, we will go,   10
    whenever you will lead the way, as comrades
      ready to seize upon that final journey together.

Neither the breath of the fiery chimaera
nor Gyges, the hundred-handed, should he rise again,
    will ever tear me away from you: such is the decree   15
      of mighty Justice and the Fates.

Whether Libra or dread Scorpio, the more
potent sign of my natal hour, looks upon me
    or Capricorn, that tyrant over
      the Western sea,   20

In an incredible agreement our stars°
both conspire. The protecting power of Jove
    gleaming bright against evil Saturn
      has rescued you and stalled fate's

Swift wings, on that day when the public in throngs   25
three times in joyful applause rattled the theater.
    But, a tree trunk falling upon my brain would have
      done away with me, had not Faunus

Deflected the blow with his right hand, the protector
of Mercury's poets.° Remember to offer   30
    victims in sacrifice and a votive shrine:
      I'll sacrifice a humble lamb.

2.18

No ivory nor gold
    ceiling glistens in my home,
nor marble beams from Hymettos°
    press on columns quarried in far-off

2.17.21-25: Maecenas was deeply interested in astrology.
2.17.30: Mercury invented the lyre and Horace frequently refers to Mercury as
    his special patron. Cf. *Odes* 1.10, 2.7.13-14, and 3.11.
2.18.3: a mountain overlooking Athens, famed for its marble and honey. See
    Vergil, *Georgics* 4.177.

Africa; nor am I a surprised heir who has   5
    usurped a palace of Attalus,
and no well-bred ladies in retinue
    trail purple Laconian gowns for me.

Instead, loyalty and a kind vein
    of talent are mine, and, though poor, the rich   10
seek me out: for nothing beyond these
    I importune the gods, and from a friend in power

I exact no greater rewards,
    happy enough with my one and only Sabine farm.
Day thrusts upon day and new   15
    moons hasten on to die:

You contract for marble slabs
    even at the brink of death, and unmindful of
the tomb you build mansions, and push
    to extend the shore   20

Into the sea roaring at Baiae,
    the mainland confining your wealth;
then the marker of the neighbor's boundaries
    and your acres you root up; in greed

For more you jump claims   25
    of your tenants. They are driven off,
carrying in their bosoms their household gods
    and scrawny children, both wife and husband.

Yet no hall more surely
    waits the wealthy master   30
than the destined bounds
    of greedy Orcus. Why strain for more? Impartial earth

Is open to the poor
    and to kings' sons, and the henchman of Death
cannot be bribed by gold to ferry back   35
    clever Prometheus. He corrals arrogant

Tantalus and Tantalus'
    race; he listens, to relieve
the poor man whose tasks are done
    whether he is called or not.   40

2.19

Bacchus on distant rocky haunts, teaching
his songs I saw (believe it, you who are to come),
    and the nymphs, his students, and satyrs
      with goat-feet and pointed ears.

Euhoe! With fear still fresh my mind trembles in awe,   5
as my breast possessed of Bacchus madly
    rejoices; Euhoe! Spare me, Liber,
      spare me, O tearful god of the powerful thyrsus.

It is ordained for me to sing of the tireless
Bacchants, the spring of wine, and streams   10
    rich in milk, and to echo in song honey
      exuding from hollow tree trunks.

It is ordained too for me to sing of the crown of your bride
blessed to be honored among the stars, and Pentheus' palace
    that collapsed into smithereens,   15
      and the ruin of Thracian Lycourgus.

You deflect rivers, you sway the savage sea,
you, flushed with wine, on distant ridges,
    in a harmless knot of serpents
      bind the locks of Thracian women.   20

You, when the impious gang of giants
scaled the heights to your father's realms,
    hurled back Rhoetus with the assumed talons
      and terrible maw of a lion,

Although you were claimed to be better fit for dances,   25
jests, and sport, and labeled unfit
    for battle; yet you were in the thick
      of war as well as of peace.

Cerberus did you no harm when he saw you°
graced with a golden horn; gently brushing   30
    his wagging tail upon you, as you were departing, he licked
      your feet and legs with his triple tongue.

2.19.29-32: an allusion to Bacchus' descent to the underworld to retrieve his
    mortal mother Semele.

3.1°

I hate the profane crowd and keep them out.
Silence, tongues! I am a priest of the Muses
    and I sing poems never heard before
        for virgins and boys.

The power of terrifying kings lies over the herds,   5
over kings is the power of Jove,
    famous for his triumph over Giants,
        shaking all things by the raising of his eyebrow.

This is so: one man sets in furrows vineyards larger
than another's; one of more birth comes down   10
    to the Field of Mars,° a candidate,
        another contests with better character

And reputation, yet a third has a bigger
mob of supporters; Necessity's impartial law
    casts the lots of the exalted and the lowest,   15
        the urn holds a lot and tosses every name.

The man above whose evil neck a drawn
sword hangs,° for him Sicilian banquets
    do not impart their delicious flavor,
        and the singing of birds and the music of a lyre   20

Will not bring back his sleep; gentle sleep does not
despise the humble homes of rustics,
    the shady river banks ,
        nor Tempe fanned by a balmy breeze.

The man who longs for just enough neither   25
the turbulent ocean disturbs,
    nor the savage attack of bad weather when Arcturus
        is setting or when Haedus is rising,

Nor the hail lashing his vineyard,
nor the cheating farm land, when his orchard blames   30
    first the rains, then the stars that roast
        his fields, then the brutish winters.

3.1: poems 3.1-6 are called the Roman Odes because the series deals with political and social subjects.

3.1.11: elections, highly contested in Republican Rome, were held in the Campus Martius (the Field of Mars).

3.1.17-18: a reference to the Sword of Damocles.

The fish feel the water constrict from the piling
of stone laid in the deep; here the contractor
   and his crew pile rubble,   35
     as does the owner who despises

The land. But Anxiety and Threats climb
to the very same spot as the master, and
   black Worry does not yield from the bronze prowed
     trireme, and sits behind her rider.   40

If neither Phrygian marble, nor the use
of purples more lustrous than a star
   soothes the troubled man, nor Falernian
     wine nor nard from Persia,

Why would I erect a lofty hall   45
with columns others would envy and in the latest
   style? Why should I trade my Sabine valley
     for the more crushing burden of wealth?

3.2

Let him learn to suffer narrow poverty
gladly, a young recruit strengthened by hard military
   training, and be a horseman feared for his spear
     who will harass wild Parthians;

Let him spend his life under the sky in dangerous   5
operations. Spying him from the enemy walls,
   may the wife of a tyrant at war
     and the grown-up virgin

Sigh: "Oh, may the royal bridegroom, green
in warfare, not provoke by touch   10
   the fierce lion whose searing thirst for blood
     drives through the center of slaughter."

Sweet and proper it is to die for one's country:
death pursues the runaway;
   it spares not the hamstrings   15
     and the spineless back of a dovish youth.

Manly courage knows no dirty defeat,°
but shines, keeps its honor untarnished;
   and it does not assume or resign the axes of power
     at the whim of a shifting public.   20

3.2.17: "defeat" refers to electoral defeat as well as to military setback.

Manly courage that opens up heaven to those who do not
deserve to die attempts a march denied to others,
    and spurns on speedy wings
        the common crowd and muddy earth.

There is guaranteed payment for silence that   25
shows faith; I will forbid him who broadcasts
    the secret rites of Ceres to remain
        beneath the same ceiling, or with me

To cast off in a risky boat. The God of Day,°
slighted, has often included the innocent   30
    among the sinful; although on halting foot, seldom
        has Punishment abandoned the sinner in the lead.

3.4

Descend from the sky, queen Calliope; come, sing
to the flute a long song,
    or with clear voice, if you choose,
        or to the strings of Phoebus' lyre.

Do you hear her? Or does a seductive madness   5
sport with me? I seem to hear her and to be wandering
    through sacred groves where
        pleasant waters and breezes flow.

Once, when I was a boy, on Mount Vultur in Apulia,
I wandered out beyond the limits set by Pullia,   10
    my nurse, and exhausted from play and sleepy,
        storied doves wove for me a cover

Of fresh leaves, a wonder to all who
live in the nest of lofty Acherontia,°
    in the glens of Bantia, and   15
        in the fat field of lowly Forentum;

So I slept, my body safe from the deadly
vipers and bears; I was blanketed
    in sacred laurel and a heap of myrtle,
        a child alive by the favor of the gods.   20

3.2.29: the God of Day is Jupiter (Diespiter).
3.4.14-16: Acherontia, Bantia, and Forentum are towns in Apulia near Venusia,
    birthplace of Horace.

Yours, O muses, I am yours, as I climb steep
Sabine hills, or I find the chill of Praeneste
    pleasant, or the slope of Tibur, or
        the clear air of Baiae.

As a devotee of your springs and choral dances,   25
neither the rank-breaking rout at Philippi,
    nor that cursed tree, nor the wave from Sicily
        at Cape Palinurus° snuffed me out.

If you be with me, gladly I'll
dare to sail the raging Bosphorus   30
    and to travel the scorching sands
        of the Syrian shore line,

I'll visit the British, savage to strangers,
and the Spaniard who enjoys mare's blood;
    I'll see the quivered horsemen and   35
        streams of Scythia untouched.

Lofty Caesar, after he has stationed in towns
the legionaires worn out from campaigning,
    longing to bring an end to his labors,
        him you refresh in your Pierian grotto;   40

You give gentle counsel, gracious ones,
and are happy in the giving. We know how
    Jove smashed with his descending thunderbolt
        the impious Titans and their monstrous mob;

He controls the motionless earth, tempers the windy   45
sea, cities, and the kingdom of mourning;
    he alone rules in just power both the gods
        and the throngs of mortals.

That gang of youths, their arms bristling, reveling
in their strength, thrust mighty terror   50
    on Jove, as also the brothers who strained°
        to pile Mount Pelion upon shadowy Olympus.

But what could Typhoeus, or valiant Mimas,
or Porphyrion of menacing stature,

3.4.28: Cape Palinurus, the promontory in Lucania, received its name from
    Aeneas' helmsman, Palinurus, who was killed on shore there.
3.4.51-6: refers to the Aloidae and lists giants who assaulted Olympus.

or Rhoteus, or Enceladus who dared   55
    to root up trees and hurl them,

Avail by their assualt upon the clanging
shield of Athena? Here stood Vulcan,
    eager; here was Juno the wife; here stood he
        who will never remove the bow from his shoulders,   60

Who washes his unbound hair in Castalia's
pure spring, who rules Lycian groves
    and his native woods,
        god of Delos and Patara, Apollo.

Power without good judgment collapses of its own weight: 65
power under control the gods themselves enhance;
    but they despise power that promotes
        wholeheartedly every kind of evil.

As witness of my opinions there is Gyges of a hundred
hands, Orion, the notorious assailant   70
    of pure Diana, who was felled
        by her virgin arrow.

Heaped on her own monsters, Mother Earth laments
and mourns her offspring hurled by the thunderbolt
    to dim Orcus; not yet has the quick flame   75
        eaten through Aetna piled on above her,

And the vulture, designated to guard his lust,
has not abandoned the liver of incontinent Tityos;
    and three hundred chains yet restrain
        the love-possessed Pirithous.   80

3.5

Thunder from heaven has confirmed our belief
that Jove is supreme: in our presence Augustus
    will be held divine after the Britons
        and the threatening Parthians are added to our empire.

Did Crassus' soldier in disgrace assume a life   5
as husband to a barbarian wife and grow old—
    perverting the Senate and our ethos—
        bearing arms for alien-in-laws,

And under an Eastern king Marsian and Apulian
blot out the memory of sacred shields,° of name, and   10
   of the toga, of eternal Vesta, while
      Jove and the city of Rome stood safe?

Farsighted Regulus protected against this,
refusing disgraceful terms of peace,
   a precedent that would spread   15
      ruin in the years to come,

Unless young men taken captive perished
unpitied: "Our banners fixed on Punic
   shrines and weapons stripped without bloodshed
      from soldiers I myself," he said,   20

"Have seen; I have witnessed the arms of citizens
twisted behind their free backs,
   and gates unbolted and fields
      once ravaged by our forces being worked again.

The soldier ransomed by gold, naturally,   25
will return the more eager for battle; to dishonor
   you add damage: wool dyed in purple
      does not recover the colors it lost,

Nor does true manly courage, when once it disappears,
care to be restored to weaklings;   30
   when the doe, disentangled from close-meshed nets,
      puts up a fight, he will be brave

Who trusted himself to treacherous enemies,
and he will trample Carthaginians in another war
   who stood still when he felt the thongs binding   35
      back his arms, and who feared death.

Ignorant of the source of his life's meaning,
he has confounded peace with war: O the shame!
   O mighty Carthage exalted higher
      by the disgraceful decline of Italy!"   40

They say that from the kiss of his virtuous wife
and from his children, as if he were disenfranchised,
   he withdrew and sternly set
      his manly gaze upon the ground,

3.5.10-12: Numa Pompilius set up twelve shields in the *regia* after a sacred shield
from heaven, sent by Mars, fell in that spot. The building was protected by
the Salii, leaping priests of Mars.

Until he strengthened the resolve of the shaky senators   45
with advice no advocate ever gave before,
    and through lamenting friends he
        hurried out, a glorious exile.

Yet he knew what the foreign torturer
was preparing for him; still he pushed   50
    aside relatives blocking his way,
        and the mass of people trying to delay his return,

As if he were leaving his clients' tedious business affairs
after a lengthy lawsuit settled,
    making for the southern lands   55
        or Tarentum, Spartan territory.

3.6

Although you are guiltless, you will keep paying for your parents'
    sins,
Roman, until you repair the temples,
    the deteriorating shrines of the gods, and
        their images befouled by black smoke.

When you conduct yourself as inferior to the gods, you   5
have power; to them ascribe the origin, the end;
    the gods neglected have brought
        many ills to grieving Italy.

Twice now the Parthian Monaeses and Pacorus' army
have crushed our ill-omened offensives,   10
    and with a grin fastened
        trophies to their cheap necklaces.

The city, gripped by civil riots,
the Dacian and Egyptian almost wiped out,
    the one superior in hurtling arrows,   15
        the other feared for her fleet.

The times, breeder of vice, have polluted first the brides,
then the children and the home;
    from this source springs a flood of slaughter
        upon fatherland and people.   20

The blossoming virgin happily learns
Ionic dances and even now practices
    her skills, and is obsessed down to her
        dainty toenail with thoughts of illicit loves.

Soon she even seeks out younger lovers   25
at the wine parties of her husband, and isn't choosy
    to whom she hastily bestows her forbidden
        fruits when the lights are out;

Summoned, her husband present and an accomplice
of it, she responds whether a traveling salesman beckons   30
    or the captain of a Spanish galleon,
        a wealthy trader in debaucheries.

Not from parents like these was born the young generation
that stained the sea with Carthaginian blood
    and felled Pyrrhus, huge Antiochus,   35
        and dreadful Hannibal,

But manly were the descendants of farm-bred
soldiers, taught to break clods
    with Sabine hoes and at the orders
        of a strict mother to chop up and bring   40

In logs, as the sun shifted the shadows
of the hills and relieved the weary oxen
    of their yokes, bringing a period of welcomed
        rest in his departing chariot.

What hasn't the ravaging day impaired?   45
Our parents' age, worse than their ancestors', has
    brought forth us, who are even more sinful, who soon
        will breed descendants yet more degenerate.

3.9

"As long as I was dear to you
    and there was no other, sweeter boy putting
his arms around your beautiful neck,
    I flourished, richer than the king of Persia."

"As long as you burned for no one else   5
    and Lydia didn't rank behind Chloe,
I, Lydia, my name renowned,
    flourished, more famous than Ilia of Rome."

"Now Chloe from Thrace rules me,
    who is skilled in sweet songs and knows the lyre;   10
for her I would not fear to die,
    if the Fates spare my soul and allow her to live."

"Calais, son of Oryntus from Thurii,°
  scorches me with mutual flame;
for him I would gladly die twice,   15
  if the Fates spare my boy and allow him to live."

"What if the old-time feeling returns
  and drives back under a yoke of bronze those now
broken up, if blond Chloe is jilted,
  and the door for cast-off Lydia swings open?"   20

"Though he be lovelier than a star
  and you are lighter than cork and angrier
than the raging Adriatic,
  with you I'd love to live, with you I'd gladly die."

3.10

Even if you drank from the distant Don, Lyce,
and were the bride of a savage, still you
would weep for me stretched out before your doors,
  exposed to your native northers.

Do you hear the creaking of the door, the windy groan   5
of the trees planted in the beautiful courtyard, and how
Jupiter with his divine power shining clear
  ices the fallen snow?

Surrender your pride unpleasing to Venus,
lest the rope spin back on the turning wheel;   10
An Etruscan father did not beget you to be
  a Penelope, cold to suitors.

Though neither presents nor prayers
nor the violet pale on the faces of lovers
nor your husband's spoiled pangs for a whore from Thessaly   15
  sway you, spare those who

Beseech you, you, no softer than rigid oak,
and no gentler at heart than African adders:
not forever will this body endure
  doorstep, sky, and rain.   20

3.9.13: in the "war of names" Lydia clearly trumps the male speaker, providing
  evocative details: in myth Calais and Oryntus are Argonauts, and Thurii is the
  renamed city of Sybaris in southern Italy, famous for its luxurious lifestyle.

3.11

Mercury—for you were the master who taught
Amphion to move stones by singing—
and you, too, tortoise shell, cleverly trained to echo
    on seven strings,

Once lacking both voice and grace, but now   5
a pleasing friend to rich men's tables and to temples,
play some tunes that Lyde will turn
    her stubborn ears to;

For like a three-year-old filly on wide meadows
she frolics about, afraid to be touched,   10
unbroken for marriage, and still unripe
    for the bawdy husband.

You have the power to induce tigers and trees
to follow you, to halt rushing streams;
the monstrous guardian of Hell's hall has   15
    yielded to your charm,

Cerberus, whose deathly head a hundred
serpents fortify and from whose
three maws foul breath and
    poisonous spittle spew.   20

Even a forced smile on Ixion's and Tityos'
face appeared; for a short time the urn
stood dry, as you soothed in delightful song
    the daughters of Danaus.

May Lyde heed the crime and punishment in myth   25
of the virgins, the jar ever empty
of water that runs out through the base,
    and the deferred fate

That awaits guilty criminals in Orcus' realm:
Evil—what greater offense could there be?—   30
evil, they dared to kill their husbands
    with hard steel.

Only one out of so many was worthy of her°
marriage torch, a glorious deceiver against
that perjurer, her father, and a virgin   35
    honored in every age.

3.11.33: the one Danaid who disobeyed her father commonly has the name
   Hypermnestra.

"Arise," she said to her young husband,
"Get up, or a long sleep from those you
least suspect will come; frustrate my father
    and sinful sisters,   40

Who like lionesses that have seized calves
rip them apart, ah, one by one; I am gentler
than they; I will not slash you nor keep you
    bolted inside.

Let my father burden me with cruel chains,   45
because I had pity and spared a wretched man,
or let him send me on ships to remote lands
    of Africa in exile.

Go where your feet and the breezes carry you,
while the night and Venus are in favor, go under   50
propitious signs and to our memory on my tomb
    carve an elegy."

3.13°

O Bandusia, fountain more lustrous than glass,
worthy of sweet wine and flowers too,
    tomorrow a kid will be your honored victim,
        its first horns swelling his forehead

Portending a life of lust and battles—   5P
but in vain—for this kid, the offspring
    of a frolicking flock, will dye your icy waters
        red with his blood.

The fierce hour of the blazing Dog Star
cannot touch you; you provide a loving chill   10
    to bulls wearied with plowing
        and to the roaming flock.

You too will become one of the famous springs,
when I celebrate in song the live oak that
    juts above your pocked rocks where cascade   15
        your prattling waters.

3.13.1: this famous hymn celebrating the *Fontinalia* immortalizes the spring.

3.21

Born in the same year as myself when Manlius was consul,°
whether you promise complaints or jokes
    or brawling or maddened loves
        or, holy jar, easy sleep,

Whatever the purpose, the Massic wine was chosen   5
for your keeping, worthy of being served on a proper day,
    so come down, as Corvinus° orders
        mellower wines to be brought to him.

He, although he soaks himself in Socratic
dialogues, will not be boorish and snub you.   10
    They tell the story that even old Cato's virtuous manhood
        often glowed hot with wine.

You apply gentle torment to a mind most often
dull; you unlock the concerns
    and inner schemes of philosophers   15
        by the power of jesting Bacchus;

You restore hope to minds that are troubled
and bring power and strength to the poor man
    who with you behind him trembles not at the enraged
        crowns of kings or at the soldiers' weapons.   20

Bacchus, and Venus, if she will happily join us,
and the Graces slow to dissolve their bond,
    and the lamps with live flame will prolong you
        until Phoebus' return routs the stars.

3.24

Wealthier than the unrifled
    resources of Arabia and the riches of India,
you can shovel your rubble on all the shoreline
    and into the sea that is shared by all,

But if dire Necessity   5
    hammers her steel nails in your highest
rooftops, you will be unable to free
    your mind from fear, or your head from death's noose.

3.21.1: an allusion to the year 65 during the consulship of Lucius Manlius
    Torquatus.
3.21.7: Corvinus is Messalla; see Glossary under MESSALLA.

The Scythians of the plains whose carts
   carry, as is their custom, their vagabond homes   10
live a better life, as do the regimented Getae
   whose acres, never divided, produce

Communal fruits and grain.
   There custom is: no more than a year at farming,
and a successor relieves the man who has   15
   finished his work, on the same basis.

There the woman does not harm but protects
   stepchildren who have lost their mother,
and no wife rules her husband with her dowry
   or surrenders to a slick adulterer;   20

Her large dowry is the virtue of her parents
   and chastity that respects another's husband,
firm in its vow, and the thought that
   it is wrong to sin, with death its price.

O whoever desires to stop   25
   unholy killings and civil madness
and looks to have inscribed on statues
   "Father of Cities,"° should have the guts

To bridle untamed license,
   a shining glory to posterity, for—oh how sinful—   30
we hate sound morals, but in envy
   seek them out when they are stolen from our eyes.

What use is gloomy complaining,
   if wrong is not pruned by punishment?
What good are laws empty of morals,   35
   if no place on earth,

Neither that part pent in by the blazing
   heat, nor the expanse flanking the Arctic
where snows that freeze the soil,
   keeps off the trader? And if clever sailors   40

Overcome the roughest oceans, and if poverty,
   that great disgrace, commands us to do
or suffer anything,
   and forsakes the way of lofty virtue?

3.24.28: "Father of Cities" refers to Augustus who was already "Father of the
   Country," and who was to assume the title of "Father of Cities" in 2.

Let us bring to the Capitol,   45
    to the cheers and applause of a favoring crowd,
or let us toss into the nearest sea
    the jewels, gems, and good-for-nothing gold,

The cause of our greatest evil,
    if we truly are sorry for our sins.   50
The seeds of depraved greed
    must be rooted up and our too delicate

Character must be molded
    by tougher standards. The freeborn boy knows
not how to ride a horse bareback,   55
    he is afraid of hunting, but is more skilled in games,

If you approve the Greek hoop,
    or prefer dice, forbidden by laws;
in the meantime his father perjures his oaths
    and defrauds his fellow investor and even his guests,   60

And he hurries to hoard money for an undeserving
    heir. His dishonest wealth, of course,
keeps increasing, yet there is always something
    lacking...enough.

3.26

I used to live fit for girls
and I fought wars with no little glory;
    now, my weapons and lyre, discharged from battle,
        this wall will keep in storage

Protecting the left side of "Venus   5
from the Sea:" here, right here, put
    the bright torches, and the levers and axes
        that threaten reluctant doors.

O goddess, who occupy rich Cyprus
and Memphis° that never experiences northern snow,   10
    O queen, with your whip lifted high
        give arrogant Chloe just one flick.

3.26.10: Aphrodite had a temple at Memphis south of the Nile Delta.

3.29

Descendant of Etruscan kings, for you,
Maecenas, a magnum of mellow wine, uncorked,
    rose blossoms, and ointment freshly
        pressed for your hair

Have long been waiting at my place; tear yourself away;   5
no more lingering; no more contemplating of moist Tibur,
    and Aefula's sloping fields,
        and the ridges of Telegonus, the parricide.°

Abandon disgusting materialism; leave
your massive edifice towering near the lofty clouds;   10
    cease to admire affluent Rome,
        her smoke, wealth, and noise.

Often change is welcomed by the rich, grateful
for simple suppers at the humble home of the poor
    lacking in tapestries and purple coverlets,   15
        meals that smooth out a forehead wrinkled with worry.

Now the shining constellation of Andromeda's father
discloses its hidden fire, now Procyon° rages
    and Leo's blazing star,
        as the sun brings back days of drought.   20

Now the weary shepherd with his languishing flock
seeks out shade and a stream and the thickets
    of shaggy Silvanus; now the silent
        river bank is bereft of random breezes.

You brood about what is the best policy for the state,   25
and you are nervous and fearful for the city,
    worried what the Seres are plotting, the Bactrians
        once ruled by Cyrus, and the rebellious Scythians along the Don.

God in his wisdom buries the outcome
of time to come in misty night;   30
    and he laughs if a mortal unduly trembles
        in fear. Remember to be calm

3.29.8: this line refers to Tusculum, a town south of Rome, purported to have
    been founded by Telegonus, the son of Ulysses and Circe. He unknowingly
    killed his father.
3.29.18: Procyon is the so-called lesser dog-star of the constellation of Canis
    Minor.

And to put in order what is at hand: everything else
is swept along like a river whose mid-bed
   peacefully glides down into the Etruscan°   35
      sea, now churns gouged stones,

Uprooted tree trunks, mixed together with
cattle and homes, and there is the accompanying roar
   of mountains and neighboring woods
      as the wild flood convulses   40

Quiet streams. He will pass his days happy
and a master of himself who can say
   day by day, "I have truly lived. Tomorrow let the father
      fill heaven's vault with dark clouds

Or clear sunlight; still he will not make   45
undone whatever is past
   nor reshape and render void
      what a single fleeting hour has brought."

Fortune, happy in her savage enterprises
and persistent in playing her haughty game,   50
   transforms shifting honors,
      kind now to me, now to someone else.

I praise her while she stays; if she shakes
her swift wings, I enter as debit what she has given
   and I wrap myself in my manhood and I   55
      court Poverty, honest but lacking a dowry.

It's not my thing, when from African storms
a ship's mast groans, to hasten to craven prayers
   and to bargain with vows
      that my merchandise from Cyprus and Tyre   60

Won't add to the rich cargo of the greedy sea.
Then, protected in my boat of two oars,
   safely through tempests on the Aegean, a breeze,
      Pollux, and his twin brother will escort me.

3.30

I have erected a memorial more lasting than bronze,
more lofty then the royal pile of the pyramids,
which no biting rain, no raging northern blast
can destroy, nor the innumerable file

3.29.35: alludes to the Tiber that flows into the Tyrrhenian (i.e. Etruscan) Sea.

of years, nor the flight of time.   5
I shall not wholly die; the greater part of me
will avoid the goddess of Death; I will grow on forever
renewed by the praise of posterity: as long as the high
priest and the silent virgin at his side ascend
the Capitoline,° I will be heralded where the wild Aufidus   10
thunders and where Daunus, scarce in water,
rules over rustic peoples, I, who rose from humble
roots, a powerful prince, the first to have spun
Aeolic song to Italian measures. Accept the proud
honor won by your merits and graciously crown   15
my hair, Melpomene, with Delphic laurel.

4.1

O Venus, do you provoke once more those wars
    long ago discontinued? Please, please spare me.
I am not what I once was when I was
    under the power of dear Cinara. Stop,

Savage mother of sweet Cupids,   5
    don't soften the hardened man of five decades
by your gentle orders; go where
    the flattering prayers of young men invite you.

More timely for you
    to travel by air on dark swans   10
to the home of Paulus Maximus,
    if you seek a suitable liver to roast.

For he is noble and handsome too,
    not reticent on behalf of his troubled clients,
a young man of a hundred talents   15
    who will carry far the banners of your service;

When, as potentate, he has mocked
    the gifts of a spendthrift rival,
beside the Alban lakes under a cedar-beamed roof
    he will erect your marble statue.   20

There you will breathe in abundant
    incense, and you will enjoy the music
of lyre and Cybele's flute,
    of woodwinds mingled with choir.

3.30.9-10: refer to a solemn procession led by the Pontifex Maximus (*high
    priest*) and Vestal Virgins to the temple of Jupiter Best and Greatest on the
    Capitoline.

There, twice every day, young boys   25
    and tender virgins will echo your divinity,
their feet chalked white beating the ground
    in the triple time of the Salii.

But for me—neither woman nor boy
    nor the hope that trusts a kindred spirit   30
pleases me now, nor wine bouts
    nor winding my temples with fresh flowers.

Yet, why, ah Ligurinus, why
    now and then trickles a tear down my checks?
Why does my tongue, so eloquent,   35
    fall in mid-words into unbecoming silence?

At night in my dreams I now
    catch and clutch you, now I follow
as you wing across the grass of the Field
    of Mars, across flowing streams, you, hard of heart.   40

4.2°

Whoever strives to emulate Pindar,
Iullus, soars on waxen wings fashioned
by the art of Daedalus and is sure to give his name
    to a glassy sea.

Like a river gushing down a mountain, which   5
rain storms have swollen above its natural banks,
so Pindar seethes and roars deep
    in his unrestrained rush.

Worthy of the laurel-crown of Apollo,
whether in bold dithyrambic metaphors   10
he sweeps along new-coined phrases surging in measures
    freed from rule,

Or sings of gods and kings, the offspring
of gods, who felled the centaurs in death
deserved, and who extinguished the fire   15
    of the frighful chimaera,

Or sings of those the palm of Elis°
brings home exalted to the sky, the boxer or horseman,

4.2.1: this poem is addressed to Iullus Antonius.
4.2.17-20: Elis is the area around Olympia, the site of the famous games.

and gives them an honor more revered
    than a hundred statues,   20

Or laments a young man snatched
from his weeping bride, and extols to the stars his strength,
his courage, and golden character, begrudging
    him to dark Orcus.

A strong breeze lifts aloft the Dircean swan of Thebes,   25
Antonius, as often as he aims his course high
among the tracts of clouds; but I in the manner and mode
    of the Matine bee

That toils hard to gather in the delicious thyme
all around the many groves and the banks   30
of moist Tibur, I, a humble talent, fashion
    my painstaking poems.

You, a poet of the grander genre, will sing
of Caesar, graced by the laurel wreath he earned
as he drags up the sacred slope in triumph   35
    the barbaric Sygambri;

Than he nothing greater or better upon the earth
the Fates and kind gods have given,
nor will they ever, even though the days of that pristine
    golden age should return.   40

You will sing of the joyful holidays and the public
games of the city celebrating the return of valiant
Augustus granted by our vows, and of the forum
    free of lawsuits.

Then, if my song be worth hearing,   45
my voice—its good part—will join in: "O beautiful
sun, O worthy of praise," I shall sing, happy
    in the homecoming of Caesar.

As you lead on, we shall sing more than once,
"Hail, god of Triumph," the entire state, "Hail, god of Triumph,"   50
and we will offer incense
    to the kind gods.

Ten bulls and as many cows will free
you of your vows; a tender calf weaned
from his mother, growing up on lush grass   55
    will fulfill mine,

His forehead resembling the crescent blaze
of a new moon that rises on the third night,
snow-white in marking,
    but elsewhere auburn.   60

4.3

Once, Melpomene, you have looked with peaceful eyes
    upon a man at his birth,
no hard labor at Isthmus°
    will make him a famous boxer, no valiant horse

Will bring him home a winner on his Achaean chariot,   5
    nor will a state of war
grace him with Apollo's leaves
    for crushing the arrogant threats of kings,

And parade him a general at the Capitol:
    but the waters that flow by fertile Tivoli   10
and the thick leafage of its groves
    will render him acclaimed for his Aeolian song.

The children of Rome, queen of cities,
    deem me worthy to be ranked
among the chorus of bards they admire,   15
    and now less often I am gnawed by envy's tooth.

O Pierian muse who modulate
    the sweet tones of the golden lyre,
O you who would give, if you pleased, the voice
    of swans even to dumb fish,   20

All this is your gift:
    that passersby point me out
as the maestro of the Roman lyre;
    my inspiration and my power to please, if please I do, are yours.

4.7

The snows have melted, now the grass returns to the fields
    and the leaves to the trees;
the earth undergoes her changes, and rivers are subsiding
    as they flow past their banks.

4.3.3: refers to the quadrennial games at the Isthmus of Greece and the epini-
cian odes of Pindar.

The sister Graces accompanied by the nymphs dare   5
    to lead the dances nude.
Hope not for immortal life, caution the year and the hour
    that rob us of the nourishing day.

Freezes melt from the western breezes, the summer tramples
    on spring, itself destined to perish as soon as   10
autumn bears its fruits and pours forth its harvests, and soon
    lifeless winter returns.

Yet swift are the changes of the moon recouping their losses in the
    sky.
    When we have descended
where pious Aeneas, rich Tullus, and Ancus Martius have gone,   15
    we are but dust and shadow.

Who knows if the gods above will add
    to today's sum tomorrow's time?
Everything you give now to your own dear soul will escape
    the greedy hands of an heir.   20

Once you have died and Minos has gaveled
    his solemn verdict upon you,
not your family, Torquatus, nor your eloquence, nor piety
    will restore you to life;

No, not even Diana can free from the dark recesses below   25
    her chaste Hippolytus,
nor does Theseus have the power to break the chains of Lethe from
    his dear Pirithous.

4.11

I have a magnum filled with Alban wine, a varietal
more than nine years old; in my garden,
Phyllis, there is parsley for weaving garlands,
    there is a wealth of ivy

For you to bind back your hair and shine;   5
the house gleams with silver, the altar wound
with sacred foliage yearns to be sprinkled with the blood
    of a sacrificial lamb;

The entire staff hurries about, here and there
scurry serving boys and girls,   10
flames dance and roll dirty
    smoke in swirls.

You should know to what festivities
you are invited: you must celebrate the Ides,
the day splitting April in half, the month   15
    of sea-born Venus,

A day rightly religious to me, almost
more sacred than my own birthday, because
my Maecenas with its dawning counts
    the flow of his years.   20

Telephus, the young man you are chasing (he's
above your station), a girl, rich and lascivious,
has claimed and keeps hobbled
    in unwelcomed fetters.

Charred Phaethon deters ambitious hopes   25
and winged Pegasus teaches a weighty lesson,
who threw off the burden of his earthly rider,
    Bellerophon:

Always pursue what becomes you, deem
it a sin to hope for more than is allowed, and   30
avoid the unequal love-match. Come now,
    last of my loves,

—For after this I shall grow hot for no other
woman—let me teach you to repeat my melodies
in your lovely voice: dark cares will become   35
    lightened by song.

4.13°

They heard my prayers, Lyce; the gods listened; the gods
heard, Lyce: you are becoming an old woman, and yet
    you yearn to look pretty,
        you keep fooling around, you drink beyond your limit,

And when you become tipsy, you arouse in quavering   5
song a reluctant Cupid; but he lies in wait
    for the beautiful cheeks of Chia in the prime
        of her youth who knows how to play the lyre.

4.13.1: one should compare 1.25 and 3.10 for the motif of the aging courtesan.

For he flies in disdain past the withered
oak trees and leaves you behind because your teeth,   10
   darkly stained, and wrinkles, and the snow
      upon your head disgrace you.

No Coan purple gowns now restore to you
nor costly jewels bring back your years that once
   and for all, stored in the archives,   15
      winged time has sealed shut.

Where has Venus fled? Ah, where have your looks gone? Where
your charming poise? What do you make of her, yes, her,
   the very one who used to breathe love,
      who once stole me away from myself,   20

Happy then, after the Cinara affair, admired for her
beautiful face and graceful skills? The Fates
   gave to Cinara brief years, but to Lyce
      they would reserve a longer time

Equal to the days of an old crow,   25
so the horny youngbloods could witness
   with roaring laughter
      a firebrand spent to ashes.

CARMEN SAECULARE
(CENTENNIAL HYMN)°

Phoebus, and Diana, powerful mistress of the woods,
bright jewel of the sky, O worshipped gods
to be honored forever, grant our prayer
   at this sacred time,

When the verses of the Sibyl have enjoined   5
chosen virgins and chaste boys
to chant a hymn to the gods who love
   our seven hills.

Nourishing Sun, you who in your gleaming chariot
usher in the day and then hide it, who are reborn   10
new and yet the same, may you see nothing greater
   than the city Rome.

1. In June of 17 Augustus commissioned Horace to compose this hymn as part
   of the celebration of the Centennial Games. This ode was sung by a chorus
   of boys and girls in the temple of Apollo.

Be gentle, Ilithyia, show your divine favor bringing on
childbirths at their proper time, protect our mothers,
approving the name Lucina   15
    or Genitalis.

Goddess, foster our young and make prosper
the laws of the fathers on weddings, the law°
on marriage destined to produce new children
    in abundance;   20

So may ten times eleven years, the fixed
cycle, bring back the singing and the games
attended by huge crowds on three clear days and
    three pleasant nights.

And you, Fates, who have chanted true prophecies,   25
may the metered march of history validate
what you have ordained, to those already fulfilled
    add happy destinies.

May the earth be bountiful in fruits and herd
and offer to Ceres a garland of wheat spikes;   30
may Jove's rains and breezes bring good health and nourish
    the newborn crops.

Put your weapon away, be gentle and peaceful,
hear the suppliant boys, Apollo;
Moon, crescent goddess and queen of stars,   35
    hear the girls.

If Rome is your doing and troops
from Troy once won the Tuscan shore, the remnant
survivors who were ordered to change household gods and city
    on an auspicious voyage,   40

For whom virtuous Aeneas, unharmed in the burning Troy,
a survivor of his fatherland, paved
a way to freedom, destined to give more
    than was left behind.

Gods, instill good morals upon the youth while teachable;   45
gods, grant peace to serene old age
and to the people of Romulus give prosperity, offspring,
    and every ornament.

18-19: refers to the Julian Laws of 18 to regulate marriage and the procreation
    of children. Cf. Propertius 2.7.

Whatever solemn entreaties he makes of you with the sacrifice of
   white bulls,
glorious descendant from the blood of Anchises and Venus,°   50
may he gain favorable response, victorious in war, yet forgiving
   of a defeated enemy.

Now the Mede fears our forces powerful
on land and sea and the Alban° axes of Rome,
now the Scythians and Indians, lately so proud,   55
   send for our answers.

Now Faith and Peace and Honor and pristine
Decency and neglected Manliness dare
to return, and blessed Prosperity appears
   with her horn full.   60

Phoebus, the mantic priest, graced with the shining bow,
and welcomed by the nine Muses,
who relieves by the power of his healing art the body's
   wearied frame,

Whenever he looks with favor on the altars of the Palatine,   65
the Roman state, and prosperous Latium,
he prolongs forever through future cycles
   ages even better;

And she who holds the Aventine and Nemi's Algidus,
Diana, guards the prayers of the priestly Fifteen°   70
Men and lends a kind ear
   to the children's prayers.

That Jove and all the gods hear this song
we carry home this sound and steadfast hope,
we, the chorus, trained to sing the praises   75
   of Phoebus and Diana.

49-50: refer to Augustus as a descendant of Iulus, grandson of Anchises, son of
   Aeneas, through the Julian clan.
54: the kings of Alba were descendants of Aeneas.
70: a Board of Fifteen priests were custodians of the Sibylline Books, a collection
   of prophecies from Etruscan times which were kept on the Palatine.

EPODES

The seventeen *Epodes* are written in iambic meter. They represent some of Horace's earliest poetic output. As he himself boasts, he introduced the iambic metrical form from Greek models, especially Archilochus, and included in several instances the sting of invective and abuse characteristic of the genre; but, as in the case of the *Satires*, the targets of his abuse are shadowy figures. Important in Horace's collection of *Epodes* is the introduction of political themes, an innovation that was to be developed more fully in the *Odes*.

2

He is happy who far from the business world,
    like the pristine race of mortals,
Cultivates his ancestral farmlands with his own bulls,
    freed from all interest owed;
He neither is aroused as a soldier by the sharp   5
    trumpet's blast nor shudders at the angry sea;
He avoids the forum too and the proud
    thresholds of VIPs.
So he either weds his tall poplars
    with the mature shoots of his vines,   10
Or in a secluded vale he looks out for
    the grazing herd of lowing cattle,
And lopping away useless limbs with his pruning hook
    he grafts on more fruitful ones,
Or in cleaned jars he stores pressed honey   15
    or shears the vulnerable sheep.
When in his fields Autumn lifts its head
    decked with ripening fruits,
How delighted he is to pluck the grafted pears
    and the purple cluster of grapes   20
As an offering to you, Priapus, and to you, father
    Silvanus, protector of boundary lines.
How delightful to recline sometimes beneath an old oak,
    sometimes on a matted turf of grass;
All the while waters cascade from high banks,   25
    birds trill in the woods,
And springs echo the splash of flowing water,
    an invitation to gentle slumber.
But when the wintertime of year and thunderous Jove
    produce the rain showers and snows,   30
Either with many dogs he drives from here and there
    fierce boars into waiting nets,
Or on a smooth pole he stretches a loose net,
    a snare for ever-nibbling thrushes,
Or he traps the trembling hare and the migrant crane   35

in his noose, pleasant prizes.
Who does not forget in such pursuits the sorrows
   and pangs that love produces?
But if a chaste wife would enjoy her role
   at home and tend to the sweet children,   40
And, like a Sabine woman or the sunburnt
   wife of an Apulian stalwart,
Would pile with seasoned logs the sacred hearth
   for the homecoming of her tired husband,
And, penning up the frisky flock in their sheepfolds made of
     wicker,   45
   would milk dry their swollen udders,
And, bringing out wines of this year's vintage
   still sweet in the demijohn, would prepare an uncatered meal,
No more would oysters from Lake Lucrino please me
   or a turbot or scarfish,   50
When winter, roaring over eastern tides,
   sweeps them to this our sea;
No African fowl, no Ionian pheasant
   would descend into my stomach,
A more savory feast than olives picked from the ripest   55
   branches in the orchard,
Or the sorrel plant that loves meadows
   and the healthful mallow good for a sick body,
Or a lamb sacrificed on the Festival of Boundaries,°
   or a kid rescued from a wolf.   60
At such a feast it is a joy to see the sheep
   hurrying home from pasture,
To see the bone-tired oxen drag along
   on weary neck the upturned plow,
And the homebred slaves that swarm a rich house   65
   in place around gleaming household gods.—
When Alfius, the usurer, had spoken this,
   always ever the future farmer,
He collected all his money on the Ides
   and set out to invest it on the Kalends.   70

12

What do you want, woman? Dark elephants are more your style.
   Why these gifts, these letters sent to me?
Me, no young hunk with a stuffed nose?
   Yet I have one sharp sense: I'm able to scent

2.59: on 23 February a yearly feast celebrated Terminus, the god of Boundaries.

The polyp or stinking goat bedding in hairy armpits   5
    more keenly than a hound where a sow hides.
What a sweat, what a rank smell engulfs her flabby limbs,°
    after the cock goes slack; she scurries
To ease her insatiable madness, her mascara
    runs, ruining her complexion chalked   10
With lotion à la crocodile turds,° and then
    at her climax she rips sheets and bedding—
Or she rips into me, disgusted, with such stinging jibes:
    "Not so limp with Inachia as with me;
Three times a night you power Inachia, but for me   15
    a soft one-timer. Damn that Lesbia!°
Who procured me a sluggard when I went looking for a bull,
    although Amyntas of Cos was right at hand;
The sinews of his invincible dick were firmer
    than a burgeoning tree deep-rooted in a hill.   20
These woolen fleeces hurriedly dyed purple again
    and again, for whom? For you, of course,
In case among your age-group there be no guest
    whose mistress would value him over you.
Oh, I am so unhappy: you avoid me as a quaking lamb   25
    wild wolves and as goats fear lions."

16

A second generation° now is being erased by civil wars,
    and Rome herself is crumbling from its own power,
Whom neither the neighboring Marsi had the power to destroy,
    nor an Etruscan force under threatening Porsena,
Nor the manliness of rival Capua, nor brutal Spartacus,   5
    nor the Allobrogian Gaul, untrustworthy in time of revolution;
Nor did barbaric Germany with her blue-eyed youth conquer her,
    nor Hannibal, hated by parents.
We, an impious generation of accursed blood, will destroy her,
    and once more wild beasts will occupy our soil.   10
Oh, the victorious barbarian will stand upon the ashes,
    and under resounding hoof the horseman will trample down the
        city;

12.11. Pliny, *Natural History* 28.108 attests to a fragrance from crocodile intestines
    that soothes and clears the complexion.
12.16: it is unlikely that the reference is to the Lesbia of Catullus' poems, but the
    reader would have had a difficult time not making the connection.
16.1: the first generation would be those Romans who fought in the civil war
    between Julius Caesar and Pompey; or, perhaps Horace is alluding to the
    period of Marius and Sulla.

In arrogance the conqueror will scatter (O horrendous sight!)
    the bones of Romulus now protected from winds and the sun's
    rays.
All of you perhaps, or the better part of you, seek a better course,   15
    to be free of evil distress.
Prefer no opinion over this: but just as the citizenry
    of Phocea swore an oath and fled into exile
From their fields and the hearths of their fatherland, and left
    their shrines to become the habitat of wild boars and predatory
    wolves,   20
Then go wherever your feet carry you or wherever across the seas
    the south or boisterous southwest wind will summon you.
Is this your decision? Or does someone have a better proposal?
    Why do we delay under favorable auspices to board a boat?
But let us take this oath: that, when rocks lifted from the bottom   25
    of the sea float, our return home not be forbidden;
That we not disdain to shift sail back toward home
    when the Po will wash the peaks of Mount Matinus,
Or when the lofty Apennine will jut out into the sea,
    when unnatural passion will couple monstrous beings in a new
    kind   30
Of lust, so that tigers will yearn to yield to deer,
    and a dove will mate with a hawk,
And trusting herds will not fear growling lions,
    and the goat, now sleek, will enjoy the salty sea.
Let us seal this with these curses and swear whatever else   35
    will cut off sweet return, yes, us, the entire citizen body, or at least
The part better than the untrainable herd, be off; may the weak
    and the hopeless lie upon their ill-fated beds.
But you who have manliness, remove this womanish grief,
    and speed off beyond the Tuscan shores.   40
Wide-spreading Ocean awaits us; let us seek the fields,
    the happy fields, and the rich islands of the blest,
Where every year the earth unplowed yields grain,
    and the vineyard unpruned blooms continuous,
And the branch of olive never fails to sprout,   45
    and the dark fig graces its native tree,
Honey flows from the hollow oak, from lofty mountains
    water lightly trickles on splashing foot.
There goats ungoaded come to their milk pails,
    and the flock willingly returns with udders swollen,   50
And at evening the bear does not growl as he circles the sheepfold,
    and earth does not puff up high with vipers,
Nor do diseases infect the flock, no sweltering rage
    from any star scorches the herd.

In our happiness we will be more astonished that the rainy   55
   Southeast wind does not wash away the topsoil with gully washers,
And fertile seeds are not burned up in dried clods,
   because the king of the gods on high moderates each season.
Not here did a ship driven by Argos' oars strive to come,
   not here a shameless Colchian set foot,   60
Not here Phoenician sailors swung their yards
   nor the toiling crew of Ulysses.
Jupiter marked out those shores for a devout people,
   ever since he debased the golden age with bronze;
First with bronze, after that with iron he hardened the ages, from
    which   65
   a happy escape is granted to the devout, as I am mantic poet.

EPISTLES

The two books of literary letters mark Horace's return to the conversational style
that characterized the hexameters of the *Satires*. The themes of these poems
center on moral and literary issues and reflect a person engaging himself in
philosophic meditation. Also in the *Epistles* Horace reveals his developing concern
and intense interest in his role and place in the literary tradition.

1.2

While you, Lollius Maximus, study rhetoric at Rome,°
At Praeneste I reread the composer of the "Trojan War."°
Yes, he states more clearly and better than the philosophers
   Chrysippus and Crantor
What is beautiful, what is base, what's useful, and what's useless.
If you've got nothing to do, listen to why I hold this considered
   opinion.   5
His story of Greece clashing with the barbarians
In a prolonged war and all because of Paris' love
Details the heated passions of stupid kings and their subjects.
Antenor votes to cut off the root cause of the war,
And Paris, what of him? He says that he cannot be forced   10
Into ruling in safety and living a happy life. Nestor bustles about to
   settle
The quarrel of Achilles, son of Peleus, and Agamemnon, son of
   Atreus:

---

1. 2.1: Lollius appears to have served in the campaign against the Cantabri of
northern Spain in 25-24 and to be preparing to enter public life. See *Epistles*
1.18.

1.2.2: the reference, of course, is to Homer, author of the *Iliad* and *Odyssey*.

Love scorches Achilles, and anger equally fires them both.
The Greeks pay the price for whatever insane folly the kings indulge
    in,
Treachery, fraud, crime, lust, and rage;   15
All these wrongs happen within and without the walls of Troy.
Yet what is the power of virtue and the potential of wisdom,
In Ulysses he has set an example useful for us.
He, the sacker of Troy, versatile and resourceful, beheld
The cities and mores of many men; far and wide over the sea   20
All the while he was contriving a return home for himself and his
    companions,
He endured many troubles, unsinkable in waves hostile to his aims.
About the song of the Sirens, the drinking goblets of Circe you know:
Had he guzzled a drink like some of his comrades, so stupid and
    eager,
He would have been enslaved by a whore; ugly and brutish   25
He would have passed his life like a dirty dog or hog wallowing in
    mud.
We are but a number, born to consume earth's fruits,
We are suitors of Penelope, good-for-nothings, Alcinous'
Young men over-busy in grooming their skin,
Who find it chic to sleep until noon   30
And to induce lazy sleep, lulled by the strum of a lyre.
Muggers get up at night to slit a throat:
Get up, get up, you! Save yourself;
Run while you're well; if you don't, soon enough you'll be sick and
    you'll have to.°
If you don't ask for a book and lamp before daybreak,   35
And don't rack your mind on studies and honorable pursuits,
You'll become an insomniac, tormented by envy and love. You are
    quick
To remove something hurting your eye, but delay
For a year taking care of any cancer of the mind.
Well begun, half done: courage! Dare to be a wise man.   40
Begin. Anyone who delays an hour of living right
Is a bumpkin waiting for a river to stop, while it
Keeps flowing, rolling, and gliding on forever.
Men pursue money, a well-dowered wife for bearing children,
And wild woods to be tamed by a plow.   45
But anyone who happens to have enough, should wish for no more.
No home, no estate, no heap of bronze and gold
Has ever relieved the fever from the owner's sick body,
Or the cares from his mind; he must be well,

1.2.34: the Romans thought that running prevented or relieved edema.

If he intends to enjoy his accumulated wealth.   50
Home and property please the man who covets and fears
As much as a man with sore eyes appreciates painting or as a man
     with gout warm
Bandages, or as one whose ears are plugged with gobs of dirt enjoys
     the music of lyres.
Anything you pour into a filthy pot gets soiled.
Spurn pleasures; pleasure is bought with pain and sorrow.   55
The greedy man is always in need: set a boundary to your desire.
The man envious of the fat possessions of another grows thin;
Tyrants of Sicily have never found a worse torment
Than envy. The man who can't control his rage
Will wish undone what his pain and mood convinced him to do,   60
When he is quick to seek violent vengeance filled with unsatisfied
     hatred.
Anger is brief madness: rule your passions; if uncontrolled,
They give the orders; rein them in, chain them up.
A groom guides and teaches the horse with a compliant neck
To go its way as the rider directs; a puppy hunting dog,   65
After it has barked at a stuffed deer in his yard,
Is ready for battle in the woods. Now drink in my words
In your youth and innocent heart, now offer yourself to your betters.
A new jar will retain for a long time the bouquet of the first liquid
Poured into it. If you linger or speed ahead of me, and if you think 70
I'm waiting around for a slow poke like you or running off to catch
     up, think again!

1.3

Julius Florus, in what far region of the world Tiberius Claudius,°
Augustus' stepson, is campaigning now, I'm anxious to know.
Do Thrace and the Hebrus ice-bound from the snow
Or does the strait in the Hellespont that runs between two
     neighboring lighthouses,°
Or do the fertile fields and hills of Asia delay you?   5
And I am curious too about what kind of work your battalion of
     scholars is up to.

1.3.1: in 20 Tiberius Claudius Nero, the son of Livia, Augustus' wife, was sent to
    Asia Minor to perform various diplomatic missions. On his staff was Julius
    Florus. Tiberius was later destined to be adopted by Augustus (4 CE) and
    then succeed him in 14 CE.
1.3.4: refers to the two tower-lights on opposite shores of the Hellespont made
    famous in the myth of Hero and Leander.

Which one of them is taking upon himself to write of the
    achievements of Augustus,
To flood the future with his glories in war and peace?
And what about Titius who is soon to be upon the lips of Rome?
He has fearlessly drunk from Pindar's spring,   10
Having the guts to reject in disdain common pools and public
    streams.
Is he well? Ever remember me? Is his muse favoring
His pursuit to fit Theban rhythms to the Latin lyre?
Or is he exhausting his rage and bluster on tragic art?   14
What is my Celsus doing? He was warned—and he should be told
    again and again—
To find his own material and to cease plagiarizing
Books which Apollo's libraries on the Palatine° hold.
So, if someday that flock of birds were to come flying back to claim
    recovery
Of their feathers, this little crow would raise a big laugh,   19
Stripped clean of his stolen colorful plumes. And what about you?
    You up to something?
What bed of thyme are you buzzing around? Your talent is not
    minute,
Uncultivated, ugly, and bristling with stubble.
You may sharpen your tongue for pleading court cases, prepare
    responses
To disputes of civil law, or compose a love poem;
Either way, you'll win first prize, crowned with victorious ivy.   25
But if you could remove the cold compresses of worry,
You would be on your way where heaven's wisdom leads you.
All of us, important or unimportant, should hurry on this task, this
    mission,
If we desire to live appreciated by our fatherland and ourselves.
You have to write back telling me if you are as concerned   30
For Munatius as he deserves, or the good will, so badly sutured,
Is beyond patching up and has split open again, or if
Your hot blood and inexperience in life torment you two
Wild, unbroken broncos. Wherever you are living,
Both of you, too excellent to break your bond of brotherhood ,   35
I'm fattening a heifer vowed for your return.

1.3.17: Two libraries, one for Greek, the other for Latin books, were part of the
    complex of the Temple of Apollo on the Palatine. Cf. Propertius 2.31.

1.5

If you can bring yourself to recline on old-fashioned couches,
Not mind eating plain vegetables on a cheap plate, be my guest,
Torquatus; I'll expect you today at my place at sunset.
You'll drink wine bottled in Taurus' second consulship° somewhere
Between marshy Minturnae and Petrinum near Sinuessa.°   5
If you've got something better, send it over, or else take what I order
    up.
The fireplace has been lit, and just for you the furniture is clean.
Drop trifling hopes, vying for wealth,
And Moschus' case:° tomorrow is a holiday (Caesar's birthday);
You're excused to sleep in; it's legal   10
To while away the summer's night in pleasant talk.
What's the point of my fortune, if I cannot spend it?
The man who is too stingy, saving for an heir, and is too austere
Sits next to a crazy man. I'm starting the drinking
And strewing flowers, and I'll put up with being called an idiot.   15
Wine drinking unseals much; it lays bare secrets;
It bids us to fulfill hopes, pushes a coward into battle,
Lifts burdens from worried minds, teaches new arts.
Who has not become eloquent from brimming goblets?
Who has not been set free from the cramp of poverty?   20
So, I take upon myself, able and willing, to provide the following:
No dirty couch spread, no soiled table napkin
To wrinkle your nostrils in disgust, no tankard and salad plate
That do not reflect in their shine the real you, no one to step outside
Betraying words entrusted to friends, and to have an equal   25
Meet and hobnob with an equal. I'll invite Butra
And Sulpicius, and Sabinus, that is if he doesn't have a prior
    engagement
And some pretty girl prevents him; there is room for a few "ghosts."°
But, mind you, party guests packed too tight reek like smelly goats.
Write back how many you want to bring; drop everything,   30
Slip out your back door, elude that client who lies in ambush in your
    atrium.

1.5.4: Titus Statilius Taurus was consul for the second time in 26.
1.5.5: these towns are on the Appian Way. See *Satires* 1.5.
1.5.9: Volcacius Moschus, a rhetorician from Pergamum, was condemned for
    poisoning, although he had been defended by Torquatus and C. Asinius
    Pollio.
1.5.28: "ghosts" or "shades" are the uninvited friends accompanying an invited
    guest.

1.6

Idolize nothing, Numicius; that is probably the one
And only thing that can make and keep you happy.
There are some who look upon this sun, the stars, the seasons
        revolving
In fixed courses: they taste not a drop of fear.°
What is your opinion of the gifts of the earth and sea enriching
        Arabs   5
And Indians far away, of the ephemeral applause
And offices that an admiring citizenry gives?
How do you view these things? How do you feel and express it?
Whoever fears their opposites, overvalues them as much
As the one who covets them; in either case their excitement is
        annoying,   10
Any unexpected appearance of fortune startles them both.
What does it matter whether anyone exults or aches, craves
Or quakes, if he stares blankly, numb in mind and body,
Whenever he sees something better or worse than he expected?
Let the wise man be labeled a madman, a just man unjust,   15
If he pursues virtue beyond what moderation demands.
Go now, admire your silver plate, antique marble, bronzes
And art-works; idolize Tyrian dyed gowns studded with jewels;
Be thrilled that a thousand eyes look upon you as you speak;
Keep busy; be off to the forum in the morning, don't come home until
        the evening
So that Mutus does not reap more grain from his dowered fields— 21
A disgrace, since his origins are from a lower class than yours—
And you end up admiring him rather than he you.
Time will bring to the light of day whatever lies beneath the earth,
And will bury and conceal things that glitter now. When you have
        become famous
And Agrippa's colonnade and the Appian Way have glimpsed your
        familiar form,
Still it remains for you to go down where Numa and Ancus went
        before.
If a severe disease attacks your side or kidneys,
Seek a remedy. You wish to live right—who doesn't?
If virtue alone can give you this, be bold, abandon your pursuit   30
Of pleasures now. If you consider virtue a mere word
And a sacred grove firewood, look out; someone else may be docking
        in ports

1.6.3-4: these lines most likely refer to those who follow the philosophic schools
    of Pythagoras and Epicurus.

Ahead of you, and you'll be losing your business from Cibyra and
    Bithynia.
Round off your sum, a thousand talents, and another thousand, and
    to that
Add a third thousand, and a fourth to make the pile square.   35
Her Majesty Money, of course, bestows upon you a wife with dowry,
    credit,
Friends, a family line and good looks.
Empress Eloquence and Lady Love grace the man who has made it
    big.
The king of Cappadocia has his wealth tied up in slaves, but lacks
    cash,
Now really you don't want to be him; Lucullus, they say,   40
Was asked if he could furnish a hundred costumes for a play;
He said: " How can I provide that many? Yet, I'll look around
And send all I have." A little later he wrote that he had five thousand
Costumes at his house, for them to take a part or all of them.
It is a poor house that lacks a lot that isn't needed,   45
So much escapes the master's notice and profits thieves.
So, if money alone can make and keep you happy,
Be the first to seek it and the last to stop the pursuit.
But if influence and popularity guarantee success,
Let's buy a slave to tell us names, to poke us   50
In the left side and to urge us over stepping stones to shake
A hand; "*He* has much pull in the Fabian voting tribe, *that* one in the
    Veline;°
Another man will give power to any candidate he pleases or take
    away the curule
Chair from him, too, if he is in a bad mood." Say, "brother" or
    "father,"
Cleverly adopt whatever term fits the age.   55
If someone who dines well, lives well, then, at daylight let's go
Where the palate leads us; let's go fishing, hunting,
As Gargilius once did: early in the morning he ordered his slaves
To bring nets and hunting spears, and to cross the forum stuffed with
    people
So that the throng might view a single mule in the train lugging   60
A boar he just bought. Gorged with undigested food we'll take our
    bath,
Forgetting what is proper and what is not, like the disenfranchised
Men on the wax tablets of Caere, like the depraved crew of Ulysses
    from Ithaca

1.6.52: the Fabia and Velina were two of the thirty-five voting tribes into which
    Roman citizens were distributed.

Who were more concerned with forbidden pleasure than with their
     fatherland.
If there is no pleasure without love and laughter,   65
As Mimnermus thinks, then live it up amid love and laughter.
Yes, live it up and good luck! If you know any better advice than this,
Kindly share it; if not, better listen to me.

1.10

To Fuscus,° a lover of the city, I, a lover of the countryside,
Send greetings. In this one matter only, as you know,
We are very different, but in other respects we are almost twins,
Kindred spirits; what one of us rejects, the other does too;
We nod mutually like two old familiar doves;   5
You protect your nest, I praise the idyllic country,
Its brooks, the rocks covered with moss, its groves.
What more to say? There I truly live and I am a king the minute I
     leave
Those haunts that you praise to the skies in approving shouts.
Like a priest's runaway slave I refuse *panforte*:   10
I need bread more than cakes sweetened with honey.
If it is proper to live in accord with nature,
Then first look for a lot to build a house.
Do you know any place better than the blessed country?
Somewhere where the winters are milder, where a more welcomed
     breeze   15
Soothes the rage of the Dog-Star and the onset of Leo,
Furious when he catches the sharp rays of the sun?
Where worry envies and interrupts sleep less?
Where grass smells fresher and shines brighter than mosaics from
     Libya?
Is the water bursting a lead pipe and gushing in city streets purer   20
Than that which gambols and murmurs through a sloping stream?
You city folk grow trees between multi-colored columns,
Praise homes that look out over distant fields.
Thrust out nature with a pitchfork, yet she will run back,
And like a thief will break through your perverse contempt and win
     the victory.   25
The expert who hasn't the know-how to distinguish fleeces
Drinking in the dye from Aquinum's lichen from Tyrian purple
Will not suffer as heavy a loss or one closer to his innards
As the man who cannot separate the false from the true.

1.10.1: for Marcus Aristius Fuscus see *Satires* 1.9.

A person who has enjoyed too much success   30
Will quake when it changes. Whatever you overvalue, you'll be sorry
To lose. Shun anything grand: for beneath a poor roof you may
    outpace
In life's race kings and friends of kings.
A stag used to get the better of a horse in a fight, driving him
From a grassy field they shared, until the loser in the long battle   35
Begged help from a man and took the bit.
But when he had won and in insolent triumph left his foe,
He could not shake his rider from his back nor dislodge the bit from
    his mouth.
Thus anyone so scared of poverty that he would rather give up
His freedom than his mines, is depraved; he will carry a master   40
And be a slave forever because he knows not how to live on a little.
Property that doesn't fit a man resembles a shoe,
If it's too big for his foot, he'll trip, if too small, it pinches.
You'll live wisely, Aristius, if you are happy with your lot;
Don't let me go without a reprimand if you see me   45
Gathering more than is enough and I seem unable to relax.
Amassed money either serves or enslaves each of us;
It ought to follow rather than lead a tight-woven rope.
I dictate this to you behind the crumbling shrine of Vacuna;
Except that you are not with me, I am happy.   50

1.12

As manager of Agrippa's Sicilian revenues, Iccius, you'll enjoy
Well-deserved gain which not even Jupiter can supply you
In greater quantity. So stop complaining.
For he is not a poor man who has enough stuff for his use.
If your stomach is OK, your lungs and feet fine,   5
The riches of kings could not add any more.
If it's the frugal life for you on a diet of grass
And nettle, you would continue living such an ascetic life
Even if Fortune's clear stream bathed you in gold—
Either because money cannot change your nature   10
Or because you believe everything else inferior to virtue.
We are amazed that Democritus' herd ate up his meager pastures
And grain fields while his quick mind roamed free without a body;
Yet you, surrounded by the leprous itch for profit,
Ever the wise man, pursue no petty course but direct your thoughts to
    lofty themes:

What checks the growth of sea; what regulates the seasons;
Whether stars move in a fixed pattern or wander by chance;
What obscures the moon, what brings its full phase;
What the harmony of discord means and what is its power;
Whether Empodocles is deranged or shrewd Stertinus.   20
In any case, whether you are butchering fish, or leeks and onions,
Welcome Pompeius Grosphus:° if he asks for something, kindly
Give it; he'll only request what is right and just.
The price for friends is cheap, especially when decent men need
    something.
Now I'll acquaint you with the state of affairs in Rome: 25
The Spaniard has fallen to the valor of Agrippa, the Armenian
To Claudius Nero's; Phraates, humbled and on his knees,
Has accepted Caesar's law and power; from her plentiful horn
Golden Prosperity pours down abundant fruits on Italy.

1.18

Knowing you as well as I do, my most candid Lollius, you will fear to
    give
Even the slightest appearance of being a toady, once you have
    claimed yourself a friend.
As a matron differs in character and dress from a whore,
So a true friend is different from a phony parasite.
But the vice opposite to this fault of flattery is almost worse,   5
That boorish, blunt, and tiresome severity
Which prides itself on hair cut down to the skin, dirty teeth,
All meant to imply that unadulterated frankness is a true virtue.
But virtue is the mean of extremes, remote from both vices.
One man sinks into abject servility, a joker at the end   10
Of the table who gets goose bumps at the nod of his wealthy patron,
Repeats his words and picks up the *bons mots* before they fade,
Such that you would think that he was a schoolboy parroting the
    lectures
Of his brutal teacher or a comic actor learning the bit part of an
    understudy;
Another wrangles over a goat's hair, armed for battle   15
He fights over trifles: "How could you not
Trust me first, and I'll bark as loud as I please,
Thank you. Another life time would be poor pay for my honesty."

1.12.22: for Pompeius Grosphus see *Odes* 2.16.

What's the dispute? Why, whether Castor or Docilis° has better skill;
Which road that leads to Brundisium is better, the Minucian or the
    Appian Way.   20
A man who has been ruined by love or stripped bare by reckless
    gambling,
Or one whom vanity dresses and perfumes beyond his means,
Or whom an insatiable thirst and hunger for money grip,
Or the one whose shame and panic of poverty, induces a rich friend—
Often himself ten times more schooled in vice— to hate and
    disgust;   25
Or, if he doesn't hate, he tries to straighten him out, and like a
    devoted mother,
Wants the man wiser and more virtuous than himself,
And approaches the truth when he says to him: "Don't try to rival
    me;
My money allows me foolish behavior; your resources are on the
    small side;
A cheap toga graces a sensible client; stop trying to compete   30
With me." Whenever Eutrapelus wanted to ruin someone,
He gave him expensive clothes: now this lucky fellow
Will don new ideas and new plans to match his new clothes:
He will sleep to noon, put off honest work
For a whore, fatten his debts, and worst of all   35
End up becoming a gladiator or a hired hand to drive a nag to the
    vegetable market.
Never pry into your patron's secrets,
But keep private anything disclosed to you, although you be wracked
    by wine or anger.
Don't praise your own interests or ridicule another's
And don't be composing poems when he is in the mood to go
    hunting.   40
The affection between the twins Amphion
And Zethus split apart until Amphion silenced his lyre
That his austere brother disliked. So, it's commonly held that
    Amphion
Yielded to his brother's ways: now you obey the mild commands
Of your powerful friend. When he leads out to his fields   45
His dogs and mules loaded with Aetolian nets,
Get up, put aside your morose and antisocial muse,
And earn your gourmet dinners paid for by work equal to his:
After all, it's a Roman custom for gentlemen to hunt, good for the
    reputation,

2.18.19: Castor and Docilis are either two actors or two gladiators.

Life, and limbs, especially if you are a fine healthy specimen,   50
Able to outrun a dog or outmuscle a wild boar;
And besides, no one else can handle manly arms
More gracefully than you; you have enjoyed the cheers from the ring
Of spectators when you do battle on the Campus Martius, and, as a
      mere youth,
You served in a bloody campaign, fought in Spanish battles under a
      commander   55
Who now is reclaiming from Parthian temples our standards°
And consigns to Roman power any territory untouched.
Don't withdraw and absent yourself without excuse:
Yes, you make it your concern never to do anything out of tune or
      time,
Yet sometimes on your father's country estate you play around;   60
An army divides up boats, you command at the "Battle of Actium"
Reenacted by slave boys in hostile fashion.
Your brother is the outlaw Antony, a pond the Hadriatic, until Victory
Speeds to crown one of you with a leafy garland.
Anyone who believes that you agree with his interests,   65
Will be your supporter, approving your sport with two thumbs up.
But more advice: if you need a preceptor—be careful
What you say, about whom you say it, and to whom you say it;
Avoid the inquisitive type: he is often a gossip;
Wide open ears don't keep secrets secret,   70
And a word once expressed flies beyond recall.
Don't tear out your guts in love with a maid or boy
Inside the marble threshold of the friend to whom you owe respect.
The patron just may present you his blessing—a little token—
Of that handsome boy or dear girl, or he may refuse and piss you
      off.   75
Anyone you recommend, check him out again and again.
For his faults may one day hammer you with disgrace.
Sometimes we misjudge and introduce a wrong person;
His own guilt will trample him; don't defend him if you've been
      fooled.
Instead, stick up for the true friend when accusations assail him;   80
Protect him, be a fortress for him who has been loyal;
And when the envious tooth of Theon gnaws at him on every side,
      can't you feel
The dangerous bites soon to sink into you?
Your own property is at stake if a neighbor's house catches fire;

1.18.55-56: Augustus led a campaign into Spain in 27-25, and in 20 he negotiated
      the return of Roman standards lost by Crassus to Parthians in the Battle of
      Carrhae.

Flames disregarded often regain strength.   85
The courting of a powerful patron seems fun for those who have
      yet to try it,
The experienced are cautious. So, while your ship is on the deep,
Take care that a shifting breeze not blow you backward.
The humorless despise jokers and jokers dislike the sober,
The quick hate the lethargic, and the lazy despise the go-getter.   90
Drinkers soaking up a Falernian varietal at midnight
Will despise you if you refuse cups proffered to you, although
You swear that you fear night fever after drinking.
Chase the cloud from your brow: many times the modest man
Takes on the appearance of the sly sneak, the silent man,
      the sneerer.   95
In all of this read and study the learned philosophers;
Following their philosophy you can live a life of peace;
Question them whether greed, a constant pauper, tosses and torments
      you,
Or is it fear and hope for things of little use;
Whether learning engenders virtue or virtue is a natural gift;   100
What diminishes worry, how to befriend yourself;
What brings pure calm: high office or a neat little profit
Or a hidden journey on the pathway of life that escapes view.
Every time the Digentia refreshes me, the cold stream
That Mandela, a village wrinkled by the cold, drinks,   105
What do you think that I am feeling, what do you believe,
      my friend, I pray for?
That I have what I have now or even less; that I may live
For myself the rest of my life, all the time remaining that the gods
      have decreed;
That I possess a good supply of books, and food enough for a year;
And that I not drift to and fro, suspended on the doubtful hope
      of the hour.   110
It is enough to pray to Jove for what he dispenses and takes away:
That he grant life and means. I'll furnish myself the calm mind.

1.19°

Maecenas, my learned friend, if you believe old Cratinus,
No poems can please or live for very long
Which are written by water drinkers. Ever since Bacchus
Enrolled insane poets among his satyrs and fauns,

1.19: Horace answers his critics who claimed that he was unoriginal in imitating
    his Greek models.

The sweet muses have been reeking with wine in the morning.   5
By lavishing praise on wine Homer is proven to be a wino:
Our father Ennius never leapt to sing of epic battles
Unless he was drunk. "The teetotalers I consign to the forum
And Libo's well: I withhold the right of singing from abstainers."
As soon as I uttered that decree, poets have not ceased to compete   10
In nocturnal drinking bouts with straight stuff and to stink during
    the day.
Now if someone with a fierce and grim look goes barefoot
And dresses up in a cheaply woven toga to imitate Cato,
Would he be imparting the virtue and character of Cato?
When Iarbitas copied Timagenes, his tongue ruined him:°   15
He was so eager and he tried so hard to be thought witty and
    eloquent.
A model that has faults easy to imitate leads us astray. But if I
    happened
To take on a pale look, poets would begin drinking cumin.
O imitators, you servile flock, how often
Your gyrations have stirred my bile and my laughter.   20
I blazed a trail planting my free footsteps over untrodden land;
My feet did not tread on another's path; who trusts in himself
Will lead and rule the swarm. I was the first to show
Latium the iambic meters of Paros. I followed the measure and spirit
Of Archilochus, but not his subjects and his words that drove
    Lycambes mad.°   25
But don't grace me with a crown of scantier leaves
Because I was afraid to change his meters and poetic technique;
Masculine Sappho shaped her muse to Archilochus' meter,
So did Alcaeus, though differing in themes and strophic structure.
He didn't hound a father-in-law to smear him with deadly verses   30
Nor fashion a noose of notorious song for his bride.
I have made this poet known here in Latin, never before sung by
    other lips;
I like to introduce poems previously unknown
To be read by the eyes of noble citizens and clasped in their hands.
If you want to know why an ungrateful reader praises   35
And loves my lyrics in the privacy of his home, but unfairly
    criticizes them in public,

1.19.15: Timagenes, a Greek rhetorician from Alexandria, immigrated to Rome.
    He was known for his eloquence and caustic wit. Iarbitas imitated his acerbic
    tongue but lacked the eloquence.
1.19.25: Archilochus wrote vitriolic poems against Lycambes because he had
    broken off the engagement of his daughter Neoboule to Archilochus.

It's because I don't go hunting for votes from a people twisting in the
    wind
By paying for dinners and doling out worn clothes.
I don't go to hear the readings of famous writers and get even with
    them,
Nor deign to court the tribes of Ph.D.s in literature at their lecterns. 40
Then the tears begin: If I say, "I'd be ashamed to read out loud
My poems to crowded halls and to treat my trifles as weighty,"
Then someone replies, "You're joking: you're keeping them
For Jove's ears° only; you really think that you and you alone
Drip the honey of poetry? What chutzpah!" At this I am afraid   45
To turn up my nose; I could get slashed by the sharp fingernail of a
    rival.
I shout, "I don't like this spot," and call for time.
This type of sport engenders furious quarrels and anger,
And the rage breeds savage feuds and deadly war.

2.1°

Since you alone shoulder so many burdens
Protecting the Italian state with arms, and gracing it with morals,
And improving it with laws, I would be amiss against the public
    interest,
If I were to waste your time, Caesar, in a lengthy discourse.
Romulus, father Liber, and Castor and Pollux   5
Were welcomed into the holy precincts of the gods after their mighty
    deeds.
But while they inhabited the earth and tended the human race,
Settled violent wars, distributed lands, and founded towns,
They complained the respect they expected did not match
Their merits. The hero clubbed the poisonous hydra°   10
And subdued storied monsters in labors imposed on him by fate;
Yet he found out in the end that only his death crushed envy.
A man's splendor burns; he weighs down the talents
Of those inferior to him: when the flame dies, then he is loved.
We lavish honors upon you still among us;   15
We erect altars to swear by your divine spirit;°

1.19.44: "Jove's ears" may be a veiled reference to Augustus and his anticipated
    deification.
2.1: this lengthy poem is addressed to Augustus. It defends modern poets
    against overvalued ancients and explores the Roman literary tradition.
2.1.10-12: refer to Hercules.
2.1.16: the line encapsulates the rudiments of emperor worship that came to
    completion after Augustus' death.

We admit that your like has never been nor will ever be again.
But your people with wise and just discernment rate you
Above all our leaders; you they also honor above the Greeks;
But in other matters they fail to discern with equal reason and
    similar sense.   20
For unless they see something which has vanished from the earth
And has lived out its time, they loathe and despise it.
So, they are a fan of anything antique, like the Twelve Tables, the
    "Commandments"°
Which the Board of Ten enacted, the fair treaties of the kings
Ratified with Gabii or with the tough Sabines,   25
The priests' sacred books, the pristine prophecies in scrolls
That they claim over and over the Muses intoned on Mt. Alba.
For if all the most ancient writings of the Greeks are also the very
    best,
And we should use the same scale for Roman authors,
Then there is not much more to say;   30
Thus the olive has no hard pit inside nor the nut a hard shell.
We have reached the height of our power: we paint,
We sing, we wrestle, more skilled than the well-oiled Greeks.
If age improves poems, like wines,
I'd like to know: how many years does it take to confer value on
    literature?   35
Should the writer who dropped off a hundred years ago
Be enrolled in the canon of the ancients or counted among the
    moderns—
The lousy authors? Fix a limit to remove any dispute.
"To be ancient and good, he must be dead a hundred years."
Well, what about the poet who is short by, say, a month or a year? 40
Do we count him in the category of the ancients? Or among those
    others
Whom the present and the future age scornfully reject?
"Put him with the ancients where he rightfully belongs,
If he is just a month or year shy."
OK, I'll take you up on your concession: suppose I pluck°   45
Hairs from a mare's tail, removing them one by one,
Then by analogy to the argument of the "diminishing heap," you'll be
    foiled and lose

2.1.23-24: the laws of the Twelve Tables enacted in 451 became a school text
    and a literary model.
2.1.45-47: the plucking of a horse's tail and the diminishing heap are logical
    paradoxes. The question asked is at what point the hairs of a tail, plucked
    one by one, cease to be a tail, or grains removed successively from a pile
    cease to be a pile.

Your case, if you trust to the calendar, judge quality by the years,
And admire nothing that the Goddess of Funerals has not hallowed.
Ennius, the wise, the powerful, and the second Homer,   50
As critics claim, appears to care but little
What becomes of the promises in his Pythagorean dreams;°
Naevius still clings in our hands and sticks in our minds
As if he were a modern: so sanctified is every poem.
There is always a dispute who is better: Pacuvius wins the prize   55
As old and learned, Accius as sublime;
Many say that Afranius' toga fits Menander,
Plautus' rapid pace follows the example of Epicharmus of Sicily,
Caecilius excels in dignity, Terence in art.
These writers mighty Rome memorizes, packs the theater full   60
To see their plays, reckons and counts them poets
From the time of Livius right down to our own day.
Sometimes the public judges right, sometimes it makes a mistake.
If it so admires and praises the ancient poets
That it prefers nothing to them and holds them beyond compare,
    it errs.   65
If it believes some of their poems are old-fashioned, and many are
    rough
In style, or confesses that much is boring,
Then it is wise and supports my view, and Jove approves.
Now I'm not really carping nor do I think Livius' poems
Should be destroyed, which I remember from my school-boy days   70
When Orbillius,° the "whip," dictated them; but I am perplexed they
    appear
Beautiful and flawless to some and all but perfect.
Sometimes a fitting phrase may sparkle,
Sometimes one or two lines are gracefully constructed,
But unfairly they carry and sell the entire poem.   75
I resent any work being criticized, not because some judge
Its style coarse or inelegant, but because it is new,
While the ancients receive honor and prizes when they need excuses.
If I doubt a play of Atta's still keeps its footing among the saffron
And flowers, almost all the elders shout that modesty   80
Is dead since I'd be undertaking to criticize those plays
In which "serious" Aesopus and "talented" Roscius acted.

2.1.52: in his *Annales* Ennius wrote that Homer appeared to him in a dream an-
    nouncing that he, Ennius, was the reincarnation of Homer. The dream was
    consistent with the Pythogorean belief in the transmigration of souls.
2.1.71: L. Orbillius Pupillus from Beneventum was one of Horace's teachers
    in Rome.

Either they consider nothing right except what has pleased them,
Or think it is a disgrace to yield to their juniors and to confess
As old men that what they had learned as beardless youths was a
    waste.   85
Now anyone who praises Numa's chant of the Salii
And desires to appear the only expert on a poem he understands
No more than I do, doesn't appreciate or applaud talents long buried.
Instead, he impugns our efforts and in spite despises them and us.
What if the Greeks had hated novelty as much as we do,   90
What would now be ancient? Or what would
Everyone of the general public have to read and thumb through?
As soon as Greece won her wars,° she began to engage herself in
    frivolity,
And to drift into decadence during favorable times;
She burned for athletic pursuits, then for horses;   95
She fell in love with sculpture of marble, of ivory, and of bronze,
And fixed her feasting eyes and mind upon painted tableaux,
One moment delighted by flautists, another time by tragic actors.
She was like a baby girl playing at her nurse's feet,
What once she passionately desired, soon, fed up, she abandoned. 100
You think what you like or dislike doesn't change?
Such was the result of long periods of peace and favorable winds.
But for a long time at Rome it was agreeable and time-honored
To rise early in the morning, open up the house, provide legal
    services to a client,
To lend money secured by honest names,   105
To listen to elders, and to explain to minors how to increase
Property and how to diminish ruinous lust.
The capricious public has changed its mind and now burns
With a single desire: to write. Boys and their stern fathers
Crown their locks with leafy garlands, and spout poems over
    dinner.   110
Even I who keep swearing to give up writing verses,
Prove myself to be more mendacious than any Parthian. I awake
Before the first light of the sun demanding a pen, paper, and a case of
    books.
A landlubber ignorant of a ship avoids sailing, and an unskilled
    layman
Does not dare give wormwood to a sick man; doctors undertake   115

2.1.93: the wars being referred to are those with the Persians in the early fifth
    century.

The work of doctors, craftsmen handle tools.
But we tribe of poets, one and all, amateurs and pros, write poems.
This craze and mild madness, however, has some virtues.
Consider this: the bard's soul is not very greedy;
He loves poetry, his one and only passion;   120
He laughs at financial losses, runaway slaves, fires;
He doesn't scheme to defraud a business partner or a young ward;
He lives on beans and stale bread;
A worthless and stupid soldier, yet he serves the city,
If you admit that small services contribute to great enterprises.   125
The poet shapes the tender and stammering speech of a child;
He turns his young ear away from dirty talk;
Soon with friendly precepts he molds his heart,
A corrector of its rawness, envy, and wrath.
He relates great deeds, instructs his successive years   130
With noble examples; he consoles the sick and helpless.°
Where would the chaste boys and unwed girls
Learn the hymnal prayers had the muse not offered up a poet?
The chorus asks for help and feels the divine presence,
Implores heaven for rain, is taught by the persuasive to pray.   135
It prevents diseases, averts fearful dangers,
Garners both peace and a year prosperous and rich in bounty.
The hymn pleases the gods above and the gods below.
The farmers of old, sturdy and content with a little,
After the harvest was stored, at festival time restored   140
Body and soul that had endured hard work in hope of its end;
In company with fellow workers, children, and a faithful wife,
They sacrificed a pig to Earth, and offered milk to Silvanus,
And flowers and wine to their Guardian Spirit who is mindful of
      life's brevity.
By this tradition licentious Fescennine verse was born,   145
Pouring out obscene, earthy slurs in responsive lines.
This freedom of speech was welcomed in the successive years
When there was playful banter; but when the jokes began to turn
      vicious
Into open rage with no check upon the threats menacing decent
      families,
The tooth drew blood and those wounded yelped with pain;   150
Even those who were unattacked had concern
About the public interest; so a law with appropriate penalty
Was enacted to forbid anyone being exposed
In vicious song; bards changed their tune in fear of being beaten to
      death;

2.1.132-133: allude to Horace's own *Carmen Saeculare*.

They reverted to singing with decorum and delighting the
    audience.   155
Captured Greece made her wild captor captive and introduced
Her arts to the fields of Latium. So, that uncouth
Saturnian measure° ran dry and elegance expunged
The offensive venom; yet for a long time
There remained, as there still remain today, traces of the rustic
    crudeness.   160
It was quite late before the Roman applied his mind to Greek
    literature,
And after the Punic Wars began to have the peace to inquire
What service Sophocles, Thespis, and Aeschylus had to offer.
He also experimented, trying to translate them in a worthy style.
He pleased himself, being naturally lofty and vigorous;   165
For he has the tragic spirit and dares to press his success,
But in his ignorance thinks to erase is a disgrace and so hestitates to
    do it.
Because comedy draws its material from everyday life, it is believed
That it demands less sweat; *au contraire*, it exacts
A more burdensome price because the audience's indulgence is less.
    Just look   170
At Plautus, how he handles character: the role of the young man in
    love,
The stingy father, the treacherous pimp,
The hungry parasite modeled on the Buffoon,°
Who runs across the stage in floppy socks.
He just wants to put money in his safe, after that   175
He is indifferent whether his play flops or lands straight on its feet.
Any poet carried to the stage on the windy chariot of Glory,
A cold audience deflates or an appreciative one puffs up:
So fickle, so trifling a thing sinks or restores a soul
That is greedy for approval. Goodbye to comic show business, if it
    means   180
That if denied a hit I come back home bone-skinny, or winning I
    return fat.
Often even the gutsy poet is routed and terrified at this prospect;
For the majority of the audience, lacking in talent and recognition,
Are ignorant, thick-headed, and ready to punch an equestrian
Who disagrees, and clamor in the middle of the production   185
For a bear or boxers, the kind of things the "dear" public enjoys.
But now even for the discerning equestrian the eyes have replaced the
    ear,

2.1.158: Saturnian was the meter of earliest Latin.
2.1.173: the Buffoon was a stock character in native farce.

Constantly relying on cheap "special effects" that jack up the
    excitement.
Curtains are up these days for four or more hours
While squadrons of cavalry and platoons of infantry dash by;   190
Soon enough captured kings are dragged on, their hands tied behind
    their backs,
Chariots, carriages, wagons, even ships hustle across,
And captive ivory and bronze statues from Corinth are paraded.
Why, if Democritus were still on earth, he'd be laughing.
If a hybrid monster, say a cross between a panther and a giraffe,   195
Or a white elephant, attracted the public' gawking,
He'd be viewing the people more than the plays
As a much more entertaining spectacle staged for him;
And he would think that the authors were composing drama
For a deaf ass. For what voices from the actors could possibly   200
Drown out the racket that redounds in our theaters?
You'd think the grove of Mt. Garganus was bellowing or the Tuscan
    sea roaring,
So much noise rises from the audience watching the plays,
The works of art, the foreign costumes richly adorning the actor
    smeared with
Grease paint whenever he has made his entrance on the stage to
    thunderous clapping.
"What did he say?" "Nothing really." "Then why the approving
    applause?"   206
"His woolen costume is stained violet with dye from Tarentum."
But don't think I shrink from praising plays, which I myself
Refuse to write, when others craft them so well;
In my eyes the poet walks a tightrope,   210
Who wrenches my heart with illusions,
Stirs it up, calms it down, fills it with false fears,
And like a magician, transports me first to Thebes, and then to
    Athens.
But think of those writers too who choose to entrust themselves to a
    reader
Rather than to bear the hauteur of a snobbish viewer;   215
Render a moment's care, Caesar, if you wish to stock the library°
Dedicated as a worthy gift to Apollo, and want to spur on poets
To seek out with even greater passion the green of Helicon.
Yes, we poets often commit some real boners—
Let me cut down my own vines—when we present you   220

2.1.216-217: a reference to the Greek and Latin libraries that were part of the
    complex of the Temple of Apollo. See note to *Epistles* 1.3.17.

A book, although you are under stress and weary; when we are cut
    to the quick,
Insulted by a friend who has dared to criticize a single line;
When, unasked, we turn back to passages already read;
When we gripe that our labors
And our poems so finely spun aren't appreciated;   225
When we hope matters will come to this: that as soon as you
Know that we are concocting poems, you will oblige us and on your
    own
Summon us in order to save us from poverty and to order us to keep
    on writing.
Yet it is worth your effort to analyze those
Who are caretakers of your virtue tried in peace and in war;   230
Don't entrust it to an unworthy poet.
Alexander the Great favored Choerilus, that hack,
Who for his unrefined and misbegotten verse
Entered as received royal issue, gold Philippics.
But just as dark inks leave a blot and stain on whatever
    they touch,   235
So writers with their ugly song smear
Glorious and heroic deeds. That same spendthrift king
Who overpaid for such a ridiculous poem
Then decreed that no one except Apelles
Could ever paint his portrait or any other than Lysippus could
    sculpt   240
In bronze the image of courageous Alexander. But if
You applied this subtle judgment of his, so discriminating in visual
    arts,
To his discernment of books and the gifts offered by the muses,
You would swear he was born in the thick air of Boeotia.
But those beloved poets of yours, Vergil and Varius,   245
Do not dishonor your judgment of them and your patronage
Which reflect much credit on you, their donor.
Features depicted on bronze statues are no better captured
Than the deeds, character, and minds of famous men expressed
In a poet's work. And I would prefer to compose epic exploits   250
Rather than these "conversations"° that creep along the ground,
To sing of the earth's faraway lands, the rivers, the citadels
Stacked high on hilltops, foreign kingdoms, of wars
Over the entire world bought to end thanks to you.
I would depict the gates that bolt in Janus, guardian of peace,°   255

2.1.251: an allusion to Horace's own *Satires* and *Epistles*.
2.1.255: in time of peace the doors of the temple of Janus were kept closed; in
    war they were opened.

And Rome under your lead feared by Parthians,
If only I could do what I wanted. But your grandeur
Does not admit a humble poem nor will my modesty
Dare to tempt a theme my powers would refuse to complete.
It is embarrassing and foolish to bother someone you love,   260
Especially if a poet prides himself on his meter and art.
For one always learns more quickly and remembers more vividly
The poem he laughs at than the one he respects and reveres.
I don't give a damn for any attention that imposes upon me, nor do I
     care
Ever to be caricatured in wax with a face uglier than the real
     thing,   265
Or to be praised in depraved verses.
Presented with a fatuous gift like that I would blush from
     embarrassment,
And, stretched out in a closed coffin along with my poet,
I'd be carried to the market street where incense and perfumes are up
     for sale,
And pepper, and anything else wrapped in waste paper.   270

PROPERTIUS

ELEGIES

There is no doubt that the Hellenistic style of poetry, particularly that of Callimachus, influenced Propertius. His frequent references to his Greek model and his allusive style verify Propertius' indebtedness. Propertius was also the heir to Roman narrative love elegy that C. Cornelius Gallus had developed. In many of his poems Propertius details his poetic affair with a certain Cynthia. Most of the poems of Book I and Book II center on the relationship with her. In the corpus, however, are interspersed poems on literary, social, and political themes with Book IV mainly devoted to etiological topics. In any case, Propertius' demanding style and wit bring an intense and refreshing reaction to his genre.

1.1

Cynthia° was the first whose eyes captured me, poor soul,
    uninfected before by any diseases of desire.
That once firmly arrogant look of mine bent to the ground
    and Love tromped and stomped on my head,
Till he taught me to hate nice girls,   5
    depraved god! and to live a senseless life without scheme.
This my madness has raged on now for a year on end,
    but the gods I'm forced to endure oppose me.

1.1.1: it is fitting that the first word of Propertius' poems is "Cynthia," in that so
    many of his poems are devoted to her and their relationship is characterized
    as a maddening enslavement.

No, it wasn't by shirking labors, Tullus, that Milanion
    crushed the savagery of the tough, hard-hearted daughter of
        Iasos.°   10
Deranged he wandered through caves of the Virgin Mountain,°
    and ventured to gaze upon hairy beasts,
And once he was struck and wounded by Hylaeus' bow,
    and groaned, as he lay maimed, to Arcadia's cliffs.
Hence, he was able to tame that fleet-footed girl;   15
    in love, prayers and good deeds work wonders.
But for me Love runs slowly and devises no schemes
    and can't remember the tricks it used to know.
So you who claim you trick and eclipse the moon from the sky,
    performing your sacred rites on magic hearths,   20
Come on, change my mistress's feelings,
    pale the glow of her face, fainter than mine!
Then I'll believe that hocus-pocus of stars and rivers
    deflected by Medean chants.
And you, friends, who seek to restore a man far gone,   25
    find me some help for a heart that is sick.
Bravely I'd suffer the knife and savage cautery
    to have the freedom to say what my fury craves;
Send me to peoples far, far away over the ocean
    where no woman would know my route.   30
But you stay, to whom god has lent a kind ear and nodded,
    be always carefully matched in a safe affair.
Against me our love plies night after bitter night;
    my lack of love is present every hour.
Avoid this disaster, I warn you; let everyone cling   35
    to his own girl, not shift his ground from well-trod love.
To anyone who listens too late to this warning,
    oh, oh, he'll echo my words with grief upon grief.

1.3

Like Ariadne lying limp on the desolate shore
    while Theseus' keel slipped away,
And like Cepheus' daughter, Andromeda, drowsing
    in the first flush of sleep, released on the flinty crag,

---

1.1.10: the daughter of Iasos is Atalanta. See Glossary under ATALANTA.

1.1.11: "Virgin Mountain" in Latin *Parthenius*, evoking the virginity of both
    Artemis (Diana) and her devotee Atalanta, and referring to the Greek poet
    Parthenios of the first century whose erotic verse served as a model for Prop-
    ertius. See Vergil, *Eclogues* 10.57.

And, no less exhausted by incessant dancing a Bacchant   5
    might collapse in Apidanus' bed, still grassy,
So she seemed to me to be breathing the same soft peace,
    Cynthia, cushioning her head on unresisting hands,
As I staggered in on drunken footsteps, heavy with Bacchus,
    in the late hour when slave boys were fanning the dying torches. 10
I had an urge—I had not yet lost all my senses—
    to approach her body soft in the mold of the couch;
I was growing hot seized by two passions,
    Love on this side, Wine on that—both demanding divine bosses—
Ordering me to assault the sleeper, to slide my arm gently under
        her,   15
    to steal kisses, and with direct hand to storm her.
Yet I didn't dare to disturb her rest,
    fearing the savage rebuttal of a rage I knew too well.
So I just stood glued, my eyes in an intense stare
    as Argus transfixed on Io's strange horns.   20
But then I dismantled the garland, my Cynthia, from my brow
    and put several ringlets so gently on your temples;
Then lovingly I tidied some curls that had drooped,
    gave pilfered apples from cupped hands:
All my gifts I lavished on thankless sleep,   25
    gifts that from time to time trickled down your open bosom.
Every time you sighed or moved ever so slightly,
    I'd freeze, believing it an empty omen,
That a nightmare was provoking you, my love, to strange fears,
    an incubus was taking you against your will,   30
Till the moon running on past the windows—
    busybody moon!—paused with its lingering beams,
And its gossamer rays unshuttered those resting eyes.
    She then spoke, her elbow propped on the soft bed:
"Bastard! So you've come at last and only because that other one,   35
    that offence to our bed, has thrown you out and bolted the doors.
Where else have you squandered the night—this night that belonged
        to me,
    creeping back here, limp, as the stars expire?
I wish that you had to endure such nights
    as I, poor soul, always suffer under your control.   40
For a while I cheated sleep by spinning a purple thread,
    and then, though tired, with Orphic songs played on a lyre,
Yet under my breath I complained to myself what it's like to be jilted,
    haunted by the thought of your frequent stays with another lover,
Till I slipped, and sleep with its wings of delight thrust into me.   45
    With worry at that I surrendered to tears."

1.5°

You, yes, you with the itching eye! Restrain your ugly words;
    leave us to make our trail on our present course as partners.
What do you want, crazy man? To feel for yourself my madness?
    Unlucky one, you speed on to know the ultimate troubles
And, poor wretch, to mark footprints over unknown fires,   5
    and to drink dry the poisons of all of Thessaly.°
She is not to be compared to flirts:
    it is not her custom to vent a gentle anger.
But if you should rush in, she is not averse to our friends,
    yes, how many thousands of concerns she will bring you;   10
She'll give you no sleep, she'll deprive you of eyes;
    she alone tames those men with wild spirits.
Ah, how often you will run to my doorstep, rejected,
    your brave words will collapse into sighs,
Shakes, shudders, and salty tears will come,   15
    and fear will trace its ugly mark upon your face;
The words you want to use to make your complaint will fail you,
    and you'll know not, poor wretch, who or where you are.
You'll be forced to learn the heavy chain of our girl,
    and what it means to be slinking home, locked out;   20
No more will you keep wondering why my pallor
    or why my body shows me a total nobody;
Nor will your nobility help you in love:
    Love knows not how to yield to ancient busts of pedigree.
And if you betray even the slightest signs of guilt,   25
    how quickly you will lose your mighty reputation—the grist of
        gossip.
Then I will be unable to provide you palliatives upon demand,
    since in my stock no medicine cures my own miserable state.
But in wretched parity we are joined by love,
    each forced to weep upon the other's sobbing chest.   30
So then, stop it, Gallus! Don't ask what my Cynthia can do.
    When beckoned, she comes with a potent penalty.

1.6

I'm not afraid to brave the Adriatic with you, Tullus,
    nor to hoist sail on the brine of the Aegean;
With you I would scale the northern peaks of Scythia
    and would trespass beyond the home of Memnon.

1.5.1: the first of a number of poems addressed to a certain Gallus. He may or
    may not be the famous poet/general.
1.5.6: Thessaly was often characterized as a place of intrigue and black magic.

But the words and embraces of my girl hold me back,   5
    her pressing pleas and ever-changing color;
For nights on end upon me she hones her shrill passions
    and complains that, if she is forsaken, there are no gods,
Denies that she is mine and in my face taunts me with threats,
    as a desperate lover does to her angry man.   10
I cannot endure an hour of such complaints;
    ah, damn him who can be slow in love.
Is it worth so much to me to gain knowledge, first hand, of learned
        Athens,
    to tour the wealthy sites of Asia,
That Cynthia, with the launching of the ship, would abuse me with
        insults   15
    and mark my cheeks with her frenzied fingers,
Claiming that we kissed only because the winds were wrong
    and that nothing is more hard-hearted than a faithless man?
You strive to surpass the high offices, deservedly won, of your uncle
    and restore the ancient laws of forgetful allies.   20
For your prime of life never had time for love,
    always your passion was for country and war.
I pray that the Boy may never impose such hardships
    as ours upon you—all the tears I know so well!
Let me lie here, as fate has willed,   25
    to squander away the breath of my worthless life.
Many have languished and died happy in love;
    may I be one of them, when the earth covers me.
I was not born for glory, nor fit for arms:
    the Fates decree that I serve beneath this other banner.   30
But you, where effete Ionia stretches, or where
    the waters of the Pactolus tinge gold the plowed land of Lydia,°
Whether you bestride the lands on foot or take the seas by oars,
    you will share in welcomed rule.
If ever there will come to you an hour mindful of me,   35
    then you'll know that I am alive, but under a hostile star.

1.7

Ponticus, while you declaim in songs the Thebes of Cadmus
    and the tragic armed conflict between brothers,°

1.6.32: the Pactolus flowed through Sardis in Lydia, and was reputed to have
    gold deposits. Cf. the myth of King Midas who washed away his curse of
    the "golden touch" in it.
1.7.2: refers to the fight for succession to the throne of Thebes between Eteocles
    and Polyneices, the sons of Oedipus. Polyneices was one of the commanders
    among the Argives (the Seven against Thebes) who attacked Thebes.

And, (may I be so bold), you challenge the first Homer—
    I hope the Fates will be gentle to your poems—
We, as usual, ply our loves   5
    and seek something for a hard-hearted lover;
I am compelled not to serve my talent as much as my pain,
    and to berate the harsh realities of this time of life.
This is the life that wears me down; but this is my glory:
    I want my verse to be renowned for this.   10
Then may refined girls praise me, their one and only source of
      pleasure,
 me, Ponticus, *me*, who often suffered many unjust rebukes.
May the spurned lover keep reading *me*
    and profit from my sorrows.
You, too, if from his bow that crack-shot of a boy should stun you, 15
    (I would not wish our gods ever to violate you),
Far away from your camps you will weep, distressed,
    while the distant Seven Battalions lie forever deaf,
And you will long to compose tender verse, but fail;
    Love so late in your life will refuse to inspire you with poems. 20
Then you will often honor me, no mean poet,
    then I shall be preferred among all Roman talents;
At our tomb young men will be unable to refrain:
    "Here you lie, great poet of our passion!"
So beware of arrogant scorn for our poems: 25
    often love that comes late arrives with a high interest rate.

1.8

What? Are you crazy? Doesn't love for me hold you back?
    Or am I less valued than icy Illyria?
And that guy, whoever he is, do you rate him so high
    that you'd leave me, to sail under any breeze?
Can you brave the roaring murmur of the raging sea?   5
    Make bed on the hard deck of a ship?
Can your delicate feet support thick layers of frost?
    Can you, soft Cynthia, stand the unfamiliar snows?
O double the length of the brumal season,
    let the sailor idle, waiting for a late spring: 10
May the sandy shore still grip your Tuscan cables,
    may no hostile wind scatter my prayers;
May I not yet see those gusts subside,
    when the surge has swept your scudding ship,
And has abandoned me rooted on the empty shore,   15
    shaking my fist and repeatedly calling you, *bitch*!
But whatever I owe you for breaking your vows,

may the nymph Galatea guard your way.
May you round rocky Ceraunia safely with auspicious oar
    and arrive in Oricos' tranquil haven.   20
For no other women will ever corrupt me to prevent
    the complaints, my life, I pour out at your threshold.
I'll constantly pester every sailor hurrying past:
    "Tell me, what port harbors that girl of *mine*?"
Then I'll say: "She may be docked on Thessaly's shores   25
    or be in Scythia—but still she will be *mine*."
She was just here! She has sworn to stay—so jeer till you burst—
    We've won! She didn't weather my ceaseless prayers.
Lustful envy, abort your delight;
    Cynthia's ours, *mine*, she has renounced her rambling ways.   30
She loves me and because of me Rome is her best-loved place;
    and she swears that without me no empire is sweet
She prefers to lie at rest with me on a narrow bed,
    and, whatever the cost, to be *mine*!
Rather than own the ancient kingdom dowered to Hippodamia   35
    and all the wealth that Elis' horses won.
Although he gave her huge gifts, and promised better to come,
    yet she did not in greed flee my breast;
Not by gold nor by Indian pearl did I sway her;
    but I wooed and won her by the charm of eloquent song.   40
Yes, there are Muses, and Apollo, too, is not slow for a lover;
    in these I trusted for love: and Cynthia rare is *mine*!
Now I can touch the highest stars with the soles of my feet;
    come day, come night, she's *mine*!
No rival can steal my own true love: 45
    that boast will see my hair turned white.

1.9

I kept saying, you mocker, that love would come to you,
    and your words would not forever be free.
Now look, you lie low and grovel to the rules of a girl,
    and she whom you once paid for now is in command over you.
In love doves from Dodona do not surpass me   5
    in foretelling which young men any girl will master.
Pain and tears have rightly made me champ—
    O to be called a raw rookie and let love begone!
What good for you now to recite your serious epic
    or to weep for those lyre-made walls of Amphion's?   10
In love a verse of Mimnermus outweighs Homer:
    a love assuaged requires polished poetry.
Go and compose those "damned" sad elegies,
    and sing what any girl would like to know.

But what if the right theme should fail to come easy to you?   15
   Now that is as crazy as looking for water in the middle of a stream.
Not yet are you pale, not yet are you touched by a real fire;
   but this is the first spark of trouble yet to come.
Then sooner would you approach tigers from Armenia
   and experience the chains of Hell's wheel,°   20
Than feel Love's bow pierce your marrow so often
   and be unable to deny your angry lover anything.
Love has never offered wings so effortless to anyone
   that he would not with the other hand fold them back.
So don't be deceived that a girl appears ready enough;   25
   when she is yours, Ponticus, all the more bitchy she becomes:
No more straying eyes:
   Love forbids you to maintain vigils under another's power;
He does not become visible till his hand has cut to the bones.
   Escape his unrelenting charms, whoever you are!   30
As both flint stones and oaks yield to them,
   you could not resist, that epic breath's too weak.
So, if you have any shame, as soon as possible confess your errors;
   for to name the one in whose love you die is often a relief.

1.10

The pleasant release, ah, when I witnessed your love-making,
   so close by that I shared the tears you shed.
That night, the memory to me is sweet joy—
   I wish I could live it again and again—
When I saw you locked in her embrace near dead with longing,   5
   Gallus, jerking out words in between long pauses.
Although sleep oppressed my drooping eyes
   and the Moon's horses blushed high in the sky,
I couldn't bear to leave your tender sport,
   so intense was the heat in the sounds alternating between you.   10
But now you've gained the courage to admit my supremacy,
   so accept these gifts, reward for consummated joys.
And it isn't just that I know how to keep the secret of your pangs;
   friend, I've a power stronger than loyal silence.
Why—I'm expert at reuniting parted lovers,   15
   and I've the power to open a lover's stubborn doors,
And power to soothe love's wound, still fresh:
   not trifling is the medicine my words contain.

1.9.20: "Hell's wheel" refers to the punishment of Ixion.

For I've learned my skills in Cynthia's school, these always do's
    and don'ts for lovers—Love has at least effected something—   20
Don't look for trouble when she is feeling moody;
    don't preach sermons; *don't* sit and sulk;
Don't scowl and *don't* say *no* when she asks a favor;
    don't underreact when she says something sweet;
If you treat her with scorn, she'll answer in righteous fury;   25
    hurt, she'll claim her just revenge—with interest.
Go ahead, abase yourself, submit to it,
    if you want to taste the fruit of love.
The only way a man can be happy with just one woman
    is to surrender his carefree heart —and his freedom.   30

1.11

As you laze, Cynthia, in the center of Baiae
    where the path lies on Hercules' shores,°
Or sometimes marvel at the bay extending south
    below Greek realms near noble Misenum,
Does our love ever sneak upon you and bring nights filled with
      memories?   5
    Is there any room still for me somewhere in the suburb of your
      heart?
Or has some creep with counterfeit passion,
    Cynthia, stolen you from our verses?
But I'd rather suppose that you rely on pygmy oars
    dallying in a tiny rowboat for one on Lake Lucrino,   10
Or that the delicate waves of Cumae's beach embrace you,
    then gently part to your hand strokes, one after another,
Than to think of you leisurely listening to whispered lies—
    laid—out on a silent collusive shore.
With chaperone gone a girl is likely to lapse,   15
    forget and betray the mutual gods she swore by.
It is not that I mistrust you—I'm not unaware of your famous virtue—
    but every love in this place produces fear.
So forgive me, if anything offends you in my maudlin poems;
    my fear will be the blame.   20
My dear mother is guarded more closely than you,
    and without you my life lacks everything;
O Cynthia, you are my home and family, all I possess,
    every season of our happiness.

1.11.2: Heracles was said to have laid a strip of land from Lake Lucrino to the
  Bay of Baiae.

So whether I'm morose when I meet my friends, or cheerful,   25
    whatever my state, I'll say: "Cynthia was the cause!"
But waste no more time, leave depraved Baiae,
    whose shores are proven grounds for divorce,
Shores where many a nice girl has slipped,
    a slur on love itself: *damn* you, waters of Baiae!   30

1.12

Why don't you just stop it, fashioning the charge of laziness against
        me,
    that Rome shares in the guilt and delays me?
My love is separated from my bed as far as Scythia's
    Bug is from Venice's Po.
No longer does Cynthia nurse me in her usual embraces of love,   5
    no more does she sound sweet in our ear.
But once I pleased her: no one at that time was lucky enough
    to love with a faith similar to mine.
We were envied. Was it some god that crushed me? Or some herb
    picked on Prometheus' ridge° that drove us apart?   10
I am no more who I was; a long trip changes girls;
    what love, ah so much, has dissolved in a time so short!
Now for the first time I must experience long nights—alone,
    forced to myself to be heavy upon my ears.
Happy the man who could weep to his girl's face;   15
    Love takes great delight in tears that are shed.
If a jilted man could change his fires,
    there are pleasures too when slavery is swapped.
For me to love another or to cease from loving her is not ordained:
    Cynthia was the first, Cynthia will be the last.   20

1.16

In the past I swung open for splendid triumphs,
    a door, famous, a model of Tarpeian chastity;
Chariots inlaid with gold thronged over my threshold,
    dripping moist with the tears of begging captives.
But now, I'm wounded by the nocturnal brawls of drunkards,   5
    and I often groan pounded by vulgar fists;
A constant clump of filthy garlands hangs upon me,
    and spent torches lie prostrate, banners of routed lovers.
I am impotent to defend the scandalous nights of my mistress,
    a noble door surrendered to obscene curses.   10

1.12.10: refers to the Caucasus where Zeus had Prometheus chained for his theft
    of fire.

Yet she receives no recall to protect her own good name,
　and she lives a life more rank than this profligate age.
Amid all this I am forced to lament bitter complaints,
　made sadder by the long vigils of a poor suitor.
For he never allows my doorjambs to rest in peace,   15
　but charms me again and again with his penetrating poems:
"O door, you are crueler than your lady inside:
　why are you so silent, so hard, and shut so tight?
Why are you never unlatched to receive my passions,
　unfeeling to smuggle my innermost prayers inside?   20
Will no end to my pain ever be granted?
　And will filthy sleep upon this half-warmed slab be mine?
The midnight hours, the stars high in their course,
　the icy breeze of the frosty dawn grieve for me prostrate here;
You alone are unmoved to pity human suffering,   25
　your hinges respond with silence.
But, oh, that my little voice could contract and enter through a chink,
　strike and wind into my lover's pretty ears.
Maybe she is more unyielding than Sicilian stone,
　perhaps she is harder than iron or tempered steel,   30
But still she'd be unable to control those dear eyes,
　and with a rise in breath she'd sigh amid unwanted tears.
Ah, now, she leans on a rival's fortunate shoulders,
　and my pleas are wasted on the nightly wind.
But you, door! are the sole and greatest cause of my pain,   35
　yes you, never conquered by my many gifts.
I never assailed you with insolent and disrespectful tongue,
　saying the usual things to an angered object,
To warrant you to acquiesce, leaving me hoarse from long laments,
　and waiting through anxious hours on a street pavement.   40
No! Instead, I have often woven you poems, originals,
　leant on my lips to kiss your steps where she trod.
Oh how often I circled, traitor, around your door posts
　and brought you due offerings with reverent hands."
Such things as these, the kinds of things all you wretched lovers
　　know,   45
　he croaks to the morning birds.
So now, because of my lady's vices and the weeping of an ever-
　　present lover,
　I am discredited, doomed to eternal hatred.

1.19

I'm not scared, my Cynthia, of the gloomy realm of the shades,
    nor am I delaying the fates owed to the final pyre.
But that my dead body may be without your love
    is a more fearful prospect than the funeral itself.
Not so lightly has Amor, this boy of ours, clung to our eyes   5
    for my dust to forget and be without love.
Down there in the sightless region the hero Protesilaus, grandson of
        Phylacus,
    could not let fade the memory of his darling wife,
But lusting to touch his pleasures with unreal hand,
    had come to his ancient home as a Thessalian shade.   10
Down there, whatever I'll be, always I'll be your specter:
    great love crosses even the shores of fate.
Down there, bring on the company of famous beauties,
    booty from Dardanian Troy, allotted to Argive heroes;
None of them are as beautiful as you, Cynthia, or would please   15
    me more; and (I pray Earth be just and permit it),
Though the Fates detain you to extreme old age,
    yet I will love and weep for your soon-to-be bones.
If only you could feel it, while you live and I am hot ash,
    then whatever I may be, death would lack a bitter taste.   20
But I fear you will scorn my grave, Cynthia,
    that hostile Love will drag you away from my dust,
And force you against your will to dry your falling tears:
    a ceaseless barrage of threats bends even a faithful girl.
So, while we may, let us love and enjoy each other: 25
    seize love; love's never long enough.

1.21°

You there, soldier! who are eager to evade the Etruscan battlements,
    wounded, and straining to escape our kinsman, Death,
Why do you roll your eyes, bulging in horror at our groaning?
    I am the next stage of your own campaign.
Look to save yourself so as to bring your parents joy;   5
    and let not your sister by your tears feel what happened: that I,
Gallus, rescued in the midst of Caesar's swords,
    failed to elude the hands of nameless men;

1.21: the dramatic setting for this poem and the next is the battle and siege
    of Perugia in 41. Octavius had three hundred prominent men of the city
    executed after the capitulation of the city.

And what bones she discovers, strewn all over
    the Tuscan hills, tell her that these are mine.   10

1.22

My status, my rank, my ancestors, my place of birth,
    you keep asking, Tullus, in the name of our long friendship.
If you have heard of Perugia—our fatherland's graveyard—
    Italy's killing field it was in those hard times,
When civil strife in Rome stirred all her citizens—   5
    (O dust of Etruria, you are my special grief,
For you strain with the weight of my kinsman's scattered limbs,
    and you leave unburied his wretched bones)—
Bordering close by here, Umbria's sheltered plain,
    lands rich and fertile, bore me.   10

2.1°

The source of my many love compositions you ask,
    the source of my book so soft upon the lips;
Neither the muse Calliope nor the god Apollo sings to me.
    It's the girl: *she* is the whole of my inspiration.
Let her strut shimmering in Coan silk,   5
    from that one gown will come a volume;
If I've spied her tresses dishevelled, tumbling across her brow,
    she is glad to walk proud to the "hymn to hair;"
If she has strummed a song on the lyre with ivory fingers,
    I adore how skilled and delicate are her hands;   10
Or, when her eyes, demanding sleep, begin to droop,
    I find a thousand new themes for my poetry;
Or, if her tunic is ripped off and she wrestles with me in nude
      combat,
    then we compose endless Iliads:
Whatever she does or whatever she says,   15
    out of nothing gushes the grandest history.
Had the Fates, Maecenas, granted me the power
    to lead hosts of heroes into battle,
I would not record in song the Titans, or Ossa piled
    on Olympus to make Pelion a stairway to heaven,   20
Or Thebes of old, or Pergama, Homer's claim to fame,
    or at Xerxes' command twin straits wedded,

2.1: a *recusatio* addressed to Maecenas. See note to Horace, *Odes* 1.6.1.

Or the pristine realm of Remus, or the pride of lofty Carthage,°
  or the German menace checked by the exploits of Marius:
No, instead, I would commemorate the wars and deeds of Caesar,   25
  and you, after mighty Caesar, would be my theme.
Yes, as often I would sing of Mutina, or Philippi,
  our common graveyards, the naval battles, the Sicilian rout,°
The sacked hearths of the ancient Etruscan people,
  the captured beaches of Alexandria, Ptolemy's tower;   30
Or I would sing of Egypt, the Nile, who, dragged into the city,
  weakly moved along with his seven estuaries captive,
Or of kings collared with chains of gold around their necks,
  and of beaks captured at Actium paraded on the Sacred Way;
My muse would always weave you into the threads of those armed
    conflicts,
                                             35
  you ever loyal in peace begun or broken:
A trust Theseus calls to witness his friend in hell, Pirithous,
  Achilles his friend, Patroclus.
But the ruckus and clash of Jove and Giant on Phlegra's plain
  Callimachus will not thunder from his slender breast;   40
And I lack the proper heart in epic verse
  to trace Caesar's name to its Phrygian roots.
The sailor spins yarns about the winds, the plowman about bulls;
  the soldier counts his wounds, the shepherd his sheep;
I, on the other hand, sing of those engaging in battles on a narrow
    bed:
                                              45
  so each man should while away the day in the skill he masters best.
To die in love wins glory; and there is another glory: to be granted the
    power
  to enjoy a single love; oh, may I, too, enjoy my single love.
She (if I remember rightly) regularly finds fault with fickle girls;
  she disapproves of the entire *Iliad* because of Helen.   50
Should I touch the cups of stepmother Phaedra,°
  philtres that would not work on her stepson,
Or should I perish from Circe's herbal magic, or should
  Medea° bubble me in her cauldron on Iolcan hearths,
Since a single woman has plundered my senses,   55
  from her home will move our funeral.

2.1.23: a reference to the three Punic Wars Rome fought with the Carthaginians.

2.1.28: the "Sicilian rout" refers to Octavius' war against Sextus Pompey waged primarily on sea in 37–36.

2.1.51–52: Phaedra fell in love with Hippolytus, Theseus' son.

2.1.54: refers to Medea who treacherously cut up and boiled Jason's uncle Pelias.

Medicine cures all other human ailments,
   only love loves not the skilled curer of love-sickness.
Machaon healed the lingering leg wound of Philoctetes,
   Chiron, Phillyra's son, the eyes of Phoenix,°   60
Aesculapius, god of Epidaurus, by Cretan herbs
   restored the deceased Androgeos to his father's hearths,
The young Telephus felt the wound from Achilles' spear,
   then experienced relief by this very weapon.
Anyone who is capable of excising my disease, only he   65
   will be able to press fruits in Tantalus' hands;
Likewise, he will refill the storage jars from the maidens'° urns,
   halting the weighty torment to necks tender from constant water
      bearing;
He will also untie the arms of Prometheus from the Caucasus rock
   and drive out the bird from his chest.   70
So, when the Fates claim my life
   and I become a little name on a small marble tomb-slab,
Maecenas, hope and envy of our youth,
   my just boast in life and in death,
If you should chance to pass close to my tomb,   75
   stop your chariot with its carved yoke, imported from Britain,
And there shed a tear and to my unresponding ashes, utter something
   like this:
"Here lies a man whose doom was a hard-hearted girl."

2.5

Is this true, Cynthia, that you flit about all of Rome
   living a scandalous, shameless life?
I have not deserved this; I expected better. I'll make you pay, you liar!
   For us, too, Cynthia, the north wind will blow.
Still, out of the many false women I'll find one   5
   who will want to win fame in my song.
She will not trample on me with a bitchy nature like yours, but will
      sting you;
   too late you will weep, you whom I have loved for so long.
Now while my anger is fresh, now is the time to part;
   when the pain passes, believe me, love will return.   10
Not so fickle are the waves of the Carpathian Sea under north winds,
   nor veers a black cloud, swept by shifting gusts from the south,

---

2.1.59-60: Machaon, the master surgeon of the Greeks at Troy, healed the wound
   of Philoctetes who had been bitten by a snake on the passage to Troy. Chiron,
   the centaur son of Philyra, cured the blindness of Phoenix.
2.1.67-68: the maidens are the Danaids.

As angry lovers with ease change at a single word:
    while there is still time, slip your neck from the oppressive yoke.
It will hurt—some—, but only on that first night;   15
    in love every pain is mild, if you just endure.
But you, my life, by the sweet rights of Lady Juno
    be careful not to let that hauteur of yours harm you.
Not only bulls hook and gore their foe;
    for even a wounded sheep counterattacks its attacker.   20
Now, I'll not rip the clothes from your cheating body,
    nor in my rage will I smash through your bolted doors,
Nor in anger would I dare to yank your carefully braided hair,
    nor brutalize and bruise you with my thumbs.
No, some clod can engage in those ugly brawls   25
    whose head no ivy has ever crowned.°
For me, I'll write what time will never erase as long as you live:
    "Cynthia, a mighty beauty; Cynthia, liar and cheat."
Believe me, however much you scorn the whispers of scandal,
    this one verse, Cynthia, will make you pale.   30

2.7

Certainly Cynthia was happy: the law was repealed:°
    when it was enacted both of us wept and wept,
Fearing that it might split us up; to separate two lovers
    against their will Jupiter himself is impotent.
"But Caesar is mighty." Yes, Caesar is mighty in war: 5
    but in love, conquered peoples don't count at all.
Sooner I would suffer this head severed from my neck
    than I would waste the fires of love on a bride,
Or, as a married man, I would pass your closed thresholds,
    looking back with moist eyes at the doors I betrayed.   10
Ah, my flute would serenade your sleeps—such as they be—
    wedding flute, an instrument more mournful than a funeral's
        trumpet.
How can I breed sons for our country's triumphs?
    No soldier will ever come from my blood.

2.5.26: a garland of ivy marked poets.
2.7.1: the law referred to is part of legislation that Augustus introduced first in
    28. The outcry against the proposed law on marriage caused Augustus to
    revise and modify the provisions that were enacted later under three other
    laws. The idea behind the legislation was to force the upper-class to marry
    and produce children by providing economic incentives and by imposing
    ruinous penalties for those who chose to remain unmarried.

But if I were serving my girl, the real war-camp,   15
    then not even Castor's horse° would prance great enough for me.
From her my glory has won me renown swelling my pride,
    renown extending to the wintry people of the Dnieper.
You are my only love, Cynthia; I hope I am yours:
    this love will mean more to me than the name of any ancestor.   20

2.8

My girl whom I love has been stolen from me;
    and you, friend, begrudge me a flood of tears?
No enmities, except love's, are bitter:
    cut my throat, I'll be a more understanding enemy.
Am I to bear watching her lean on another man's shoulder?   5
    She who once was said to be mine now will not be called mine.
All things revolve: definitely love changes;
    you lose some, you win some: this is the wheel of love.
Often mighty leaders, mighty tyrants have fallen,
    Thebes once stood and lofty Troy was—once.   10
How many gifts I gave her, what poems I composed!
    Yet she, the iron maiden, not once said: "I love you."
For too many years I was a rash fool, putting up with you,
    bitch, and with your household.
Have you ever thought of me as free, not some servant   15
    upon whose head you cast abusive words?
So, Propertius, are you to die in your prime?
    But yet, die, so she may exult in your passing!
Let her hound my shades, haunt my shadowy spirit,
    dance on my pyre, trample on my bones.   20
On Antigone's tomb Haemon of Boeotia collapsed,°
    mortally wounded by his own sword;
He mingled his bones with the bones of his girl;
    without her he refused to return home to Thebes.
But you will not escape; you too must die;   25
    the gore of both of us will drip from the very same sword.
Though my death will be dishonorable,
    a truly shameful death, still you will die.
Even great Achilles, left alone, after his girl was seized,°
    endured in his tent, his arms rusting;   30

2.7.16: Castor and his brother Pollux were famous for horsemanship and were
    the tutelary gods of the Equestrian class in Rome.
2.8.21: Haemon, the son of Creon, king of Thebes, committed suicide when he
    discovered Antigone, daughter of Oedipus and his fiancé, dead.
2.8.29-38: summarizes about two-thirds of the *Iliad*.

He watched the Greeks scattered in flight along the shore,
　he watched the seething of the Dorian camp torched by Hector;
He saw Patroclus mudspattered, stretched out dead on the sand,
　his hair matted and bloodied—
All this he endured for the sake of lovely Briseis,　　　　　　35
　so great was the pain that raged over his lost love;
But when at long last she was returned to him as recompense,
　he dragged the brave Hector behind his Thessalian stallions.
I really can't compete with him either in mother or in battle;
　is it any wonder that Love naturally triumphs over me?　　　40

2.12

Whoever he was who painted Love as a boy,
　don't you think he had marvelous, creative hands?
He was the first to imagine lovers living without scheme
　and squandering great fortunes on fickle desires.
He aptly added windy wings　　　　　　　　　　　　　　5
　to hover in the hearts of humans;
So we are tossed about from wave to shifting wave,
　and the breeze does not persist for us, steady in one spot.
He was right, too, to arm his hand with barbed arrows
　and to sling a Cretan quiver across the shoulders.　　　　10
Until the sniper strikes, we feel safe, not perceiving him as enemy;
　no one walks away clean from his wound.
In me the weapons stick; that image of the boy stays;
　yet he has lost his wings for sure,
Since from my heart he does not fly elsewhere,　　　　　　15
　and in my blood he wages unceasing wars.
What fun do you get residing in dried-up bone marrow?
　Shame on you! Hurl your arrows at someone else.
You should try those uninfected by your poison;
　it is not I, but the wispy shadow of myself that is being flogged;　20
If you destroy me, who will sing songs like this,
　(this slender muse of mine is your great glory),
Who will elegize her head, her fingers, her dark eyes,
　how nimbly my girl's feet are wont to go?

2.15

O happy me! O shining night, O little bed,
　scene of my dreamy delight!
How many stories we told by flickering lamplight,
　what a great brawl there was when we put out the light.
One moment with nipples naked she wrestled me,　　　　　5
　then with her tunic as cover she balked;

She opened my eyes that had slipped off to sleep
    with a kiss and murmured: "Why lie so—sluggish?"
Shifting our arms, we made new embraces; how long
    my kisses lingered upon your lips!   10
It's no fun seducing and then spoiling Venus in blind rumbling;
    if you're curious: in love eyes are the best guides.
Why, Paris himself, they say, perished at the sight of Helen nude
    rising up from Menelaus' bed;
Endymion naked aroused Apollo's sister°   15
    and lay with the goddess nude.
So if you have an idea of stretching out with clothes on,
    my hands will tear them into shreds;
And if I'm provoked to too much anger,
    you will have bruised arms to show your mother.   20
Sagging breasts don't yet stop you from playing,
    that's the shame of one who has already given birth.
While the fates grant us leave, let us feast our eyes on love;
    a long night is approaching and day will not return.
As we cling together like this, bind us with a chain   25
    that no day could ever dissolve.
Take the pattern of a pair of mating doves,
    male and female in perfect union:
He is wrong who seeks to set bounds to the madness of love;
    true love knows not how to keep any limit.   30
Sooner the earth will fool the plowing farmer with false fruits,
    the sun spur on black horses,
The rivers begin to call back their waters to the source,
    and fish lie parched on a dry ocean bed,
Than I would have the guts to transfer our pains elsewhere.   35
    Hers I will be so long as I live, hers I will be in death.
But if to me she grants such nights with her as this,
    a year will be a lifetime;
If she bestows many, I'll live eternal,
    when in a single night any man would be a god.   40
Should all men desire to wind down in an easy life,
    to lie resting their limbs drunken after much wine,
There would be no savage sword, no ship of war,
    the sea waves of Actium would not be churning our bones,
Nor Rome, beleaguered by self-inflicted triumphs,   45
    would be drained from tearing out hair in mourning:°

2.15.15: Diana, Apollo's sister, visited the shepherd Endymion in the dark during
    the period between the old and new moon.
2.15.45-46: refer to Rome's numerous civil wars fought in the first century,
    including that between Octavius and Antony.

Then, no doubt, coming generations will justly praise us,
    that our cups offended no gods.
While daylight lasts, don't neglect the fruit of life;
    all the kisses you give me will still be too few.   50
As petals from the drying garlands fall
    and float, visible, scattered here and there in the wine bowls,
So for us, who dare draw deep breath—alive to make love—
    perhaps tomorrow's day will close in our death.

2.16

The praetor has just arrived, Cynthia, from somewhere in Illyria:°
    huge profit for you, big trouble for me.
If he'd lost his life on some rock of Mt. Ceraunia,
    ah, Neptune, I'd be lavishing you with a flood of gifts!
Now there are parties going on, food and drink galore—but not for
        me;   5
    now all night long his door lies open—but not for me.
So, if you are clever, don't let the tendered fruits slip away;
    fleece the fool, a sheep with a prime coat for shearing;
Then, when he has exhausted his cash and stands a pauper,
    tell him to sail off to other Illyrias.   10
Cynthia does not court the axes of power nor care for political offices;
    as no other does, she always weighs her lover's wallet.
But you, Venus, help me now in my distress,
    make him bust his balls in non-stop sex!
So then love is for sale, on the market for gifts;   15
    Jupiter, my girl ruins herself, sold for shoddy gifts.
She's always sending me to look for pearls in the Persian Gulf,
    and orders me to fetch presents from Tyre.
I wish there were not a single rich man in Rome, and our leader
    lived in a hut of wattle and daub with a thatched roof.   20
Girl friends would not then put themselves up for sale for a gift,
    and a girl would grow gray in the same house;
Never would you sleep apart for a whole week,
    while embracing in your lovely arms a man so foul;
And I have done nothing wrong—I swear that to you—   25
    but beautiful girls have always been a friendly mix with infidelity.
The barbarian paces to and fro,° shut out along with his prick,
    and suddenly he's lucky enough to usurp my kingdom!

2.16.1: after a year in office the praetor often served as a governor of a prov-
    ince.
2.16.27: Propertius depicts his rival as a former slave on the block.

Note what bitter pain Eriphyle found in presents;
  and the torments the bride Creusa° suffered when she was burned
    alive.   30
Will no outrageous conduct of yours calm my weeping?
  Or does this pain of mine know not how to escape betrayals?
Many days have passed since I have felt any desire for the theater
  or Campus Martius; not even a good spread tempts me.
Shame, yes, shame on me, unless, as they say,   35
  disgraceful love falls upon deaf ears.
Mark the general, who has lately filled with useless cries°
  the waters off Actium for his doomed men:
His infamous love prompted him to turn his ships and his back
  in flight and seek escape at the end of the world.   40
This was Caesar's test of courage, this Caesar's glory,
  that with the very hand he conquered, he buried his weapons.
I'd like to see all those gifts of clothes, emeralds,
  and topaz of golden gleam,
Wafted into empty space by swooping storm-winds,   45
  and that you find some of them turned to earth and some to water.
A calm Jove does not always laugh at perjured lovers,
  overlook their prayers, and turn a deaf ear.
You have seen thunder rolling through the sky
  and lightning-bolts dance from their ethereal home.   50
Neither the Pleiades nor rainy Orion cause them,
  nor does the angry thunderbolt fall for no reason;
At such times he is usually punishing lying girls,
  since he, too, although a god, has wept after he was deceived.
Therefore, don't value a dress from Sidon° so highly as   55
  to fear every time the sirocco gathers a cloud.

2.19

Although against my will, Cynthia, you are departing Rome without
  me,
  I am glad that you will be visiting out-of-the-way spots in the
    country.

2.16.29: Eriphyle was bribed by Polyneices to convince her husband, the seer
  Amphiareus, to join the ill-fated expedition of the Seven against Thebes.
2.16.30: Creusa is the usual name given the princess of Corinth whom Jason
  married. The jilted Medea had a poisoned robe sent to Creusa which killed
  her when she put it on.
2.16.37-40: refer to Mark Antony, Cleopatra, and Octavius' victory over them
  at Actium in 31.
2.16.55: like Tyre, Sidon in Phoenicia was famous for its dyed garments.

There in pure fields no young seducer will appear
   to coax you, ruining your upright name;
Before your windows no brawling will start   5
   nor will shouts, hailing you, sour your sleep.
You will be alone, Cynthia, and you will gaze at lonely hills,
   and sheep, and the fields of a poor farmer;
There no games can corrupt you,
   no temples—a frequent cause of your wandering ways.°   10
There you will watch the bulls laboriously plowing,
   and with skilled hook the vine being pruned and dressed of its
      leaves;
And there you will bring incense to an unadorned, seldom-visited
      shrine,
   where a kid will fall before the rustic altars.
Then you can bare your thighs and imitate the local dances,   15
   provided everything is protected from some interloper.
I'll go hunting myself! Now I want to take up the sacred rites
   of Diana° and lay aside Venus' worship.
I'll start tracking wild game and affixing their horns on a pine tree
   as trophies, and tallyho the hot-pursuing hounds;   20
Not that I'd dare to stalk huge lions
   or rush to go *mano a mano* with wild boars.
Yet I'm brave enough to trap gentle hares,
   and with a sectioned rod stick a bird,
Where Clitumnus and his grove shade his beautiful waters,   25
   washing the snow white bulls;
And you, my life, if you try something, remember:
   I'll be there in a few dawns.
Here, not the lonely woods nor the twisting brooks
   that pour from mossy hills could ward me off,   30
But will hear me echoing your name again and again;
   for when a lover is away, everyone is out to poach upon his
      bailiwick.

2.25

Unique, my most beautiful source of trouble, she was born to bring
      me pain;
   since my lot in life excludes the phrase: "Come often,"
My elegies will glorify that famous beauty of yours—
   your pardon, Calvus, by your leave, Catullus.°

2.19.10: apparently Cynthia has used temples for romantic rendezvous.
2.19.18: Diana is the goddess of the hunt.
2.25.4: Calvus and Catullus are famous predecessors of Propertius whose lovers
   parallel Cynthia.

The veteran lays down his weapons and sleeps alone,   5
    the aged oxen refuse to pull plows,
On an empty beach the ship rests and rots from disuse,
    and an old shield, once warlike, now vacations in a temple.
But old age will never rob me of my love for you,
    be I as long-lived as Tithonus or as Nestor.   10
I would have been better off the slave of a cruel tyrant
    and bellowing, savage Perillus, in your bull;
Better, too, to be turned to stone after one look from a Gorgon,
    or even to suffer the vultures of the Caucasus.
Yet I will resist. Rust corrodes the iron blade,   15
    and often, too, a steady drip of water wears away flint;
But no threshold of a lover wears down love,
    no, it stays and endures the threats it didn't deserve to hear.
Jilted, the lover asks for more and confesses he did wrong,
    when he himself was wronged, and he keeps coming back on
        reluctant feet.
Now as for you who put on arrogant airs, smug in your fulfilling
    love,   21
naïve you are, for no woman is stable.
Does anyone pay vows in the middle of a storm
    when a smashed ship often bobbles in a harbor?
Or claim winnings before the race is over   25
    and his chariot wheels have seven times° skillfully shimmed the
        turning post?
In love favorable breezes trick and lie:
    mighty is the fall, if it comes late.
You there, in the meantime, although she may love you dearly,
    keep your joys locked up tight in a silent heart.   30
You see, in love somehow, some way, a man's
    biggest boasts come back to hurt him.
Although she invites you often, remember, go only once;
    for if it incites envy, it usually doesn't last.
But if the ways and customs existed today which pleased the girls of
    yesteryear,
    I'd be what you are now: the times defeat me.   36
This damned age will never change my habits;
    every man will know how to pursue his own path.
But those of you who again and again summon up your services for
    many loves,
    what pain torments your eyes.   40

2.25.26: a chariot race normally ran for seven laps.

You have seen a young girl, pretty, pure, and of delicate skin;
    you have seen one dark: both colors are attractive.
You have seen a Greek beauty stroll by,
    you have seen our Roman girls: either form captivates you.
She may be dressed drab and plain or in scarlet: 45
    either one is a sure road to trouble and hurt.
Since a single girl is all you need to bring you insomniac eyes,
    one woman is trouble enough for any man.

2.26A

I saw you, my darling, in a dream, shipwrecked,
    dragging your weary hands in the Ionian deep,
Confessing every falsehood leveled at me,
    unable to lift your water-weary hair,
Tossed in the dark waves like Helle   5
    whom the golden ram carried on its fleecy back.
O how I feared some sea someday would bear your name,
    and the sailor gliding over your waters would weep.
I prayed to Neptune, Castor and his brother,
    and to you, Leucothoe, recently a goddess.   10
But, barely stretching your fingertips above the engulfing water,
    as you were sinking, you often called my name.
If by chance Glaucus had seen those dear eyes,
    instantly you would have become "The Girl of the Ionian Sea,"
And the Nereids, white Nesaee and blue Cymothoe,   15
    out of jealousy would be taunting you.
But then I saw a dolphin speed to help you,
    the very same one, I believe, that had once rescued the lyre of
        Arion.
High on a rock I was readying to hurl myself down,
    when my terror shattered this nightmare.   20

2.31°

You ask why I come to you so late? Phoebus'
    golden portico has just been opened by mighty Caesar.
It was quite a spectacle: African columns aligned in rows;
    between them the whole female gang of old Danaus.
Then there appeared before my eyes Phoebus in marble, more
        beautiful   5
    than the god himself, gaping a song on a silent lyre.
Around the altar stood four bulls, the herd
    of the artist Myron, statues that breathed life.

2.31: Cf. Horace, *Odes* 1.31.

There in the middle bright with marble soared the temple,
    more precious to the god than his native Delos;   10
High on the gable was the chariot of the Sun;
    the doors were double, splendid work of Libyan ivory,
One depicted the Gauls dislodged from Parnassus' peak,°
    the other Niobe mourning over her dead children.
Then between his mother and sister the god himself,   15
    the Pythian in long garb resounding his songs.

2.33

They're back again, those rites so dismal for us:
    ten nights of worship now Cynthia fulfills.
Damn those sacred rituals that from the balmy Nile Io
    (Inachus' girl) imported for Italian matrons,
A goddess who has so often split lustful lovers,   5
    whoever she was, she was a bitter dreg.
In your secret love affair with Jove, as Io, you surely
    learnt what it is like to set out on many journeys.
For Juno gave you, still a girl, the order to sprout horns
    and to spoil your human speech with a heifer's harsh lowing.   10
You galled your mouth on oak leaves
    and chewed a cud of wild strawberry in your stall—wherever—
But, since Jupiter has erased that rustic look from your face,
    is it for this reason that you have become an arrogant goddess?
Aren't you satisfied with Egypt's dusky children?   15
    Why did you ever take the long road to Rome?
What do you possibly gain, if girls sleep without men?
    Believe me, horns you'll receive again;
Or we will rout you from our city, damn beast;
    Tiber and Nile have never been a friendly mix.   20
But you, Cynthia , our pain has already overly appeased,
    for these nights we have lost, let us triple the journey of love.
You do not listen; you let my words slip by, while the oxen
    of Icarius already bend the lingering stars around the pole.
You drink on, indifferent; the midnight hours fail to break you;   25
    will your hand never tire of rolling dice?
Damn him, whoever he was, who discovered clusters of pure grapes
    and who first tainted water's innocence with divine wine.
Served you right, Icarius, when Attic farm folk slit your throat;
    you learned well that the grape-leaf's bouquet is bitter;   30

2.31.13: in 278 a group of Gauls led by Brennus attacked Delphi, but were
    repulsed.

And you, Centaur Eurytion, died because of wine,
    and you, too, Polyphemus, from strong Ismarian.
Wine ruins beauty, wine destroys youth;
    in wine a lover often fails to know her man.
O poor me, even after many glasses of Bacchus' brew she has not
       budged.   35
    Drink on! You're beautiful, wines become you!
Your garlands wilt and droop in your beakers,
    and you read my poems in a well-spun voice.
Pour out a Falernian varietal, slosh and soak the table,
    and in your golden goblet top off the delicate foam.   40
Yet no girl retires to bed alone by choice;
    there is one thing that Love compels you to seek.
Always love's heat will teem more powerfully for an absent lover;
    constant access breeds contempt for ever-present men.

2.34

Why now would anyone entrust a beautiful sweetheart to Amor?
    That's how he almost snatched my girl from me.
I speak from experience: in love no one can be trusted;
    rarely does any man not go after a pretty girl for himself.
That god pollutes relatives and divides friends,   5
    and provokes colleagues to bitter arms.
The guest who came to Menelaus' hospitality was an adulterer;°
    and Medea of Colchis followed a foreigner.
Lynceus,° you liar, you had the gall to touch
    my love; at that point didn't your hands drop?   10
It's good that she stood firm, loyal, and unfaltering;
    how could you have lived otherwise in so much shame?
Run a blade through my chest, end my life with poison,
    but keep yourself away from my woman.
Share my life, be ally of my body,   15
    I entitle you, my friend, to all my business:
Only from my bed I beg you refrain, just this one bed I ask;
    I cannot even bear the thought of Jupiter as a rival.
When I am alone, I am jealous of my own shadow, a mere nothing,
    fool that I am, I tremble and shake with baseless fear.   20
Yet there is a single reason why I excuse your criminal behavior:
    your words rambled off course because you drank too much wine.

2.34.7: the adulterer is Paris.
2.34.9: Lynceus is a fellow poet and friend of Propertius who has made advances
    upon Cynthia. He has dabbled in philosophy (27), astronomy (28, and 51-54),
    tragedy (29-30 and 41), and epical mythology (33-40).

But never will your frowning wrinkle and your prudish life deceive
    me:
  everyone knows by now how sweet it is to love.
My good buddy himself, Lynceus, rages, reeling in love—at last.   25
    I'm delighted to welcome you of all people to our gods.
Now what good to you is all that knowledge from Socratic dialogues?
    Or to be able to declaim on the nature of the universe?
Or what good is that poetry, 'Selected Works from Athens?'
    Deep in love your old fuddy-duddy provides no pleasure.°   30
You should model yourself on Philetas, the Muses' favorite,
    and on the dreams of the unpretentious Callimachus.
So, although you sing again the story of how vast love
    broke the flow of Archelous,
And how the loops of the Menander, convoluted on the Phrygian
    plain,   35
    trick and deceive the direction of its labyrinthine channels,
Of Arion, the talking steed of Adrastus that mourned the funeral
    of Archemorus,° though he was the victorious horse,
The fate of Amphiareus' chariot and the crash of Capeneus
    that pleased Jove won't help you a bit.   40
Stop composing your verses for the tragic buskin of Aeschylus,
    stop it; loosen your limbs in step with gentler dances.
Begin now to forge your poems on a narrow anvil,
    come, stern poet, come to your own fires.
You will fare no better than Antimachus or even Homer: 45
    a shapely girl despises mighty gods.
As a bull does not yield to the heavy plow
    until you lock his horns in strong nooses,
So you will not endure, unaided, loves so painful;
    yet, still wild, we'll have to break you in.   50
No girl really wants to know the universe's imperative;
    why the moon eclipses before her brother's horses;
Whether we survive as something beyond the waters of the Styx;
    if thunder and crashing lightning have a meaning.
Just look at me, no family fortune was left to me,   55
    no grandfather celebrated a triumph in war fought long ago;
But here I am king of banquets, crowded by girls, all around me—
    by that very talent which you scorn.
I like languishing, buried in yesterday's garlands,
    touched to the bone by the shaft of the unerring god.   60

2.34.30: perhaps a reference to Aratus.
2.34.37-38: the infant Archemorus was the first to die in the campaign against
    Thebes.

Vergil can sing of Actium's shores where Apollo keeps watch°
   and of the courageous galleys of Caesar;
He is now arousing Trojan Aeneas to arms,
   and the walls being built on the Lavinian beaches:°
Make way you Roman poets, make way you Greeks,   65
   something greater than the *Iliad* is coming to birth.
You, Vergil, sing too of Thyrsis and Daphnis wearing away their
      pipes in song°
beneath the pines that shade the Galaesus river;
And how ten apples can seduce girls,
   so too a kid just weaned from suckling udders.   70
Lucky you who with ten apples barter love at bargain prices!
   Even Tityrus himself could afford to sing to a rejecting girl;
Lucky is Corydon who attempts to pluck the virgin fruits
   of Alexis, the sweetheart of a farmer;
He may rest tired out from his piping on oaten reed,   75
   yet among the good-natured woodland nymphs he is exalted.
You, yes, you, Vergil, sing the precepts of the ancient poet of Ascra:
   the best soil for wheat to grow green, the best slope for the grape.
Your poetry on the artful lyre is like the music
   of Apollo himself strumming over the strings.   80
But a reader will come upon something pleasing to him
   in these my verses, be he crude or skilled in love.
For I, like the melodious swan, though less in volume, but no less
   in creative powers, out-sing the untrained goose.°
Here, Varro, after Jason's quest was ended, sported,   85
   Varro, ablaze with flames for his Leucadia.
So lascivious Catullus sang these same themes;
   because of him Lesbia out-Helens Helen herself;
And the pages of learned Calvus confessed in song
   the funeral rites of lost Quintilia;   90
And Gallus, just now dead, in the waters of the underworld bathes
   his many wounds, still smarting from beautiful Lycoris.
Cynthia too is praised in the verse of Propertius—
   if fame will kindly put me among this company.

2.34.61: refers to the temple of Apollo at Leucas, the island that overlooks
   Actium.
2.34.63-64: allude to the opening lines of Vergil's *Aeneid*.
2.34.67-80: Propertius selects themes first from the *Eclogues* and then the *Geor-*
   gics.
2.34.83-84: a notorious crux in Propertius. I have provided one possible read-
   ing. The controversy revolves around the symbolic meaning(s) of the swan
   and goose.

3.1

Shades of Callimachus and sacred rites of Philetas of Cos,
  permit me, I beg, to enter into your cultic grove.
For I am the first to step from the clear spring, a priest
  consecrated to bring Italic mysteries via Greek dances.
Speak, what cave was it where you modulated your refined song?   5
  With what foot did you enter? What water drink?
Good riddance to him who wastes Apollo's time detaining him in
    arms!
  Let your verse go smooth and polished by pumice.
That's why Fame lifts me from the earth on high, while my offspring,
  the muse, rides in triumph on garlanded horses;   10
And with me in the chariot sit six pixie Cupids,
  as a crush of poets follows behind my wheels.
Why do you rush out so fast in competing against me—in vain?
  No one speeds on a broad road in the race to the muses.
Many others, O Rome, will add to your glory in their annals;   15
  they will sing that in time to come Bactria will mark the boundary
    of empire.
My page has brought down from the mountain of the sister Muses
  by a route untrod the work you now read in peace.
Pegasids,° offer tender garlands of flowers to your poet;
  a hard crown does not suit my head.   20
Whatever the envious mob begrudges me in life,
  fame will repay with double interest after death;
In death the passage of long time renders all things magnified;
  after the funeral rites one's name comes greater to the lips.
Who would not know of the towers battered by a wooden horse,   25
  the rivers grappling hand to hand with the Thessalian hero,°
The Simois flowing from Mount Ida, or Scamander, child of Jove,
  and the wheels that defiled Hector three times over the plains.
Their own land would hardly know of Deiphobus, Helenus,
    Polydamas,
  and Paris° (such as he was) in arms.   30
A theme of little substance, small talk, you would be now, Ilion,
  and you, Troy, captured twice by the divine power of Oeta's god;°

3.1.19: the Pegasids are a reference to the Muses; the spring of Hippocrene on
  Mt. Helicon where the Muses dwelled was storied to have sprung from a rock
  struck by a hoof of Pegasus, the winged horse tamed by Bellerophon.
3.1.26: a reference to Achilles who fought the Simois and Scamander rivers near
  Troy.
3.1.29: lists prominent Trojans well known from the *Iliad* and epic cycle.
3.1.32: Oeta's god is Hercules.

But Homer, that poetic preserver of your fall,
   has felt his work grow great with time.
Rome too will honor me among her grandsons yet unborn;   35
   I solemnly prophesy that day, when I am ashes;
No stone will mark my bones in a forgotten tomb—
   that has been ordained, my vows approved by Lycian Apollo.°

3.3

I dreamed I was lying in the gentle shade of Helicon,
   where flowed the stream of Pegasus, Bellerophon's horse.
For your kings, Alba, the exploits of your rulers,
   so huge a task, I strained my mouth with all my powers;
I put my puny lips to those mighty springs   5
   where father Ennius had once before quenched his thirst,
Singing of Curii brothers and the pikes of the Horatii,°
   the trophies won from a king paraded on Aemilius' ship,
The victorious strategy of Fabius, the Delayer, the ill-starred defeat
   at Cannae, and the gods who turned to hear our devout prayers, 10
The Lares routing Hannibal from the hearth of Rome,
   and Jove saved by the voice of a goose;
But Phoebus Apollo spotting me from a tree near Castalia's grottoes
   leaned on his golden lyre and spoke to me:
"What right have you, demented fool, to a stream like this?   15
   Who gave you orders to touch upon the poetry of heroic labor?
You cannot hope to win any fame here, Propertius:
   your small wheels should crush delicate meadows,
So your slender volume may be tossed on a bench
   to be read by a lonely girl who waits for her lover.   20
The verses on your page have gone careening off the right tracks,
   and you should not overload the canoe of your talent.
One oar should skim the water, the other graze the sands; that way
   you will be safe: in the middle of the sea is the roughest turmoil."
He spoke, and with his ivory plectrum motioned me to a seat   25
   along a path, newly made from the mossy earth.
Here was a verdant grotto, studded with a mosaic of tiny stones,
   and tambourines hung from rusticated domed rocks,
Sacred objects of the Muses, the image of father Silenus
   fashioned in clay, and your pipes, Arcadian Pan;   30
And birds of mistress Venus, my folk, the doves,
   dipped their red beaks in the Gorgonean° lake;

3.1.38: Apollo had a famous temple at Patara in Lycia.
3.3.7-12: these lines include themes from Ennius' *Annales*.
3.3.32: Propertius alludes to Hippocrene, formed by Pegasus, offspring of the
   gorgon Medusa.

And the nine maidens, each allotted her own jurisdiction,
  were plying their gentle hands to their proper gifts:
One gathering ivy for the sacred staffs, one tuning her songs to the
      lyre's   35
  strings, and another with both hands weaving a garland of roses.
One of these goddesses put her hand upon me
  (From her looks, I think it was Calliope):
"You will be content, if you always travel on snow-white swans;
  never let the thundering hooves of a war horse lead you to battle.40
It is not for you to blast on the loud trumpet the summons to arms,
  or to dye the Aonian grove with Mars' gore,
Or to relate the fields where under the standard of Marius
  stood firm the lines and Rome smashed the Teutonic power,
Or how the barbarian Rhine dyed through with German blood   45
  swept along in its sorrowful stream the mangled bodies.
No! you will sing of garlanded lovers at another's threshold,
  the drunken signs of a rout at night;
Through you the lover will learn the spells that charm girls
  behind locked doors, even how (with panache) to outwit surly
      husbands."   50
So stated Calliope, and with water drawn from the spring
  where Philetas once drank, she bathed my lips.

3.4°

God Caesar is pondering war against wealthy India,
  splitting with his fleet the straits of the sea rich in pearls.
Men, great is the reward; the world's end is already preparing the
      triumphal processions;
  both Tigris and Euphrates will flow beneath your power.
It will come late, but it will happen, a new province for Italian *fasces*. 5
  Parthian trophies will become inured to Latin Jove.
Come, onward! Set your sails on a ship well-tried in war,
  and you, horses decked in armour, do your duty!
I sing, the omens are good! Atone for Crassus, atone for the defeat.
  Go, and take thought for Rome's history.   10
Father Mars, and fateful fires of sacred Vesta,°
  I pray that day may come before I pass away,

3.4.1: an amusing and skillful adaptation of the *recusatio*. After heralding Augustus' glorious triumphs of future campaigns, Propertius will contribute applause as he watches them with his girl.
3.4.11: the Vestal Virgins saw to keeping a fire lit in the small temple of Vesta in the Roman Forum.

When I may behold Caesar's wheels heaped with spoils of war,
   his horses stopping to pause for the crowd's applause;
And I, leaning on the bosom of my darling, will watch   15
   and read from the placards the names of captured cities;
I'll look upon the weapons of the mount swift in flight-tactics, the
      bows
   of the trousered soldier and the captive chieftains seated beneath
       their arms.
You, o Venus, protect your offspring for the rest of time,
   keep forever the stock you now see surviving from Aeneas.°   20
Let this booty be theirs whose toils have earned it;
   I'll be content enough to clap my hands on the Sacred Way.

3.8

How sweet it was! That brawl yesterday beside lamp after lamp,
   that dirty-talking from your crazy lips,°
When in a drunken rage you shoved away the table
   and with insane hand hurled at me brimming goblets.
Come, show some guts, attack my hair,   5
   rake my cheeks with your beautiful nails,
Grab coals aflame and threaten to burn out my eyes,
   rip off my tunic from my body and bare my chest!
Surely these are tell-tale signs of love's true heat,
   for no lady ever smarts except from oppressive love;   10
The woman who spits out insults from a rabid tongue
   grovels at the feet of mighty Venus,
Around her as she goes throng flocks of "bodyguards,"
   or, like an enthused Maenad, she haunts the streets;
Frequent nightmares terrorize her timid soul,   15
   or a girl portrayed in a painting affects her.
Of these kinds of delusions I am a true diviner:
   I have learned that the signs of true love are often these.
In love no trust is guaranteed unless you provoke it to quarrels:
   to my enemies may a girl turn out to be frigid.   20
Let my peers see the gashes bitten on my neck;
   may a bruise prove that I have had it out with her.
Either I want to feel the pain of love or hear you are suffering,
   or to feel my own tears or to see you crying,
Whenever your eyebrows send me back a coded message   25
   or your fingers trace words that best remain unspoken.

3.4.19-20: see note to 2.1.42.
3.8.2: lit: "the abuse from your frenzied mouth."

I hate sighs that never puncture sleep;
    may I always be pale because of an angry lover.
The fire of love for Paris was sweeter, when in delicious combat
    he serviced and pleasured Helen who then was his;   30
While the Greeks were winning, while savage Hector resisted,
    he waged his most glorious battles in the lap of Helen.
Either with you or with rivals, for your sake I'll always war;
    with you I desire no peace.
Go on, be happy, for no other is as beautiful: you'd be upset,   35
    it there were one; but for now you can go proud.
But for you, who have woven and spread nets for our bed,
    may your father-in-law live forever, and your house come with a
        mother.
If you were ever granted the resources of a stolen night,
    she gave them as an insult to me, not as a pleasure to you.   40

3.9

Maecenas, equestrian from the blood of Etruscan kings,
    zealous to stay within your own rank,
Why do you launch me onto a sea of writing so vast?
    Huge sails are not fit for my boat.
It is a disgrace to entrust to the head a load unbearable   5
    and then, overloaded, buckle at the knees, and turn tail.
Not everyone is equally comfortable with every theme,
    and not just one prize is won from the same summit.
Lysippus wins glory by sculpting statues that breathe,°
    to me Calamis trumpets his exquisite horses;   10
Apelles claims his fame in his picture of Venus;
    Parrhasius wins first place for his miniatures;
Mythic subjects adorn most of Mentor's designs;
    but Mys scrolls acanthus in a narrow band;
Phidias' Jupiter dresses himself in ivory;   15
    marble from his own city advertizes Praxiteles.
Some contend in the prize-winning chariot of Elis,
    others are destined to gain glory by running fast.
One man is born for peace, another fit for the weapons of the military
        camps:
    each man pursues the seeds sown by his own nature.   20
But I have absorbed your rules of life, Maecenas,
    so, I am compelled to refute you by the examples you yourself set.

3.9.9-16: eight Greek artists illustrate Propertius' point of the preceding couplet.

Although you may post the imperial axes in office at Rome
    and issue law in the middle of the forum;
Or march through the hostile spears of the Medes,   25
    and nail up trophies to grace your home;
And Caesar may strengthen your success, and wealth
    with ease snake into your pockets already bulging,
Yet you restrain yourself and retreat humbly to modest shadows,
    and tack your billowing sails.   30
Believe me, that judgment will make you equal with the mightiest
    Camilli:
    and you, too, will be heralded on the lips of men;
You will match, step with step, the fame of Caesar,
    Loyalty will be Maecenas' true memorial.
As for me, I don't cut across the swelling sea in a ship bellying under
    sail;   35
    I dally all my days on a shallow stream.
I'll not bemoan Cadmus' citadel collapsed on ancestral ashes,
    nor the seven battles that ended in mutual slaughter;°
And I'll not repeat the story of Scaean gates, of Pergama, Apollo's
    citadel,
    the return of the Greek armada in the tenth spring of war,   40
When the victorious wooden horse, designed by Pallas' art,
    with a Greek plow smashed and leveled Neptune's walls.
For me I'll be content to bring delight in company with the small
    works
    of Callimachus and to sing, divine poet, in your meters.
May these poems of mine set boys afire, may they set girls afire,   45
    to proclaim me a god and to offer sacrifices to me.
Lead on, Maecenas; I'll sing of Jove's arms, Coeus' threat
    to heaven, the Giant Oromedon's attempt upon Phlegra's heights;
I'll weave in the lofty summits of the Palatine cropped by Rome's
    bulls,°
    and its walls fortified by Remus' murder;   50
I will chant: "Troy, you fall, but you, Trojan Rome, will rise from its
    ashes;"
    and I'll sing of the many burials on land and sea,
Of the pair of kings nursed by an udder from the forest;
    my talent will grow to your command;
I'll extol chariots in triumph from shore to distant shore,   55
    Parthian arrows shot back in clever flight,

3.9.38: a reference to the Seven against Thebes.
3.9.49-58: references to the story of Rome's foundation and topics in recent Ro-
man history, particularly regarding Antony.

The fort at Pelusium overwhelmed by the Roman sword,
  and the heavy hands of Antony bringing his own doom.
Be the supporter of my early manhood; take the gentle reins
  and with your hand signal my speeding wheels.   60
You grant me this distinction, and by your leave I gain
  the renown of being in your coterie.

3.11

Why are you surprised that a woman manipulates my life
  and drags me into her power like an indentured servant?
And why do you keep fashioning ugly charges of cowardice against
    me,
  that I'm unable to break the yoke and smash my chains?
The sailor better forecasts impending death,   5
  the soldier learns to fear wounds.
In my youth I bragged in outrageous language:
  you now, from my example learn to fear.
Medea of Colchis drove fire-breathing bulls beneath yokes of adamant,
  and sowed armored fights in the soil,   10
And shut the savage maw of the guardian snake
  so golden wool could go to Aeson's home.
Fierce Penthesilea of Scythia once dared to attack
  the Greek fleet with arrows shot from her horse;
When her golden helmet exposed her forehead,   15
  the splendor of her beauty conquered her conqueror.
Omphale advanced to such a distinguished degree of beauty—
  as a girl this Lydian dipped in Gyges' lake—
That the hero who laid the pillars of the world he pacified
  spun baskets of soft wool with his rough hand.   20
Semiramis founded Babylon,° capital city of Persia,
  raising high a solid mass of baked bricks
So two chariots driving in opposite directions along the walls
  could not graze or side-swipe their axles;
She directed the Euphrates through the middle of the citadel she
    built,   25
  and Bactra bowed its head at her command and power.
Now, why should I drag heroes to trial or why gods?
  Jupiter dishonors both himself and his entire home.
What of her° who has recently brought scandal upon our arms,
  a woman fucked out by her own servants?   30

3.11.21: Queen Semiramis was the reputed founder of Babylon.
3.11.29-34 and 39: Cleopatra of the Ptolemaic dynasty traced her lineage back
  to Philip of Macedon, the father of Alexander the Great.

As price for so revolting a marriage she demanded the walls of Rome
  and the city-fathers indentured to her power.
Guilty Alexandria, land most ripe for treacherous guile,
  and Memphis, so often a gory damage to us,
Where Pompey sank in the sand that robbed him of a triple
    triumph,°   35
  no day will ever erase this stigma from you, Rome;
Better you had met death on the Phlegrian plain
  or had offered up your neck to your father-in-law.
And yes, the queen, that whore of incestuous Canopus,
  that singular stigma branded on Rome from Philip's bloodline,   40
Dared set barking Anubis upon our Jove,
  and compel the Tiber to endure the Nile's threats,
Drive out the Roman trumpet with the rattling sistrum,
  and pursue the beaks of our Liburnian warships with Egyptian
    punts,
Spread her vile, gauzy canopies on the rock of Mt. Tarpeius,   45
  and dispense laws amid the statues and the arms of Marius.
What's the good now to have broken the axes of Tarquinius,
  whose arrogant life brands him with like sobriquet,
If we had to suffer a woman? Sing out the triumph, O Rome,
  you have been saved; pray for a long life for Augustus.   50
Yet you, woman, fled to the coiling streams of the frightened Nile:
  your hands received Roman chains.
I witnessed your arms bitten by the sacred snakes,
  and the secret course of the coma ambush your limbs.
"When you have a citizen like this, no need to fear me, O Rome!"   55
  Spoke the tongue buried in constant wine.
The city, lofty upon its seven hills, which now governs the entire
    world,
  was in a panic, fearing the threats of a female Mars.
Where now are Scipio's fleets, where the standards of Camillus,
  or those recently captured, O Bosporus, by the hand of Pompey?   60
The spoils of Hannibal, the monuments of conquered Syphax,
  and Pyrrhus' pride smashed at our feet?
Curtius erected his own memorial in the gaping chasm he filled,
  and Decius spurred on his horse to break through the battle lines,
A narrow street attests the chopping down of Cocles' bridge,   65
  and to someone a crow gave his name:

3.11.35: Pompey triumphed over Marians, Sertorius, and Mithradates. After
  his defeat at Pharsalus in 48 he fled to Egypt where he was murdered as he
  reached shore.

These walls the gods founded and the gods protect them now:
   as long as Caesar lives, Rome need not fear even Jove.
Apollo of Leucas will commemorate the routed forces:
   a single day expunged so mighty a war effort.   70
But you, sailor, bound for port or on the way out,
   on all the Ionian Sea remember Caesar.

3.16

Midnight—a letter arrives from my lover,
   ordering me to be at Tibur without delay,
Tivoli, where white gleaming peaks disclose twin towers,
   and the Anio River cascades into spreading lakes.
What to do? Entrust myself to enveloping shadows of the dark   5
   and not be afraid of criminal hands aimed at my limbs?
If I put off these directives because of fear,
   her weeping will be more savage than any nocturnal mugger.
Once I made a mistake and was banished for an entire year:
   she doesn't treat me with a gentle touch.   10
Now, no man's alive who would injure lovers—they're sacred:
   so, they can travel down the middle of Sciron's road.
Any lover can stroll on Scythia's shores,
   no one would be so barbarous as to harm him:
The moon attends his way, the stars point out the potholes;   15
   Amor himself fans the lit torches in front of him;
Savage rabid dogs turn aside their gaping jaws—no bites;
   for him and his ilk at any time, day or night, the road is safe.
What criminal would splatter himself with a lover's trifling blood?
   Venus herself graciously escorts even rejected lovers.   20
If certain death follows my ventures,
   for such a death I'd pay the price.
She'll bring unguents and deck my tomb with garlands,
   and she'll sit watch beside my grave.
Gods, see to it that she does not contract my bones to a
   much-frequented earth   25
   where a crowd beats a constant path.
Thus after death are lovers' tombs mocked. So may a secluded plot of
   earth
   beneath the shade of a spreading tree cover me,
Or may I be buried walled in by unmarked mounds of sand:
   on the street I want no inscription with my name.   30

4.1°

All that you see around you, stranger, the grandeur of Rome,
    was once, before Aeneas of Phrygia, grass and hills;
And up there on the Palatine where stands the sacred shrine
    to Commodore Apollo, in exile Evander's bulls huddled together.
These golden temples spired from gods of clay;   5
    there was no disgrace in a simply designed hut.
The Father thundered from a bare rock on Mount Tarpeius,
    and the Tiber was a foreigner to our cows.
Where Remus' house has risen above a flight of steps,
    once was a single hearth, a whole kingdom for brothers.   10
The Curia, which now gleams proud with a senate in the bordered
        toga,
    then held Fathers dressed in skins, peasant spirits;
The sound of a horn summoned the pristine citizens to debate:
    those hundred often formed a Senate in a meadow.
No billowing awnings draped the hollow theater;   15
    no stages exuded the aroma of ceremonial saffron.
No one cared to seek out foreign gods,
    since the anxious masses trembled in suspense at an ancestral rite,
And bonfires of hay yearly celebrated the Foundation Day,°
    as docking the tail of the October Horse nowadays renews and
        purifies.   20
Garlanded little donkeys pleased a poor Vesta,
    and scrawny cows carried cheap sacred emblems;
Fattened pigs lustrated the small wards of the city,
    a shepherd offered the guts of a sheep to the sound of his pipes;
The plowman, clad in skins, plied his shaggy thongs,   25
    hence, the rites of the riotous Fabius, a Lupercan.
No rude soldier glittered in hostile weapons;
    au naturelle, they joined in battles with a charred stake.
Lycmon set up the first headquarters wearing a helmet of hide,
    and much of Tatius' power derived from his sheep.   30
Such were the Tities, the Ramnes, and the Luceres°—real men,
    hence Romulus drove in triumph his four white horses.
Bovillae° (now a suburb) then was bigger than small-town Rome,
    and Gabii, which now is no consequence, teemed with people;

4.1: Propertius guides a visitor, the astrologer Horos, through Rome.
4.1.19: see PALES in the Glossary for "Foundation Day."
4.1.31: the three original tribes of Rome corresponding to Sabine, Roman, and
    Etruscan elements respectively.
4.1.33: Bovillae, Gabii, Alba, and Fidenae are all Latin towns near Rome.

Alba stood a mighty power, born from the omen of the white sow;   35
  and Fidenae was a long way to travel.
The Roman foster-child has nothing of his father's—except the name:
  he would never imagine that a she-wolf nursed his bloodline.
You did well, Troy, to send here your exiled Penates:°
  what a mantic sign that Dardan ship sailed under!   40
Even then the omens were pledged in good faith—the opened belly
  of the fir horse did no harm to it,
When the trembling father hung on his son's neck,
  and the flame feared to burn those devout shoulders.
Then came the courage of Decius, the axes of Brutus,   45
  and Venus in person brought the weapons of Caesar, her son,
Carrying the victorious arms of resurgent Troy.
  Happy the land that received your gods, Iulus;
For the tripod at Avernus of the quaking Sibyl
  prophesied that Remus of the Aventine should sanctify the
      fields;°   50
The chants of the prophetess from Pergama,° believed too late,
  came true, uttered to the aged head of Priam:
"Turn away your horse, Greeks! You win in vain. The land of Ilion
  will live on; Jupiter will arm these ashes."
She-wolf of Mars,° best of nurses for our fortunes,   55
  what walls have sprung from your milk!
The very city-walls I try now in reverent poetry to lay in order:
  but, ah me, weak is the volume in my tiny voice.
Whereas a rivulet flows in a trickle from my puny breast,
  yet all of it will be at the service of my fatherland.   60
Let Ennius wreathe his words with shaggy garland:
  Bacchus, stretch out to me your leaves of ivy;
Umbria then will swell with pride because of my books,
  Umbria, native land of the Roman Callimachus!
Let him who will view the towers ascending out of the valley   65
  honor those walls because of my innate talent!
Rome, bless this work that soars in your name; citizens, show
  bright omens; may the good-luck bird sing approval of my
      undertakings!

4.1.39-40: refers to Aeneas' voyage to Italy bringing his household gods (Penates).

4.1.50: the expiatory death of Remus was in the prophecy of the Sibyl of Cumae. Remus occupied the Aventine Hill to observe omens for the foundation of Rome.

4.1.51: i.e. Cassandra of Troy.

4.1.55: a she-wolf suckled Romulus and Remus, twin offsprings of Mars.

I shall celebrate in song sacred rites, festal days, and the names of
    places lost in lore:
        toward these goals my horse should sweat.   70
Foolish Propertius, where are you rushing, dashing off-course to
    soothsay destinies?
        Such threads have not been spun on a favorable loom.
Your singing will evoke tears—Apollo is averse.
        From your unwilling lyre you demand themes you'll regret.
I shall reveal true prophecies, relying on true authorities, or else
    I am a seer   75
        who knows not how to chart the constellations on the bronze globe.
Orops of Babylon, offspring of Archytas, begat me,
        Horos: I trace my house back to great-grandfather Conon.
The gods bear witness that in me the family has not degenerated;
        in my books nothing comes before honesty.   80
Nowadays the gods are the set price for business, and Jupiter is
    suborned
        for gold; the constellations of the Zodiac wheel in renewal:
Propitious are the stars of Jupiter, rapacious those of Mars,
        Saturn's a serious weight upon every head;
What "Pisces" means and the spirited sign of the "Lion" symbolize, 85
    why "Capricorn" bathes in the Western sea....
When Arria was escorting her twin sons and set to fitting them for
    arms,
        even though a god said "No", I prophesied:
"It is destined they not bring back their spears to ancestral gods of the
    family."
        Now two graves mark proof of my reliability.   90
First, Lupercus was shielding his horse's wounded face,
        when to his surprise the stallion pitched forward and threw him;
And Gallus on camp-guard duty protecting the standards entrusted to
    him
        fell before the eagle's bloody beak:
Doomed boys, two victims of a mother's greed!   95
        True was the fulfillment of my reluctant prophecy.
Likewise, while Cinara was in labor pains,
        and the weight within her womb, slow to descend, was delaying
        birth,
"Vow to Juno," I said, "to win her consent."
        She gave birth—and my mantic books won the palm!   100
Jove's sandy chamber in Libya° does not expound better,
        nor the entrails that speak volumes on the gods entrusted therein,

---

4.1.101: the oracular shrine of Jupiter of Ammon at the oasis of Siwah.

Nor anyone skilled in observing the winged movements of a crow,
  not the ghostly spirits that appear like magic in bowls of water.
For the truth, study the highway of heaven, the infallible zodiac;° 105
  credibility will also rest on the five celestial zones.
Calchas serves as a grim example: he launched at Aulis
  the ships still clinging to devout rocks;
He also stained his sword in the neck of Agamemnon's girl;
  thus, the son of Atreus hoisted bloody sails;   110
Yet the Greeks never returned: O Troy sacked,
  restrain your tears and look back upon the harbors of Euboea;
Nauplius, under the cover of night, along the coastline lit the fires of
    revenge,
  and Greece floats, awash with her own spoils.
You, conqueror Ajax, son of Oileus, go ahead, assault and rape a
    prophetess,   115
  wrench her from Minerva's gowned statue against the goddess'
    command.
So much for ancient history; now I deign to stoop to your horoscope:
  compose yourself to weep amid fresh tears.
Ancient Umbria bore you; your family's gods are renowned—
  Am I wrong? Or do I hit upon the borders of your native
    land?—   120
Where misty Mevania° bedews the hollow plain,
  and the waters of Lake Umber in the summer become warm,
Where the wall of soaring Assisi towers high,
  a wall made even more famous by your genius,
You gathered the bones of your father at an age too young,   125
  and you were forced to a narrow living;
For many bullocks had once plowed your fields,
  but the grim surveyor's rod° confiscated your cultivated wealth.
Soon, when you had set aside the golden amulet from your unrefined
    neck
  and assumed the toga of freeborn citizens before the gods of
    your mother,   130
Then Apollo proclaimed to you several verses from his repertoire
  and banned you from thundering speeches in the insane forum.

4.1.105: according to ancient astronomical belief the five zones of the heavens cor-
  respond to the equatorial and the two temperate and frigid zones of earth.
4.1.121: Mevania is a town in the plain just below Assisi.
4.1.128: the rod was used to survey the land confiscated after the Perusine War
  of 41.

Go, fashion elegies, deceptive work—this is your camp—
    to provide a model for the scribbling crew.
You will endure the service of Venus in the charming armor of
    love,   135
    and you will be an enemy, fit target for Venus' young crowd.
For all those victorious "scores" you worked so hard to attain,
    a single girl makes a mockery of your conquests.
Although you can shake loose from the hook that is fixed in your chin,
    it will do you no good: a clamp in your nose will squeeze you
        tight.°   140
Come day, come night, she'll be in charge;
    not one lone teardrop will trickle from your eyes without her
        command;
No help for you to post a thousand guards or to seal the doors;
    once she has convinced herself to cheat on you, a crack is all she
        needs.
Your ship may be tossing in the middle of the sea,   145
    you may be marching unarmed against an armed foe,
Or the hollow of the earth may shake and the ground gape wide open,
    always beware the ominous sign of the eight-legged Crab.

4.3

Arethusa sends this letter to her dear Lycotas—
    if you can be mine when you are away so often—
Now if a smear prevents you from reading it,
    the blot will be derived from my tears;
Or if you fail to make out an indistinct shape of a letter,   5
    it will be a sign of my dying right hand.
Bactra has seen you now on a second morning,
    lately, too, the hostile mounted Chinese cataphract,
And the wintry Getae, Britain in the painted war chariot,
    and the dark Indian stained in the waters of the East.   10
So, this is a husband's vow, the kind of nights promised to me,
    when, innocent, I surrendered to your pressing love, your conquest?
The torch that led my wedding procession and heralded good luck,
    was lit from the smoky black fires of a ruined funeral pyre;
I was sprinkled with water from Lake Styx, and askew   15
    was the ribbon for my hair; I was married without the god's
        attendance.
Upon all the gates hang my offering—vowed to no avail:
    a fourth overcoat I have woven for your campaigns overseas.

4.1.139-140: the Latin metaphor is from construction work with stone.

Damn him who yanked a palisade stake from an innocent tree,
    and who fashioned mournful trumpets out of blaring bones,   20
More deserving that sideways-sitting Ocnus° to twist a rope
    and to feed forever his donkey's hunger!
Tell me, does your breastplate rub raw your tender arms?
    And the heavy spear wear blisters on your hands unsuited for war?
Rather these burns than a girl's teeth-marks   25
    planted on your neck to make me cry.
They say that your look is gaunt and thin: I hope
    that pale color is from missing me.
When the evening has brought bitter nights upon me,
    I kiss your weapons—those left lying around;   30
Then I complain that the bed-blankets don't keep still,
    and birds, the heralds of the dawn, fail to sing.
On winter nights I work and work on camp clothes for you
    and stitch Tyrian woolen strips for your officer's wear.
I learn where flows the Araxes, your next military mission,   35
    and how many miles a Parthian horse can speed without water.
I am compelled to learn the world from maps painted on a panel,
    what this creative arrangement of the skilled god is like,
What land is numbed by ice, which is stifling from the heat,
    what wind best brings sails to Italy.   40
A single sister sits with me, and my nurse, pale with worry over me,
    lies, swearing that the wintertime causes your delay.
Lucky Hippolyta! with a nipple exposed she warred;
    a barbarian's helmet covered her soft head.
How I wish Roman girls could join up for camp life;   45
    I would be faithful baggage in your tour of duty.
The heights of Scythia would not slow me down when the Father
    sweeps the deep and freezes the water into ice.
Every love is mighty, but even mightier when love's partner is at
      hand;
    so Venus in person fans the flame of live passion.   50
For what good is it for me to glow in the purple of Punic gowns
    and crystal rings, clear as water, grace my hands?
There is dumb silence everywhere; not used to kalends coming at
      long intervals
    a single girl opens the closed cupboard of the Lares;
I welcome the whine of my puppy dog Craugis: 55
    she claims your side of the bed all for herself.

4.3.21-22: Ocnus suffered this punishment because he allowed his extravagant
    wife to squander his money.

I garland little shrines in flowers, I drape the crossroad altars with
   herbs,
  and sweet marjoram crackles on ancient hearths.
If a hoot owl, perched on a nearby beam, screeches at night,
  or, if a sputtering lamp has approved a touch of wine,   60
That day demands the blood of this year's lambs,
  and suppliers for the sacrifice grow hot for fresh profits.
Do not overvalue, I pray, the glory won by scaling Bactra's mountains
  or the gauzy linen torn from a perfumed fop of a prince,
When sling-shots of lead are whirled   65
  and the insidious bow twangs from horses in flight.
But, when you have tamed the sons of Parthia's soil,
  follow your triumphing horses carrying the spear of valor;
Preserve and never violate the treaty of my bed.
  Only on these terms would I want you back;   70
And when I dedicate your weapons at the Capena Gate,°
  I'll write this underneath: "From a girl grateful for her man's
    homecoming."

4.4

Tarpeia's grove, Tarpeia's tomb—her disgrace—
  and the capture of pristine Jove's sacred thresholds, I'll sing.
A lush wood there was, enclosing a grotto overhanging with ivy,
  and a thicket echoed the babble of a natural spring;
Silvanus made his home among the branches and there the sweet
    strains   5
  of a shepherd's pipe bade the sheep to water in refuge from the
    heat.
This spring Tatius fences with maple stakes
  and secures his camp with a mounded ring of earth.
In those days Rome was not Rome, when a trumpeter from Cures
  blared long and loud, shaking Jove's nearby rocks.   10
And where laws are now issued for conquered lands
  once stood Sabine spears in the Roman forum.
For walls they had the hills; and where now the Curia is fenced,
  a war horse drank from a spring.
From this very spot Tarpeia drew spring-water for the goddess
    Vesta: 15
  for it she balanced a clay pot upon her head.
Surely, a single death is not enough for an impious girl
  who chose, Vesta, to betray your flames.

4.3.71: the Capena Gate was important because the Appian Way entered Rome
  there.

She spied Tatius sporting on the sandy field,
   and, when he lifted his blazoned helmet graced with yellow
      plumes,   20
She was stunned by the king's beauty and his kingly armor,
   and her urn fell, slipping through her forgetful hands.
She often claimed bad omens from the moon—it was not the guilty
   one—
   stating that she had to rinse her hair in running water;
Often she brought shimmering lilies to the graceful nymphs,   25
   praying that no spear of Romulus ruin Tatius' beauty:
And while she ascended the Capitol engulfed in the first misty smoke,
   she returned with arms scratched by thorny brambles,
And sitting down in tears on Tarpeia's crest she lamented
   the love-pangs that Jupiter would not countenance: 30
"O campfires and headquarters of Tatius' troops,
   Sabine weapons so beautiful to my eyes,
I wish I could be sitting a prisoner before your household gods,
   and be paraded a captive of my Tatius!
Goodbye, you hills of Rome: goodbye, Rome, set upon those hills;   35
   and goodbye, Vesta—before you I should feel ashamed of my sin;
That horse, yes, that very horse, will restore my love to the camp,
   the one whose mane Tatius himself grooms to the right.
It's no wonder Scylla savaged her father's hair
   and her glistening loins metamorphosed into wild dogs.   40
It's no surprise the horned monster, although a brother, was betrayed
   and gathered thread disclosed the way out of the maze.
I will commit a crime dishonorable to Ausonian girls,
   I, though chosen to serve her, will profane the virgin's hearth.
If anyone wonders why Pallas' fire° has gone out,   45
   may he forgive me: my tears inundated her altar.
Tomorrow, as the rumor has it, the whole city will be on a binge:
   seize the dewy spine of the ridge filled with brambles.
Slippery and treacherous is the entire path; the cliff conceals
   the deceptive ooze from springs unheard and constant.   50
How I wish I knew the Muse of magic spells,
   then this tongue too could help my handsome lover.
Your embroidered toga becomes you; better than that motherless
      changeling
   suckled on the hard tit of an inhuman she-wolf.
So I'd be a feared foreign queen in my own country's palace: 55
   Rome betrayed yields no mean dowry for you.

4.4.45: the image of Pallas Athena, the Palladium rescued from Troy, was kept
  in the shrine to Vesta in the forum.

If not that, don't let the rape of the Sabines go unpunished;
  rape me, pay back in kind, tit for tat.
I can disengage the lines already committed to battle; enter now
  upon a treaty of peace that my bridal gown mediates.   60
Marriage God, strike up your chords; trumpeter, hush your harsh
    blare;
  trust me, my marriage-bed will soften your weapons.
And now the fourth bugle call heralds the coming dawn;
  the stars sink, slipping into Ocean.
I'll try to fall asleep and look for you in my dreams;   65
  come as a gentle shade to my eyes."
After these words she yielded her arms to capricious sleep
  unaware that a new madness lay beside her.
For Venus, blessed keeper of Troy's embers,
  fuels her crime and in her bones banks more fires.   70
She rushes about like Strymon's female above swift-flowing
    Thermodon,
  her blouse ripped open, her breast bare.
The city had a holiday which our ancestors called the Parilia,
  it was the anniversary of Rome's walls;
Every year there are parties held by shepherds, there are games in the
    city,   75
  and village trays overflow with rich food and drink;
Over bonfires of hay, set at intervals,
  a drunken gang leaps, darkening their feet with soot.
No guard duty for the holiday, Romulus decreed,
  no reveille from bugles, in camp all quiet.   80
Tarpeia, reckoning this is her moment, meets the enemy:
  she strikes a bargain—she herself is part and partner of the terms.
The hill was treacherous in the climb and lax in security because of
    the festivities;
  in a moment with a sword she silences the barking dogs.
Everything was conducive to slumber; but to exact his penalty with
    revenge   85
  Jupiter alone decided to keep watch.
She had betrayed the trust of the gate and her prostrate fatherland,
  and she asks him to choose the wedding day.
But Tatius, although an enemy, gave her no honor for her betrayal;
  "Marry," he said, "and mount my royal bed."   90
Without another word he buried and crushed her beneath the shields
    of his soldiers.
  This, Vestal Virgin, was the fit dowry for your services.
From Tarpeia, the guide, the rocky hill has won its name:
  O sentinel, you have your reward, an unjust fate.

4.7

There are ghosts after all: death does not end it;
  the pale shade escapes, overcoming the pyre.
Cynthia I saw, leaning over my bed-support, yes her,
  just recently buried near the murmuring road's end,
When sleep hung suspended over me after the death rites of my love, 5
  and I was complaining of the cold realm of my bed.
There was the same hair which she had on the day of the funeral,
  the same eyes: the shroud was charred to her body
And the beryl ring on her finger, her favorite, the fire had gnawed;
  the waters of Lethe had shriveled her facial features.   10
She flashed her temper and voice just as she did when she breathed
      alive,
  and in rebuke snapped her bony fingers at me:
"Liar! What else could any girl expect from you?
  Can sleep so soon possess powers over you?
Already gone the memories of those furtive dates under the Subura's
      spying eye,
  my windowsill worn smooth by our nocturnal subterfuges?   16
From there I often dangled on a suspended rope for you,
  hand over hand lowering myself into your arms.
We used to make love on alley corners; breast to breast
  our clothes warmed up the pavement.   20
Well, so much for our secret compact! Mere words, lies,
  that the unheeding winds have blasted away.
Ah, no one cried out my name as my eyes were growing dim—
  a call from you would have gained me an extra day:
No guard rattled a split reed on my behalf,   25
  instead, a broken tile propped against my head hurt me;
No one saw you bent over with grief at our funeral,
  soaking your black toga in hot tears.
If it was too much of a bother for you to pass beyond the city gates,
  at least you could have ordered my bier to proceed more slowly. 30
Why didn't you personally pray for winds, you ingrate, at the pyre?
  Why not scent my flames with perfume?
Was this too a burden? To scatter a few hyacinths (bought at cost),
  to break duly a wine jar, propitiating my ashes?
Burn Lygdamus°—get the branding iron red-hot for a slave—   35
  I perceived it when I drank the paling wines spiked in treachery—
Or Nomas—let her slyly store out of sight her mysterious slimy
      concoctions—
  a glowing hot potsherd will declare her hands guilty.

4.7.35: Lygdamus is Propertius' slave. See 4.8.79.

And she, just recently open to the public for cheap nights,
    now in gold-embroidered gown marks a trail on the ground.   40
Any girl who in idle chit-chat says something about my beauty
    pays the unfair price of a heavier load of wool in her baskets.
Old Petale,° because she brought garlands to my tomb monument,
    now feels the shackles, hobbled to a filthy clog;
And Lalage, strung up by her twisted hair, gets whipped   45
    because she dared to ask a favor in my name.
You allowed *her* to melt down the gold from my bust,
    so she would have a dowry from my blazing funeral pyre.
Yet, I do not hound you, Propertius, although you deserve it;
    in your books long was my reign.   50
I swear by the song of the Fates that no one may unravel,
    (may the three-bodied dog's growl be gentle for me),
That I have kept faith. If I lie, may a viper
    hiss on my tomb and brood above my bones.
Over the foul river there are allotted two seats;   55
    by separate routes of water rows the entire crowd of the dead.
One stream conveys the adultery of Clytemnestra, another the
        debauchery
of the Cretan Pasiphae, the wooden monstrosity of a counterfeit cow.
Look, another group is swept along in a festooned boat
    where the balmy breeze caresses the roses of Elysium,   60
And the rhythmic flute and bronze cymbals of Cybele
    and Lydian lyres resound in tune with turbaned dancers.
Andromeda and Hypermestra,° wives without deceits,
    narrate their courage famous in history:
The former complains of the bruises upon her arms caused by her   65
    mother's chains and of hands undeserving of icy rocks;
Hypermnestra relates the enormity her sisters dared,
    that she lacked the heart for their crime.
Thus, with tears in death we heal the loves of life:
    for I keep hidden the many charges of your infidelity.   70
But now I entrust to you my mandates, if by chance you are receptive,
    and not yet Chloris' drug has taken complete hold of you:
Don't let my old nurse, Parthenie, lack for anything in her trembling
        years;
    she could have been, but was not, greedy at your expense;
And as for my dear Latris, (her name means "servant"),   75
    don't let her hold out a mirror for a new mistress;

4.7.43, 45, 73: the names of the servants are significant. Petale means "petal,"
    Lalage means "prattler," and Parthenie means "virgin."
4.7.63: Hypermnestra is the Danaid who spared her husband. Cf. Horace *Odes*
    3.11.

Whatever poems you composed in my honor,
    burn them for me: cease to win praises because of me;
Pull the ivy from my tomb which in pregnant clusters
    twines in twisted tendrils around my softening bones;   80
Where the Anio, teeming with apples, broods on the wooded fields,
    and the divine power of Hercules prevents the yellowing of ivory,
In the middle of a stele scratch this couplet honoring me,
    but be brief, so a traveler from the town speeding by may read:
'Here in Tibur's soil lies golden Cynthia,   85
    glory to your bank, Anio.'
Do not spurn the dreams that come from pious gates;
    when reverent dreams come, they have significance.
We are night wanderers; night frees the shades imprisoned;
    unshoot the bolt, even Cerberus himself prowls.   90
At dawn we return to Lethe's pools, obedient to cosmic laws;
    we are the freighted passengers, the cargo the ferryman reviews at
        reveille.
Now let other women possess you; soon I'll get you back all to myself;
    you will be with me and your bones on mine I'll grind to dust."
When she had finished this complaint and indictment against me,   95
    her shade slipped from my many embraces and vanished.

4.8

Listen, I'll tell you of the panic last night on the watery Esquiline:
    a pack of neighbors from the new quarters° came running to the
        scene,
An ugly brawl echoed from a backstreet bar
    that stained my name, and I wasn't even there.
Now Lanuvium is an old site guarded by an ancient serpent,°   5
    unusual and an hour's stop is not a waste.
There's a black yawning pit that drops sheer to a holy spot
    where a virgin must penetrate (be careful of the descent, maiden)
To offer in obeisance to a hungry snake the food it demands every
        year
    as it writhes and hisses in the deep core of the earth.   10
Young girls are sent to perform the rite: they pale
    entrusting a hand to the fearful gamble of a snaky maw
That gobbles like bait the morsels the maiden tenders,
    making the very baskets tremble in the virgin's hands;

4.8.1-2: for the "new quarters" see note to Horace *Satires* 1.8.
4.8.5-16: describe the rites of Juno Sospita at Lanuvium.

Those whose maidenhood is proven intact return to embrace their
    parents' necks,
    and the farmers shout: "Fruitful will be the year!"   16
Here my Cynthia went, driving a team of ponies, closely clipped,
    on a visit, so she claimed, to Juno—more likely to Venus—
Speak up, O Appian Way, please, that triumphal procession you
    witnessed,
    her driving of chariot wheels hurtling across your pavement;   20
And what a sight she was, leaning over the tongue pole,
    recklessly shaking the reins over the foul potholes.
That smooth-skinned dandy, I leave to silence—him and his
    fashionable
    two-seater draped in silk, and his Afghans decked with jeweled
        collars;
Soon enough he will be fated to sell his life for the rationed slop of a
    gladiator   25
    when a beard (O shame) will disfigure his hairless cheeks.
As this was one other occasion I'd been rooked of our bed,
    I decided to strike camp and to change bed-operations.
A girl named Phyllis is a neighbor of the goddess Diana on the
    Aventine,°
    not much fun when sober, but a real charmer after some drinks;   30
And then there's Teia, who lives next to Tarpeia's grove,
    a beauty, but when she's tipsy, one man is not enough.
I decided to invite them over to while away the night with me,
    and to infuse some variety into my love life.
On the lawn, well-concealed, spread a couch just for three,   35
    if you're wondering about the logistics, I was snuggled in the
        middle.
Lygdamus tended to the cups serving the wine from a glass carafe,
    strictly
    for summer use, a vintage of excellent bouquet from Lesbos;
The Nile provided a flute player; Phyllis was the castanet clacker:
    roses arranged in guileless elegance were ready for strewing,   40
While Goliath, a dwarf compacted into knotted joints,
    with stumpy hands beat time to the flute carved from boxwood.
But: the flame kept flickering out, though I had filled the lamps;
    and the table legs collapsed flat,
And when I tried for "Lucky Venus" on the dice,   45
    everything I rolled came up those "Damn Dogs."°

4.8.29: there was a famous temple to Diana on the Aventine Hill.
4.8.45-46: the best throw was called "Venus," the losing throw "dogs." Cf.
    Horace *Odes* 2.7.25.

As for the two, I was deaf to their singing, blind to their naked
    breasts:
  I was all alone—by the gates of Lanuvium.
When suddenly I heard the loud creaking of door hinges
    and the hum of voices in the vestibule dedicated to Lares.   50
Instantly Cynthia rushed in flattening the folding-doors;
  there she was, her hair dishevelled, but beautiful in her wild rage.
The goblet slipped from my limp fingers,
  I gaped and my wine-dribbled lips turned pale.
Her eyes flashed thunderbolts; she fumed savagely as a woman can, 55
  the scene was no less vivid than the sacking of a city.
With her furious fingernails she ravaged Phyllis' face;
  in terror Teia screamed "Fire! Fire!"° to the neighborhood.
The brandishing of flambeaux soon awoke and alarmed the locals;
  and the whole alley resounded to the midnight donnybrook.   60
With their hair torn out in bunches, their tunics all a mess,
  they raced to that bar, first up in a back street.
Then Cynthia stormed back, victorious, delighted by her plunder;
  she slaps my face with a smarting backhand,
Plants her teeth into my neck biting till she drew blood,   65
  and my eyes (they especially deserved it) she beats again and
    again.
And after her arms wearied of the barrage of blows,
  from his hiding niche, under the left-hand headboard of the bed,
She rooted and hauled out Lygdamus who appealed to my guardian
    spirit;
  but I could do nothing at all, Lygdamus; I, too, was a captive.   70
So I sued for peace, throwing my suppliant palms
  about the feet she'd hardly permit me to touch.
"If what you want is my forgiveness for your offence," she said,
  "then here are the terms of the contract: take it or leave it.
No more strutting all dressed up in the shade of Pompey's portico,° 75
  no sauntering through the sandy forum during carnival;
No craning your neck in the theater up towards the balcony;
  no dilly-dallying around to gawk into an open litter;
And above all—no Lygdamus! He goes, the main cause of my
    complaint;
  put him up for sale—shackled in double leg-irons."   80
I accepted promising to abide by her terms as asserted.
  She laughed, flaunting the power I had given her.

4.8.58: the Latin has "water" instead of "fire." Teia screams for people to bring
    water to quench a fire.
4.8.75: Propertius refers to the large colonnaded courtyard of Pompey's The-
    ater.

Then anything or any spot those interlopers had touched
    she fumigated, and she wiped clean the doorstep with clear water.
She ordered me to change the oil in all the lamps,   85
    singed my head three times with burning sulfur,
Then started to change the linens, one by one:
    I cooperated. And we made peace—all over the bed.

4.11°

Cease, Paullus, to burden my tomb with tears:
    the black gate of death opens to no prayers.
When the buried dead have entered within Hell's bailiwick,
    routes stand blocked with unrelenting adamant.
Although the god of the dim court° may hear your prayer,   5
    the shores will surely drink unfeeling of your tears.
Vows move the gods above—here, once the ferryman° has taken his
    fee,
    the dank gate bars the grassy pyres.
So the mournful trumpets played, as the malignant torch
    fired my bier that collapsed, bringing down my head.   10
What good have they done me? —The marriage to Paullus,
    the triumphing chariot of my ancestors, the great testimonies to my
    fame?
Cornelia too has met unkind fates,
    and I am the load that five fingers may gather.
O nights of the damned, you swamps, slow pools,   15
    and all the waters that entwine my feet,
Although before my time, yet I have come here, not guilty;
    may the Father here grant gentle judgment upon my shade,
Or if an Aeacus sits the judge with the urn at his side,
    let him be the champion of my bones when the ball is drawn;   20
May his brothers sit with him, and next to Minos' chair, as advisors,
    the grim group of Eumenides, while the court remains engrossed.
Sisyphus, leave your stone; may Ixion's wheel halt in silence;°
    may Tantalus catch you up, teasing water;
And today let not impious Cerberus attack the shades,   25
    but lie still, his chain slack, the bolt silent.

4.11.1: the "queen of elegies" spoken by Cornelia, daughter of Publius Cornelius
    Scipio and Scribonia, who later married Octavius and bore their daughter
    Julia.
4.11.5: refers to Pluto, the god of the underworld.
4.11.7: the ferryman is Charon, who transports souls across the river Styx.
4.11.23-28: Propertius lists the canonical sinners punished in the underworld
    for their heinous crimes against gods and humanity.

I plead my own defense: if I perjure myself, may my punishment
  be that of the Danaid sisters, a luckless urn pressing upon my
    shoulders.
If anyone has ever won glorious fame through trophies of ancestors,29
  then the African kingdoms speak the names of my Numantine
    grandfathers,°
The other clan makes my mother's family, the Libones, their equal,
  each house propped up by its own glorious record.
When my bordered toga was set aside for the marriage torch
  and a different kind of fillet bound my coiffured hair,
I joined myself then, Paullus, to your couch—destined now to leave
    it;   35
  on this my tombstone read it, that I was the bride of one man only.
I call upon you to bear witness the ashes of my ancestors, objects of
    your worship,
  Rome, beneath whose published victories Africa lies crushed,
And I call to witness him who smashed Perses, that pretender
    Achilles,
  and all his proud house puffed up by its great-grandfather
    Achilles,   40
That I never softened the censor's law nor because of any taint
  of mine have your hearths ever blushed.
Cornelia has not been a stain on spoils so illustrious;
  she herself was a model to a mighty house.
I have not changed; all of my life has been without reproach: 45
  between the wedding torch and the torch of death I lived nobly;
Nature provided me with laws of conduct derived from my bloodline;
  nor can you become better out of fear of a judge.
The urn will bring me whatever stern verdicts it may;
  no one will be disgraced by appearing in court seated at my side,50
Not you, Claudia, who pulled by rope the stalled Cybebe,
  rare priestess of the goddess with the crenelated crown,
Nor she° whose fine linen dress proved the hearth-fire alive,
  when Vesta was demanding flames that had been snuffed out;
Nor have I harmed you, my sweet head, mother Scribonia: 55
  would you want anything changed in me except my fate?
I am eulogized by the tears of a mother and the laments of a city;
  my bones have secured the defense of Caesar's groans;
He loudly laments that a worthy sister of his own daughter has lived
    and died,
  and we have seen the god shedding tears.   60

4.11.30: a reference to Publius Cornelius Scipio (Aemilianus) who successfully
  besieged Numantia (Spain) in 132.
4.11.53-54: the Vestal Virgin Aemilia.

Yet, I have earned the prolific honors of my special dress;°
  my abduction did not occur from a sterile home.
You, Lepidus, and you, Paullus, my hope after death,
  you embraced me when I closed my eyes.
We have seen my brother twice take the chair of state;   65
  he was consul° in a festive season when his sister was snatched
      away;
O daughter, born to be the reminder of your father's censorship,
  imitate me, your mother, and keep only one man as husband.
All of you, in turn shore up our bloodline: I am happy that my boat
  is being launched, for many of my descendants will anoint my
      burial site.   70
This is final reward for a woman's triumph, when her fame,
  that of a free-born woman, honors her deserving tomb.
Now to you I entrust the children, our shared pledges;
  this my love breathes still, branded in my ashes.
But you, the father, will have to perform a mother's role: 75
  your neck will have to bear that entire crew of mine;
Whenever you kiss away their tears, add the kisses of their mother;
  the whole family begins now to be your responsibility.
If you ever have cause to grieve, let them not witness it;
  when they come to you, fool their kisses with dry cheeks.   80
May there be nights enough, Paullus, for you to fret on and on about
  me,
  and dreams that you often believe have my likeness;
And when you speak in secret to my portraits,
  speak expecting me to reply to each and every sentence.
Yet if the door sees a change of bed across the room,°   85
  and a wary stepmother sits upon our couch,
Approve, my sons, and accept your father's new union:
  she will, like a captive, surrender to your gentle manners;
Do not over-praise your mother; once compared to her predecessor,
  she will construe words spoken candidly as an offence.   90
If he will be happy to stay faithful to my shade
  and hold my ashes dear,
Learn now how to sense his old age ever approaching,
  leave not a single avenue for a widower's worries.

4.11.61: according to a provision of the Julian Law of 18 the "special dress" was
  afforded to a woman who had borne at least three children.
4.11.66: the consul of 16 was Publius Cornelius Scipio. This line sets the dra-
  matic date of the elegy.
4.11.85: the marriage bed was placed in the atrium of the house. It faced the
  front door.

May the years robbed from me be allotted to yours,   95
    so through my children may Paullus be happy in his old age.
It has been good: I never wore the robes of mourning as a mother;
    the entire clan has come to my funeral rites.
My case is pleaded; arise, witnesses, and shed tears over me,
    while the grateful and welcomed earth weighs the verdict of my
        life.   100
Even heaven lies open to virtues; may your judgment find me worthy,
    and my bones be transported on the waters of honor.

TIBULLUS

ELEGIES

To Quintillian (ca 35 – ca 95 CE), Tibullus was the most refined and elegant of the Roman elegists. His easy style and his handling of multiple themes and conventions that he blends into a harmonious whole lend credence to Quintillian's judgment. And many modern readers would agree with him, although Tibullus may be lacking the wit, the allusive power, and the verve in language and imagery of Propertius. Yet, he was well appreciated by his contemporaries Horace and Ovid who both dedicated moving poems to him upon his death.

1.1

Let some other man pile up riches, his hoard of gleaming gold,
   and possess many acres of cultivated soil,
And let him endure unremitting work and suffer the terror when an
      enemy is near by,
   whose sleeps the blasts of Mars' trumpets rout.
May my poverty support me in a life of leisure,   5
   while my hearth glows with constant fire.
I, myself a rustic, with effortless hand in the proper season
   shall plant the delicate vines and large fruit trees.
May hope not flag, but forever furnish bushels
   of fruit and new wine thick in a brimming vat.   10
For I am reverent to a stump deserted in the fields
   or to an old rock at crossroads garlanded with flowers;
And whatever fruit the new year may yield for me
   is offered before the farmer's god.
Golden Ceres, may you have from our farm a crown of wheat   15
   spikes to hang before the doors of your shrine;

Priapus, stand red in the fruit gardens, on guard
    to frighten away birds with your ferocious hook.
You too, O Lares, protectors of a field once rich,
    but now poor, receive your gifts.   20
A slain calf once purified innumerable bulls,
    now a lamb is but the small sacrifice of a scanty field:
A lamb will fall for you; around it youth from the country
    will shout: "O grant fruitful crops and fine wines."
Now, now, may I be able to live content with a little   25
    and not always be consigned to a long march,
Avoiding the summer risings of the Dog Star beneath the shade
    of a tree near brooks of water streaming by.
Yet may I not feel ashamed sometimes to take up a hoe
    or with a whip to crack slow oxen;   30
And may I not regret to bring home cradled in my bosom
    a lamb or kid deserted by a forgetting mother.
Play fair, thieves and wolves, and spare my meager
    flock: you should pursue prey from a larger herd.
Here, year after year, I purify my shepherd   35
    and by custom sprinkle a calmed Pales with milk.
Be propitious, O gods! And spurn not gifts
    from a poor table or from clean earthenware.
A farmer of old first made for himself such earthenware
    cups; he fashioned them from pliable clay.   40
I do not covet the wealth and produce of parents which
    a stored harvest bequeathed to a grandfather of old;
A small crop is enough; it is enough to be allowed to rest
    in bed and to relax limbs on the familiar couch;
How inviting to lie listening to fierce winds   45
    and to clasp a lady in soft embrace,
Or, when the wintry south wind pours its icy showers,
    without a care to catch sleep by a seductive fire.
So may it happen to me! Let him be rich, rightly, who can
    endure the fury of the sea and the saddening rains.   50
Damn to hell all the gold, all the emeralds in the world,
    before any girl should weep over my journeys.
Yours, Messalla, to war on land and sea
    so that your home may wear the spoils of an enemy;
Mine—the chains of a beautiful girl keep me bound—   55
    I sit a doorman before her hard-hearted doors.
I care not to earn praise, my Delia;° when I can be
    with you, I'll be called a lazy bum, and like it.

1.1.57: the delayed mention of the name of the speaker's loved one, hinted at
    in 46.

May I gaze upon you, when my final hour comes,
     and, dying, clasp you with failing hand.   60
You will weep for me, Delia, when I am laid upon the burning pyre;
     you will mingle your kisses with mournful tears.
You will weep; your heart is not surrounded by hard steel
     nor in that tender chamber dwells flint.
From that funeral no young man, no young girl,   65
     will be able to bring home dry eyes.
Do not offend my shades, but spare your disheveled
     hair, and spare, Delia, your soft cheeks.
So, while the fates allow, let us join our love.
     Death shrouded in darkness comes soon enough;   70
Soon will creep upon us that inactive time of a white-haired head,
     indecent for lovemaking and purring sweet nothings.
Now is the moment for buoyant Venus, while it's no shame
     to smash in doors and it's fun to start brawls.
In this war I am a general, a good soldier; you, O standards, and
     trumpet blares,   75
     go far away! Wound ambitious men;
Bring them wealth: for me, untroubled, with my heap secure
     I shall despise riches and scorn hunger.

1.2

Over here, more wine! Unmixed! Wash down my new sorrows with
     drink
     so sleep may seize and overcome my exhausted eyes.
Don't any of you rouse my temples pounded by so much wine
     while unhappy love is resting.
You see, a savage guard has been stationed over our girl   5
     and her door is locked firm with a hard bolt.
Door of a harsh master, may a shower of rain pelt you;
     may thunderbolts hurled at the command of Jove seek you out.
Door, be won over by my complaints, open now only for me;
     but don't make a sound when you furtively swing your hinge.   10
And if in my dementia I have ever cursed you,
     forgive me: I pray those same curses upon my own head.
You should remember all the many prayers in the voice of a suppliant
     I expressed when I offered your doorpost my flowery garlands.
And you, Delia, don't be timid; deceive the guards.   15
     Now is the time for daring: it is Venus who helps the bold.°
She favors any young man who braves new thresholds,
     or any girl who with a fitted key unlocks the door;

1.2.16: a humorous elegiac twist on the adage: "fortune favors the bold."

She teaches a girl to steal softly from a bed,
 the ability to step without a sound,   20
How in the presence of her man to confer nods that talk,
 and to conceal sweet-nothings in signals prearranged.
She does not instruct all, but those whom laziness neither hampers
 nor fear prevents from arising in the deep of night.
Look, when I mosey through the city, somewhat anxious, 25
 <I know I'm safe>.° Love does not permit
Anyone coming up to me seeking to wound my body
 with an iron blade or to grab my clothes in search of money.
Whoever is under the aegis of love goes safe and sacrosanct
 anywhere he pleases without improper fear of attack. 30
The numbing cold of a wintry night does me no harm,
 not even when a rainstorm drenches me.
This type of labor does not injure me, if only Delia will unlock
 the door and without a word summon me with the snap of her
   finger.
Avert your glance, if you meet a man or a woman: 35
 Venus loves to conceal her subterfuges.
Do not fear the sound of footfalls or ask for a name
 or bring torches of glowing fire close by.
If anyone in ignorance catches a glimpse, let him keep it secret
 and by all the gods swear to forget;   40
For the tattletale will encounter the goddess born from blood,°
 Venus who emerged from the rushing sea.
Him your spouse will not believe, so a truthful witch
 during her magical rite once promised me.
I have seen her charm down stars from the sky,   45
 reverse the course of a rapid river,
And with her chanting split the soil and conjure up from their tombs
 dead spirits, summon bones down from a funeral pyre still warm.
With her magical screeching she controls crowds from Hell
 and orders them bedewed with milk to turn back.   50
At her whim she scatters clouds from a dismal sky;
 At her whim she summons snows from the summer sky.
She alone, they say, controls Medea's evil herbs,
 she alone has tamed the wild hounds of Hecate.

1.2.26: a lacuna in the text filled in by a likely statement.
1.2.41: refers to Uranus whose bloody castrated member fell into the sea, from
 which Venus was born.

This sorceress has composed chants for me, which you could use for
    witchcraft: 55
    chant three° times, spit three times after uttering them.
That man of yours will not believe anyone, no matter what he says
    about us,
    not even if he himself were to see us on a soft couch.
Yet you should keep away from others; for he will discern
    all other things: only about me will he perceive nothing.   60
Why should I believe her? Why, just recently this witch said
    she could dissolve my love by her chants or herbs,
And she purified me with sulfur torches, and on a calm night
    a dark victim fell to the gods of magic.
I didn't want to be rid of love completely; but I prayed that it be
    mutual;   65
    nor would I like you to be powerless.
That guy was iron-hearted and stupid who, although he could possess
    you,
    instead preferred to pursue arms and the rewards of booty.
He may drive ahead of him the conquered crowds of Cilicians
    and pitch war camps on captured soil;   70
Woven completely in silver, completely in gold,
    let him set ambushes spying from a swift steed;
If only I can be with you, my Delia, let me
    yoke bulls and on a desolate mountainside pasture a flock;
As long as I may hold you in tender embrace,   75
    may my sleep be soft on unworked ground.
What good is it to lie back on a couch fitted in purple without sunny
    love,
    when sobbing comes during a wakeful night?
For then neither downy pillows nor ornately dyed spreads
    can induce slumber or evoke the sounds of calming water.   80
I did not violate the majesty of mighty Venus,
    nor has my tongue been impious enough to warrant punishment.
I am not charged with approaching the homes of the god, unholy,
    and stealing garlands from the sacred hearths.
If I deserved it, I would not hesitate to prostrate myself at the
    temples   85
    and give kisses to holy thresholds;
I would creep a suppliant upon the ground on my knees
    and beat my miserable head on a sacred doorpost.
But you who smugly laugh at my troubles, yourself
    beware: not just against one person will the god rage.   90

1.2.56: for the idea of the number three used in magic see Vergil, *Eclogues*
    8.74-76.

I have witnessed an old man, who made fun of the unhappy loves
    of young men, bearing on his neck the chains of Venus,
And in quavering voice composing sweet-nothings
    and wanting to hand-fix his graying hair himself;
Shamelessly he stood before the doors of his dear girl,   95
    and detained her maid in the middle of the forum.
Against him rubbed a boy, and a youth in a tight crowd,
    who spat° into the soft folds of their garments.
Spare me, Venus; always in my mind I have been your
    devoted slave: why are you bitter and why do you burn your
        harvests?   100

1.4

"Yes, I hope you get a shady roof, Priapus,
    so neither suns nor snows can harm you.
What is your clever trick that has captivated handsome boys?
    Certainly your beard doesn't shine, your hair is unkempt.
You endure the freezes of winter nude,   5
    and nude the seething days of the summer Dog Star."
So I said: then the country child of Bacchus responded to me,
    the god armed with his pruning hook.
"Don't entrust yourself to the tender throng of boys;
    for they produce a phony pretext for a true and constant love.   10
You prefer one because he reins in his horse tight,
    another because his snow-white breast strokes calm water;
Another captures you because he is brave and bold; and in that other
        one
    a virgin blush appears upon his tender cheeks.
Don't despair; if at first he should say no,   15
    little by little he'll offer his neck to the yoke.
To teach lions to obey a man requires a long day;
    it requires a long day for soft water to eat through stones;
A year ripens grapes on sunny hillsides;
    a year directs the shining constellations in regular pattern.   20
Don't be afraid to swear; winds waft the useless lies
    of love over lands and deep seas.
Glory be to Jove: why, the father himself attests and has proven void
    whatever fickle love has sworn in desire.°

1.2.98: the spitting is an apotropaic reaction to the old man's absurd fool-
    ishness.
1.4.23-24: Jupiter swore to Juno that he was innocent in the affair with Io.

Diana Dictynna by her arrows lets you promise   25
   without paying, Minerva by her locks.
You'll be making a mistake, if you are slow; life will pass,
   and quickly too! Not at all sluggish is day; and it doesn't come
      back.
How quickly the earth loses its crimson colors,
   how soon the tall poplar its beautiful leaves.   30
When the fates of feeble old age have come, time lays low
   the horse that once bolted from the starting gates at Elean Olympia.
I have seen a young man, when pressing middle age was upon him,
   mourn that he was stupid to neglect the days.
Cruel gods! A snake sheds the years, renewed;   35
   the fates have granted no such reprieve for beauty.
To only Bacchus and Phoebus Apollo is youth eternal:
   uncut hair is the proper mark of both these gods.
Now you! Whatever your boy desires to try,
   comply; love will conquer most things by giving in.   40
Don't refuse to accompany him, although the road stretches long,
   and the Dog Star toasts the fields with burning thirst,
Though the rainbow fringing the heaven with a rusty border
   shrouds the coming storm.
Or if he wants to cross the blue sea by ship,   45
   with yourself at the oar propel a light boat through the waves.
Nor should you be ashamed to undergo laborious jobs
   or rub raw your hands on labors unfamiliar;
And if he likes to enclose deep valleys with animal snares,
   to get what you please, don't let your shoulders begrudge a load
      of nets.   50
If he wants weapons, try to play the sport with a weak hand;
   for him to win often, expose a naked side.
Then he will become gentle toward you; you'll be able to steal
   dear kisses: he'll resist, but will give you your due;
At first he'll give the kisses stolen, then, if you ask, he'll offer them on
   his own;   55
   and then he will wish to wrap himself around your neck.
Ah, today's world trades in evil and troubling arts:
   even a tender boy has gotten the habit of desiring gifts.
But you who were the first to teach that love is up for sale,
   whoever you are, I hope an unlucky stone grinds your bones.   60
Love the Muses of Pieria, boys, and the erudite poets;
   don't let gifts of gold outweigh the Muses.
In song Nisus' lock is purple: if there were not songs,
   ivory would not have gleamed from the shoulder of Pelops.
Whomever the Muses echo in song will live as long as the earth   65
   supports oaks, the sky the stars, and rivers carry water.

But he who fails to heed the Muses, who sells love,
    let him follow the chariots of Ops of Mount Ida,
Fill three hundred cities with his wanderings,
    and cut off his worthless parts to the measures of Phrygian
        music.   70
Venus herself wills a place for sweet-nothings: for she favors
    the laments of suppliants, the tears of the love-sick."
In oracular voice the god uttered such things for me to sing to Titius.
    But Titius' wife forbids him to recall it.
He should obey her. But you, attend me, your master,   75
    you who get mistreated by the deft skill of a crafty boy.
To each his own boast: mine, that spurned lovers
    seek my advice; our door is open to all.
There will be a time when I, an old man, will trumpet the precepts of
    Venus
    as an attentive crowd of young men escort me home.   80
But oh my, with what a slow love Marathus° tortures me!
    My skills fail, my tricks don't work.
Spare me, please, boy, so I don't become a disgraceful story
    to be mocked —for my mastery nullified.

1.5

I was tough, in denial, asserting that I was bearing up well over the
    separation:
    but now that boast of mine is way out of line.
For I am driven, lashed over level ground like a spinning top
    which a young kid with customary skill whirls quick.
Burn the beast, torture him; don't let him say anything   5
    pretentious after this: tame his shaggy talk.
Yet forgive me, I beg you by the vows of our furtive bed,
    by Venus, and by your coiffured head.
When you were lying near death from a dreadful disease, they say that
    I was the one by my vows to have saved you.   10
I myself thrice lustrated° around you with purifying sulfur,
    after an old witch had chanted her magic formula;
It was I who prayed that no raging nightmares would harm you,
    dreams that had to be averted three times with holy meal.
It was I who veiled myself with fillet and with clothes unbelted   15
    in the silence of the night made nine prayers to the goddess of the
        crossroads.

1.4.81: the delayed mention of his lover Marathus, who frustrates his reverie.
1.5.11: the rite of lustration has the magic associated with the number three.

I rendered all that was due: now someone else relishes your love
   and, lucky him, takes advantage of my prayers.
But for myself, if only you escaped safe, I was crazy to keep
   fashioning a blessed life, a lunatic opposed by a disapproving
      god;   20
My dream: to cultivate the country, and my Delia to be there as
   guardian of crops,
   while in the boiling sun the threshing floor will crush the harvest
      grains;
Or she will protect for me the grapes in full vats
   and the gleaming must pressed by an eager foot.
It will be her custom to count the herd; a talkative young slave will
      grow   25
   accustomed to sport in the bosom of my loving mistress.
In honor of the farmer's god she will learn to bring the grape for the
      vines,
   for the crops the wheat spikes, a feast for the flock.
May she control everybody, may everything be her concern:
   but for me I'd like to be a total nobody in all the house.   30
Here will come my Messalla, for whom sweet fruits
   Delia will pluck from choice orchards.
May she worship so great a person, gladly tend him,
   prepare and personally serve his foods.
I kept imagining all this in my dreams, blown away by the southeast
      and south winds
   which now toss them amid the perfumes of Armenia.   36
How often I tried to dispel my misery with wine,
   but my pain changed all the wine to tears.
Sometimes I held another woman; but when ultimate joys came, oh,
      so close,
   Venus admonished and deserted me.   40
Then as she left, the lady said that I was bewitched,
   and (O shame) she claimed that my woman knows the
      unspeakable.
Our girl does not put the hex on me with her words,
   but with her face, her tender arms, and blond hair,
As did the blue Nereid, Thetis, who, reining in a dolphin,   45
   once was carried to the Thassalian Peleus.°
This is what hurts: that a rich lover is always hovering,
   that a clever old bitch comes to ruin me:
May she eat bloodied food and with a gory mouth
   drink bitter cups laced with gall;   50

1.5.45-46: Thetis, daughter of Nereus, married the hero Peleus in a ceremony
on Olympus. Their son was Achilles.

May specters whining of their fate always flit around her
    and a violent owl screech from the rooftops.
Let her rage on, driven by hunger to look for weeds at tombs
    and bones abandoned by savage wolves;
Let her bare her thighs running naked and howling throughout
        cities,   55
    and may a wild pack of dogs from the ghostly crossroads hound
        her from behind.°
It will happen: god gives the signs; for a lover there are divinities;
    a Venus forsaken rages against an abused law.
But you, quick now, forget those precepts of a greedy witch;
    for every love is conquered by gifts.   60
However, a poor lover will always be at hand for you; a poor lover
        will be
    the first to approach you and will be ever fixed in your soft side;
A poor lover will be your faithful companion in a dense crowd
    and will extend his hands to clear you a path;
A poor lover secretly will coax you toward his sly friends   65
    and remove lacings from a snow-white foot.
How vainly we sing; words fail and the door still
    remains shut; a hand must be full of gold to strike it.
But you, who now have the upper hand, fear my subterfuges:
    fickle fortune turns on a swiftly revolving wheel.   70
Ah, some luckier lover already stands persistent
    at your threshold, frequently looks about, turns away
Pretending to pass by the house, and then soon runs back,
    alone, and right in front of the doors, coughs.
Sly love is preparing something; take advantage of it, I beg you,   75
    while you may; for your boat is in clear water for now.

1.6

You keep casting alluring looks to hook me,
    then, Love, you get upset and tough on lovesick me.
What means your savagery against me? Is the glory so great
    for a god to have concocted plots against a mortal man?
The nets are set against me; my sly Delia now in secret   5
    during the silence of the night fondles someone else.
She's sworn that she didn't do it, but it's hard for me to believe her,
    after all, she is always denying me to her husband.
I am the wretch who taught her how she could trick
    guards; oh, oh, now I am netted by my own artifice.   10

1.5.53-56: the witch becomes so frenzied and wild that she becomes a creature
of Hecate, the goddess of the crossroads.

Now she has learned how to fashion pretexts for lying alone,
    how deftly to turn the double doors on a quiet hinge.
Once I gave her herbal juices to soothe the bruise
    caused by a tooth planted during our one-on-one sex.
But you, heedless spouse of a deceptive girl,   15
    watch me too, so she may never go wrong;
Be on guard; don't let her in lengthy conversation praise young men,
    or lie down at table with her breasts exposed from loose garments;
Don't let her deceive you with a nod, or with a finger trace
    spilled wine and draw notations on the round table top.   20
Every time she goes out, fear it, even if she claims to be visiting
    the sacred rites of the Good Goddess, off limits to all males.
But if you trust me, I alone shall follow her to the altars
    so, seeing her with my own eyes, I may dispel any fears of my own.
Often, as if to test her gems and signet ring,   25
    as a pretext I remember touching her hand.
Often I used wine to engender sleep for you; for myself I kept drinking
    sober cups, substituting water to make me a winner.
Unthinking, I have injured you, I confess; forgive me.
    Love ordered it; who should bring arms against the gods?   30
I am the one and (I will not be ashamed to speak the truth now)
    yes, your dog used to menace me all night long.
Why do you need a young wife? If you don't know how to protect
    your own goods, it is useless to lock doors.
While she embraces you, she sighs for an absent lover,   35
    then suddenly fakes a headache.
You should entrust me to watch over her: I do not refuse
    savage blows nor do I unbind the fetters from my feet.
Hey, you fops keep far away, any of you who artfully style your hair,
    who furl a billowing fold of a loose toga: 40
That none of you who meet her may be charged with a crime,
    stand off or stand far away—on another street.
So the god orders it; so the great priestess
    divined to me in her holy song.
Inspired to movement and possessed by Bellona, in her frenzy   45
    she fears no sharp flame, no torturous whips;
With a doubled-bladed ax she violently slashes her own arms,
    unhurt she splatters the goddess with profuse blood;
She stands, her side pierced by a shaft, she stands, her chest lacerated,
    and she chants the prophetic future as the great goddess foretells:50
"Do not violate the girl Amor protects;
    it would be a shame to have to learn this the hard way.
Should one touch her, he'll lose his wealth, as sure as blood flows
    from our wounds, as the winds snatch and scatter these ashes."

She has leveled, my Delia, some punishment against you: 55
    if you admit it (and him), I pray she be gentle.
I forgive you not because of you, no, but for your dear mother
    who moves me; this golden old lady softens my wrath.
In the darkness she brings you to me and in great fear
    secretly and silently joins our hands: 60
She waits for me at night clinging to the doors and recognizes
    the far-off sound of my approaching steps.
For my sake, live long, sweet old lady! Were it right,
    I'd contribute to you fitting years from my own.
Always I'll love you, and because of you your daughter;   65
    whatever she does, still she is your blood.
Teach her to be chaste, although a fillet does not bind
    and intertwine her locks nor a long gown cover her legs.
Make rules so strict for me, that I couldn't possibly
    praise another girl without her attacking my eyes;   70
And if she ever thinks I have committed a wrong, haul me
    by the hair and unjustly hurl me headfirst into the streets.
I wouldn't want to beat you, Delia, but if that raging fury comes,
    I'd hope to lack hands.
Don't be chaste out of savage fear, but out of a sense of faithfulness:75
    In my absence let our love for each other keep you true.
She who was faithful to none later succumbs to old age,
    and in her poverty spins twisted spindles with a trembling hand,
And weaves steady threads on a rented loom,
    as she weighs out clumps drawn from a snow-white fleece.   80
Crowds of young men rejoice to see her thus;
    they recall that rightly she, now an old woman, bears so many
        troubles.
From high on Olympus Venus spies her weeping
    and warns the unfaithful how vindictive she can be.
May these curses befall others; may both of us, Delia,   85
    be a model for love when our hair has grown white.

1.8

I cannot be fooled; I know what the nods of a lover mean,
    the mild words with their soothing sound.
I don't read guts that know the divine and I don't have oracles
    nor any bird to sing melodies to me of things to come.°
Venus herself has tied up my arms in a magic knot   5
    and taught me through and through with many lashes.

1.8.3-4: refer to different forms and approaches to divination to interpret signs
of love.

Stop the pretense: the god reserves a crueler burn
    for those he sees reluctant to yield to him.
What good now for you to have tended your soft hair
    and to have repermed your curls so often dyed?   10
What good your cheeks adorned in bright rouge, what good
    your nails trimmed by the skilled hand of an expert?
Useless now to update your wardrobe, to change your cloaks,
    and to bind your feet tight with a pinching lace.
She's a charmer, though she comes without a face all made up,   15
    and has not adorned her shining hair with time-consuming artifice.
Did an old woman with chants or paling herbs
    bewitch you in the stillness of night?
Chanting brings forth fruits from neighboring fields,
    chanting obstructs the path of an angered snake,   20
And chanting tries to spin out the moon from her chariot,
    and would cause it, were it not for the reverberating clash of
        bronze cymbals.°
Oh, why should I moan that chanting or herbs have hurt lovesick me?
    Beauty does not need the aids of magic.
But it hurts to have touched that body, to have given   25
    long kisses, to have planted thigh to thigh.
But you, Pholoe, remember not to be mulish to the boy:
    Venus punishes grievous acts with vengeance.
Don't ask for gifts: let the gray-haired lover give them,
    thus to snuggle his cold limbs in a soft bosom.   30
The young man is more precious than gold whose smooth face
    gleams, whose embraces no rough beard abrades.
Put your glistening arms upon his shoulder
    and scorn the great wealth of kings.
But Venus will discover a furtive way to lie with the boy,   35
    and, while he trembles, to plant close together tender breasts,
To give him wet kisses as he gasps and as tongues collide,
    and to fix teeth-marks upon his neck.
No precious stone, no jewels help her who sleeps alone
    in the cold unwanted by any man.   40
Oh, too late one calls back love, too late youth,
    when white-haired age infects an old head.
Then begins the pursuit of beauty: then a change of hairstyle
    to conceal the years, tresses tinged from the green bark of a nut;
Then the concern to pluck out white hairs by the root,   45
    to strip some skin to reveal a new face.

1.8.22: alludes to the practice of raising a racket during a lunar eclipse in order
    to avert its cause.

So you, while the age of your early years blooms,
    use it; it slips away on swift foot.
And don't rack Marathus: what glorious boast in conquering a boy?
    Be tough, girl, on old men.   50
Spare the naive boy, please; his case is not serious;
    but intemperate love stains his body with a yellow pallor.
How often the lovesick kid hurls his complaints against you
    when you are gone, and everything drips full of tears.
"Why does she reject me?" he says. "The guards could have been won
    over;   55
    the god himself has bestowed upon lovers the technique of deceit.
Furtive love is within my ken, how to draw a light breath,
    how to give stolen kisses without a sound;
In the middle of the night I can even creep in
    and secretly without a creak unlock the doors.   60
What good are skills, if a girl scorns her lovesick lover
    and brutally flees from her very bed?
Or after she has promised, suddenly and deceitfully breaks her vow;
    then I must spend the night awake in many a misery;
While I fool myself thinking that she'll come, whatever moves,   65
    I believe is the sound of her feet."
Stop crying, boy: she's not broken,
    and your eyes are already swollen and weary from weeping.
Pholoe, I'm warning you, the gods hate arrogance,
    and it does no good to offer incense on holy hearths.   70
This guy Marathus once played games with poor lovers,
    unaware that behind his head was an avenging god.
The gossip is that he often laughed at the tears of one in agony
    and feigned delay to keep a lover waiting.
Now he hates all disdainful airs, now he loathes   75
    any hard door bolted tight against him.
But payback is waiting for *you*, unless you stop being arrogant.
    With prayer upon prayer you'll want to recall this day.

1.9

If you had intended all along to injure a lovesick lover, why, by the
    gods,
    did you make pledges only to violate them in secret betrayal?
Oh, even if someone at first manages to hide his perjury,
    Retribution, however late, comes on silent feet.
Pardon him, heavenly ones: once without penalty you can justly   5
    let the beautiful injure your divinity—just once.
In pursuit of profit the farmer joins bulls to the handable plow
    and presses his hard work upon the earth;

In pursuit of profit over seas obedient to the winds
  unstable vessels trust the unerring stars;   10
My boy has been captivated by gifts. I hope that god
  will turn them to ashes and running water.
Soon enough he will pay the price to me; dust will detract
  from his comeliness, his hair disheveled by the winds;
The sun will burn his face and hair;   15
  a long road will wear down his delicate feet.
How often I warned you: "Don't pollute your beauty with gold.
  Usually myriad troubles accompany gold.
If any lover corrupted by money has violated his love,
  Venus is harsh and obstinate against him.   20
Better to brand my head and attack my body
  with a blade and cut open my back with a pliant whip.
Forget the hope of concealing any betrayal you are planning;
  the god who forbids deceptive secrets knows.
This very god has allowed the silent servant   25
  to express smooth words freely after much wine;
This very god has ordained those subdued by sleep to mutter sounds
  and to speak against their will of matters best hidden."
I said such things: now I am ashamed to say I wept
  and lay prostrate at your tender feet.   30
But at that time you swore more than once that you wouldn't sell
  your faith for any weight of enriching gold or for any jewels,
Not even if Campanian land were ceded to you as reward,
  not even if Falernian territory, Bacchus' bailiwick.
With those words of yours you could have robbed me of the gleam 35
  of heaven's stars and the clear flowing of rivers.
Yes, you wept; but I, untaught in the ways of deceit,
  in total trust wiped your wet cheeks.
What am I to do? Unless you're in love with the girl?
  Like your own example I pray she be fickle.   40
O how often, so that no one would be a witness to your words,
  late at night I pandered bringing you lamp after lamp.
As part of my service she came to you unexpectedly
  and lay in wait with head covered behind closed doors.
I died then, stupidly entrusting myself to love: 45
  for I could have been more cautious of your snares.
Yes, in my thunderstruck state I used to sing to you of noble deeds;
  but now I'm ashamed of our affair and my muses.
I wish Vulcan in his devouring flames would toast
  those poems, or a river of clearing water wipe them out.   50
Stay away from here, you, who like to sell your beauty
  and pull in a hefty price.

But for you who have dared to corrupt a boy with gifts, I hope your
   wife cuckolds you
     again and again and makes you a laughing stock—and gets away
     with it;
And, after she has wearied a young man with her furtive practice, 55
   interposes her clothes as she lies languid next to you.
May there always be traces of another on your bed
   and your house be open to horny lovers;
Let no one claim that her raunchy sister drank more cups
   than her or exhausted more men.   60
Gossip has it that she often holds wild parties to Bacchus
   until the rising wheel of the Morning Star challenges the day;
No other is able to use up the night more than her
   or to deal out the various delights of love's labors.
But your wife has learned through and through, yet you are too
   stupid to perceive   65
   her know-how, although she shakes her body for you with rare
   skill.
Do you really think that she coifs her tresses just for you
   or with a thick comb strokes her soft hair?
Does that face of yours persuade her to lace her arms in gold
   and to strut forth arrayed in Tyrian garment?   70
Not for you, but for a young man she wants to appear lovely,
   for him she curses your wealth and your home.
She does this out of no fault of her own; a cultivated girl avoids
   the body and the embraces of a gouty, ugly old man.
Yet our boy has lain with this guy: I do believe   75
   that he could mate with wild beasts.
Have you dared to sell to other bidders those sweet-nothings
   belonging to me?
   Dared, too, you crazy boy, to convey my kisses to others?
You will cry one day when another boy keeps me bound
   and usurps proud kingdoms in your realm.   80
Then your punishment will be my joy, and a golden palm
   attached to deserving Venus will mark my misfortunes:
"To you, Tibullus, freed from deceiving love,
   dedicates this and asks you, O goddess, to be kindly disposed."

2.3

The countryside and farmhouses, Cornutus, have a grip on my girl:
   he is of iron, oh, oh, whoever stays in the city.
Venus herself now has fled to the broad fields
   and Love is learning the rustic idiom of a plowman.

If I should catch sight of my lady there, how bravely   5
    I would churn the fat soil with a strong hoe,
And in the manner of a farmer follow the plow's handle
    as the sterile oxen plow up the acres to be planted;
Nor would I complain of the sun burning my graceful limbs
    or of a ruptured blister injuring my tender hands.   10
The handsome Apollo once quivered at the bulls of Admetus,
    his lyre and unshorn hair of no use to him;
Nor could he heal his own problems with healing herbs:
    whatever was his curative skill, love vanquished it.
This was the very god who drove heifers from stalls   15
    and who taught the process of mixing rennet with fresh milk,
And of hardening the milky mix into cheese,
    and then of squeezing the whey through narrow interstices.
O how often, as he was carrying a calf through the field,
    his sister met him and blushed for shame.   20
O how often, while he was echoing a song beneath a high valley,
    the cattle dared to break up the skillful singing with their lowing.
Often leaders during anxious crises sought out his oracles;
    often the crowd returned home fruitless from his temples.
Often Latona° grieved to see his holy locks disheveled,   25
    which even his stepmother Juno admired before.
Anyone who would look upon his shaggy head and loose locks
    would be seeking vainly for Phoebus' coiffure.
So where is your Delos, Phoebus, where now your oracular Pytho of
    Delphi?°
    Right now Love bids you to live in a small shack.   30
Once, as the story goes, when the eternal gods openly
    were not ashamed to be slaves of Venus, men were happy.
Now that god is a scandalous story: but the man who has a girlfriend,
    prefers to be a scandal of legend than to be a god without love.
But you, whoever you are, Cupid with a severe frown   35
    orders your command posts in our home.
Now the ages of iron praise not love but money;
    money means many evils;
Booty has equipped wild battalions with the arms of civil discord:
    from it comes gore, from it slaughter and death ever nearer and
        nearer.   40
Booty has forced the doubling of risks on a restless sea,
    furnishing the beaks of war to hesitant ships.
The lover of booty desires only to besiege huge estates
    to feed his enormous sheepfold on many acres;

2.3.25: Latona is the mother of Apollo and Diana.
2.3.29: Delos and Delphi are well-known cultic sites of Apollo.

He longs for a stone imported from abroad; in the hustle and bustle of
    the city   45
    a thousand teams in all their might transport his single column;
A causeway blockades the untamed sea, and fish are careless,
    neglecting the approach of winter's threats.
Yet for me, may Samian pots bring me happy banquets,
    and earthenware made from clay on a Cumaean wheel.   50
Damn! I see girls delight in rich men:
    if Venus chooses riches, bring on the money,
So my Nemesis may flow in luxury and throughout the city
    strut in full view draped in my gifts.
May she wear sheer negligees which a woman from Cos   55
    has woven and arranged with strips of gold leaf.
May she have dark-skinned companions from the heat of India,
    those whom the fire of the Sun and his yoked horses have tinged
        dark,
Who vie to furnish her choice colors,
    red from Punic Africa and purple from Tyre.   60
I speak of things everybody knows; the very man who now possesses
    a kingdom,
    more than once the barbarian slave-block has forced him to bear
        chalked feet.°
In you, harsh crop, who have lured my Nemesis from the city,
    may the earth have no faith and deal you out barren seeds.
And you, soft Bacchus, planter of the pleasing grape,   65
    yes, you, Bacchus, curse and abandon the vats.
You can't get away with hiding beautiful girls in accursed fields;
    O father Bacchus, your vintages are not worth that much.
Good-bye, fruit crops, no more country life for girls:
    let the acorn be food, and in the old way water be the drink.   70
The acorn once nourished those of old, and everywhere those old-
    timers loved it.
    What harm to them that they did without planted furrows?
For then Love breathed upon them and openly gentle Venus
    provided joys in a shaded valley.
There was no guard, no door to shut out pained lovers: 75
    if it is right to say, I pray the return of that lifestyle...
    when a shaggy cloth covered hairy bodies.
Closed and rare now the opportunity of my seeing her;
    oh, poor me, what joy is there in a toga fitted loose?
Come, lead on: we will plow furrows in the fields at the command of
    a mistress: 80
    I do not reject chains or whips.

2.3.62: slaves on the block for sale had their feet chalked with gypsum.

2.4

So it's slavery time for me, I see, and a domineering woman too;
 now it's goodbye to that ancestral freedom of mine.
Yes, grim slavery is my lot; chains are fettering me,
 and Love refuses to unloose the bonds from lovesick me.
Whether I deserved it or did nothing wrong, it burns.   5
 I'm on fire right now, ouch! Take away the torches, savage girl.
O, I wish I couldn't feel such pains;
 I'd rather be a stone on any icy mountain
Or a crag standing exposed to raging winds
 pounded by a shipwrecking wave of the vast sea!   10
Now the daytime is bitter, bitterer still the dark of night,
 for all my time drips with grim gall.
No good are elegies, no good Apollo, the maker of song:
 she keeps asking for money with a bottomless hand.
Go away, Muses, if you are no use to a lover: 15
 I do not cultivate you to sing wars;°
I don't trace the ways of the sun nor how, when she completes
 her circle, the moon wheels her horses and drives them back off.
I'm looking for easy ways to approach my lover via songs:
 go away, Muses, if they're worth nothing.   20
But I must get hold of some gifts by murder or crime
 so I won't lie a weeping wretch at her locked house,
Or steal some sacred objects hung in holy shrines;
 but Venus before all others I ought to violate.
She is the one leading me on to evil and crime; she gives me over   25
 to a gold digger of a girl; she should experience my sacrilegious
  hands.
Damn him who collects green emeralds
 and tinges snowy-fleeced sheep with Tyrian purple dye.
Silky gowns from Cos provide other reasons for greed among girls,
 as does the shiny pearl from the Red Sea.   30
These items have made women bad: hence the door felt a key
 and a dog began his defense of a threshold.
But if you bring money for a big bribe, the guard is overcome,
 and keys fail to keep you out, and the dog, too, is quiet.
Oh whatever heavenly one gave beauty to a greedy girl,   35
 what a good job he did for a ton of trouble!
From this weeping echoes out and brawls reverberate; this is the
  reason
 that the god, Love, now has become infamous.

2.4.16-18: the poet has no inclination to compose epic or didactic poetry.

But for you, who shut out lovers overwhelmed at the price,
    may wind and fire snatch away your savings account.   40
And may young men watch with joy those fires on your property
    and no one budge to pour water on the flame.
If death comes to you, there will be no one to mourn
    or to offer a service to your gloomy final rites.
But the good girl who has not been greedy, though she live to be   45
    a hundred, will be wept for at her burning pyre;
And some elderly gentleman, respecting his long-standing love,
    will offer yearly wreaths upon a mounded tomb,
And will say as he departs: "May you rest well and in peace,
    and may the earth be light upon your resting bones."   50
I utter true warnings, but what good is the truth to me?
    We must cultivate love by her law.
Should she order me to sell the estates of my grandparents,
    then, under her control, Household Gods, up for sale you go .
Whatever poison Circe has or whatever Medea's got,   55
    or whatever herbs the land of Thessaly grows,
And that "horse madness," when Venus breathes love into unbroken
      herds,
    which drips from the cunt of a mare in heat,
As long as my Nemesis gazes at me with a serene look,
    should she mix those and a thousand other herbs, I will drink.   60

SULPICIA

ELEGIES

The six epigrammatic elegies from Sulpicia provide us with a brief encounter with the female voice among the Augustan poets.

1

At long last love has come. I'd have greater shame concealing it
    than laying it bare to anyone.
I entreated the goddess of Cythera in my poetry:
    Voilà! She brought him and plunked him in my bosom.
Venus has paid off her promises; let him narrate the story
    of my happiness who has lost his own love.
I don't want to entrust anything to sealed tablets
    for just anyone to read before my lover does.
I enjoy my peccadillos. It's a big bother to put on faces for my
      reputation;
    gossip about me will say that I was deserving of a deserving man.

2

I hate it! My birthday is upon me, which in the boring country
    I must spend in misery and without Cerinthus.
What is sweeter than the city? How could a farmhouse befit a city-girl
    or a cold stream in the plain of Arezzo?°

2.4: Arezzo, in Latin Aretium, birthplace of Maecenas in northern Tuscany.

Be calm now, Messalla; you are too solicitous of me;   5
    roads, my cousin, are not always seasonable for travel.
Abducted against my will I leave behind here my heart and feelings,
    since a force does not allow me my own decisions.

3

Have you heard? That grim journey has been lifted from your girl's
    heart.
She can now be in Rome on her birthday.
Let us all then celebrate that birthday together,
    which perhaps comes as a surprise to you.

4

I'm happy that you allow yourself so much peace on my behalf
    so I won't suddenly collapse a total klutz.
Better for you to care for your toga or that whore burdened by her
    work basket
    than for Sulpicia, daughter of Servius:
But some are worried on my account and who are in pain for me,   5
    because I am giving way to the bed of an ignoble woman.

5

Do you have, Cerinthus, a loving thought for your girl,
    for the fever that now racks my weary body?
Ah, I would not ever struggle to survive dire diseases
    unless I thought you too wanted me to.
But what good would it do me to survive any illness, if your heart   5
    remains unmoved by and unfeeling of my fate.

6

May I not ever be, my light, so hot a lover
    as I feel myself to have been a few days ago,
If in all my youth I have ever done anything so stupid,
    anything I would confess a greater regret for,
Than the fact that I left you alone last night   5
    desiring to conceal from you my ardor.

OVID

HEROIDES

The *Heroides* is an innovative poetic work of an epistolary form that seems to derive from Propertius' experimental letter of Arethusa (4.3). The work consists of fictionalized letters of mythological female figures sent to lovers or husbands. The dramatic monologues of the figures involved are cast at crucial times in their mythic lives and are mostly drawn from the tragic and epic tradition. In almost every case impassioned pleas and speeches, desperate or angry, and from one emotionally hurt or devastated, fill the texts of the poems.

1 (PENELOPE TO ULYSSES)

Your dear Penelope sends you this letter as you tarry, Ulysses;
    You needn't write me back: just come yourself.
Troy, hated by Greek girls, is fallen; to be sure
    Priam and all of Troy were hardly worth so great a cost.
O gods, I wish that adulterer,° when he was on his way to Sparta,   5
    had been sunk in raging waters!
I would not have lain so long, cold on a deserted bed,
    nor would I be complaining, abandoned, that the days drag on so
        slowly,
Nor, as I try to beguile the spacious night,
    would I be wearing out my widowed hands on the hanging web of
        the loom.   10
There was no time I didn't fear dangers more serious than the reality.
    Love is an estate filled with worrisome fear.

1.5: the adulterer is Paris.

I imagined violent Trojans were about to attack you,
   at Hector's name I was always pale.
If a story teller related that an enemy had laid low Antilochus,°   15
   Antilochus was reason for my terror;
Or that Patroclus, son of Menoetius, had fallen in armor meant to
    deceive,
   I wept that trickery could fail;
Tlepolemus' blood warmed a Lycian spear:°
   Tlepolemus' death renewed my worry.   20
In sum, whenever a throat was slit in the Argive camp,
   the heart of your loving wife became colder than ice.
Yes, there is a just god: he has favored my faithful love;
   Troy has been reduced to ash and my husband is safe.
The Greek leaders have returned, the altars smoke;   25
   barbarian booty is dedicated to the gods of the fatherland;
Brides bring gifts in thanks for their husbands' lives.
   Those men now sing the fates of Troy conquered by their destiny.
Just old men admire and girls tremble,
   a wife hangs upon the war-stories from the lips of a husband,   30
And someone outlines on the table the ferocious battles
   and depicts all of Troy with a drop of wine.
"Here the Simois flowed; over there is the plain of Sigeum,
   here stood the lofty palace of old man Priam,
Over there Achilles, grandson of Aeacus, pitched his tent, right there,
    Ulysses;   35
   here mangled Hector terrified horses into a gallop."
The aged Nestor, you see, reported everything to your son sent
   in search of you; and he reported it to me.
[He also related that Rhesus and Dolon had died by the sword,
   how each was betrayed, one by sleep, the other by deceit.]   40
You were much too forgetful, yes, much too forgetful of your loved
    ones,
   when in reckless daring you entered the Thracian camp in a nightly
    ruse;
When you and your single assistant killed so many men.
   But—you were very cautious and mindful of me before.
Fear fluttered in my bosom until I heard that you, in victory,   45
   brought Thracian horses through friendly lines.
But what good does it do me to hear that Troy has been smashed and
    leveled
   by your muscles, that what once was wall is now top soil,

1.15: Antilochus was one of Nestor's sons, killed by Memnon.
1.19: Tlepolemus was the King of Rhodes; he died fighting Sarpedon, king of
   Lycia and an ally of Troy.

If I remain now just as I was when Troy was holding firm,
　and if my husband is still absent, and there's no closure for me? 50
For others Troy's citadel lies in ruin where a victorious settler plows
　with a captive bull; only for me Troy still stands.
Yes, where Troy was is now a field crop, the sickle has to prune away
　the overgrowth, lush and fecund with the blood of Phrygians,
Curved plows strike the half-buried bones   55
　of heroes, weeds hide the ruin of homes.
In victory you left, but I can't find out why you delay return so long,
　or where in the world you hide yourself and your heart of iron.
When a foreigner docks his ship upon these shores,
　I inquire in detail about you, and before he departs,   60
So he may hand it over to you, if ever he meets you somewhere,
　I give him a letter written by my own hand.
We sent to Pylos, land of Neleus passed on to aged Nestor;
　the report sent back from Pylos leaves some doubt.
We sent to Sparta: Sparta too knows nothing of the truth.   65
　What lands are you living in? Where do you tarry so far away?
Better for me if the walls built by Apollo were even now still
standing.
　Oh, I get angry, so fickle are my prayers.
I'd know where you were fighting, and I'd only fear the battles:
　my laments would be the same as those of many wives.   70
Now, I don't know what to fear; yet in my deranged state I fear
　　everything,
　and broad is the scope exposing my worries.
The risks inherent in the sea, the dangers of land,
　these are the true causes, I suspect, of your delay that is so long.
While I was foolish to fear these, yet I know you men and your
　　lust;   75
　the love of a foreign woman can bewitch you.
And perhaps you would relate to her how provincial and countrified
　　is your wife,
　the type who only objects to coarseness in wools.
I hope I am wrong and this charge I lay vanishes into thin air,
　that you, though free to come back home, are absent against your
　　will.   80
My father Icarius tries to force me to abandon my widowed bed
　and carps on and on about my endless postponements to remarry.
Let him carp forever! I am yours and should rightfully be called
　　yours:
　I am always Penelope, always Ulysses' wife.
Yet, my devotion, my prayers, and my self-control break him
　　down,   85
　and he tempers his impulses.

Suitors from Dulichium, from Same, and those raised on lofty
    Zacynthus,°
  a gang of dissolute spendthrifts, descend upon me.
None here stop them from usurping your palace;
  they tear apart our vitals, consume your resources.   90
Need I tell you of cruel Pisander, Polybus, and Medon?
  Eurymachus and Antinous° who have greedy hands?
And all the others? To your disgrace you yourself, although absent,
  are feeding them
  from the store of goods won by your blood.
The beggar, Irus, and Melanthius,° the keeper of the flock to be
    consumed,   95
  the ultimate shame and disgrace, add to your losses.
In number we are three weak souls, I, a wife without power,
  Laertes, your old father, and Telemachus, your boy.
I almost lost him to a recent ambush,
  as he was ready to travel to Pylos against everybody's wishes.   100
I pray the gods ordain this: that in the due course of fate
  he close my eyes in death, and he close yours.
On our side are the cowherd, your aged nurse,
  and third, the faithful warden of the dirty pig sty.
But Laertes, since he is of no use in armed fighting,   105
  lacks the power to hold on to the kingdom against so many
    enemies;
Telemachus will grow to a stronger age—only let him live—
  but *now* his father should be standing by him and protecting him.
I lack the power to drive these unwanted suitors from the halls;
  come quickly, a port and sanctuary await you and yours.   110
You have a son and I pray you may hold him still; he should have
    been instructed
  with his father's training during his tender years.
Take a concern for Laertes: so you may be the one to bury his eyes in
    death,
  he endures to postpone the final day of his destiny.
I, a mere girl when you departed,   115
  though you return right now, will surely appear an old woman.

1.87: Dulichium, Same, and Zacynthus, islands not far from Ithaca, are considered
  to be part of Ulysses' kingdom.
1.91-2: a list of prominent suitors of Penelope. Medon was to be spared in
  Ulysses' onslaught against the suitors.
1.95: Melanthios, a goatherd, sided with the suitors.

5 (OENONE TO PARIS)

Are you reading this? Or does your new wife forbid it? Read it.
  It is not in handwriting from a Mycenaean hand.
I, Oenone, fountain nymph, most honored in the forest of Phrygia,
  but wronged, complain about you, my own—if you allow this
    address.
What god has exercised his divine power to oppose my prayers?   5
  That I not remain yours because some fault of mine blocks the
    ways?
You should bear calmly whatever you suffer deservedly;
  punishment that comes undeserved comes with pain.
Not yet were you so important when I, a nymph born from
  a mighty river god, eagerly joined myself to you as my husband. 10
Now you are the son of Priam—let not any respect for rank hinder
    the truth—
  but then you were a slave, and while a slave, I, a nymph, deigned
    to marry you.
We often whiled away the time resting among the flocks beneath the
    shade of a tree;
  grass and leaves made up our bed.
Often, as we lay upon of a bed of straw and a pile of hay,   15
  a humble hut protected us from the hoary frost.
Who used to show you the glades best for hunting?
  The rock cliff where a wild animal would hide her cubs?
As your attendant I stretched the nets of intricate meshes,
  and often I drove the hounds over long ridges.   20
Beech trees you carved still bear my name;
  and "OENONE", notched by your hooked knife, can be read.
[And a poplar tree, as I recall, planted in a river bed,
  has a letter incised on it that recalls our memory.]
My carved names grow as the tree trunks grow;   25
  o trees, grow and rise straight to become my memorials.
Poplar tree, planted on the edge of the bank, I pray, live on,
  who have in your furrowed bark this epigram:
"When Paris is still able to breathe, if Oenone is abandoned,
  the waters of the Xanthus will turn around and flow back to their
    source."   30
O Xanthus, flow in reverse, and turn around, waters, and flow back:
  Paris has deserted his Oenone and withstands it.
That day pronounced my pitiable fate; from that moment
  began the coldest winter storm of changed love,
When Venus, and Juno, and Minerva, who would have been more
    lovely   35
  had she assumed her armor, came naked for your judgment.

My bosom fluttered, astonished, a cold tremble ran
    through my bones, as you told me the story.
My fear was not moderate; I consulted old women
    and old men: they agreed that it was a sacrilege.   40
A fir was felled, beams were sectioned, a fleet was built;
    the blue waters of the sea received the ships caulked with wax.
You left in tears; don't you dare deny that.
    Your love now should shame you more than that for love past.
You cried and you saw my eyes weeping;   45
    we both mingled our tears with our sighs;
Not so intertwined is the elm bound with vines
    as your arms which embraced my neck.
O how often when you wailed that the wind was holding you back,
    your comrades laughed! There was a favorable wind.   50
How often you sent me away only to call me back to kiss me!
    Your tongue was barely able to say: "Goodbye."
A light breeze puffs up the sail furling on the hard mast
    and the water churned by the oars foams white;
Unhappy, I follow with my eyes, as far as I can, the departing sails; 55
    my tears moisten the sand.
I pray to the sea-green Nereids that you come quickly,
    yes, that you may come quick to my loss.
So, intending to return in answer to my prayers, have you returned
        for the sake
    of another? Oh, me! I was persuasive on behalf of an ill-omened
        whore.   60
A natural breakwater faces the immense deep;
    it was a crag, a barrier against the waves of the sea.
From it I first recognized the sails of your ship,
    and my first impulse was to run through the surf to you.
While I was hesitating, a gleam of purple on the top deck struck my
        eye.   65
    I was afraid: it was not from your attire.
The ship comes closer and beaches under a swift breeze;
    with trembling heart I saw the cheeks of a woman.
Wasn't that enough? I was utterly mad to hang around—
    a shameless "girlfriend" was clinging to your breast.   70
Then I ripped my blouse, I beat my breasts,
    and I cut my wet checks with a hard fingernail;
I filled holy Ida with wailing and howls;
    there to the rocks I knew, I brought those tears.
I pray that Helen will feel such pain and weep when she has been
        abandoned   75
    by her husband, that she will endure everything which she has
        inflicted on us.

Now they suit you—those women who would follow you
    across the seas and desert their legitimate husbands;
But when you were an impoverished herdsman driving herds,
    no one but Oenone was the wife of that poor nobody.   80
I do not admire wealth, nor does your royalty impress me;
    and I will not be called one of Priam's many daughters-in-law.
Surely Priam would not refuse to be the father-in-law of a nymph
    nor would I be ignored as daughter-in-law by Hecuba.
I am worthy of becoming the wife of a powerful prince;   85
    I have hands which can grace scepters.
Don't scorn me because I used to lie with you on a bed of beech
    leaves;
    I am more than fit for a purple bed.
In short, my love is risk free: from it no wars
    begin; nor does the sea bring ships seeking revenge.   90
The runaway daughter of Tyndareus is being reclaimed by hostile
    arms;
    she comes into your bed chamber arrogant with that dowry.
Whether she should be restored to the Greeks, ask Hector,
    your brother, or Delphobus,ᵛ or Poulydamas.
Consult with others: what serious Antenor thinks, what even Priam
    himself   95
    argues. Both these men have the experience of long age as teacher.
Disgraceful is your first lesson—preferring an abducted woman to
    your fatherland.
    You should be ashamed; her husband is starting a just war.
Be smart, don't trust that Spartan woman to be faithful,
    who so quickly turned to your embraces.   100
Just as the younger son of Atreus now loudly bemoans the violation
    of the marriage bond,
    and is in pain, hurt by her love for an interloper,
So you, too, soon will wail; chastity once violated is repaired
    by no art; it is lost once and forever.
You think she is on fire for your love? Once she loved Menelaus like
    that.   105
    Now that gullible man lies a widower in their bed.
Fortunate is Andromache who married a faithful husband!
    You should have taken your brother as model when you embraced
    me as wife.
You are lighter than leaves that flit about weightless,
    their sap gone, dried by the shifting winds;   110

5.94: Deiphobus was also a son of Priam and brother of Paris. He "married"
Helen after the death of Paris.

There is no more substance in you than the tip of a wheat stalk
   which, charred by continuous suns, dries, hardens, and becomes
      light.
Yes, once your sister (and now I repeat it) with her hair disheveled
   in a raging fit sang this prophecy to me:°
"What are you up to, Oenone? Why do you plant seeds in sand?   115
   You are plowing shore lines with bullocks that will bring you no
      crop.
A heifer arrives from Greece to ruin you, your country, and your
   home.
   Stop her, I say! A Greek heifer is on her way!
While you can, sink the immoral ship in the sea!
   Oh, she sails bringing with her so much blood for Phrygia!"   120
Her words were in mid-course: servants seized her in her raving;
   my golden hair stood on end.
Ah, too true of a prophet of my misery you were;
   look, already that heifer takes possession of my pastures!
No matter how beautiful she is, she is still an adulteress;   125
   seduced by her guest, she has abandoned her marriage gods.
Theseus, if I am not mistaken of the name, yes, some fellow Theseus
   once before abducted her from her fatherland.
Can you really believe that she was returned a virgin by a man both
     young
   and hot-blooded?° How I discovered this you can well ask: I am in
     love.   130
You may call it rape, but with this term you would be concealing the
     blame;
   she has been raped so often because she has exposed herself to
     rape.
But Oenone remains chaste, even to a deceitful husband,
   and yet could have cheated by the very rules you set.
Swift-footed satyrs, that raunchy throng, were quick to chase me,   135
   but I hid myself in the woods,
And also Faunus, wearing on his horny head a pointed pine cone,
   where Mt. Ida swells on enormous ridges.
The wall-builder° of Troy, resplendent carrying his lyre, made love to
     me:
   he has the honor of my stolen virginity,   140
And that, too, after a struggle. Yet I tore his hair with my nails,
   I disfigured his face with my fingers.

5.113-114: a reference to the prophecies of Cassandra, sister of Paris.
5.127-130: Theseus had kipnapped Helen who was rescued by her brothers
   Castor and Pollux.
5.139: a reference to Tros, the eponymous founder of the walled city.

I made no demands for jewels and gold as the price for his wanton
    sex:
    it is shameful to buy the body of a freeborn woman with gifts.
He thought me worthy to transmit to me his skills in medicine   145
    and gave my hands access to his gifts.
Every herb capable of healing, every root useful to a doctor,
    growing all over the world, is now mine.
O poor me! Love cannot be cured by herbs;
    skilled in the art of healing I fail in that very art.   150
[The story is told that the inventor of the healing art himself pastured
    cows in Pherae
    and was wounded by the fire of love that I feel.]°
Since neither the earth, so fecund in bearing plants,
    nor a god can help, you can bring me a cure.
Yes, you can do it, and I deserve it: pity a worthy girl!   155
    I do not come with Greeks bringing bloody war;
But I am yours and was with you from your childhood years,
    and I pray to be yours for the rest of my life.

7 (DIDO TO AENEAS)

As a white swan, when the fates of death call, lights upon moist
    grasses
    and sings to the shallow waters of the Meander,°
I address you, not because I would expect my prayer
    could move you—I have begun it with a god against me—
but, since I have utterly wasted my just services, my reputation, and
    the modesty   5
    of both my body and heart, it is a light matter to waste words.
Have you already decided to go, your mind made up to leave hapless
    Dido,
    and will the same winds drive your sails and carry off your faith?
Are you determined, Aeneas, to cast off your ships and break your
    promise,
    to seek Italian realms not even knowing where they are?   10
Does new Carthage no longer touch your heart, or her walls rising
    high,
    or the fortunes of power handed over to your control?
You run away from things achieved to seek things to achieve, to find
    another land
    in the world when you have already won one.

5.151-152: a reference to Admetus whom Apollo served for a year.
7.1-2: refer to the story of Cycnus, a musician king in Italy who was transformed
    into a swan and catasterized (i.e., made into a constellation) by Apollo.

Well, suppose you find this land: who will hand it over to you to
    control?   15
    Who will give his own fields for strangers to cultivate?
I suppose another love waits for you, another Dido,
    another promise for you to make and then to break again.
Is it ever likely that you will found a city as magnificent as Carthage,
    and view your peoples, high on a citadel?   20
Although all this may come true, I pray the gods not delay your
    solemn wishes.
    Where will you get a wife to love you as much as I do?
I burn, blazing like wax candles coated with sulfur,
    like holy incense placed upon the smoking hearths.
Aeneas always clings upon my eyes, ever awake;   25
    night and rest ever bring back Aeneas to my mind.
He is really an ingrate, deaf to my kindnesses, the kind of man
    I'd like to be rid of, if I weren't such an idiot.
Yet I do not hate Aeneas, although he is a conniver;
    I complain about his lack of faith, but even as I complain I love him
        more madly.   30
Spare me, Venus, your daughter-in-law; embrace your hard-hearted
    brother,
    brother Amor;° let him soldier in your camp.
Or let me, who began it, do all the loving—I don't think it unworthy
    of me—
    and let him supply the fuel for my love.
I delude myself, and the fantasy flits before me in my deluded
    state: 35
    so different is he from the nature of his mother.
A rock, mountains, oaks sprung from lofty crags,
    or savage wild animals gave you birth,
Or the sea like the one you see now churned by the winds,
    on whose smashing waves nevertheless you make ready to sail.   40
Where are you off to? The winter obstructs you: here's to the winter!
    Cheers!
    Look, see the east wind drive and churn the waves.
Let me owe to the storms what I had preferred to owe to you;
    the wind and waters are more understanding than your heart.
I am not so important—surely you don't think you're being judged
    unfairly?—   45
    that you die on your flight from me over broad stretches of sea.
You indulge a hatred at a very high price and cost,
    if to rid yourself of me, you forfeit the value of life.

7.31-32: as the son of Venus, Aeneas was then the half-brother of Amor, god
    of love.

Soon the winds will subside, the waves level out flat,
    and Triton be riding over the sea on his blue steeds.   50
How I wish that you too were as changeable as the winds,
    and, unless the hardness of your heart surpasses oaks, you will be.
Why—as if you didn't know the raging power of the seas—
    why do you trust waters on which you have suffered so many
        trials?
Although you may cast off the cables and the sea point the way,   55
    yet the broad expanse of the deep possesses many grim dangers.
It's no good for those testing the seas to violate faith,
    that vast region exacts punishment against a lying traitor,
Especially when love has been wronged; after all they say that
    the Mother of Loves, herself, emerged nude in the waters off
        Cythera.   60
Ruined, I fear ruining him, hurting the hurter,
    and I shudder at the thought of my enemy shipwrecked, drinking
        the waters of the sea.
Live, oh, please! For me to ruin you is a better revenge than your
    death out there.
    Instead you will be indicted as the cause of my death.
Come, imagine a rapid storm pulling you down—may no weight   65
    be found in this omen—what will be on your mind?
At once there will come to you the perjuries of your lying tongue,
    Dido driven to her death by Trojan treachery.
Before your eyes will stand the mournful image of a deceived wife,
    her hair disheveled and bloody.   70
What is so important for you then to say: "Enough! I deserved it!
    Forgive me!"?
    And for you to think that whatever thunderbolts fall have been
        hurled against you?
Grant a short time for the savagery of the sea and of your own to
    pass;
    a safe journey will be worth some time well spent.
Although you don't give much of a damn for these matters, pity your
    boy, Iulus.   75
    It should be enough for you to have the credit for my death.
What did Ascanius do to deserve this? What have your gods, the
    Penates, done?
    Will a wave overwhelm those gods rescued from the fires?
You liar, you are not taking with you all that you brag to me about;
    and your father and the sacred images did not burden your
        shoulders,   80
All lies—and I am not the first to be deceived by your tongue
    nor the first to suffer your blows.

The mother of handsome Iulus, if you ask,
  is dead, abandoned by her hard-hearted husband.°
You told me this story and it shook me. Torture me,   85
  I deserve it: my punishment will be milder than my blame.
I have no doubt in my mind that your divinities will damn you:
  For seven winters you had been buffeted across sea and land;
I saved you from the waves, shipwrecked, and gave you safe haven,
  and hardly had I heard your name when I surrendered my
      kingdom.   90
I wish I had been content with these services,
  my lying with you would not have buried my reputation.
That day ruined me when in a cave beneath a slope
  a sudden storm from heaven forced us together.
I heard voices: I thought nymphs were howling;   95
  but it was the Furies sounding signals of my doom.
Exact the penalty, my lost chastity; violated are the rights
  of my marriage bed; my reputation ruined right to the ashes of my
      grave;
And you, my shades, and spirits and ashes of Sychaeus,°
  to which I go in misery filled with shame.   100
I have dedicated a marble shrine sacred to Sychaeus;
  leafy garlands and white woolen fillets hang over and cover it.
From it I heard a familiar voice sigh four times hailing me;
  in faint sound it said, "Elissa,° come!"
I do not hesitate; I come, I come as wife pledged to you.   105
  Yet I am slowed by the shame of my crime.
Forgive my mistake: a suitable authority deceived me;
  he removes the ill will from my offense.
His divine mother, his aged father, the bundle of his devoted son,
  his men who duly would remain gave me hope.   110
If I had to stray, my error has honorable causes;
  then too there is his reliability; in no respect will my lapse be a
      shame.
The course of my destiny, as it was before, lasts to the very end
  and follows the final moments of my life.
A husband fell, slaughtered at the altars of the house,   115
  and a brother reaps the rewards of a most foul crime.

7.83-84: in Vergil *Aeneid* 4 Creusa, Aeneas' wife, gets lost in the turmoil and confusion of the sack of Troy. Here Dido claims that Aeneas deliberately deserted her.

7.99: Sychaeus, Phoenician husband of Dido, was killed by her brother, Pygmalion.

7.104: Elissa is another name of Dido.

I am driven into exile; I leave behind the ashes of a husband and a
    fatherland;
  an enemy pursues me as I travel over doubtful routes.
I land upon these shores, escaping brother and sea;
  I buy this shoreline which I gave to you...liar.   120
I established a city, built its walls spreading far,
  the envy of the neighboring communities.
Wars swell; a stranger and a woman, I am tested by wars,
  and I barely make ready crude gates and arms.
A thousand suitors found me desirable; they joined together to
    complain   125
  that I preferred some one else over marriage to any of them.
Why do you hesitate to bind and hand me over to Iarbas, the
    Gaetulian?°
  I would submit my arms for you to do this wicked deed.
There is my brother, too, whose unholy hand, spattered with the
    blood of my husband,
  demands to be stained with mine.   130
Put down the images of your gods and the sacred emblems you
    profane with your touch;
  your right hand is too impious to worship the heavenly ones.
Since you were destined to be a worshipper of gods who escaped the
    fire,
  the gods regret their escape from the flames.
Perhaps, too, you would desert a pregnant Dido, you bastard!   135
  A part of you lies enclosed in my body.
That pitiable infant will join the fate of his mother,
  and you will be the executioner of your son unborn;
The brother of Iulus will die along with his mother,
  a single punishment of fate will take away two joined together. 140
"But a god orders me to go." I wish he had forbidden your coming,
  and that Punic soil had not been touched by Trojans!
Of course, this is the god guiding you as you are tossed by malevolent
    winds
  and waste so much time on a raging sea.
You would have hardly labored so hard to return to Troy,   145
  if it were the same great city it was when Hector was alive.
You do not seek the Simois of your fatherland but the waves of the
    Tiber.
  When you arrive where you desire, you will be a complete
stranger.

7.127: Gaetulia refers broadly to the interior of Africa.

For the land you seek lies concealed and avoids your ships.
  You will almost be an old man by the time you reach that
    "promised land."   150
Instead, receive these people here as my dowry—no more
  misdirection—
  and accept the wealth of Pymalion that I brought here with me.
More fruitful it will be for you if you resettle Ilion to my Tyrian city;
  in the role of king take hold of the state and sacred scepter.
If in your heart you are eager for battle, if Iulus asks   155
  from where will come the triumph to be won by his prowess
in war,
We will present an enemy for him to conquer, should one be lacking.
  This area offers a range for terms for peace and weapons for war.
By your mother, by the spears and arrows of your brother,
  by your comrades in flight, and by the sacred objects of Troy and
    her gods—   160
So may they survive, the men of your people whom savage Mars
  escorts home, and may your losses from that war be limited to a
    few,
And may Ascanius fulfill his years in a happy life,
  and the bones of aged Anchises be gentle in the earth—
You, I pray, pity the home which surrenders itself to your control. 165
  What crime do you claim was mine except falling in love?
I was not born in Phthia° or mighty Mycenae,
  nor did my husband or father stand against you.
If you are ashamed to have me as your wife, I'll reject the name of
  "bride," happy to be
  called "hostess"; as long as Dido is yours, she'll bear any title you
    want.   170
I know the straits that pound the coast line of Africa;
  they grant and deny a voyage at fixed times of the year.
When a breeze offers you passage, you will furl your sails to the
    winds;
  now only light seaweed detains your ships driven ashore.
Entrust me to observe opportune weather: you will go more secure, 175
  and I will not permit you to stay, even if you desire to.
Besides, your comrades need rest, and your battered fleet
  requires a little delay for more repairs.
For all the benefits I gave you and for any that I will yet extend to you
  I ask a little time, not out of the hope of marriage,   180

7.167: Phthia, a city in Thessaly, the birthplace of Achilles, was a possible threat
  to Aeneas.

While the seas and my love calm down, while I learn, with the
     passing of time
   and with an adjustment to the idea, how to face and deal bravely
       with my grief.
Otherwise, I intend to breathe out the last of my life;
   no longer can you be cruel against me.
I wish you could see the sight of me as I write;   185
   I am writing with a Trojan sword lying on my lap,
Tears flood across my checks and fall upon the drawn weapon,
   soon to be stained with blood rather than tears.
How well your gifts suit my fate!
   You are building my tomb and the price is cheap.   190
Not for the first time does a weapon strike my breast;
   that spot shows the scars of savage Love's wound.
Anna, my sister, my sister Anna, accomplice of my offense,
   soon you will give the final services to my ashes.   194
When I have been consumed upon the pyre, the epitaph, "Elissa, wife
     of Sychaeus"
   will not be inscribed; only this epigram will be on the marble stone
       of my tomb:
"Aeneas caused my death; he even provided the sword;
   Dido by her own hand used it for her demise."

10 (ARIADNE TO THESEUS)

I have found every species of wild beasts to be more tender than you
     are:
   I could not have been worse off trusting myself to any of them than
       to you.
I am sending you the letter you are reading, Theseus, from the very
     shore
   where the sails carried off your ship without me.
Here my sleep badly betrayed me, and so did you,   5
   ambushing my sleep by your shameful act.
It was the time when a crystal frost sprinkled the earth
   and birds sheltering under leaves complained.
Half-awake and sluggish from sleep I turned,
   half-lying down, moving my hands to embrace Theseus.   10
He was gone! I pull back my hands and try again,
   moving my arms all over the bed: he was gone!
Fear shook me from my slumber; terrified, I spring up,
   bolting from my widowed bed.
With the flat of my hands I pounded my breasts that rang out from
     the blows;   15
   I tore my hair still tangled from the sleep.

There was a moon: I look to see if there is anything in sight besides
    coastline;
  my eyes find nothing except the shore.
Now here, now there, every direction I run in aimless search;
  the deep sand slows my girlish feet.   20
As I shouted along the entire stretch of shore "Theseus,"
  the hollow rocks echoed your name.
Many times I called you and every time that place redounded the call:
  Yes, that very spot wanted to help me in my wretched state.
There was a high cliff: on top here and there are visible some
    shrubs;   25
  from here hung a rock eaten out by noisy waves.
I climb it—my will gave me strength—and far and wide
  I survey the deep expanse in my gaze.
Then I saw (for I experienced winds as cruel as you)
  the sails furled to a brisk south wind.   30
When I saw a sight I thought I did not deserve to see,
  I turned colder than ice and almost fainted.
Pain did not allow me to feel faint for long; I arouse myself;
  frantic, I call Theseus loud and clear: 34
"Where are you going?" I scream; "Come back, Theseus, come back,
    you bastard!
  Turn back the ship! It lacks its full complement."
This said, when my voice failed, I set about beating my breast again.
  My words and blows harmonized.
In case you couldn't hear, you could at least see,
  I waved my hands high to give signals;   40
I also tied white strips of clothing to a long branch
  to alert those who had obviously forgotten me.
Soon enough you were snatched away from my eyes. Then I wept at
    last;
  my soft cheeks had previously been dull with pain.
What else could my eyes do except weep for me,   45
  when I despaired seeing your sails?
Either I ran about aimlessly, alone, with hair streaming loose
  like a Bacchant° enthused by the Theban god,
Or looking out over the sea I sat cold on a rock,
  and I was as much a stone as my stone seat.   50
Often I return to the bed which had embraced us both,
  but is destined no longer to welcome participants.

10.48: Bacchants were the female worshippers of Bacchus (Dionysus) who was
  born from Semele, princess of Thebes.

I feel, not you, but your imprint on the bed,
    and the covers that your body had left warm.
I lie upon the bed dripping wet with the tears I had shed,   55
    and I cry out, "We two made our imprint on you; now restore the
        two of us.
We came here together; why do we not depart together?
    Deceitful little bed, where is he, that greater part of me?"
What am I to do? Where will I go all alone? The island has no
        habitation:
    I see no evidence of men, no evidence of oxen;   60
The sea surrounds the land on every side: nowhere a sailor,
    no ship off course about to journey here.
Imagine I somehow had a ship, a crew, and winds,
    what course am I to take? The land of my father denies docking.
Although I may glide over calm waters on a fortunate ship,   65
    and though Aeolus control his winds, I will be an exile.
I shall not look upon you, Crete, land of a hundred cities,
    site known to Jupiter when he was a child.
By my deed I have betrayed my father and the country ruled
    by a just parent—father and country, both names dear to me.   70
I kept you from dying in the wandering maze when I gave you the
        ball of thread
    to guide and direct your steps to victory:
You told me then: "I swear by these perils I risk
    that you will be mine as long as we both shall live."
Well, Theseus, we are both alive, but I am not yours, if you
        suppose   75
    that a woman buried by the guile of a lying mate is alive.
Had you killed me with the same club as you slaughtered my brother,
        you bastard,
    the promise which you gave would have been absolved by my
        death.
[Now I ponder not only what I am to suffer,
    but everything an abandoned girl can expect to endure.]   80
A thousand forms of death come to mind;
    the wait for death is harsher punishment that death itself.
I suspect that wolves soon will rush from every direction
    to rip open my guts with greedy teeth.
Perhaps this land breeds tawny lions;   85
    who knows? Maybe Dia° harbors a savage tiger.
They say the straits here cast large seals ashore.
    Who can protect me from swords being plunged through my side?

10.86: Dia is a small island in the Aegean where Theseus abandoned Ariadne.

I hate the thought of being taken captive and bound by a hard chain,
    being assigned tedious manual tasks as a slave,   90
I, who have Minos for a father, and for a mother the daughter of
    Phoebus,°
    and, what I remember most, you to whom I was engaged.
Whenever I see the sea, the lands, and the shores stretching far,
    against me many are the threats on land, many the threats on water.
The sky remains an option for me; but I fear the images of the gods. 95
    I am left resourceless, prey and food for rabid wild animals.
And if men do cultivate and live here, I distrust them.
    I have learned from my hurt to fear foreign men.
I wish Androgeos were alive! And that you, land of Athens,
    had not paid for your impious crimes with your deaths,   100
That you had not slaughtered with that knotty club, wielded
    high in your right hand, that man part bull, that bull part man,
Nor that I had given you the thread to show you your return,
    the thread, retraced and rewound by your hands.
Now I'm not surprised that Victory stood by you,   105
    and the beast was laid low and crashed upon the earth of Crete.
His horn could never have pierced your iron heart;
    although no gear protected you, you were protected by your heart.
There you brought flint, there steel,
    there you have Theseus, the man who out-flints flint.   110
Your father is not Aegeus; you are not the son of Aethra,
    Pittheus' daughter; rocks and sea bred you.
Cruel sleep, why did you hold me fast and keep me doing nothing?
    I should have been buried once and for all in everlasting night;
And you, too, winds, were cruel, over-prepared   115
    to hurl your blasts that work me into tears;
Cruel was the right hand that murdered my brother and me,
    and cruel your promise to me—an oath without meaning.
Sleep, wind, and promises have conspired against me,
    one girl betrayed by three treasons.   120
I'll die, never to see the tears of my mother;
    no one here will close my eyes at my death.
My soul will have no goal as it flits into unknown air;
    no friend will anoint my body laid out on the pyre;
Birds from the sea will circle around to prey upon my unburied
    bones.   125
    Are these the burial rites my gifts deserve?
You will reach your native port of Athens, be received by your
    fatherland,
    stand tall in the sight of the crowd flocking around you,

---

10.91: Pasiphae was the daughter of the Sun (Phoebus).

And you will gloat over your success, the killing of the man-bull,
    the maze made of stone, cut into intricate paths.   130
Be sure to add how you abandoned me here on this lonely land;
    I must not be stolen from the records of your career.
I wish the gods had made you see from the top deck of the ship,
    that my mournful figure had moved your expression.
Look upon me now, not with your eyes but with whatever
        imagination you can,   135
    as I cling to a rock smashed by promiscuous waves.
Look upon my hair unkempt and in disarray like one in mourning,
    and my clothes soaked with tears as if by a heavy rain.
My body shivers like wheat crops swept by north winds,
    and the letter that I trace keeps slipping from my trembling
        fingers.   140
I beseech you not out of my service to you, since it has turned out
        badly for me;
    for what I have done no gratitude is due,
But no punishment either. Even if it were not true that I rescued you,
    still there is no reason for you to cause my death.
These hands, wearied from beating my sorrowful breasts, in futile
        gesture   145
    I now stretch across the long strait to you.
In mourning I show you this hair of mine that remains.
    By the tears which your actions caused I beg you:
Turn the ship around, Theseus, reverse the sail and glide back here.
    If I die before you arrive, you will be taking my bones.   150

11 (CANACE TO MACAREUS)

Some of this script may be unclear; smudges make it illegible.
    True enough: the text will be smeared from the gory death of the
        composer.
My right hand holds the pen, the left has a drawn sword,
    and in my lap lies a loose sheet of paper.   4
This is the scene: the writer is fashioning a letter to her brother, the
        son of Aeolus.
    I imagine I may be pleasing our implacable father.
I wish he could be here to witness my death first hand,
    and view the work that he has initiated and achieved.
Cruel as he is, and more savage than his own winds,
    he'd look at my wounds, his checks dry.   10
Living with fierce winds has some effect:
    his temper matches the nature of his own subjects.
Within his power he controls the south wind, the west, and the north
        from Thrace,
    and he controls your wings too, blustering east wind.

Yes, he reins in the winds, but his anger swells beyond his control;   15
  he possesses realms too small for the arrogance of his power.
What good does it do me, promoted to the sky by the repute of my
    grandfather,
  to be able to list Jupiter among my family?
Is the iron blade, the gift of death—to be sure not my choice of
    weapon—
  less deadly, which I hold in my womanly hand?   20
O Macareus, I wish that the hour that joined us as one
  had come after my death.
Why, I ask you, did you, my brother, ever love me more than as a
    brother?
  Why was I something to you which a sister ought not to be?
I also became hot for love; some god—I used to know him only by
    hearsay—   25
  I felt in my heart that warmed to him.
Color drained from my face; my limbs shrank, losing weight;
  my mouth, forced to eat, took in the minimum of food;
No sleeps were easy, and night seemed like a year to me,
  and hurting I uttered a groan unconscious of any pain.   30
I couldn't render myself a good reason why I was experiencing these
    reactions,
  nor did I understand what it meant to be in love; but in love I was.
My nurse first sensed it; that old woman's mind intuitively grasped it;
  my nurse anticipated me: she was first to say: "You are in love
    with Macareus."
I blushed; in shame I cast down my eyes to my bosom: 35
  these signs were enough of a confession, though I said nothing.
Already the heavy swelling of my deflowered womb betrayed me;
  my limbs were weak, bearing the burden of my secret.
The nurse administered all kinds of herbs, all kinds of drugs;
  it was a risk for her to supply them. But she was unafraid.   40
Our purpose: to abort—only this fact we concealed from you—
  the growing fetus from deep inside my womb.
The baby clung tenaciously to life, resisting every device
  we tried, and remained safely protected from a hidden enemy.
Nine times the most beautiful sister of Phoebus arose,   45
  and now Luna began the new drive of her horses that bring the
    moonlight.
I didn't understand the reason for sudden pains in me,
  I was a young and raw recruit in matters of giving birth.
I couldn't restrain my painful voice: "Why betray your guilt?" my
    accomplice said,
  the old woman nurse who then covered my screaming mouth.   50

What to do, unhappy me? Birth pains are forcing me to moan;
  but fear, the nurse, and my shame forbid it.
I hold in the groans and I try to restrain the words escaping from me,
  and I am compelled to swallow my own tears.
Death was before my eyes; Lucina, goddess of childbirth, was refusing
  her help.   55
  If I died, death, too, was a serious indictment against me.
Leaning over me, your tunic and hair ripped,
  you pressed my breast against your own and warmed me again.
You then spoke to me: "Live, sister, O sister most lovely!
  Live! Do not destroy two people in the body of one!   60
Hope gives strength: you will be your brother's bride;
  you will be the wife of him who has made you a mother."
Though dead—believe me—yet I revived at those your words;
  from my womb the guilty burden descended.
No place for you to be a happy father: Aelous sits inside the
  palace.   65
  The evidence of the crime has to be secretly removed from our
    father's eyes.
The old nurse gets busy; quickly she conceals the infant in wheat
  spikes
  garlanded with white olive twigs and soft fillets;
She feigns a sacred rite, chanting a prayer.
  People make way for the holy emblems, our father too.   70
She was just at the threshold when our father's ears heard
  the baby's cry; the infant himself betrayed the fraud.
Aeolus seizes the child and lifts the veil from the phony sacred
  articles.
  The palace echoes with his outbursts of rage.
As the sea shimmers buffeted by a light breeze,   75
  as the ash tree, battered by a warm south wind, shakes,
So my paling limbs appeared to tremble;
  the very bed quaked from the shiver of my body lying upon it.
He bursts in shouting—revealing to all asunder our shame;
  he barely keeps his hands from my pitiable face.   80
I myself was too shamed to do anything except flood my cheeks with
  tears.
  My tongue was numb, blocked up by icy fear.
He had given the order to expose his own grandchild to wild dogs
  and birds,
  to be left as prey in a desolate spot.
Then that poor one began to bawl—you would have thought he
  sensed his fate—   85
  pleading with his grandfather over and over with such voice as he
    could.

What do you think was my state of mind, my brother?
  —you can infer it from your own feelings—
When our father, our enemy, snatched up in front of me my flesh and
    blood
  to be devoured by mountain wolves high up and deep in the
      woods?   90
He left my bedroom; then I started beating my breast
  and clawing my cheeks with my nails.
Meanwhile an attendant of my father came in with a mournful look
    on his face
  and uttered these shameful words:
"Aeolus sends this sword to you," —he handed it to me—   95
  "and orders you to judge what its purpose is."
I understand: I will act with courage to use the violent sword,
  to bury my father's gift in my chest.
These are the gifts you send, father, to my wedding?
  The dowry that will enrich your daughter?   100
Off with you, deceiving Wedding God, and take your marriage
    torches with you,
  leave this cursed household on troubled feet!
Furies, bring me the dark torches you carry;
  my funeral pyre will blaze bright from the fire you light!
My sisters, marry happy and with better fortune,   105
  but remember me after I have gone.
What crime did he commit, my child born only a few hours ago?
  What deed, scarcely born, to offend his grandfather?
If he possibly deserved death, let him be judged to have deserved it;
  but the poor thing is wrongly implicated in my crime.   110
O my son, grief of your mother, and prey of mad beasts,
  ripped apart on your day of birth, oh, oh,
My son, miserable token of ill-starred love,
  this day was your first, this day your last.
I was not allowed to shed tears over you,   115
  to come to your burial bringing shorn hair.
I didn't lean over you and cull cold kisses;
  hungry wild animals are mauling my own flesh and blood.
With a strike soon I, too, will escort the shades of our infant,
  not for long shall I be called a mother or one deprived of a
      child.   120
But you, whom I, your wretched sister, longed for in vain,
  please, I beg you, gather the scattered limbs of your son,
Bring them to his mother and place them in our shared tomb,
  and let one urn, however small, contain us both.
Live! Remember me, shed tears over the wounds of my body,   125
  and do not recoil from the loving body of the one you love.

I charge you, perform the last requests of your sister loved too much;
   I myself shall execute the orders of our father.

AMORES

Ovid's elegies present to us the persona of a rake and a self-conscious exploration and parody of the lover poet. In the *Amores* Ovid manipulates and pushes to an extreme the conventions and possibilities of narrative elegy. In style he is both elegant and witty, sharing characteristics of both Tibullus and Propertius. In his elegies Ovid portrays his lover poet as a *bon vivant*, knowledgeable and appreciative of the urban scene, its atmosphere, its salacious undertone, and its diverse experiences. Like his *Metamorphoses*, Ovid's *Amores* has enjoyed a kind reception in the Western literary tradition.

1.1

Arms and violent wars in ponderous style I was venturing
   to compose, with meter matching theme.°
I had completed the second line equal in length to the first when
     Cupid,
   they say, laughed, and sneaked in to steal a foot.
"You little savage, who gave you jurisdiction over poetry?   5
   We are the bards of the Muses, not members of your gang.
Now suppose Venus should grab hold of blond Minerva's arms
   and Minerva fan the flames of love's torches;
Who would approve Ceres ruling the forests along mountain ridges,
   or by some legal ploy the virgin goddess with the quiver
     cultivating farm lands?   10
Just imagine Apollo, remarkable for his long hair, learning to fence
   with a sharp saber,
   or Mars strumming the lyre on Mt. Helicon.
You already have a mighty empire, boy, too much power.
   Why are you so ambitious to claim a new line of work?
Or is everything in the world yours? Even the valleys of the Muses?15
   And as for poor Phoebus Apollo, hardly can he keep his own lyre
     safe from you.
My first line on page one arose lofty,
   but the next one flat out unstrung my tone.
I do not have the proper subject for light verse—
   no boy, no pretty girl with styled long hair."   20
So much for my protest: instantly he unhooked his quiver
   and drew out an arrow custom-made for my ruin.

1.1.1-2: Ovid refers to the meter and themes of epic.

Flexing his bow against his knee, he bent it, moon-shaped:
  "OK, bard," he said, "I'll send you something to sing about—take
    this."
Poor me! That boy hit the bull's eye with his arrows.   25
  Now I am on fire and Love is the ruler in my vacant heart.
Up, my work! Rise in hexameters and end in five feet!
  Goodbye to iron wars; farewell to your lines of six beats!
Wreathe your golden-haired temples with myrtle° from the seashore,
  my Muse, singing in measures of eleven counts.   30

1.4

That "man" of yours is coming to the very same party as us—
  Well, I hope it will be his last meal.
So what about me? Am I just to ogle the girl I'm in love with,
  a mere guest, as someone else gets to enjoy "touchy-feely?"
Will you, so perfectly spread beneath him, be fondling his chest?   5
  Will that guy, whenever he wants, be caressing your neck?
No wonder that after a round of wine the beautiful Hippodamia
  attracted the centaurs, those men of ambiguous form.
I don't make my home in the woods, and my members do not cling to
    a horse:
  still I have a hard time keeping my hands off you.   10
Learn what you have to do, and don't allow my words
  to be wisped away by the balmy breezes, east or west.
Get there before your "man" arrives—not that I see what good
  it can do, but come early before he does anyway.
When he reclines on the couch, and with a shy look you go   15
  to lie beside him, give my foot a secret touch.
Watch me for nods, for my every look that speaks;
  catch my furtive signs and return them.
I'll talk with my eyebrows, not utter a single word;
  I'll spell out words for you with my fingers, dipping them in
    wine.   20
When the thought of our "games of Venus" sneaks upon you,
  touch your blushing cheeks with your soft thumb.
If in your silent thoughts you become a little cross at what I do,
  rest your finger-tip lightly on the lobe of an ear.
If, on the other hand, what I'm doing or saying pleases you, light of
    my life,   25
  keep turning the ring on your finger.

1.1.29: myrtle was associated with Venus, the goddess born from the sea.

Put your hand on the table the way people touch it when they pray:
    that means you wish your "man" a lot of bad luck—well-deserved
        too!
When he mixes wine for you, be smart, order him to drink it himself;
    discreetly ask the waiter for the kind that you like.   30
Every time you return the cup to him, I'll take the first sip as it passes
    by;
    I'll drink from that very spot where you drank.
If your "man" happens to offer you a dish that he has tasted first,
    reject any food that his mouth has touched.
Don't allow him to fondle your neck or squeeze you in his arms;   35
    don't put your soft head upon his hard chest;
Keep his fingers off your bosom and nipples so caressable,
    and most of all don't give him a single kiss;
If you do, I'll show myself your lover and shout:
    "Those are mine!"—then stake my claim.   40
These things, of course, I'll see, but the acts that the dress conceals,
    those will cause all my blind fears.
Don't rub thigh to thigh nor cling leg to leg,
    nor let your delicate foot touch his hard toes.
I fear much, wretched because I have done as much in my wild
        past,   45
    yes, I am tormented with fear because of the example of my own
    life.
Often my girlfriend and I have had to rush pleasure
    and perform love's sweet labor beneath the cover of a dress.
This you will not do; still to avoid the suspicion,
    slip the guilty cloak from your back.   50
Let him drink on; keep urging and coaxing him—only no kisses;
    while he's drinking, keep pouring (secretly, if you can) the straight
        stuff.
Once he passes out, dead drunk,
    time and circumstance will provide us a plan.
When you rise to go home, and the rest of us rise too,   55
    try to move in the thick of the crowd;
You'll find me there in the throng or I'll find you:
    whatever part of me you can find to touch, touch it.
Oh, poor me! What advice I've said is good for only a few hours;
    now comes the separation from my lover at the command of the
        night.   60
Late at night your "man" will lock you in; I, tearful and gloomy,
    will lurk, following as far as I can, right up to those cruel doors.
Then he will take kisses and get more than kisses;
    what I receive from you by cheating, he wins by brutal right.

Give in against your will—that you can do—and as if under duress; 65
   no exchange of sweet-nothings, just silence and Venus in spite.
My most powerful prayer and hope: that he doesn't enjoy it;
   next, that you do not have any fun at all.
Yet, whatever the night may chance,
   tomorrow, convince me—deny, deny, deny.   70

1.5

It was sizzling hot, high noon.
   I plopped my limbs on my couch for a rest.
One part of the window's shutter was open, the other closed;
   almost like the light shimmering in the woods,
Or like the twilight gleaming when the sun goes down,   5
   or after the night has passed, just about the break of day,
The kind of light nice girls should take advantage of
   in hope of screening their shy modesty.
And look, in came Corinna,° wearing a loose dress;
   her hair was parted hanging down over her white neck,   10
Just as beautiful as queen Semiramis (so they say) when she entered
   her bedroom, or as Lais, woman of many lovers.
I pulled off the dress, being thin, it didn't do much to hurt the view
     anyway—
   but she resisted, fighting to keep it on.
Her struggle, however, was half-hearted, as if she didn't want to
     win.   15
   So she was easily overpowered, done in, betrayed by herself.
Her slip of a dress removed, she stood before my eyes;
   on all her body was not a single flaw.
What shoulders, what arms I saw and touched!
   The shape of her breasts, her nipples, ready and waiting for
     fondling!   20
Beneath her firm bosom a stomach smooth and flat,
   her waist long and slender, her thighs of a young girl.
Why catalogue the details? I saw nothing objectionable;
   I pressed her naked body to every inch of my own.
For the rest, everybody knows: worn out, we both languished in rest. 25
   Hot noons like that I'd welcome every day.

1.5.9: Corinna is the pseudonym Ovid gives to his elegiac lover.

1.6

Doorkeeper—it's undeserved that you are bound by a huge chain—°
    please, turn the hinge and open your stubborn door.
I'm asking for a little thing—just a crack for entry;
    standing sideways, my side can make it through.
Lots of loving has thinned my body for this purpose   5
    and slimmed down my frame to produce the right-sized limbs.
Love has shown me how to walk lightly past the vigils
    of guards, and has kept my nimble feet from stumbling.
Why, I used to be afraid of the shadowy phantoms of the night,
    to wonder who would go out in the dark.   10
But Cupid laughed, so did his tender mother, and I could hear
    them whisper: "Courage, even you can be brave!"
Love came without delay: now I fear not the specters flying in the
        dark
    nor the hands of muggers aimed at my life.
You are the only thing I fear, only you, too slow to my seductive
        line.   15
    Yes, you have the (thunder)bolt to destroy me.
Look, (but you have to unbar and to open the ruthless barrier to see),
    how the door has become stained, wet from my tears.
Hey, it was I, when you once stood stripped of clothes for a
whipping,
    who brought your trembling words to our lady.   20
Yes, a lot of good my kindness on your behalf did me:
    Damn it, doesn't that count for a little?
So render in turn what is deserved; you'll get from it what you want:
    The hours of the night go by; unlock the bar from the door.
Unlock it. Then may you be relieved forever of the long chain,   25
    and not forever drink the water of a slave.
Doorkeeper with an iron heart, you do not listen to me and my pleas.
    The door remains stiff, propped up by hard iron bars.
Cities under siege need barred gates, fortified bolts,
    but in time of peace what do you fear from arms?   30
What will you do to an enemy, when you treat a lover like this,
        banishing him outside?
    The hours of the night go by; unlock the bar from the door.
I have not come here in arms and accompanied by soldiers.
    I'd be completely alone, save for savage Love.
Though I should wish it, I cannot send him off;   35
    sooner I would split off my own limbs.

1.6.1: the scene is that of the excluded lover; the slave doorkeeper was often
    chained to his post.

Love escorts me, and a little wine, and around my temples
    a garland, slipping down my moist hair.
Who would fear these weapons? Who would be afraid to face them?
    The hours of the night go by; unlock the bar from the door.   40
You are tough; or is it your sleep (damn you!) that scatters
    to the winds the lover's laments rejected by your ear?
But I remember the first time when I was trying to escape your notice,
    you were wide awake, on guard, until the stars at midnight.
Possibly your girlfriend now lies sleeping with you;   45
    oh, so much better your luck, so much worse my fate!
For that luck, put the hard chains on me.
    The hours of the night go by; unlock the bar from the door.
Is it a trick, or did I hear the sound of a turning hinge, or the
    doorposts?
    Or was it a raucous clang upon the door?   50
Yes, I am fooled; it was a wild wind beating the door panel.
    Ah, me: far away a gust has wafted my hope.
If you remember, Boreas of the north wind, the girl Orithyia you
    carried off,
    blow here, blast these unanswering door frames.
In all the city silent and dripping with crystalline dew   55
    The hours of the night go by; unlock the bar from the door.
Otherwise, I myself, better armed with iron and fire
    and torch in hand, will assault this arrogant house.
Night and Love and wine brook no moderation:
    Night lacks shame; Love and the Wine-god show no fear.   60
I've used up every device; neither my prayers nor threats
    have moved you; you are even harder than your door.
For you to guard and protect the doorsteps of a beautiful girl is just
    not the way
    it should be; you deserve to be keeping watch in a restless prison
    cell.
Now the morning star sets the frosty axles of dawn in motion,°   65
    now the cock rouses poor souls to their toil.
But you, my garland, torn from my unlucky hair,
    lie on the hard threshold this entire night.
In the morning when she sees you tossed here,
    you will be witness to the wasted time I spent.   70
Farewell, and know that in my departure I pay you just respect;
    steadfast, you did not disgrace yourself, letting in a lover—
    goodbye.

1.6.65: the Morning Star drives a chariot across the dome of heaven, like the
    Sun-god and Dawn.

And you, too, cruel doorpost, unyielding lintel,
    and protecting panels, hard wood all, farewell.

1.7

Tie up my hands—they deserve chains—
    till the madness has faded, friend, if friend you are.
Mad frenzy provoked me to raise reckless hands against my lover.
    My girl is weeping, hurt by my crazy attack,
So mad I could have violated my dear parents   5
    or lashed out in fury against the holy gods.
Now didn't that lord of the sevenfold shield, Ajax,
    rout and lay low flocks in open fields?
Did not Orestes, to champion his father, take evil revenge on his
    mother,
    and dare to demand arms against the goddesses of the secret
        future?   10
So, by analogy, I had the right to pull out her hair that she had
    arranged?
    Hey, she still looked great even with the disheveled look.
Yes, she was beautiful, as striking as Atalanta, I would say,
    hunting wild game in Maenalia with her bow;
Or as Ariadne of Crete who wept over the promises and sails   15
    of perjured Theseus as they were swept off by the southern wind,
Or as Cassandra—except ribbons were binding her hair—
    who knelt in your shrine, chaste Minerva.
Everyone screamed at me: "Madman, barbarian!"
    She said nothing; trembling fear muted her tongue.   20
Her silence and her looks exposed my guilt.
    I stood accused by the silent tears upon her face.
I wish my arms had dropped from my shoulders;
    I'd been better off without them.
I was a madman, spending my strength to my own loss,   25
    and I prevailed, my bravery bringing my own punishment.
Now what, hands, you servants of murder and crime?
    Handcuff me; I deserve it for my sacrilege.
Had I struck the basest of Roman citizens, I'd be beaten
    in punishment; so will I have a greater right over my lover?   30
Diomedes,° son of Tydeus, has provided the worst model for crime.
    He was the first to strike a goddess. I'm the second.
But he was less guilty than I who hurt the one I professed
    to love; Diomedes was savage against an enemy.

1.7.31: Diomedes wounded Venus (Aphrodite) who was fighting on behalf of
the Trojans. Cf. Homer, *Iliad* 5.330.

Go now, victorious general, celebrate those magnificent triumphal
    processions,   35
  crown your hair with laurel and render vows to Jupiter.
A crowd of followers will attend your chariot
  cheering: "Hurrah, brave hero, victor over a girl!"
She will proceed you, her hair a mess, a pitiable captive,
  all beautiful except for the welts on her cheeks.   40
It would have been better if I had implanted bruises from kissing
  and her alluring neck had shown the mark of my bite;
Or if I were being swept away like a teeming torrent,
  or if blinding anger had made me its prey,
Surely it would have been enough to have just shouted at the
    frightened girl,   45
  and not thundered out unyielding threats,
Or shamelessly to have ripped her dress from her neck all the way
  to her waist or to the girdle that might have assisted her midriff.
But no! I grabbed and yanked her hair from her forehead
  and marked her freeborn cheeks with iron fingernail.   50
There she stood, dazed, her face bloodless and white
  as the marble stone quarried from Paros' cliff;
I saw her limbs lifeless, her whole body quivering
  as do poplars when their leaves stir in the breeze,
As a slender reed sways to the gentle west wind,   55
  or as the crest of sea wave is swept by a balmy gust from the south.
Then her tears, which she held in check for some time, flooded her
    face
  like water flowing out of melting snow.
I began to sense my first guilt.
  Those tears she shed were drops of my blood.   60
Three times I wanted to throw myself a suppliant before her feet,
  three times she pushed away my appealing hands.
Waste no time—revenge will soften the pain—
  dig your nails into my face;
Spare neither my eyes nor hair;   65
  rage will make your weak hands strong.
But, lest there remain any grim signs, reminders of my wrong,
  straighten up and fix that hair.°

1.7.68: the imagery of the Latin is military. Ovid is suggesting that she get
  herself ready (stationed in battle array) for another assault.

1.8

If you want to know an old hag, I have one for you.
  Listen, the old bitch's name is Dipsas.°
Her name speaks for itself. For she has never been sober enough to
    see
  black Memnon's mom, Aurora, on her steeds of rosy-
    fingered dawn.
She knows and practices magic, the incantations of Circe;   5
  with her skill she reverses the flow of rivers to their source.
She knows the use of herbs, the whirl of a wheel snapped by a leash,°
  the "love potion" exuded by a mare in heat.
When she wills it, clouds ball in the sky,
  when she wills it, clear sunshine brightens the sky.   10
Believe it or not, I have seen stars drip with gore
  and the face of the moon turn the royal red of blood.
I suspect that she flies through the shadows of the night
  metamorphosed, her old crone's body covered in feathers.
I suspect, and gossip supports it, that her eyes have two pupils that
    flash lightning   15
  and from her eyeballs darts light.
From tombs of ancient times she summons the souls of ancestors
    generations dead;
  her long chants cast spells upon the hardened earth to crack open.
This witch took it upon herself to corrupt our innocent bed,
  her tongue spewing a lot of persuasive poison.   20
Pure luck offered me the chance to witness her as she talked; I was
    hiding,
  shielded by the double door, when she gave this advice:
"You know, my dear, yesterday that handsome young buck was hot
    for you.
  He was glued, mesmerized by your looks.
And why not? You're pretty with a shape second to none.   25
  It's a real pity you don't have the clothes and bearing worthy of
    your body.
I want you to be well off to equal your exquisite beauty;
  If you become rich, I won't be poor.
Mars was in opposition, a sign of trouble for you;
  but Mars is in descent, Venus now is in ascendant, just the right
    sign;°
        30

1.8.2: Dipsas means "thirsty."
1.8.7: refers to a practice intended as a love-charm.
1.8.29-30: some astrological lore that is a reworking of the philosophical idea
  of the opposition between the cosmic powers of Love and Strife. See lines
  41-42 for the humorous elegiac variation of this theme.

Her rising means profit; just look: here's a rich lover
  who is lusting for you, wanting to provide your every need.
He is handsome too, a good match for your beauty.
  Why, we'd have to buy him, if he weren't so eager to buy you.
Ah, she blushed! True enough that blushing from modesty suits a
    light complexion.
  It's a help if you fake it; if it's for real, then usually it's a hurdle.   36
Be demure, keeping your eyes fixed upon your lap;
  measure a man by how much cash he brings.
Maybe in the days when Tatius was king, frumpy Sabine women
  refused to make themselves available to more than one man.   40
Nowadays Mars hones his fighting spirit in foreign campaigns,
  but in the city of her son Aeneas Venus reigns supreme.
Pretty girls play around; call her chaste who is never asked out.
  Only country gaucheness would prevent a girl asking first.
Shake off the frowns; they bring wrinkles to the forehead of those   45
  who wear them; out of wrinkles drops many a guilty conscience.
Penelope tested the virility of her young suitors by a bow;
  they drew that bow of horn to prove it.
Winged time slips by; speeding on, it goes unnoticed, deceiving us;
  galloping horses quicken the year's gliding course.   50
Bronze glistens with use; nice clothes need wearing;
  a house neglected molders in squalid rot.
Beauty unused soon fades, old before its time without a lover
  to ply it; and one or two are not enough to matter.
The more the merrier, more loot, the talk no more vicious.   55
  For gray wolves steady is the prey from a flock.
Now look at that 'bard' friend of yours. What gift does he send you
  except his latest elegy? You'll receive many thousands from a
    proper lover.
The god of poets appears distinguished in a golden gown,
  and strums melodious strings on a lyre inlaid with gold.   60
Homer is great, but the man who gives cash, I think, is better for you.
  Believe me, giving is an art.
Don't look down on a slave who has bought his person for cash;
  the stigma of chalked feet is a trifling matter.
And don't be fooled by ancient wax busts of pedigree all around the
    living room.   65
  A poor poet, then, out you go! And take your great-grandfather
    with you.
Don't let a lover wheedle a night without pay just because he's
    handsome.
  Make him beg a gay friend for a loan so to hand over the money to
    you.

Offer a discount until you set the trap: you don't want them to get
    away.
    After you catch them, then roast them in any recipe you like.   70
It doesn't hurt to pretend you're in love; allow him to think you love
    him;
    and be careful not to let this love come gratis.
Hold out some nights; pretend to have a headache,
    and sometimes, too, Isis' worship will provide excuses.
Take him back after a while before he gets used to enduring.   75
    Love rejected too often cools off.
Bolt your door, deaf to a beggar, but open wide for a gift-giver.
    Let your lover welcomed inside hear the words of the excluded one
        outside.
If he's wronged, get angry as if you were injured first.
    His charge countered by yours will disappear.   80
Never prolong your anger;
    anger harbored often causes grudges.
Also, teach your eyes to cry upon command,
    to drench your cheeks jealous of first one and then another.
Don't be afraid to lie, if you are cheating on him;   85
    Venus adjusts her deaf divine powers to games of love.
Rehearse a slave and clever maid for their roles
    to teach him what's the best buy for you.
They can ask for gratuities; asking many for just a little
    they will build, one straw at a time, a huge pile.   90
Get your sister, your mother, and your nurse, too, to fleece a lover.
    Plunder comes quickly when many hands make the grab.
When you start running out of excuses in asking for presents,
    say it's your birthday and produce a cake for proof.
Don't let him take your love for granted, thinking he has no rival;   95
    love does not last long, if you remove competition.
Let him see imprints on the bed, traces of another man;
    and let him notice a few love-marks bruised upon your neck.
Above all, let him get a glimpse of presents someone else has sent
    you.
    If no one has done so, order them from the fashionable Sacred
        Way.   100
No matter how much you've taken him for, if he has something left to
    give,
    ask him for a loan—which , of course, you'll never repay.
Let your tongue disguise your intention; charm him as you harm him.
    Sweet honey masks unholy poison lurking below.
If you fulfill to the letter what I've learned from long experience,   105
    and if my words aren't blown away by gusty winds or fickle
        breeze,

Again and again, while I'm alive, you'll bless me; time and again,
    after I have expired, you'll pray my bones rest gentle."
She was droning on in mid-monotony, when my shadow betrayed
    me.
    I barely restrained my hands   110
From tearing out what little white hair she had left, from gouging out
    her eyes bleary from wine, and clawing her wrinkled cheeks.
May the gods curse you with no home and an impoverished old age
    and long winters and, finally, a continual thirst.

1.9

Every lover is a soldier, and Cupid keeps his own camp,
    Atticus; trust me on this one, every lover is always at war.
The age most conducive to war is the same as that for love.
    It is disgusting: an old man as soldier; disgusting, too, as a lover.
The fighting spirit that the brass demand in a brave soldier,   5
    a pretty girl wants in her lover.
Both keep watch all night long; both bivouac on the ground:
    one before the door of his girlfriend, the other at his captain's
        headquarters.
A long march is a soldier's job; send a girl off,
    and the tireless lover hounds the road without end.   10
He'll cross mountains in his path, rivers swollen double
    by rain, trudging through deep snow;
He'll take to the deep making no excuse of squalling winds,
    and use the stars for guides to steer the seas.
Who but a soldier or lover would endure   15
    the freezing cold of night, snow, thick sleet, and rain?
One is sent to spy on dangerous enemies,
    the other keeps his eyes peeled for his rival.
One lays siege to fortified cities, the other to the threshold
    of a hard-hearted girl; one smashes gates, the other pounds
        doors.
     20
It often works to attack a sleeping enemy
    with an armed force, striking down the unarmed foe.
Thus the wild herd of Rhesus was captured while he slept;
    those Thracian stallions deserted their master.
Lovers use these tactics for the slumbers of husbands,   25
    and launch their weapons upon an enemy lulled to sleep.
They elude squads of guards, bands of patrolling sentries.
    This is the ever-trying task of both soldier and hapless lover.
Mars is a doubtful prospect, and Venus is a gamble; the beaten rise,
    and those you say could never fail, fall.   30
So don't ever claim that love is a lazy vocation:
    Love is the test of true mettle.

Achilles sulking over the taking of Briseis was on fire with love,
　(that was your chance, Trojan, to have smashed the power of the
　　Greeks);
Hector went off to battle from the embrace of his wife,
　Andromache,　　　　　　　　　　　　　　　　　　　　　35
　who personally used to fit the helmet on his head.
Agamemnon, leader of leaders, was bewitched (so they say)
　by the sight of Cassandra's wild streaming hair.
Mars, too, caught in the chains of the divine smith, felt love.
　No story in heaven was more well-known.　　　　　　　40
I was a lazy guy, born for those leisures that require clothes off.
　A bed and a shade had sapped my spirit.
Love for a beautiful girl pushed me from my lazy life;
　I earned my medals in her camp under her command.
Now you see me alert, waging mid-night wars.　　　　　45
　If you want to give up the lazy life, then go fall in love.

1.14

I told you over and over: "Stop dyeing your hair!"
　Right now you haven't any hair left that you can dye.
If you had only let it be, it would be so profuse.
　It had reached all the way below the waist.
It was so fine you'd fear to dress it,　　　　　　　　　　5
　like the silk veils the Chinese have,
Or the gossamer strands that a delicate spider spins,
　weaving his gauzy work beneath a neglected ceiling beam.
Its color was not black nor golden,
　but a blend of both colors and yet neither,　　　　　10
Like the color that a tall cedar in the dewy valley of hilly Ida
　has after its bark has been stripped.
Your hair was easy to style and suitable for a hundred fashions,
　and never caused you pain or grief.
No hairpin nor the teeth of a comb frayed it.　　　　　15
　Your hairdresser was always secure;
I often watched her set it and never once
　did you snatch a pin and jab her arm.
And often in the morning with hair not yet arranged
　you lay propped up on your purple pillow,　　　　　20
Lovely, too, even disheveled, like an exhausted Bacchant
　relaxed and languishing on a patch of green.
Delicate and soft as down,
　how many tortures and ordeals your hair endured.
How patiently it braved curling iron and fire　　　　　25
　to curl and coil it into tight spirals.

"It's a crime," I cried, "to singe those locks;
  they are charming as they are. Take mercy, iron maiden, on your
    head.
No violence—no more burning! It's just not right.
  The tongs can learn a lesson from your hair."   30
That beautiful hair is ruined, hair that Apollo would envy,
  that Bacchus would wish crowned his head.
I'd compare it to the hair in the painting of Venus,°
  naked, holding it up by her dripping hand.
Why do you complain that the hair that you wrecked is now
    ruined?   35
  Why, silly girl, do you put down the mirror and then grieve?
You look at yourself with eyes unused to the sight;
  so, to be attractive now, you should forget yourself.
No enchanted herbs of a rival have impaired you;
  no old hag of a treacherous witch has bathed you in water from
    Thessaly.   40
No disease—heaven forbid!— has crippled you;
  no envious tongue has damaged your hair.
It is your fault; it is by your own hand that you suffer the loss of your
    dense locks;
  you yourself concocted the poisons for your head.
Soon Germany will be sending you curls from a prisoner;   45
  you'll go safe, coiffured in a gift from a people we triumphed over.
When they all admire your hair, you'll blush
  and say: "It's my purchased goods they are attracted to;
Instead of me they are complimenting some German girl;
  yet I remember still when I merited that admiration."   50
Oh, my! She does a poor job of holding back her tears; she covers
  her face with her hand to hide the blush spread upon her free-born
    cheeks.
Her lap holds her original hair; she keeps staring at it,
  a god-given gift regrettably out of place.
Make up your face, make up your mind: the loss is not fatal.   55
  Soon you'll be ogled for your home-grown hair.

1.15

Why, gnawing Envy, do you carp against me for wasting my years,
  and call my poetry the work of a talent both lazy and useless?

1.14.33-34: refer to Apelles' famous painting of Aphrodite (Venus) Anadyomene.
  It is said that Augustus acquired the painting and placed it in the Temple of
  Divine Julius located in the Forum.

Not for me the tradition of my ancestors to pursue, while I am in the
    vigor
    of youth, the medals of a soldier earned in the dust;
Not for me to learn by rote the jargon of law; not for me   5
    to prostitute my voice in the ungrateful forum.
The work you pursue is mortal; I seek undying fame,
    to be alive and sung over and over throughout the whole world.
Homer lives as long as Tenedos and Mt. Ida stand,
    and the Simois rolls its waters in torrents into the sea.   10
Hesiod of Ascra will also be alive as long as the grape swells with
    juice
    or Ceres reaps her wheat that falls to the curved pruning hook.
Callimachus will sing on and on throughout the world;
    although in genius he lags behind, in art he is supreme.
No loss will ever come to Sophocles, poet of the tragic buskin;   15
    Aratus will be around as long as there is a sun and moon.
While the cheating slave, the harsh father, the depraved pimp,
    and the charming hooker live, Menander will survive.
The rustic art of Ennius and the impassioned voice of Accius
    have a fame undying, undiminished by time.   20
What generation does not know of Varro, of the first ship, Argo,
    of the hero Jason, and his quest for the golden fleece?
The verse of sublime Lucretius will perish
    only on that day the world comes to an end.
Virgil's Tityrus, his crops, and the arms of Aeneas will be read
    as long as triumphant Rome stands as head of the world.   26
While Cupid's weapons, torches and bow, survive to strike us,
    your lines, polished Tibullus, will be learned;
Gallus will be known in the West, Gallus will be remembered in the
    East,
    and Gallus' Lycoris will also earn a name.   30
So, although time destroys stone and the hard iron
    of a plow, poetry is deathless.
Let kings and the triumphs of kings yield to poetry,
    and all the gold of Tagus'° gentle banks.
Cheap goods may attract the vulgar crowd, but for me golden
    Apollo   35
    serves cups filled with the water of Castalia;
For me I pray my hair may wear a garland of myrtle that fears the
    cold,
    and I may be read much by a tormented lover.

1.15.34: the Tagus river is in Roman Spain.

Envy feeds on the living; on graves it rests;
   each one keeps the honor won by merit.   40
Therefore, when the final fire has devoured me,
   a great part of me will survive; yes, I shall live!

2.4

I would not dare to defend my faults and lack of morals,
   nor fight phony wars on behalf of my vices.
I confess, if any confession of wrongs helps;
   now I rush about like a madman admitting my flaws.
I hate what I am, yet despite my desire to change, I cannot be   5
   other than what I hate; it is quite a burden to bear what you want
      to drop.
I lack the strength, the self-control to guide me.
   I'm swept along like a ship battered in raging waters.
One? The alluring beauty who attracts my love is not a definite *one*.
   There are hundreds who give me reason to always be in love.   10
If one is modest, of shy eyes,
   I'm on fire, snared by her bashful innocence.
If she be wanton and forward, I'm captivated because she is not a
      hick;
   I imagine her bouncing ability on a soft bed.
If she seems tough and behaves like austere Sabines,   15
   I suspect that underneath she is suppressing her real desires.
If she is educated, I'm delighted by her rare culture;
   if unrefined, how sweet her unspoiled naivete.
If any girl claims Callimachus' poetry is rustic compared to mine,
   that I like, pleased by this discriminating critic.   20
Someone else objects to my songs, finds fault with my poetic self,
   I'd love to lay her (thigh of) objection to rest.
One has a graceful walk, I'm taken by her fluid motion; another is
      hard,
   the touch of a man will soften her up.
One sings sweet—a perfect soprano—   25
   I imagine myself stealing kisses in mid-aria.
Another with facile finger strums elegiac strings,
   who wouldn't love those practiced hands?
One is a dancer; in perfect rhythm she sways her limbs,
   ah, the delicate art in the subtle movements and twists of her
      hips.   30
Enough about me! I am swayed by every type.
   Put Hippolytus in my spot—he will rise a Priapus.
One is tall, a peer of the ladies of epic,
   how much she occupies lying full on the bed.

Another adjusts to her short size; by either one I am broken: 35
  tall or short, both suit me fine.
One dresses poorly, imagine her dressed to the nines;
  another is all decked out; she accentuates her natural assets.
The blonde, the redhead, each captivates me;
  yes, I love brunettes too!   40
When dark curls fall over a neck snowy-white,
  I envision her a black-haired Leda.
Golden colored—that's Aurora of the saffron hair:
  my love adapts to all the beauties in history, literal translations.
The young one drives me crazy, the older also attracts me;   45
  one wins by her looks, the other by her *savoir-faire*.
In the city there are girls galore to please every taste;
  my love is a candidate for the votes of them all.

2.7°

Not again! Am I forever to defend myself , facing new charges?
  So I win, so what? I tire of all the judicial battles.
I shoot a glance at the balcony in the marble theater,
  and you choose any one of the girls there to get upset over.
A pretty woman without a word from her mouth catches sight
    of me,   5
  you claim that silent look is some sort of signal.
If I compliment one girl, you attack my poor hair with your nails;
  If I criticize her, you believe that I'm covering up a cheating crime;
A glow on my face, you say I'm cold;
  a little pale, you accuse me of dying in another's embrace.   10
How I wish I were guilty of some infidelity;
  those who have deserved it suffer the punishment best.
But now your rash charges and gullible credulity
  make your anger tiresome and weaken your case,
Like the pitiable lot of the long-eared donkey (note it!)   15
  that responds slowly to the constant beating of a lash.
Now look: a new charge; you accuse Cypassis,° handmaiden
  to your hair, of violating our bed with me.
O gods, if I truly lusted to cheat, would I
  find pleasure with a damned low-class slut?   20
What freeborn man would want to screw a servant,
  to hug the body of one whose back showed the marks of a whip?
And besides, her job is arranging your curls,
  a skilled hand-service which pleases you.

2.7.1: this poem is paired with the following one.
2.7.17: Cypassis means something like "mini-skirt."

Surely, I wouldn't hit on the trusty maid who was devoted to you! 25
    What for? To be indicted and then betrayed?
I swear by Venus and the bow of the winged boy-god
    that I am innocent of this charge!

2.8

Skilled in a thousand ways of coiffuring hair, Cypassis,
    and worthy of giving goddesses perms,
Refined and not at all rustic in our furtive pleasure,
    how well you suit your mistress, but you suit me even better.
But who, what tattletale, who was the informer of our carnal
      relations?   5
    How did Corinna sense the "whole lotta shakin' going on?"
Did I ever blush, make some slip of the tongue
    to give away telltale signs of out secret love?
What if I did maintain that one who could fall
    for a servant girl was a dim-wit?   10
Achilles was on fire for the beautiful Briseis,
    and Agamemnon fell in love with the slave girl Phoebas.°
I'm not greater than either of these epic heroes;
    why should I believe what kings find decent is disgraceful?
When she zeroed in her angry eyes on you,   15
    I saw you blush, all your cheeks turn red.
If you remember, I was in more control;
    I swore by mighty Venus that I kept love's faith—
Venus, my goddess, I was pure of heart;
    order the warring south winds to blow those lies across the
      Aegean Sea.   20
You, Cypassis, pay me back today for those services,
    a few sweet fucks, my dark-haired beauty.
Why are you shaking your head? Why do you pretend to be afraid,
    ungrateful girl? Once more is enough.
You are stupid to deny me: I'll confess to our previous liaisons,   25
    I'll go inform on me and betray myself,
I'll give her all the details, Cypassis, where, how many times,
    what methods and how many positions.

2.8.12: Phoebas was a priestess of Apollo. The story of Agamemnon's love for
    her is not common.

2.10

You, yes, you, Graecinus,° I remember it well; it was you who said
  no one could love two girls at the same time.
What a lie! Because of you I have been duped, because of you caught
    defenseless.
    Well here I am, ashamed and embarrassed: I'm in love with two
      girls.
They're both beautiful, both sophisticated and elegant,   5
  and which is more expert is hard for me to distinguish.
One is prettier than the other, or is it the other way around?
  Each of them delights me, depending on which of the two I'm with.
I flounder about like a canoe tossed by winds at war,
  first one love, then the other, keeps me divided in half.   10
Why, O Venus of Eryx, do you double my endless heartache?
  Wasn't one girl hell enough?
Why add leaves to the trees, stars to the sky already full,
  water to the deep seas?
Still, it's better having two loves than lying unloved without one.   15
  I wish upon my enemies the Spartan life;
Let my enemies sleep alone on an abandoned bed
  and relax their limbs in the middle with lots of room to spare.
But for me, give me savage Love to shatter my languid slumber,
  that I not be alone, the only weight in my bed.   20
May my girl emasculate me, and no one be there to stop her;
  one may be enough, if not, then I'll take on two.

I can handle it: my limbs are slender but very vigorous,
  skinny I may be, but my body has stamina.
Raw sex is the food for virile action;   25
  no girl has ever been frustrated by a failure on my part.
Many times I have spent a night in libidinous romping;
  the morning after, I was fit and strong, able to be of service.
Lucky the man who dies in the mutual duels of love!
  May the gods grant me a death from such a duel!   30
Let the soldier face the enemy's spears aimed at his chest,
  and his blood buy him a name, remembered forever.
Let the greedy trader, to obtain his money, weary the seas,
  risk shipwreck, and drink in his swindling mouth the very water
    he dies in.
But for me, I want to die exhausting myself in the movements
    of Venus   35
  and fade out, expiring in mid-Love's labors.

2.10.1: Gaius Pomponius Graecinus became a consul.

At my funeral let a mourner in tears say:
  "Your death was a perfect match for the way you lived."

2.15

Go, little ring, to grace the finger of a beautiful girl,
  not worth much except as a token of the giver's love.
Be a special gift for her; I wish you a happy welcome,
  and that right away she slips you on over her knuckles.
I hope you fit her as snugly as she fits me,   5
  and hug her finger in just the perfect size.
O lucky little ring! You'll be fondled by my lady!
  I'm already in bad shape, jealous of my gift.
I wish I could suddenly become my own present,
  metamorphosed by Circe's or old Proteus' art.°   10
Then I'd like you, my lady, to touch your nipples
  and insert your left hand inside your dress;
I'd slip from your finger, although I had been clinging tight,
  and working loose by magic drop down your bosom;
Or, so I could seal secret letters   15
  and not clog and cake my dry jewel,
I would first touch the moist lips of my pretty girl;
  But I'd decline to seal any letter that would hurt me.
When she thinks to store me away in her jewelry box, I'll refuse to
    come off,
  shrinking and tightening the circle around her finger.   20
I will never embarrass you, my life,
  and may your delicate finger never refuse my little weight.
Wear me when you soak your body in a warm bath;
  don't fear damage to the stone from the flow of the water.
Seeing you naked, I think my member will rise, erect with lust,   25
  and I, a mere little ring, will play the man's role.
Pure fantasy! Go on your way, little gift;
  with you she should feel my love pledged true.

2.19

You fool! If you don't guard your girl for your own sake,
  guard her for mine to make me want her more.
What's allowed is boring; what's forbidden sets me afire with intense
    heat.
  He is an iron-hearted man who loves what another lets him.

2.15.10: for Proteus and his art see Vergil, *Georgics* 4.441-443.

We lovers should hope and fear in equal amounts;   5
    a rejection or two should give a chance for our dreams.
What good is a beauty who never bothers to cheat on me?
    I don't love something which doesn't ever hurt me.
Clever Corinna saw this weakness of mine:
    she knew all the cunning tricks to catch me.   10
How often she faked a headache when she was feeling fine,
    and ordered me to leave, slow-footed and hanging around.
How many times she pretended guilt—as much as an innocent
    woman could—and displayed the look of a cheater.
So, in that way, when she had stoked and rekindled my lukewarm
       fires,   15
    again she was nice and obliging to my every desire.
Oh, the many endearing words and sweet-nothings she used to cook
       up just for me;
    and kisses—god almighty—long and many she used to give.
And you, too, who just recently ravished my eyes,
    watch out for my plots, and, when I ask you, sometimes say no;   20
Let me lie stretched out on the threshold before your door,
    suffering the frosty cold long into the night.
That way, my love lasts firm and grows stronger through the long
       years;
    I like that, it is the diet for my soul.
Love that is fattening and too cloying turns boring to me,   25
    and like sweet food too rich upsets the stomach.
If a bronze tower had not confined Danae,
    Jove would have never made Danae a mother.
While Juno watched Io transformed and sprouted with horns,
    to Jove she was more appealing than she had been before.   30
Whoever wants that which is licit and easy should pick
    leaves off trees, drink water from a big river.
A girl who wants to be in control long, should deceive her lover.
    (I'm a sap—I may come to be tortured by own advice).
Come what may, compliance makes me a wreck: 35
    she who follows, I run away from; she who flees, I follow.°
But you, so sure of your pretty girl,
    begin now to lock the door at nightfall;
Begin to ask who is making those furtive taps at your threshold
    so often, why the dogs are barking in the still of the night;   40
Ask what letters her clever maid keeps bringing and returning,
    why she frequently sleeps alone on a bed empty of you.

2.19.36: a Latin version from a famous epigram of Callimachus.

That love of yours sometimes should gnaw at your bone marrow.
    Give me a chance and material for my tricks.
A man can make love with the wife of a fool   45
    as easily as he can steal sand from a deserted shore.
Now I warn you flat out: if you don't begin
    to guard your girl, she'll begin soon to cease to be mine.
Long enough I've put up with a lot; I often hoped that,
    if you guarded her tight, I could deceive you with ease.   50
You are slow and you bear things that no husband ought to endure.
    For me, if love is allowed, that's the end of it.
Hey, will I never be refused entree and be out of luck?
    Will every night be without reprisals?
Never to be scared? Never to heave sighs during my slumbers?   55
    Will you never give me an excuse to wish you dead?
What do I need with a husband so easy, a pimp,
    whose depravity spoils our fun?
Find someone else who likes your saintly patience;
    if you want me to be your rival, use your veto.   60

3.2

I do not sit here because I'm gaga over the thoroughbreds.
    Still, I hope that your favorite will come in a winner.
I have come to talk with you, to sit next to you,
    so you may know what love you are causing in me.
You watch the races, I watch you; let's both of us watch   5
    and feed our eyes on what pleases each.
Lucky stiff, the jockey you favor!
    Pure luck he's got your attention.
I wish that would happen to me; right out of the starting blocks
    I'd send the horses galloping, driving them as intensely as
        I could.   10
I would give them free rein, sometimes cracking their backs with the
        whip;
    and I would shave the turning post with the inside wheel;
And catching sight of you as I sped by, I would hesitate;
    I'd let the reins loose, let them fall from my hands.
Why, Pelops almost fell to the Pisaean spear of Oenomaus,   15
    while he gazed upon your face, Hippodamia.
And yet he won with the support of his girl,
    as I hope your favor will spur us, driver and me, on to victory.
Why are you edging away? It's no use: the groove dividing our seats
    makes for a tight fit.
    That's the advantage of the seating here in the Circus.   20

Hey, you! You there on the right! Who do you think you are? Be
    careful of shoving her:
the push of your body rubbing up against her is hurting the girl.
And you, the spectator behind us, pull in your legs!
    Aren't you ashamed of yourself? Stop jabbing your hard knees into
      her back.
My, my, your dress now is trailing a little on the ground;   25
    lift it—or look, I'll lift it a bit for you.
You are a spiteful piece of cloth to hide such pretty legs,
    and the more one looks—oh, you spiteful dress, you—
Legs like speedy Atalanta's which Milanion
    dreamed of lofting in his arms;   30
Legs like those that painter depicted of Diana girt for the chase,
    and out-daring her wild prey.
Even before I saw them, I was on fire, and now that I've seen them,
    what's next?
    You are adding fire to fire, pouring water into the sea.
I imagine from that one glimpse that all the rest that lies hidden   35
    beneath your thin and gauzy dress can only be delightful.
But do you want to catch a gentle breeze?
    My program makes a nice fan for us;
Or is this the heat of my heart, and not from the air,
    that captivates and fires my breast with passion for a woman.   40
While I was talking, just then a speck of dust settled upon your white
    dress.
    Away, dirty dust—get off that body white as snow.
But look! Now comes the parade.° Pay attention, be quiet.
    Okay, now we can clap; the golden parade begins.
First, they bring in Victory, her wings spread wide.   45
    Come over here, goddess, and bring victory to my love.
Cheer for Neptune, all you sailors who over-trust the seas.
    The sea is not my thing; I'm a landlubber through and through.
Give a hand for your Mars, soldiers; I hate war and weapons.
    I prefer peace; in peacetime love abounds.   50
You prophets, do homage to Phoebus Apollo; you hunters to Diana;
    craftsmen, applaud Minerva.
Farmers, rise up and cheer for Ceres and tender Bacchus.
    Boxers honor Pollux, equestrians Castor.
I cheer for enticing Venus and her boy, the powerful bowman.   55
    O goddess, nod approval of my ventures,

3.2.43: before the races began effigies of the gods were carried on wagons
    around the course.

Inspire my girl to consent to my love.
    She nodded; with a shake of her head she has given me signs of
        success.
I ask you to make good the promise the goddess made:
    with Venus' permission I'll make you a goddess greater than
        she.   60
By all these spectators as witnesses, by this parade of gods I swear to
    you:
    forever you will be my lady.
But your legs are dangling: you can, if you so please,
    rest your feet over the edge of the railing.
The track is cleared, now the officer has started the feature event;   65
    the four-horse chariots are off from the starting gate.
I see the one you are betting on; anyone you favor will win;
    even the horses seem to know what you want.
Damn it all! Look, the guy has taken the pole too wide!
    Hey, you! What are you up to? The team behind is closing in.   70
Yes, you, what are you doing, you sap? You're breaking the girl's
    heart.
    Pull on the left rein, hard, hard, I tell you.
We have backed a real loser. Recall them, citizens;
    wave your toga everywhere—that's the signal to restart.
Look, they're calling them back.° But, so a waving toga not muss up
    your hair,   75
    lean your head upon my chest—you can do that—
And now the gates are unbolted, and they're off again,
    a blur of colors° from the racing horses flash by.
Come on! Take the lead, and widen it down the stretch!
    Make my hopes come true, make my lady's dream real.   80
My lady's hopes are fulfilled; my wishes are still in wait.
    He has his victorious palm; my prize is yet to be won.
She smiled; her sparkling eyes flirted a promise.
    Enough here—pay me the rest of the bet in another place.

3.7

Well, was she so ugly? Inelegant? She was gorgeous!
    The object of my desire, I believe.
But there I lay holding her, useless and limp,
    a burden, a shame, on her bed without any action.

3.2.75: the sponsor of the races could have a race restarted either for a false start
    or if he was influenced by the crowd.
3.2.78: four colors, red, white, green, and blue, represent the four factions or
    stables that sponsored the games.

I wanted it and the girl too was equally hot;   5
  but I couldn't enlist the aid of my lifeless cock to enjoy her.
Sliding her ivory arms beneath my neck she embraced me,
  arms whiter than the snow in Scythia;
She planted kisses filled with desire, kisses that rumbled our tongues;
  her lusty thigh she slid beneath my thigh,   10
And she cooed sweet-nothings and called me her "daddy,"
  and uttered other provocative phrases that all know.
But my member, as if dipped in icy hemlock,
  didn't budge, deserted my desire.
I lay there, a block of inert wood, a mirage, a useless lummox;   15
  I could not tell if I were body or ghost.
What will old age be like for me, should I reach old age,
  if in my youth I can't keep the beat.
I am humiliated, ashamed of my years. My vaunted youth? My
    virility?
  From me my girlfriend got neither.   20
She got up like a Vestal Virgin about to approach the sacred and
    eternal fire,
  like a sister respected by a dear brother.
And just think, recently twice with Childe, the redhead, three times
    with blonde Pitho,
  and three with Libas° I performed continuous duty;
And I remember in one brief night Corinna demanded   25
  and got me up for a record nine times.
Can it be that my body lies limp, cursed by the poison of a Thessalian
    witch?
  That some spell or magic herb is emasculating me?
Or a Phoenician sorceress has incised my name in wax
  and has stuck thin needles in my liver?   30
When Ceres is cursed with a spell, she withers into barren weed;
  by magic spells springs run out of water,
Acorns fall from oaks, grape clusters drop from the vines,
  and apples fall in a flood though no one shakes the tree.
Who is to say my fibers can't be sapped by the arts of magic?   35
  Perhaps that is the reason my crotch is without feeling.
Add to this the shame of it all, the humiliation, and the hurt,
  the second cause of my infection.
What a girl! But I only looked and touched,
  just as close as her nightgown touched her.   40

3.7.23-24: the three Greek names, Childe, Pitho, and Libas, suggest freedwomen
  and/or professional call girls.

Her touch could rejuvenate old Nestor,
   and make Tithonus more potent than his years.
She was mine to take, but no man was hers.
   What new vows, what prayers can I conceive now?
I think the mighty gods are sorry for the gift they brought me,   45
   since I made such shameful ill-use of it.
I was hoping for a welcome—and I got it—
   I wanted her kisses, I took them; I wanted to be next to her, I was.
But what good did that good luck do me? What good is a kingdom
     unused?
   I possessed wealth, holding on to it like a miser.   50
That is just how Tantalus, that gossiper of secrets, parches in his pool
   and has fruit he can never reach.
Now, who rises in the morning from the bed of a tender girl
   pure enough to approach the holy gods?
I am sure she wasted her charm and her best kisses   55
   on me, and tried by every trick to arouse me.
She could have moved mighty oaks, softened hard diamonds,
   could have moved deaf rocks with her teasing words.
To be sure she was worthy to move all living men,
   but I was neither living nor a man, as I was before.   60
What's the use of a Phemius singing to deaf ears?
   What good is a painting to a blind Thamyras?°
Yet in my mind I silently pictured many erotic scenes,
   imagined and fantasized on variations and positions.
But my prick lay prematurely dead,   65
   a disgrace, drooping limper than yesterday's rose.
Look at it now, erect, vigorous, burgeoning out of season;
   now it's demanding action, ready for battle.
Lie still, you shameful and villainous part of me!
   I've been a prisoner to your promises before.   70
You failed me and I'm the boss; because of you I'm now defenseless,
   caught by surprise, shamed, and suffering bitter losses.
My girl also did not disdain
   to arouse you, gently stroking with her hand.
But when she saw that no skill, no trick, could make you rise,   75
   and that you just lay there, indifferent to her,
She said, "Why are you playing around with me? Are you crazy?
   Who ordered you
   to invite yourself here and dump your prick on my bed?

3.7.62: Thamyras was blinded for challenging the Muses to a singing contest.

Either a poisoner like Circe has put a curse on you with binding
    threads,
  or you come here exhausted by another lover."   80
She wasted no time; she jumped up, wrapped herself in a loose gown,
  (how stunning she looked, rushing off in her bare feet),
But so that her maid would not suspect that I hadn't touch her,
  she douched with some water to disguise the disgrace.

3.9°

If mother Aurora wept for Memnon and mother Thetis for Achilles,
  and if the sad lot of mankind touches the hearts of mighty
      goddesses,
Loosen your hair and weep, tender Elegy,
  true namesake of sorrow.
The body of your poet laureate, Tibullus, your glory,   5
  is burning, consumed by flames, on a high funeral pyre.
Look, here comes Venus' boy, bringing his quiver reversed,
  his bow broken, his torch spent.
See how sadly he walks, his wings drooping,
  beating his naked breasts with his fists.   10
His tears fall upon the hair disheveled upon his neck,
  and loud sobs shake his face.
So they say he seemed at the rites of his brother Aeneas,
  when he left handsome Iulus' home.
Venus now grieves for the death of Tibullus,   15
  as she mourned for Adonis when the wild boar slashed open his
      groin.
We poets are called sacred, the care of the gods;
  some think that we are divinely inspired.
But death comes at the wrong time and profanes everything sacred;
  it lays its murky hand on all.   20
What help were father Apollo and mother Muse to Orpheus of Thrace?
  What good the song that tamed and muted wild beasts?
The same father, deep in the woods, sang a dirge for Linus,
  so they say, to his unresponsive lyre.
Even Homer, the fountain of inspiration forever,   25
  bathing the lips of poets from the stream of the Muses,
Drowned in black Avernus on his last day;
  only his poetry lives on, escaping the greedy pyre.
His work endures, the story of the toils at Troy,
  the slow weaving unraveled by deceit in the night.   30

3.9.1: an elegy on the death of Tibullus who died in 19 BCE.

So Nemesis' and Delia's fame will last:
  Nemesis his last love, Delia his first.
The sacred rites of Isis from Egypt, the hum of the sistrum° failed
    them;
  they're each sleeping alone in an empty bed.
When malicious fates snatch away the good—forgive my candor— 35
  I am moved to believe that there are no gods at all.
Live a pious life—you die; observe the sacred rites—during your
    worship
  heavy death drags you from temple to tomb.
Trust in polished poetry—take a look at Tibullus, lying dead;
  a small urn holds the little that remains.   40
The flames of the pyre have consumed even you, O sacred poet,
  and had no compunction devouring your heart.
The fire that could desecrate one so fine
  would gut the golden temples of the holy gods.
From the heights of her Eryx Venus turned her face aside   45
  to hide the tears some say she couldn't restrain.
Better, I surmise, to have died here in Rome than a stranger in the
    land
  of Phaeacia, buried in a cheap grave.
Here at least your mother closed your blank eyes
  and brought the final offerings to your ashes.   50
Here your sister shared in the grief of your mourning mother
  who came tearing out her unkempt hair.
Yes, Nemesis and your first love, Delia, came and added their kisses;
  both attended the pyre.
At parting Delia cried, "I was the lucky one to be loved by you.   55
  The fires of my love brought you life."
But Nemesis replied, "Mine is the loss you express in grief;
  dying, he held me by his failing hand."
But if we humans survive beyond a name and shade,
  Tibullus lives in the vale of Elysium.   60
There coming to him, their temples wreathed in ivy, will be
  learned Catullus and his pal Calvus,
And Gallus too (if the charge is a lie that he betrayed a friend,)
  who wasted his life and soul.
Your shade will be their companion, if spirit survives the body;   65
  elegant Tibullus, gracing their august numbers.
I pray your bones find peace and rest, protected in your urn,
  and that the earth weighs light upon your ashes.

3.11

I have been a martyr too long, my patience shot because of your
    deceit.
   Go, leave my weary breast, shameless Love.
Yes, I've slipped the chains and now I am free,
    and I am embarrassed by what I endured without shame.
I've won and I have given the boot to defeated Love.   5
    Horns, though late, have sprouted upon my head.
Be tough, endure it, Ovid. Someday this pain will do you good.
    Often bitter juice has restored the sick and weary.
So how did I stand it? So often rejected from your door,
    laying my freeborn body on the hard ground?   10
And, while you were hugging some nobody, did I actually
    sleep like a slave in front of your locked door?
Well, I saw your wreck of a lover coming out the door,
    dragging his weak and spent and burned out body home.
Worse than that, he saw me,   15
    a disgrace I would wish only on my enemies.
I used to cling to your side, firm and patient,
    your personal escort, your man, your friend,
Yes, my company caused people to be fond of you;
    my love for you made many others love you.   20
Need I mention the dirty lies from your deceitful tongue?
    The gods you falsely swore by to fool me?
The silent nods of young guys at parties
    and the coded words that belied the signs?
I heard that you were sick; in a panic I ran right over, out of
    my mind;   25
   I arrived to find you well enough to be with my rival.
I've become hard from enduring these insults and others unspeakable.
    Find someone else instead to be your willing martyr.
My ship is now in, votive garlands hanging all over,
    hesitant to listen to the swelling roar of the sea.   30
So no more sweet stuff and stop wasting words that used
    to control me. I am not the damn-fool jackass I used to be.

3.14

Since you are so beautiful, I don't insist you not cheat,
    but, please, I do not necessarily want to know it.
My sense of moral conduct doesn't require you to be faithful,
    but it does demand that you at least try to pretend you are.
A woman who can say she has not cheated, doesn't cheat;   5
    only guilt confessed brings a scandalous reputation.

It is utter madness to confess in broad daylight what lies hidden at
      night,
   and to publicize what you do in private.
A whore, before joining her body to a citizen she doesn't know,
   keeps the people out by locking her door.   10
You, on the other hand, expose your guilt to scandalous gossip,
   and play the role of self-incriminating informer.
Have better sense, or at least act like faithful girls act,
   and, although you are not, let me think you are pure.
Do all that you do, only say that you haven't done it.   15
   Don't be ashamed to speak with decorum in public.
There is a proper place for hanky-panky. Fill it full
   of every pleasure; keep modesty standing far away.
As soon as you leave from there, abandon all thoughts
   of lascivious behavior; confine your sins to your bed.   20
There it is no disgrace to take off your dress
   and to plant thigh under thigh.
There bury your tongue in moist red lips,
   and imagine love's many configurations.
There coo on and on, sweet talk all you want,   25
   and shake the bed posts in lusty movement.
But when you put on a dress, put on moral make-up too,
   and wear the modest look that denies dirty work.
Trick the people; fool me. Let me be in ignorant bliss,
   and enjoy my foolish illusions.   30
Need I see so often the messages being sent and delivered?
   The bed imprinted in the middle and on both sides?
Need I witness your hair all in disarray, tangled by more than just
      sleep?
   And a bite-mark on your neck?
You all but parade the guilty act before my eyes;   35
   if you hesitate to spare your own reputation, at least spare mine.
I go crazy and I die every time you confess that you've cheated;
   and a cold sweat flows over my limbs.
I love you then, but then I hate, frustrated because I cannot help
      loving you.
   And then I feel like dying—but only along with you.   40
I'll ask no questions, and whatever you scheme to hide,
   I will not pursue; being fooled will be like a favor.
Even if you get caught *in flagrante delicto*
   and I have witnessed your indecency with my own eyes,
Flatly deny it, saying that I did not see what I saw so well.   45
   Your words will triumph over my eyes.
It is an easy victory: to beat a man who wants to be beaten,
   if only your tongue remembers to say: "Not Guilty."

Since two words can win your case, speak up; although the case
   is materially weak, you'll win because the judge is in your
      pocket!   50

THE ART OF LOVE

The *Art of Love* is Ovid's humorous mocking of the didactic poem. The poet/
speaker assumes the role of a preceptor in the art of seduction and erotic intrigue.
The first two books advise men about women, whereas in Book III the roles are
reversed. Written in elegiac couplets, the poem draws heavily upon the *Amores*
and Augustan elegies for atmosphere and themes. The choice of meter indicates
a purposeful distinction from main didactic poetry written in epic hexameters.
Unfortunately for Ovid, Augustus appreciated neither the artistry nor the humor of
the poem. The publication and public acceptance of a work that seemed openly
to defy the Augustan moral program contributed to Ovid's exile in 8 CE.

BOOK I

If anyone in this population does not know the art of loving,
   he should read this and, well-trained after he has read it, let him go
      out and love.
It is through art that ships, both under sail and propelled by oars,
      move fast,°
   it is through art that chariots run light; through art love must be
      guided.
Automedon was skilled in the chariot and pliant reins,   5
   Tiphys was master of Jason's ship:°
Venus has made me a master artisan, a preceptor of tender love;
   I can be called the Tiphys and Automedon of Love.
Now he is really wild and often resents me;
   yet he is a boy, of a tender age that's easily controlled.   10
When Achilles was a boy, Chiron taught him the lyre,
   and through art tamed and soothed his wild spirits.
So he who many times terrified friends and enemies alike,
   was himself, so they say, scared of a decrepit old man;
The hands that one day Hector would feel he furnished for
      rappings,   15
   whenever his master-teacher ordered.
As Chiron was Achilles' teacher, so I am the preceptor of Love,
   each of them a young savage, each one born of a goddess.
Yet, as beneath the plow the bull's neck feels the weight of a yoke,
   and the wild horse is broken by bridle and cutting bit,   20

1.3-4: the images of the ship and chariot convey the metaphor of poet as helms-
   man and charioteer. Ovid ends this book with the image of the ship (772).
   See Propertius 3.1.9-10 and 4.1.70 for the metaphor of the charioteer.
1.5-6: Automedon was Achilles' charioteer, Tiphys the helmsman of the Argo.

So Love will yield to me, although he wounds my heart with arrows
    shot
    from his bow, and at me hurls his flying torches;
The more violently he pierces and toasts me,
    all the more I'll avenge the wound that he has made.
I'll not pretend that you, Phoebus Apollo, gave me my powers of
    art,   25
    nor say that I was warned by the voice of a bird from the sky,
Nor that in a vision Clio and her sisters inspired me
    as I was tending sheep in the valley of Ascra;
No, experience inspires this work of mine; heed me, a skilled bard,
    I shall sing the truth. Mother of Love, stand by my labors.   30
Keep away, you women who wear finely-woven fillets, symbols of
    chastity,
    and you who wear long skirts to cover ankles:
I shall sing of safe affairs, love's lawful thefts;
    in my poem will be no charge of a crime.
First, my raw recruit, prepare for a new battlefield; strive   35
    to find what you really want in matters of love.°
Your next duty is to win over the girl who is the object of your desire,
    and then to see to it that the love lasts.
That is my limit; this is the territory my chariot will traverse,°
    to this goal my wheels will aim.   40
While you are free and able to go anywhere, slacken the reins,
    choose one to whom you can say: "You are my only sweetheart."
She will not come to you dropping out of thin air;
    you must use your eyes to get the right girl.
The hunter knows where it is best to spread his nets for deer,   45
    he knows the haunts where the wild boar gnashes his teeth.
Fowlers know their bushes; the fisherman knows where to bait
    his hooks in waters where swim the many fish.
So you, too, in your quest for material intended for long-lasting love,
    first learn the spot where girls frequent.   50
I will not order you to hoist sails for your search;
    you don't have to tread far and wide to find her.
Perseus brought back Andromeda° from dusky India,
    and she was a Greek woman whom the Phrygian Paris abducted.
Rome will offer you all the beautiful girls you want,   55
    so many, you'll say: "This city has the pick of the world."

1.35-36: see *Amores* 1.9 for the developed metaphor of Love as War.
1.39-40: the images of the ship and chariot convey the metaphor of poet as
    helmsman and charioteer. Ovid ends this book with the image of the ship
    (772). See Propertius 3.1.9-10 and 4.1.70 for the metaphor of the charioteer.
1.53: Andromeda is most frequently depicted as Ethiopian.

The number of crops in Gargara, the grapes of Methymna in Lesbos,
    the fish in the sea, the birds that take cover under leaves,
The stars in the sky, do not equal the many girls your Rome pos-
    sesses.
In the city of her son, Aeneas, mother Venus resides.   60
If you are hooked on nymphets, still budding,
    you'll find a genuine girl before your eyes;
If you desire one in the prime of youth, there are thousands to please
    you.
    You'll be hard pressed to choose your heart's desire.
Or perhaps an older and wiser woman pleases you,   65
    believe me, you'll have a host of these too.
Just take a leisured stroll in the shade of Pompey's portico°
    when the sun approaches Leo, Hercules' lion;
Or where a mother has bestowed her own gifts to the endowments°
    of her son, a work adorned and rich in foreign marble.   70
Don't avoid the colonnade filled with art works of the old masters
    that bears the name of its patron, Livia;°
Nor the statues of the Danaids who dared to ready murder
    for their hapless cousins, and where stands their savage father with
        sword drawn;°
And don't let pass the holy precinct of Adonis, bewailed by Venus,°75
    and the sacred shrine where on the Sabbath a Syrian Jew worships;
Don't shun the temple of Isis from Memphis, the Heifer, dressed in
    linen
    (she makes many women what Jove made of her);
The markets too are conducive to love (who'd believe it?),
    and in the shrill forum the flame of love is often found.   80
Where the Appian fountain hard by the marble temple of Venus
    gushes and sprays its waters into the air,
There in that spot Love's lawyer is snared,
    who just recently defended others but now cannot himself defend.

1.68: the colonnade of Pompey's Theater opened in 55.

1.69: refers to the portico of Octavia, sister of Octavius/Augustus.

1.71-72: Livia, the wife of Augustus, built a large colonnaded arcade on the
southwestern section of the Esquiline in 7. It honored a triumph of her son
Tiberius.

1.73-74: refer to the Temple of Apollo in whose portico were placed statues of the
Danaids. See Propertius 2.31. The allusions to the many building complexes,
shrines, and temples refer to conspicuous monuments of the Augustan period.
For Ovid they serve as convenient places to meet and pick up girls. This
flippant attitude, no doubt, did not sit well with Augustus and his family.

1.75-78: catalogue foreign cults and shrines encouraged by Augustus in a grow-
ing cosmopolitan city governing the Mediterranean littoral.

In that same spot words often fail the glib speaker;   85
    though new cases arise, he must plead his own.
From her temple nearby Venus laughs at him
    who a moment before was a lawyer, but now longs to be a client.
But do your best hunting in the curves of the theaters;
    they are precincts rich beyond your dreams.   90
There you'll find someone to love, or someone you can play around
      with,
    someone you'd love to touch just once, or someone you'd like to
      hold on to.
Just as a long column of ants keeps going back and forth,
    carrying in their mouths a load of grain, their usual food,
Or just as bees swarm over their glades and scented meadows   95
    and flit above the tops of flowers and thyme,
So to the games with their crowds in a rush flock the most sophis-
    ticated women;
    so many in number that they deter my judgment.
They come to see; they come to be seen.
    This spot causes the loss of shame and chastity.   100
You, Romulus, first made the games scandalous
    when the rape of Sabines delighted your wifeless men.
At that time no awnings hung over a marble theater,°
    no spraying saffron drenched the platformed stage.
The woods of the Palatine provided foliage; arranged in simple
    design   105
    it adorned the artless stage.
The people sat on steps created from sod,
    shading their foreheads and shaggy hair with leaves.
They scanned with their eyes, and each one marked for himself
    the girl he wanted; in his silent heart stirred many feelings;   110
And while the Etruscan° flute was sounding a crude melody,
    and an actor stamped the level ground three times,
Amid the applause—even cheering applause was natural—
    Romulus, the king, gave the sign to the men waiting for their
      booty.
Up they leapt, their shouts attested to their intention;   115
    they grabbed the women in their lustful hands:
As frightened flocks of doves flee the eagles,
    and the youngest lamb flees the sight of wolves,

1.103-108. Augustan poets exploit with nostalgia the simplicity of primitive
Rome. See Propertius 4.1
1.111: the Etruscans were credited with introducing drama to early Rome.

So these girls feared the men as they rushed about helter-skelter.
    Not one of them maintained her color.   120
The fright was the same, but each expression of fear was different:
    some tore their hair, others sat bewildered.
One is silent in grief, another calls uselessly for her mother;
    one moans, another is in shock, one stays, another flees.
The girls were seized and led away, the prize for marriage,   125
    and fear made many of them more attractive.
If one struggled too much or refused her captor,
    he lifted her up and held her to his lustful breast
And said: "Why do you spoil your tender eyes with tears?
    What your father is to your mother, I will be to you."   130
You knew, Romulus, how to give prizes to soldiers;
    if you offer me a prize like that, I'll sign up for a tour of duty.
From such a tradition theaters stand today celebrated,
    where snares still await beautiful women.
And don't avoid the thoroughbred races:°   135
    the track packed full of people offers many opportunities.
You don't need to use your fingers to communicate secret codes,
    no need of nods to get her to know you.
No one stops you; take a seat next to a lady,
    press your side to her side as close as you can.   140
And it's fine, even if she is against it, the barrier forces close contact;
    it's a ground-rule that you have to touch the girl.
At this point you should try to find an opening line of conversation;
    speak out in public your first impulses:
Eagerly ask: "Whose horses are on the track?"   145
    Don't waste time, bet on whomever she bets on.
Then when the parade proceeds with the many ivory images of the
        gods,
    clap and cheer for Queen Venus.
If some specks of dust, as it happens sometimes, drop on the girl's
        lap,
    flick them off with your fingers.   150
And, if there is no dust, flick anyway what isn't there.
    Use any old excuse for your concern.
If her skirt droops and trails on the ground,
    gather it up, carefully lifting it off the dirty surface.
There and then, if the girl permits it, as a reward for your
        attention,   155
    your eyes will get a view of her legs.

1.135-162: Ovid reworks *Amores* 3.2.

Take a look back at whoever is seated behind you;
    Don't let him prod his knee into her soft back.
Small things captivate gentle hearts: it is very helpful
    to arrange her pillow with adroit ease;   160
And it counts a lot to fan the breezes with a slender program
    and to set a hollow stool beneath her tender feet.
As the track provides such approaches for a new lover,
    so too the worrisome forum spread with sand, grim for gladiators.
Often Venus' boy fought on that sand,   165
    and he who has watched the wounds receives a wound himself:
While he was talking, touching a hand, asking for a program,
    and inquired who was winning after he had placed his bet,
Wounded, he groans to feel the swift arrow:
    from spectator he became a part of the show.   170
When Caesar has staged a mock sea battle
    in which he has engaged Persian and Athenian ships,°
When young men and young women from east and west
    have come and all the world is in the city,
Who in the crowd doesn't find someone to love?   175
    O how many men a foreign lover has put to the rack!
Look! Caesar is ready now to add to his power the world
    he has not yet conquered: now, far east, you will soon be ours.
Parthian, you will pay the penalties due; and the Crassi, long buried,
    will cheer when the standards, mistreated in barbaric hands,
        return.°   180
The champion is already here; in the early prime of life he heralds
        himself the avenging
    general; youthful, still a boy, he undertakes wars not to be con-
        ducted by a boy.°
Cease, you fretful ones, to count the birthdays of the gods.
    The manliness of a Caesar predates its day.
The genius of the divine soars faster than its years   185
    and scorns cowardly delay.
Hercules was a baby at Tiryns when he choked the two snakes
    with his bare hands, proving in his cradle his worthy descent from
        Jove.

1.171-172: refer to a mock sea battle of the Greeks and Persians at Salamis (480
    BCE) that Augustus staged to dedicate (2 BCE) the opening of the Temple
    of Mars the Avenger in his imperial forum.
1.180: the standards captured by Parthians at the Battle of Carrhae in 53 had
    already been restored (in 20) after intense diplomatic negotiations.
1.182-216. the reference is to Gaius Caesar, grandson and adopted son of Au-
    gustus.

Bacchus, who is still a youth, was not very big
    when he conquered India which quaked at his wands. 190
With the blessing and courage of your father, you will take to arms
    and, though just a boy, win under that blessing and courage of
        your father.
Under so mighty a name you are due a practice victory,
    you, now the leader of the youths,° soon to be prince of elders.
Since you have brothers, avenge the wrongs suffered by your
        brothers; 195
    since you have a father, defend the rights of that father.
Your father and the father of the fatherland have armed you
    against an enemy that seizes kingdoms from your parent.
You will bear righteous weapons, the enemy the arrows of crime.
    Justice and Right will serve as your standards. 200
Losers of their cause, may the Parthians lose in battle:
    and may my general add the resources of the East to Latium.
Father Mars and Father Caesar, one of you a god, the other soon to
        be,
    bestow your divine grace upon him when he goes.
Yes, I prophesy that you will win; and I'll vow proper songs to
        you, 205
    my mighty lips will herald your praises.
When you halt the troops, you'll use my words to inspire the men
    (O may no words of mine fail your courageous heart!).
I shall sing of Parthian backs turning in rout before Roman breasts;
    I shall sing of weapons hurled by the enemy from a horse turned in
        flight. 210
O Parthian, what do you lose in defeat, if you flee to win?
    Parthian, already your tactic in war has an ill-omened repute.
So, there will come a day when you, the glory of our empire,
    behind four snow-white horses and dressed in the gold of a victor-
        will pass in triumph.°
Ahead of you will go chieftains with chains weighing down their
        necks; 215
    no possible flight and safety as before.
Happy young men and happy girls, too, will watch,
    every heart that day will be imbued with joy.
If one of the girls asks the names of the captured kings,
    the locales, the mountains, or rivers on display, 220

1.194: in 5 Gaius had been made the "Prince of Youth" (*princeps iuventutis*), a
    type of *Jugenkorps* meant to train young men for military leadership.
1.214-216: unfortunately, in 4 CE Gaius died from a wound that he received in
    the siege of Artagonia (Armenia). He never celebrated the triumph heralded
    here.

Answer them all, even if she doesn't ask for them;
   whatever you don't know, make it up as if you knew it well.
That's the Euphrates wearing a crown of reeds,
   and the one with long blue hair, that'll be the Tigris.
Those over there, make them Armenians, and right here Persia,°
     descendant of Danae;
   and that one was a town somewhere in the valleys of Media.   226
This one here, that one there, is a general: speak out their real names,
   if you can, if not, then make an apt one up.
Parties, too, when the tables are set, offer an approach;
   there, you can get something besides wine.   230
Often, when Bacchus places himself there at rest, purple-hued Love
   has caressed him with tender arms;
And when wine has drenched Cupid's drunken wings,
   he stays weighed down, and stands a captive in his place;
He quickly shakes his wings dripping wet,   235
   then the heart bedewed with love feels the hurt.
Wine readies minds and makes them susceptible to the heat of pas-
     sion;
   wine in plenty dissolves and puts cares to flight.
With it laughter comes, then a poor man takes on wealth;
   pain, worries, a frowning wrinkle on the forehead vanish.   240
Then simplicity, that rarest commodity of our time,
   opens hearts; the god expels all forms of pretense.
At that point girls often captivate the hearts of young men;
   when you have Venus in wine, you have fire in fire.
Do not put excessive trust in a deceptive lamp: 245
   night and wine impair the judgment of beauty.
In daylight and under an open sky Paris judged the three goddesses,
   where he declared to Venus: "You win, Venus."
Nighttime hides flaws and forgives every fault.
   The hour makes any woman a beauty.   250
Depend upon the daytime for judgment about jewels and wool dyed
     purple,
   for evaluation of face and body.
No need for me to list for you the gathering-places for women who
     are right
   for your hunts: the number I could give you surpasses the grains of
     sand;
No need to mention Baiae and the shores bordering it,   255
   where hot sulphur gurgles up with water and steam.

1.225: Perses, son of Perseus and Andromeda, was the eponymous founder of
   Persia.

More than once a man has brought back from there a gashing wound
   in his heart and has exclaimed: "These waters aren't so healthy as
      advertised."
Right outside the City there stands Diana's sylvan temple,°
   where a murderous hand and violent swords win a long reign. 260
The goddess is a virgin, she despises the weapons of Cupid:
   yet many wounds she has caused, and many more she will give.
So far, you have been reading where to set your nets, hunting for a
     lover;
   my Muse, riding on a chariot wheeled in couplets, has been your
     teacher.
Now you must learn the skills by which to capture your heart's
     desire.   265
   It is the art in my mighty effort that can tell you.
Men, whoever you are, wherever you are, be receptive and pay
     attention:
   and you ordinary guys, too, stand by, favor my promise.
First, have confidence; fix it in your mind that all women
   can be caught; just spread your nets, and you'll bag them.   270
Sooner birds in spring, cicadas in summer, would be silent,
   a hound of Arcadia turn tail from a pursuing hare,
Than a woman, approached and properly wooed, would refuse a
     young lover:
   she even will say "yes" whom you thought would say "no."
Venus on the sly thrills a woman as much as a man;   275
   a man's no good at pretense; but she likes to hide her lust.
Were it not the convention that we males ask a woman first,
   the female would assume the role of the asker.
The heifer lows for the bull in soft meadows,
   the mare always whinnies for the horn-shod stud.   280
In us—human males— lust is rarer and not so mad and wild;
   the fire of masculine passion has a rightful boundary.
I cite the case of Byblis who burned for the forbidden love of her
     brother:°
   she atoned for her wrong, bravely submitting to the noose.
And Myrrha loved her father, but not as a daughter ought;°   285
   now she is held, pressed in the bark of a tree

1.259: "Diana's sylvan temple" refers to the famous sanctuary of Diana Nemo-
rensis at Lake Nemi a little south of Rome.

1.283: Bibylis fell in love with her brother Caunus (Ovid, *Metamorphoses* 9.454-
668).

1.285: Myrrha bore Adonis by her father Cinyras (Ovid, *Metamorphoses* 10.298-
518).

Whose scented tears which the tree distills
    we use as ointment, the drops of unguent that bear her name:
        myrrh.
Once in shady glades beneath groves on Mt. Ida
    was a white bull, the glory of the herd,   290
Between its horns on the forehead a thin black mark;
    it was a blemish, all the rest was milky-white.
Heifers of Cnossus and Cydonia° desired him,
    wanting him to mount their backs.
Pasiphae longed to become the adulterous mate of this bull;   295
    she envied and hated the beautiful cows.
I sing of matters well-known; Crete, land of lies,
    and nurse of a hundred cities, cannot deny it.
They say that with unpracticed hands she cut fresh leaves
    and the juiciest meadow grass for the bull.   300
She goes in company with the herd; love for her husband, Minos,
    does not stop her going; so he too was conquered by a bull.
What is the point of putting on your expensive clothes, Pasiphae?
    Your adulterous mate perceives no wealth.
What good does it do you to take a mirror on your search for herds in
        the mountains?
    Why, you fool, do you adorn and readorn your hair?   306
Yet have faith in a mirror that shows you are no heifer;
    nor, despite your fondest wish, do horns sprout from your brow!
If you were pleased with Minos, you would not go looking for a
        lover.
    If you choose to cheat on a man, then do your cheating with a
        man.   310
Leaving her bedroom the queen goes to glade and glen
    driven like a Bacchant enthused by the god of Aonia.
Ah, how often she gazed at a cow with spite on her face
    and asked: "How can she satisfy my lover?
Look at her gamboling in the tender grass in front of him;   315
    I don't doubt that the fool believes she is beautiful."
With these words she ordered her to be led from the huge herd
    to haul curved plows—a fate which she did not deserve;
Or she had one struck down a victim before altars under some
        trumped up
    sacred rites, then held up in her jubilant hand the entrails of her
        rival.   320
How often she slew her sexual rivals to appease divinities
    and exclaimed as she lifted up the entrails: "Go now, and satisfy
        him, my lover."

1.293: Cnossus and Cydonia are cities in Crete.

Sometimes she prays to be Europa, sometimes Io,
  the latter because she was a cow, the other because she rode a bull.
Yet finally, the leader of the herd, deceived by a maple cow,   325
  impregnated her, and the birth of her son, the Minotaur, betrayed
    the father.
If Cretan Aerope had abstained from her love for Thyestes
  (quite a task it is to please one man),
Phoebus would not have interrupted his course, wheeled his chariot
    around,
  and reversed his horses to approach the dawn of the East.°   330
Nisus' own daughter, Scylla, robbed him of his purple locks;
  around her groin and loins now mad dogs press.
Atreus' son who escaped war on land and the wrath of Poseidon on
    the sea
  met the direst end, a victim of his wife.
Who has not lamented the flame of Creusa of Corinth,   335
  and the bloody, violent mother, murderer of her own sons?°
Phoenix, son of Amyntor, wept from eyes without sight;
  mad horses ripped apart Hippolytus.
Why, Phincus, did you stab out the undeserving eyes of your own
    sons?
  That same punishment will devolve upon your head.   340
All these crimes were motivated by a woman's lust,
  more intense and raging with madness than ours.
So, up! Don't hesitate; put your hopes in all the girls:
  there will scarcely be a single one out of many who would refuse
    you.
Those who assent, and those who say no, all like being asked: 345
  although you may be rejected, your defeat is without harm.
But why should you be rejected? A new pleasure is a delight,
  those belonging to others captivate hearts more than one's own.
The crop in somebody else's field always is richer;
  a neighbor's flock produces a greater yield.   350
First take care to get to know the maid of the girl you want to seduce.
  She will smooth your approach.
Make sure that she is always privy to your lover's schemes,
  a trusting confidante of the secrets of her playing around.
Spoil her with promises and spoil her with pleas;   355
  with her good will, what you seek, you'll easily find.

1.329-330: Phoebus, the Sun-god, turned back his course across the heaven in hor-
  ror and shock of Aerope's adultery with Thyestes, her husband's brother.
1.336-339: four examples of female lust and malicious vindictiveness. After
  Jason left her, Medea killed her two sons.

She will choose the proper time (as doctors observe critical periods)
  when easy and ripe for capture is her lady's heart;
Her mind will be right for the taking, when, like a crop
  in rich soil, she blossoms in joy over her state of affairs.   360
When hearts are happy and pain does not tighten around them,
  then they are wide open and Venus with charm and art sneaks in.
For years arms defended Troy during doom and gloom;
  with joy she received the horse pregnant with soldiers.
Then again, you should try an assault when she is hurt and in pain
    over a rival.   365
  Perform your operations to avenge her.
The maid, while combing her hair in the morning, can urge her on,
  helping you by adding, so to speak, oars to the sail;
With a sigh and soft murmur let her whisper:
  "You could do nothing else, I suppose."   370
Then let her talk about you, adding, to be sure, some words of
    persuasion,
  and swearing that you are mad for her and dying of love.
But hurry! The sails may collapse and the breezes subside:
  anger, like brittle ice, melts with time.
Could it do any good to seduce the maid, you ask: 375
  such an enterprise is dicey, a big risk.°
One is eager after the love-making, another too slow;
  one maid readies you to service her lady, but another does it for
    herself.
Some luck is involved, and it may mean some bold risks,
  but my advice is to choose to abstain.   380
I will not proceed over precipitous and steep summits,
  nor will I lead any young man into a trap.
Yet, if the maid pleases you, giving and receiving notes,
  her body as attractive as her careful work on your behalf,
Catch and take the lady first, then follow up with the maid.   385
  your love-making should not begin with the maid.
I add this one piece of advice: if you trust my skill at all,
  and if my words are not driven across the sea by a hurricane,
Either do it right or don't even try: you remove her as a tattling in-
    former
  as soon as she becomes a partner of your "crime."   390
A bird with lime glued to its wings cannot with success fly off,
  a wild boar has a problem escaping the mesh of nets;
And hold on to the fish once hooked;
  so, press the attack upon her, and don't go away until you emerge
    a winner.

1.375-376: see *Amores* 2.7 and 2.8 for the working out of this theme.

Sharing your guilt then she will never betray you,   395
    all of her lady's acts, all her words, you will know.
But keep her under wraps, if you make her your undercover informer;
    she will always be a friendly news reporter for you.
He is wrong to think that the seasons are to be observed only by
      farmers
    laboring in the fields, and by sailors.   400
Not always should grain be entrusted to the treacherous soil,
    nor a hollow ship to the green water of the sea.
So it is not always safe to go hunting for tender girls:
    often it is better at a suitable time.
If it's her birthday coming up, or the first of the month   405
    when Venus' celebration has succeeded March,
Or if the Circus is not decorated with its usual emblems,
    but displays the gathered wealth of kings,
Put off your chase: the winter is gloomy, the Pleiades threaten,
    the young Haedus sets in Ocean's stream,   410
That's the time to pause: whoever entrusts himself then to the deep
    barely saves the shipwrecked remnants of his shattered boat.
Begin on the day mourned for the defeat at the Allia
    which ran with blood from the wounds of Latins,
Or on the day when business is suspended, the Sabbath,   415
    as worshipped by the Jew of Palestine.
Treat your girlfriend's birthday like a taboo:
    it is a black day when you have to give presents.
Even if you avoid it as best you can, still she robs you.
    Women have perfected to an art form the fleecing of a lustful
      lover.   420
A peddler will come by, easygoing, to a lady who loves to shop;
    he displays his wares as you sit near by;
She asks you to inspect them to make you think you're in the know,
    then she'll kiss you and coax you to buy.
She swears she'll be happy with just this one item for many years, 425
    claiming she can't do without it and it's on sale to boot.
If you offer the excuse that you have no money on you,
    she'll demand you write a check—(don't you wish you had never
      learned to write?).
Often she'll ask for cash for a birthday cake:
    quite often she gets herself born as suits her need.   430
She pretends sadness, complaining she has lost something valuable,
      making up
    a cockeyed story that an earring of precious stone has slipped from
      her earlobe.
Sometimes they ask for a big loan, but refuse to pay back the debt;
    you lose the money and get no thanks for the loss.

For me to detail the impious acts of prostitutes   435
   ten mouths and ten tongues would not be enough.
Send tablets smoothed with wax to test the water;
   let the wax-tablets go as the guidelines of your mind.
Let them carry sweet nothings and the bogus words of lovers;
   whoever you are, add a lot of prayers.   440
Achilles, moved by the prayers of Priam, restored Hector to him;
   even an angry god bends to the praying voice.
Make promises: for what harm is there in promising?
   Anyone can be rich in promises.
Hope endures for a long time, if once she is trusted;   445
   she is a goddess, useful to be sure, but also a cheat.
If you give a gift, then in all probability, you'll be dumped:
   she'll win out and not lose a thing.
Don't give, but always give the impression that you are going to do
   so,
   like a barren field that often frustrates the hope of its owner,   450
Like the gambler who does not cease to bet to recover his loss,
   when his greedy hands cannot surrender the dice.
That is the task, that is your labor: to screw her without that first present.
   She'll always keep giving, if she feels she hasn't given for free.
So scratch out your flatteries and send her the letter   455
   to test her feelings and to blaze your trail.
A message inscribed on an apple tricked Cydippe;
   she was a girl unaware that her own words netted her.
I advise you, young men of Rome, to learn the liberal arts,°
   not just to defend defendants in fear of their life.   460
As the people, a serious judge, and the elected senate will surrender,
   so a girl, overcome by eloquence, will succumb.
But conceal your powers, and don't wear the professional look;
   avoid using tedious sentences.
Who but a cretin would declaim to a young girl?   465
   Often a pretentious letter has been the cause of dislike.
Your style should be colloquial, natural, using common words,
   yet coaxing as though you were speaking in the flesh.
If she refuses a letter and sends it back unopened and unread,
   hope that she will read one someday. Stick to your course.   470
In time recalcitrant bullocks come to the plow,
   in time horses learn to bear pliant bridles;

1.459-470: Ovid gently pokes fun at Roman rhetorical doctrine and principle that
   in theory emphasized a well-rounded education and stressed that the style of
   speaking should be appropriate to the subject and circumstance.

Constant wear eats away an iron ring,
    the curved plow rusts away from the continual work in the soil.
What is harder than rock or softer than water?   475
    Yet soft water hollows out the hardest rocks.
Persist and in time you will win over even Penelope:
    although captured late, you see Pergama captured nonetheless.
Suppose she reads your letter but refuses to write back: don't force it.
    Keep her reading your sweet nothings.   480
To what she has decided to read someday she'll be willing to reply;
    such things come by degrees and in steps.
Perhaps the first letter to arrive will sadden you,
    which asks that you not bother her:
In truth, she fears what she asks and hopes that what she does not
      ask   485
    you will insist upon: press on, in time you'll gain your heart's
      desire.
Meanwhile, if she happens to be lying on her accustomed seat, being
      carried in a litter,
    find a pretense to approach the woman's sedan.
To insure that no one overhears words offensive to the ears,
    be cunning and, when you can, in ambiguous metaphors, disguise
      the meaning.   490
If she whiles away her time taking a carefree stroll in a spacious col-
      onnade,
    join her there at a leisurely pace;
Sometimes proceed a little ahead, sometimes linger behind,
    at one point hurry, and then just mosey along;
Don't be bashful: pass between the columns now and then,   495
    or saunter side by side.
Also, take a seat by her in the curving theater as she is watching the
      show;
    her arms and shoulders will conjure up something for you to look
      at.
It's okay to look at her, to admire her,
    use your eyebrows to speak volumes, use signs;   500
Applaud the dancer who plays the part of a girl,
    and whoever has the role of a lover, clap for him.
When she gets up, you get up, but keep your seat while she sits:
    while away your time as suits the whim of your lady.
But don't coif your hair with a curling iron,   505
    or scrape smooth your legs with coarse pumice:
Leave that to those who howl and harmonize
    the Phrygian strains that celebrate the Great Mother, Cybele.
The neglected look becomes men; Theseus stole away
    Minos' girl without pinning up his hair.   510

Phaedra fell in love with Hippolytus who didn't doll himself up like a
    dandy,
    and Adonis, dressed for the woods, won a goddess' love.
Cleanliness counts, and bodies tanned from exercise on the Campus
    attract;
    keep your toga fitted well and spotless.
Brush your teeth to prevent decay and rot,   515
    don't flop around in loose leather shoes.
Long, stiff hair, badly cut, makes you look ugly;
    let the skilled hand of a barber cut your hair and trim your beard.
Maintain your nails, pared and cleaned of dirt;
    watch out for hair sprouting and bristling in your nose.   520
And check your breath for smelly odors from your mouth,
    and let not the whiff of a billy goat offend any nostrils.
Leave the lusty girls to do the rest,
    and any man who shamefully seeks to take another man.
Look, Bacchus summons his bard: he too aids   525
    lovers, and fans the flame whose heat he himself has felt.
Out of her mind Ariadne of Cnossus wandered over the deso-
    late sands
    of tiny Dia beaten by the waves of the sea:
Just as she was awakened from sleep, with her clothes loose upon her,
    her feet bare, her yellow hair unbound,   530
To unresponsive waves she kept calling: "Theseus, you bastard!"
    As a shower of shameful tears furrowed her soft cheeks,
She cried out and wept, but her cries and tears were becoming;
    she was not uglier because of her tears.
Again and again, beating her gentle breasts with her hands,   535
    she wailed: "That liar has gone; what's to become of me?"
"What's to become of me?" she repeated. Along the entire coast line
    echoed the sounds of cymbals, the beat of drums pounded by fren-
    zied hands.
She broke off her last words and fainted from fright:
    all the blood drained from her lifeless body.   540
Look, Bacchants come with hair streaming down their backs;
    a gang of satyrs comes, frolicking ahead of the god.
Then comes old Silenus, drunk on his swaybacked ass,
    barely able to keep on, tightly gripping and hanging on to the mane.
He chases the Bacchants; at times they run off, and at times they at-
    tack him;   545
    While with a stick the tipsy rider was prodding his mount,
He slipped from the long-eared beast and fell on his head;
    the satyrs shouted out: "Come on, get up, get up, old dad."
Now the god himself in his chariot, wreathed and draped with grapes,
    was plying the golden reins fastened to a team of tigers.   550

The girl had lost her color, her voice, her Theseus;
  three times she tried flight, three times her fear held her back.
She shook like stripped wheat stalks tossed by wind;
  she quivered like a slender reed in a marshy swamp.
To her the god spoke: "Look, I am here, a more faithful lover
    for you.   555
  Cast aside your fear, you will be Bacchus' wife from Cnossus;
Take the gift of heaven: you will be seen as a constellation in the sky;
  often you, the Cretan Diadem,° will be the guide for a floundering
    ship."
With these words, lest she fear the tigers, he leapt from his chariot;
  the sand left his prints as he strode.   560
He held her tight in his arms—she lacked the strength to struggle—
  and bore her away; for a god everything is easy to do.
Some sing out: "Hail, Hymeneus!" Others shout: "Hail, Bacchus!"
  So god and bride join on the sacred marriage-bed.
Thus, when the gifts of Bacchus are set before you,   565
  and a woman shares your bed,
Pray to Bacchus, the father, and to the holy powers of the night,
  not to allow the wine to give you a hangover.
At night you can hint in ambiguous phrases
  messages which she can surmise are for her;   570
Trace lightly in wine some flirtatious enchantments outlined on the
    table
  for her to read that she is your girl;
Gaze into her eyes with eyes that confess your fiery passion:
  often the silent look speaks volumes of words.
Be the first to seize the cup that her lips have touched,   575
  and drink from the lip where your girl sips;
And whatever food she has tasted and offers with her fingers for you,
  take it, and while you are at it, touch her hand.
Vow to make your girlfriend's husband like you:
  if he becomes a friend, he will be quite useful.   580
Suppose you are drinking in an order determined by lot, let him have
    the first turn,
  give him the garland meant for your head.
Whether he is sitting at the end of the table or at the head, let him
    take every dish first,
  don't hesitate to flatter him.
Deceiving in the name of "friend" is a protected and well-trodden
    road,   585
  it may be a safe and well-trodden road, still it is wrong.

1.558: the Cretan Diadem is the constellation Corona, the crown of stars given
  by Dionysus to Ariadne when they were married.

The broker too often brokers too much,
    and thinks he should oversee more than his share.
Now, I will set you a definite limit for your drinking;
    let both mind and feet each perform their respective function.   590
Avoid at all cost brawls incited by wine
    and hands too ready for wild fights and blows.
Stupid Eurytion fell from excessive drinking of wine.
    The table and wine are meant for wholesome fun.
If you have a voice for it, sing; if you have supple limbs, then
       dance;   595
    and whatever talent you have to please with, use it to please.
Getting drunk is harmful, but pretending to be drunk is real fun.
    Stutter a little; slyly let your tongue make a slip or two;
So, if you say or do something a little too risque,
    they'll think that too much wine was the reason for it.   600
And toast your lover, and toast him as well with whom she is
       sleeping,
    but beneath your breath curse the bastard.
But when the table is cleared and the party breaks up with the guests
       all leaving,
    the milling of the crowd will offer you a spot and opportune
       access   604
To plant yourself among the group and, as you move through and as
       she is on the go,
    to pinch her lightly and to touch her foot with yours.
Now is the time for conversation; off with the rustic demeanor,
    off with bashful shame: Fortune and Venus favor the bold!
My rules are unneeded; let your own eloquence rise to the fore,
    you need only desire and automatically you will be eloquent.   610
You should play the role of the lover, feigning wounds of the heart;
    seek with every art to make it seem true and believable.
It's not a difficult task to be believed: every girl thinks
       herself desirable.
    She may be the ugliest hag around, but she's not displeased by her
       own sex appeal.
Often too the role-player falls in love for real,   615
    he becomes the character which he only pretended to be.
So, girls, go easy on those whom you suspect to be pretending:
    love that began as a lie will soon become true.
Flattery, like a thief, takes the mind by surprise,
    like flowing water that subtly eats away a steep river bank.   620
Don't forget to praise her face, her hair,
    her elegant fingers, her delicate feet.
Even "nice" girls are delighted to hear commendations of their
       beauty,
    and virgins attend to their looks with fastidious care.

Why do you suppose Juno and Pallas even now feel the sting   625
   of the lost verdict in Phrygia's forests?
Praise Juno's bird, the peacock, and it spreads its tail;
   watch it in silence, and it keeps buried its feathered glory.
Lightning-fast thoroughbreds between the races of the track
   love their manes combed and their necks stroked.   630
Don't be too bashful to promise: promises attract the girls;
   in your promise call to witness any of the gods you please.
Jupiter from on high laughs at lovers' lies
   and commands the winds directed by Aeolus to waft them away.
More than once Jupiter swore falsely by the Styx to Juno;°   635
   now he approves of his own example.
Gods are convenient to have around; so, let's conveniently believe
   they exist.°
   Bring to their pristine altars incense and wine.
No peace and carefree quiet in seeming slumber keep them aloof:
   live an innocent life, then divinity is at hand.   640
Pay back what you've borrowed; respect the code of proper conduct.
   Avoid fraud, keep your hands clean of blood.
If you are smart, play the deceiver with girls only—that's free of
   charge—
   truth in this one case is more shameful than deceit.
Cheat on these cheaters: for the most part they are an irreverent
   tribe,   645
   unprincipled: let them fall into the traps that they themselves have
   set.
They say that Egypt once lacked the welcoming rain to inundate the
   fields
   and that there was drought for nine years.
Thrasius visited Busiris then and pointed out that Jove°
   would be appeased if the blood of a stranger were shed.   650
To him Busiris replied: "Fine, you first will be the victim to Jove,
   the stranger to water Egypt's land."
Then, too, Phalaris roasted that brute Perillus, limbs and all,
   in a bull, a contraption he devised for his own doom.
Both were right, for no other law is more just   655
   than that artisans of death perish by their own art.

1.635-646: Ovid employs a divine example to show that when it comes to love
   one can commit perjury. See Tibullus 1.4.23-24.
1.637-640: The Epicureans believed that it was proper to observe public wor-
   ship for political and social stability, but that the gods played no part in the
   governing of the universe.
1.649-654: Ovid appreciated the myths of Busiris and Phalaris; he reused them
   in *Tristia* 3.11.39-54.

So, women who lie deserve to be deceived by lies;
    a woman should hurt, inflicted with a wound of her own making.
Try tears: they work. With tears you can melt steel;
    make sure, if you can, that she sees your cheeks all moist.   660
If tears fail to come—they don't always rise to the occasion—
    moisten your hands and rub your eyes.
Be smart enough to mix kisses with flattery.
    If she refuses to return them, then take them as if she had.
Perhaps she'll resist at first and call you a cad,   665
    that battle she will gladly lose.
Be careful that you not crush her tender lips snatching those kisses.
    Don't give her the excuse that they were too hard.
Whoever takes kisses and does not follow up to take the rest,
    deserves to lose all that he has gained.   670
By a long shot kissing misses the full completion of your heart's
    desire.
    Not shyness but the manners of country bumpkin cause this.
Call upon brute force: girls like it;
    what they enjoy, they pretend to give unwilling.
She who is violated by a sudden rush for love welcomes the forcible
    attack,   675
    and considers her wantonness an attractive gift.
But she who leaves untouched, when you could have forced her,
    will be a gloomy girl, though feigning looks of joy.
Phoebe suffered outrage, and her sister, too, was ravished;
    both violators delighted their abducted captives.   680
Then there is the story, an old one, but worthy of recounting:
    the girl of Scyros° joined in love with the hero Achilles.
Sometime before that the goddess had bestowed her fatal reward,
    the goddess who triumphed beneath Mt. Ida over her two rivals;
Then Helen came to Priam a daughter-in-law from a distant part of
    the world,   685
    a Greek wife within the walls of Ilium;
All the Greeks swore allegiance to the injured husband.
    The grief of a single man became the cause of an entire people.
It was a disgrace. Achilles responded to his mother's prayers;
    he wore the long dress of a woman to disguise his being a man. 690
What's up with you, grandson of Aeacus? Spinning wool is not your
    game.
    You seek glory from Pallas' other art.
What are baskets to you? Your hand is made for carrying a shield;
    Why do you hold balls of yarn in the hand that will fell Hector?

1.682: the girl of Scyros is Deidamia, whose story is intricately involved with
    that of Achilles' attempt to avoid the Trojan War. See Glossary under
    DEIDAMIA.

Throw away the spindles, the toilsome threads of the warp;   695
    brandish instead a Pelian spear in your hand.
The princess, Deidamia, shared a bed with him
    and there discovered, after his ravishment of her, that he was a man.
They would have us believe that the girl was taken by force,
    but she willed it: by force she wanted to be overcome.   700
Often, when Achilles was hurrying to leave, she begged, "Stay!"
    for he had by then exchanged the distaff for weapons of manliness.
Tell us, where's the force? Why the coaxing words to delay
    the perpetrator of a rape against you, Deidamia?
Of course it is a shame for the woman to be the forward one,   705
    but she's delighted by the experience when a man starts it.
A young man puts too much trust in his own looks
    who waits around for the girl to ask first.
The man should make the first approach, do the asking out;
    Let the girl kindly listen to his flattery and requests.   710
Just ask to win her: she truly wants to be asked out.
    Give her a reason, a basis, for your interest.
Jupiter himself humbly approached the girls of myth;
    no girl seduced mighty Jove.
If, however, you perceive your request met with puffed-up pride, 715
    then stop what's begun and retreat a few steps.
Many girls covet the shy, but some detest the aggressive type:
    proceed with caution and you remove her antipathy towards you.
Don't always profess your hope of love on your first date;
    conceal your budding desire under the name of friendship.   720
I have witnessed this M.O. succeed with a prude of a girl;
    he who was "just a friend" became a passionate lover.
White is a color that disgraces a sailor: he ought to be dark
    from the waves of the sea, sunburnt by the rays of the sun;
And likewise a farmer who toils over a bent plow   725
    and heavy rakes in the light of day churning up soil;
And an athlete who seeks the fame a garland of olives bestows
    wears the disgrace of a totally white complexion.
Pale should be the look of every lover: this color suits the man in love;
    it adds charm, though many would dispute its appeal.   730
Orion was pale when he was strolling in the woods of Side,°
    pale was Daphnis for the love of a reluctant Naiad.
Leanness shows proof of your feelings; don't think it a shame
    to wear a scarf over your shining hair.
Sleepless nights wear down the bodies of young men in love,   735
    worry and pain are the hallmarks of mighty passion.

1.731: Side was the first wife of Orion.

To win your heart's desire, look miserable
    so that anyone who sees you will say: "You've got a bad case of
        love."
Should I complain and warn that right and wrong are all confused,
    that friendship is an empty name, faith a fruitless word?   740
It is not safe to praise your girlfriend to a buddy;
    once he believes you in your praise, he'll sneak in to supplant you.
"But Patroclus did not betray the bed of Achilles;
    Phaedra was true and chaste out of respect for Pirithous;
Pylades loved Hermione in the same way Phoebus did Pallas,°   745
    and as Castor, your twin, Helen, was loyal to you."
Anyone hoping for a relationship of these types, should expect thistles
        to bear
    apples and look for honey in the middle of a river.
Only a base act pleases: his own pleasure is each one's goal.
    All the more sweet if it comes at the expense of another's pain.   750
Damn it! A lover should not fear an enemy:
    avoid those you trust and believe in; then, you'll be safe.
Watch out for the cousin, the brother, and dear ol'chum:
    this gang will cause you real fear.
I was about to finish up—but how different are girls' hearts;   755
    a thousand minds require a thousand means and methods.
The earth produces varying crops; one soil is just right
    for vines, another for olives, and elsewhere grains thrive.
Hearts have as many moods as there are faces in the world.
    The wise lover will adjust to innumerable natures,   760
And, like Proteus,° now will melt into flowing water,
    now become a lion, then a tree, then a bristly wild boar.
Some fish are caught by spears, some by hooks,
    while others hollow nets with fine mesh pull in.
One approach for all ages will not always fit you;   765
    from afar the deer that's been around awhile will spot the trap.
If you seem learned to a dolt or crass to a prude,
    she will lose confidence in herself and be wretched.
So what happens? She fears to commit herself to an honorable man,
    but goes running off to the embrace of some inferior clod.   770
Part of my labor is finished, part of my enterprise remains;
    here let's drop anchor to hold firm my vessel.°

1.745: Hermione became the wife of Orestes. Ovid's point is that Orestes' good
    friend Pylades did not intrude upon the relationship of Orestes and Hermione.
    Pylades treated Hermione like a sister.
1.761: for Proteus see Vergil, *Georgics* 4.441-443 and Ovid, *Amores* 2.15.10.
1.772: a good example of "ring composition." The image of the ship takes us
    back to lines 3-5 at the beginning of the book.

TRISTIA

The *Tristia* ("sufferings" or "sorrows"), written in elegiacs, are literary letters addressed to Ovid's wife and assorted friends and acquaintances. The poems serve not only to detail the sorrows associated with Ovid's exile to the Black Sea area but also to argue for a reconsideration of his relegation. Neither Augustus nor Tiberius was persuaded to commute the harsh sentence. Not unexpectedly, many of the poems of the *Tristia* defend his poetic career, although numerous letters depict the harshness of Ovid's present life, include many ethnographic details, and portray his psychological state that seems to worsen day by day and to lead to Ovid's utter despair. In poem after poem images of illness, torpor, decay, and approaching death serve as a metaphor for Ovid's poetry and life in the barren waste of his banishment.

1.1°

Little book of mine, you're off (and I don't begrudge it) to the City
    without me;
  I'm upset because your author (that's me) can't go.
Yes, go on, shabby-looking as suits the work of an exile,
    put on the clothes of mourning of this my time of life.
No purple or raspberry-colored jacket for you—   5
    those colors do not befit grief;
No title in rubrics, no pages scented by cedar,°
    no white bosses marking your dark scroll.
Lucky books should be trimmed with these frills;
    you should remember my fate.   10
No polishing your two rolls with brittle pumice;
    you should appear shaggy with disheveled hair.
Don't be ashamed of blots; whoever sees them
    will perceive they were made from my tears.
Go, little book, and with my words greet the places I enjoy;   15
    I'll touch them with any foot I can.
And if there is someone among the populace who remembers me,
    someone who perhaps asks what I'm up to,
You will tell him that I'm alive, but not well:
    that my being alive is only the gift of a god.°   20
But keep quiet; anyone wanting to know more must read you.
    And don't by chance say anything unnecessary.

1.1.1: this poem was sent from Tomis shortly after Ovid's arrival there. It out-
    lines the poet's main themes of his exile: his physical and mental suffering, his
    awareness of his guilt and punishment, and his prayerful hope of restoration
    through his poetry.
1.1.7: cedar oil helped preserve papyrus.
1.1.20: the god is Augustus.

Once reminded the reader will right away remember the charges
 against me,
 and I'll be judged guilty by the public wherever I may go.
And don't defend me, although you are stung by words: 25
 the case is too damaging for any advocacy.
You'll find someone who will sigh over my demise
 and not be able to read these poems of mine with dry cheeks;
And one who will, so no malicious sort may hear, pray in silence to
 himself
 that Caesar relent and abate the punishment against me. 30
Whoever he may be, I too pray that he will not suffer
 who wants the gods to indulge those who are in misery.
May he receive approval of whatever he wants, and may the anger of
 Caesar
 subside so I may be able to die on ancestral soil.
Although you may execute my orders, little book, perhaps you will be
 blamed   35
 and reckoned unworthy of my talent.
A judge's job is to look into circumstances and time.
 If the context checks out, you'll be safe.
Poems are the well-spun fruits of a mind at peace:
 our brows are clouded with sudden, terrible storms.   40
Poems require a writer's safe haven and blocks of leisure time:
 ah me, the sea, the winds, and a savage winter toss me about.
My every fear hinders my creative powers: I am desperate;
 I keep thinking a sword is about to be thrust into my throat.
A fair-minded judge will be amazed at the poems that I compose 45
 and will pardon them when he reads them such as they are.
Now take Homer: let him see all around him my many misfortunes;
 every bit of his talent would collapse under the weight of the
  troubles.
Finally, my book, remember to go secure in honor,
 and don't worry if your words displease.   50
Fortune does not favor me so much
 that you must keep a ledger of your praise.
While I was secure and safe, I used to be impassioned for fame,
 and in my ardor I just had to acquire a great reputation.
If I now refuse to hate the poems and the pursuit that harmed me, 55
 let it suffice; it is my talent that has brought me exile.
So, you go in my place, you, as you may, be my eyewitness of Rome:
 Great gods! I wish I could be my book!
And just because you arrive in the big city from abroad,
 don't think you can go about unrecognized by the people. 60
Although you lack a title, your style will make you known;
 pretend as you like, clearly you are all mine.

O.K., enter incognito so you won't be hurt by my poems:
    they do not find as much favor as they once did.
If someone thinks that you should not be read   65
    because you are mine, and tosses you aside,
Tell him, "Look at the title.° I am not the preceptor of love;
    that work has long paid the penalty it deserved."
Perhaps you may be waiting for me to send you to the lofty Palatine,°
    to order that you climb up to Caesar's house.   70
August the site and its gods —may they pardon me—
    it was from that very height a thunderbolt struck my head.
Yes, how I remember the deities in those abodes—
    most gentle they were; but I fear gods who have already hurt me.
The dove, once slashed by the talons of a hawk,   75
    is frightened by the slightest whirr of a wing;
The lamb does not dare to stray from the folds
    if she has escaped the shock of a wolf's rapacious fangs.
Phaethon would certainly avoid the sky, were he alive, and refuse
    to touch the horses which he once foolishly coveted.   80
And me, I confess fearing Jove's weapons—I have felt them all too
    well—
When he thunders, I reckon lightning is bolted against me.
Any Greek sailor who escapes Cape Caphareus
    always trims his sails away from Euboean waters.
My boat too, once smashed by a fierce storm,   85
    shudders to sail back to that spot where it was struck.
So, my little book, beware; carefully and with some fear look about
    you;
    make it enough to seek readers among average people.
In his quest for the heights Icarus soared too high on flimsy wings;
    he gave his name to the Icarian deep.   90
Yet, it remains difficult to say whether you should use oars or sail
    with the wind.
    The circumstance and place will improvise the best plan.
If you can, get introduced to someone at leisure; note all
    gentle movements, when his anger has abated and lost its strength;
Or, if someone, as you hesitate and fear to approach him,   95
    passes you on and introduces you in a few words, then go.
On a beautiful day, luckier than your author,
    may you arrive there to ease my misfortunes.

1.1.67: Ovid alludes to the *Art of Love*.
1.1.69-82: Ovid depicts the Palatine as Olympus and suggests that his punishment
    from Augustus parallels Jupiter's thunderbolting of sinners. The myths that
    Ovid mentions after this passage suggest arbitrary and unjust action at the
    hands of hostile divinities.

Yes, either no one can, or only the person who wounded me,
    like Achilles, can heal my trauma.   100
Now take care, don't injure me in your wish to assist me.
    Know that in my heart my hope is less than my fear.
Don't stir and rekindle the rage that was at rest
    and become another excuse for further punishment.
But when you have found admission into my den   105
    and have reached your home, my round bookcases,
You will see your brothers there, all arranged in order,
    every one of them I lucubrated over with the same passionate
        attention.
The rest of the group will clearly display titles
    and openly on the front bear labels.   110
Far off hiding in a nook you will see three books:
    they instruct what every man already knows—the art of love.
Shun these books or, if you have courage,
    call them Oedipus or Telegonus.°
And of these three, I warn you, if you have any love for your
        parent,   115
    don't choose any, although it will masterfully instruct you in
        loving.
There is also the *Metamorphoses* in fifteen volumes,
    a poetic work rescued from my funeral rites.
I entrust it to you to tell them that among the figures transformed
    the face of my fate can be reckoned.   120
You see, in a blink it was metamorphosed, very different from its
        previous state,
    now something pitiable that was once joyful.
I had it to send you more orders, if you really are eager to know,
    but I fear I have held up your journey.
Now if you, my little book, were to pack everything that comes to my
        mind,   125
    you would be one heavy suitcase to lug around.
The trip is long; hurry along: as for me, I'll be living
    at the world's end, in a land far, far away from my own.

1.1.114: examples of parricides. Oedipus unknowingly killed his father Laius
    as Telegonus killed Ulysses.

1.3°

Whenever I envision that most tragic night reminding
    me of my final hour in the City,
When I recall the very night I abandoned so many of my treasures,
    even now a teardrop sneaks its way from my eyes.
It was almost dawn of the day on which Caesar had decreed   5
    me to leave the far frontiers of Italy.
I had no time, I was mentally unprepared:
    long delays had numbed our hearts.
I lacked the will to choose slaves, attendants,
    clothes, outfits that an exile would need.   10
I was in shock—like someone smashed by Jove's lightning bolts who
    survives and yet is in the dark of his very life.
But when my pain removed the storm-cloud over my mind
    and in the end I recovered my senses,
As I was about to leave, I said some final words to my sad
        friends—   15
    there were only one or two left.
My loving wife weeping so painfully held me tight as I cried:
    a shower of tears flooded our undeserving cheeks.
Beneath the skies of Libya's far-off coast our daughter resided,
    separated and uninformed of my fate.   20
Wherever you looked, were the sounds of grief and moans,
    inside the house it was like a noisy funeral.
Woman, man, slaves, all were mourning my funeral rites;
    every nook in the house was shedding tears.
If I may compare my slight case with a mighty one,   25
    it had the look of Troy in the hours of its sacking,
All had become quiet, no sounds of men and dogs,
    and Lady Moon was driving her nocturnal horses high;
Looking up at her and by her light spying the Capitoline,
    which to no avail was right next to our home,   30
I stated: "You deities who dwell on sites neighboring mine,
    and whose temples never again will be seen by these eyes of mine,
And you gods whom I must abandon and whom the lofty city of
        Quirinus worships,
    welcome my greetings for all time to come.
I have suffered wounds; and although too late I take up a shield,   35
    yet, O gods, free me from hatred in this my exile,
And to that divine being tell what mistake duped me
    so he doesn't think my fault to be a crime.

1.3.1: in this poem Ovid suggests a comparison of his experiences with Aeneas'
    departure from Troy.

And may he, the perpetrator of the penalty against me, become aware
    of what you know.
    I cannot be unhappy, if a god is appeased."   40
With this prayer I appealed to the powers above: my wife offered
    many more
    amid the sobbing that choked off her words.
She even lay prostrate before the Lares, her hair loose,
    and kissed with her trembling mouth the hearth-altar grown cold;
And against adverse household gods poured out a torrent of words 45
    that would not prevail on behalf of the husband she mourned for.
The waning night denied room for delay,
    already the Great Bear° was wheeling around the North Pole.
What was I to do? An irresistible love for my country restrained me:
    but that night was my last; I was ordered to leave in exile.   50
Oh, how often I spoke up when someone was hurrying me, "Why do
    you press me?
    Look where and whence you are hastening me to go."
Oh, how often I lied to myself that I had set an hour
    which would be fixed and appropriate for my journey.
Three times I reached the threshold, three times I checked myself; 55
    I dragged my feet, matching my mood.
I said many goodbyes, then continued to talk;
    I gave final kisses as if on the way out.
I repeated the same instructions and deluded myself,
    looking back upon my loved ones.   60
At last, I said, "Why am I in a hurry? It's Scythia where I am being
    sent;
    I have to leave Rome. Each is a just excuse for delay.
A wife alive is forever denied to me as long as I live,
    and home, and the sweet members of a faithful household,
Friends I have loved like brothers,   65
    hearts bonded to me with the faith of Theseus.°
While I can, I will hug them, perhaps never again will I be allowed to
    do so.
    Every hour granted to me is a gain."
No more delay, I left the words of my sentence unfinished,
    and embraced everything dear to my heart.   70
While I was talking and we were all weeping, Lucifer,
    high heaven's brightest star, but my albatross, arose.
I was being ripped apart as if I was losing my limbs,
    a part of me seemed to be torn away from my body.

1.3.48: the Great Bear is the Big Dipper.
  1.3.65-66: a reference to the well-known friendship between Theseus and
Pirithous.

Such pain Mettus suffered when the horses avenged   75
    his betrayal and ripped him in two.
Yes, then arose the wailing and groans of my loved ones,
    the beating of bare breasts with mournful hands;
Then, ah yes, as I was leaving, my wife° hugged and clung to my
    shoulders;
    my tears mingled with these her parting words: 80
"You cannot be wrenched from me. Together, yes, together, we leave
    here.
    I shall follow you to be the exiled wife of an exile.
The journey is mine too; I too am a captive in a distant land.
    I will be small baggage added to your ship of exile.
It is Caesar's wrath that decrees your banishment from the country; 85
    my devotion commands me; this my love will be Caesar for me."
Such attempts she made, as she had tried before;
    with reluctance she gave up, beaten by practical concerns.
I took my leave, carried out like a body without a funeral,
    dirty, unshaven, and with hair disheveled.   90
They say that she was crazy with grief, her mind darkening,
    half-dead, that she fainted, slumped in the middle of the floor.
When she recovered, her hair was dirtied by the foul dust,
    and from the ground she arose, her limbs icy-cold.
She wept first for herself, then for the deserted household gods,   95
    and again and again called out the name of her banished husband;
She groaned as if she had witnessed the funeral pyre
    piled with the body of her daughter and husband.
She wanted to die, to efface her senses in death.
    Yet her love for me prevented her perishing.   100
May she live and, as the fates have willed it,
    let her live to help me, far away in exile.

1.5

You will always be recalled as my most faithful friend,
    and one who especially saw my fate as your own;
You, as I remember, my dearest friend,° were the first to dare
    to have consoled and helped me when I was thunderbolted,
Who gave me gentle counsel to live on   5
    when my wretched heart longed for death.
You well know to whom I refer since I have set clues for your name;
    and my debt to you does not go unnoticed.

1.3.79-102: Ovid details the role of his wife in his exile; she is to be his repre-
    sentative and defender in Rome.
1.5.3: many see that Ovid is alluding to his friend Carus with the word *caris-
    sime*, i.e. "dearest."

I will keep these services fixed deep forever in my marrow,
  and forever I will owe you this my life.   10
Sooner my spirit will evaporate into empty air
  and abandon my bones on a tepid funeral pyre,
Before forgetfulness of your merits enters my mind
  and in long time the thought of that loyalty of yours ebbs.
May the gods bless you and grant you a fate   15
  that lacks no resource and is unlike mine.
Yet if this my ship were traveling under a friendly wind,
  perhaps that trusting nature of yours would remain unknown.
Pirithous would not have experienced his friendship°
  had Theseus not gone alive to the waters of the underworld.   20
Pylades has provided a model of true love
  which your furies, unhappy Orestes, fashioned.
If Euryalus had not fallen against Rutulian enemies,
  there would have been no glory for Nisus.
Just as red gold is tested by fire,   25
  so in hard times loyalty should be tested.
So long as Fortune helps with a serene smile upon her face,
  all things pursue undiminished wealth.
But as soon as it thunders, they vanish, and no one knows
  the man who had just been surrounded by throngs of pals.   30
What I once suspected from earlier examples of old,
  now from my own misfortune I know for real.
Of all my "friends" only two or three are left;
  the rest are Fortune's crowd, not mine.
So all the more, you few, support my exhausted state of affairs,   35
  and offer the shipwreck of my life safe shores,
And don't tremble from excessive fear untrue,
  afraid that a god be offended by such devotion.
Caesar has often praised loyalty even in those who took arms against
    him;
  he loves it among his own, approves it in his enemy.   40
My case is stronger: I have never supported armed insurrection;
  because of my naivete I earned exile.
I beg you to be vigilant for my troubles,
  if the anger of the deity can somehow be assuaged.
Should anyone desire to know all my misfortunes,   45
  he looks for more than circumstances allow.°

1.5.19-24: examples of friendship.
1.5.45-46: Ovid could not divulge the details of his "mistake." See 4.10.100.

Innumerable are the troubles I have endured, as many as the stars
    that shine in the sky,
  and as there are tiny particles of dry dust.
Unimaginable and incredible are the ills I have suffered,
  and although they have happened in fact, they lack trustworthy
    belief.   50
A part, as well, should die with me;
  I'd truly like to keep it covered, only to pretend its reality.
If I had an unbreaking voice, a diaphragm stronger than bronze,
  many tongues and mouths,
Still I'd not embrace the whole story;   55
  the subject far surpasses my powers.
Instead of that commander from Ithaca, you learned poets
  write of my sufferings; I have out-suffered that Ithacan by far.
He wandered about for many years in a short space
  between the homes of Dulichium and Troy: 60
I have traveled a sea under distant stars;
  my lot has brought me to the gulf inhabited by Getae and
    Sarmatians.
Ulysses, at least, had a trusty crew of faithful companions:
  my comrades deserted me in my exile.
He sought his fatherland, a happy winner.   65
  I, a defeated exile, am banished from my country.
My home is not Dulichium, Ithaca, or Samos,
  places that are no great punishment to be separated from.
No! but it is the City of the Seven Hills that overlooks the whole
  world,
  Rome, seat of empire and of the gods.   70
His body was toughened and inured by his labors:
  my strength is slight, home-nurtured.
He was buffeted by the constant lash of savage war,
  I accustomed myself to gentler pursuits.
A god has crushed me; no one has come to relieve my suffering,   75
  whereas the warrior goddess° favored him with her help.
The god who rules the swelling seas is Jove's inferior;
  Neptune's wrath assailed him, Jupiter's anger overwhelms me.
What's more, most of his troubles are mere fiction,
  but in my misfortune lies not a single myth.   80
Finally, he reached the home of his household gods that he searched
  for,
  regained the lands that he quested for so long.
But for me, I am forever to lose my native land,
  unless the injured god abates his wrath.

1.5.76: the warrior goddess is Pallas Athena.

1.11

Every letter that you read in my entire book
  was written during a troubling time of my journey.
The Adriatic witnessed me writing on the open sea
  as I shivered in the icy month of December;
Or, after we passed the Isthmus of the two gulfs°   5
  and transferred to another vessel for my exile,
I think the Cyclades in the Aegean were astonished
  that I kept writing verses among the savage murmurs of the sea.
In fact, I wonder myself that in all the tumble of mind and sea
  my inspiration did not sink.   10
Who knows if it was shock or madness that was the proper label for
    this my pursuit;
  this activity relieved me of my every care.
Often I was in doubt, buffeted about by the storms of Haedus,
  often tossed by the menacing sea and lightning from the sky.
The protector of Ursa Minor often darkened the sky,°   15
  or the west wind scattered late winter storms.
Time and again sea waves poured onto the deck; yet my hand,
  trembling, kept spinning poems—so to speak.
The taut rigging whistled in the north wind,
  curving billows, like huge mounds, soared high.   20
The helmsman too raised his hands toward the stars,
  his skill forgotten, he begs, he prays for help.
Wherever I looked, there was nothing but the image of death
  which in my cowering mind I feared, and in fear I prayed for.
If I reach a port, I'm terrified by that port;°   25
  the dry land holds more terror than the savage sea.
Both men and sea constantly harass and plot against me;
  sword and wave double my fears,
A sword, I fear, hopes to shed my blood for booty,
  a wave wants to mark my death.   30
On the left a barbaric sector, inured to greedy plunder,
  always occupied with bloodshed, murder, and wars.
As the sea tosses its wintry waves,
  all the more agitated is my heart, more turbulent than the sea
    waves.
All the more, kind reader, you ought to forgive these poems,   35
  if they fall short and disappoint you as they are.

1.11.5: alludes to the Corinthian and Saronic Gulfs separated by a narrow isthmus (Isthmus of Corinth).
1.11.15: refers to the constellation of Bootes.
1.11.25-32: anticipate the theme of the dangers from plundering tribes that recurs often in the *Tristia*. See 3.10 and 4.1 for examples.

I have not composed them, as I once did, in my garden,
    my body relaxed on a favorite couch.
No, instead I'm tossed about on the untamed deep in winter's light,
    and every page of paper is spattered by dark surf.   40
Depraved winter, indignant that I dare
    to write on, threatens and smashes me hard.
Winter may defeat a man, but, I ask, may I end
    composing my song at the same time as it ends.

3.3°

If perhaps you're wondering why my letter
    has been written by someone else's hand, I have been ill;
Yes, sick, and in the remotest parts of an untamed world
    I was quite unsure of my survival.
What do you think I now feel lying here in this dreadful   5
    region among Sarmatians and Getae?
I can't bear the climate, and I haven't gotten used to the waters,
    even the landscape grates on me.
Housing is inadequate, and the food here makes a sick person sicker;
    there is no doctor who has the skill to cure someone sick,   10
No friend to console me, to beguile in storytelling
    the hours that creep slowly by: no friend at all.
Exhausted, I lie among these remotest peoples and places
    and in my illness I imagine all that is not here.
You, my wife, win out in all my haunting thoughts,   15
    you occupy more than the outskirts of my heart.
Though you are absent, I am always talking to you; from my mouth
        you are
    the only one I name. Without you I pass no night, no day.
And then too they say I only spoke of you
    in my delirium, only your name was on my lips.   20
If I am failing and my tongue becomes numb, and beneath my palate
    I can hardly be revived by swigs of wine,
And if someone announces that my lady has arrived here, I'll get up,
    and the hope that you bring will be a reason for my renewed vigor.
So, as my life is in doubt, can you perhaps be spending   25
    a pleasant time there, unaware of my fate?
You are not, I'm convinced. It's very clear, my dearest,
    that the time you spend without me must be truly a sad one.
But if I have fulfilled the allotted years of my life,
    and the end is very near that comes too soon,   30

3.3: an ill Ovid writes to his wife. Many compare this letter to Tibullus 1.3.

O great gods, what would be the cost to divine plans to spare one
    about to die
  so that at least I may be buried in native soil?
If only my punishment had been postponed until the hour of my
    death,
  or a premature death had prescribed my banishment;
I could have given up this light of day, untainted;   35
  but as things are now, I have been granted life only to die in exile.
So, I shall die far off on unknown shores,
  a fate gloomy because of the site;
My limbs will languish on an unfamiliar bier,
  once buried, no one will be present to weep over me;   40
No tears from my lady will drop upon my face
  to bring a few moments of respite to my spirit.
I will not give last instructions; there'll be no final wailing,
  no hand of a friend to close my swimming eyes;
No funeral rites, no honor of a tomb, this head,   45
  unmourned, a barbaric land will cover.
And when you hear the news, your mind will be tormented,
  and you'll beat your faithful breasts with a trembling hand.
Then you will flail your arms toward this place,
  shouting the empty name of your pitiable husband.   50
Yet don't tear your cheeks or rip out your hair;
  this will not be the first time, my light, I have been torn from you.
When I lost my country, believe that it was then that I died:
  that was my first death and one that was more grievous.
If by chance you can—but, of course, you cannot, most excellent
    wife—   55
  be happy that with my death my troubles have ended.
You can do this: assuage the misfortune by enduring it with
    courageous heart;
  you have a heart trained for it.
I wish our bodies and souls would perish together,
  and no part of me escape the greedy pyre.   60
If the deathless spirit flies high in the empty air,
  and if the words of old Pythagoras from Samos are reckoned
    worthy,
A Roman shade will wander among Sarmatian ghosts,
  always to be a stranger among uncivilized spirits.
Yet see to it that my bones be brought back in a small urn: 65
  thus in my death I will not be an exile.
No one forbids this: even the Theban sister° buried
  her slain brother, although the king forbade it.

3.3.67: refers to Antigone burying her brother Polyneices against the decree of
  Creon, the king of Thebes.

Mingle my bones in the leaves and powder of balsam
   and bury them in soil near the city   70
So a traveler with hurrying eye may read
   carved in large letters these verses on the marble tombstone:
"Here I lie, playful poet of tender loves,
   I, Naso, done in by my own genius.
You, passerby, if you have ever loved, don't resent   75
   saying that Ovid's bones lie gentle."
That is epitaph enough. My books are a greater
   and more enduring monument for me.°
Although they have ruined me, I trust that
   they will gain for their author renown and eras of fame.   80
You, however, perform the yearly funeral rites
   and offer garlands dripping wet from your tears.
Although fire will transform my corpse into ashes,
   a sorrowful ember will feel your careful service.
I'd like to write more, but my voice is weary from speaking,   85
   my tongue is dry lacking the strength to dictate.
Accept what may be the final word from my lips,
   which the sender himself does not have— "Fare well."

3.4b

That portion of earth nearest to the Great Bear constellation
   detains me, a land charred with searing ice.
Beyond to the north are the Bosporus, the Don, and marshes of
    Scythia,
   and a few names of an area hardly known at all.
Farther than that is nothing but uninhabitable cold.   5
   How near I am to the end of the world!
And far away is my country, far away my dearest wife,
   and after those two all that which was sweet to me.
Yet, they are here, although I can't physically touch them:
   I imagine all of them in my mind's eye.   10
Before my eyes flit home, city, the outline of landscapes;
   every one of them yields events peculiar to the locale.
Before my eyes is the vision of my wife, just as if she were present;
   it is that vision that both burdens and relieves my troubles,
Aggravating since she is absent, mitigating because of her gift of
    love,   15
   and because she steadfastly bears the burden imposed upon her.
And you, too, my friends, cling to my heart;
   I long to mention each and every one of you by name,

3.3.77-80: Ovid's thoughts on his illness and impending death lead naturally to
   reflection on the immortality of his verse.

But my fear and caution restrain my sense of obligation, and, I
    believe,
    you yourselves don't want to be included in my verse.   20
Before, you used to wish it; it was a welcomed honor
    that your names be read in my poems.
Since it is risky now, I will address each of you in my heart.
    I will not be the cause of fear for anyone.
My verse does not reveal or indict friends who cautiously   25
    conceal themselves. Let anyone who loves me in secret continue to
        love me.
Yet know, however distant I am banished from you,
    you are always in my mind.
Each of you, in any way that you can, lighten my troubles;
    don't begrudge me, an exile, a loyal hand.   30
So may prosperous fortune be with you, and may you never be
    afflicted with a fate like mine that causes you to make the same
        appeal.

3.10°

If there is anyone who still remembers Ovid, the banished man,
    and if my name survives in the City without my presence,
I want him to know that I have been plunked beneath stars that never
    touch
    the sea, living in the middle of barbarity.
Sarmatians, a wild people, Bessi, and Getae surround me,   5
    all names unworthy of my talent.
As long as a balmy breeze blows, we are protected by the Danube
    between us;
    its clear waters ward off hostile attacks.
But when grim winter thrusts forth its squalid face,
    and when the land becomes white, like marble, with ice,   10
And when wind and blizzards from blue northers prevent habitation,
    then these peoples are crushed by a shivering sky.
Fallen snow piles up; neither sun nor rains melt the deep cover
    which the north wind packs and hardens forever.
So, before the first snowfall has melted, another comes,   15
    and in many areas stays for two years.
So savage is the force of northern gales that it levels
    lofty towers to the ground, rips apart roofs, and hurls them off and
        away.

3.10.1: the very descriptive and poignant poem of the bitter and harsh life among
    barbarous peoples of the Black Sea has an implied contrast with the bounty,
    pleasant climate, and civilized life of Italy.

Men ward off the bitter cold with furs and sewn pants;
   of their entire bodies only their faces lie exposed.   20
Often icicles hanging from their hair shake and tinkle;
   their beards glisten white with packed frost.
Wines stand exposed, preserving the shape of their jar;
   so, they swig not drinks but clumps of wine.
I could talk about rivers frozen solid by the cold,   25
   and waters able to be split, chopped from a frozen lake.
The very Danube, which is no narrower than the papyrus-breeding
     Nile,
   flows through many mouths into a vast sea,
Whose dark waters freeze hard from gales,
   snakes along to the Black Sea under a cover of ice.   30
Where boats once traveled, now people go on foot, and horses'
     hooves
   pound waves petrified by the cold.
Across new bridges, as the water glides beneath them,
   Sarmatian oxen haul barbarian wagons.
I'd hardly be believed, but, since there are no rewards   35
   in lying, one should trust my testimony:
I saw the vast sea solid ice,
   and a slippery crust keeping the water still underneath;
And I have not just seen it. In fact, I have trampled the solid expanse
   and with dry feet trod its surface.   40
If you, Leander, had had that sort of strait,
   the narrow sea would not have been charged with your death.
At those times dolphins cannot leap and curve into the air;
   the hard freeze of winter prevents their attempts.
Although the north wind howls and flaps its wings,   45
   no billow will form on the frozen deep;
Ships will stand encased in ice as in marble,
   and no oar will be able to split the stiffened waters.
I witnessed fish fastened and stuck in ice,
   and some of them were still alive.   50
Whether the savage power of northern blasts hardens
   the waters of the sea or the overflow of the river,
When the dry winds of the north have leveled the Danube,
   a barbarian horde rides on swift horses;
The enemy, experts in horsemanship and skilled in shooting arrows
     far,   55
   lay waste extensive territory of their neighbors.
Some neighbors flee; with no one staying to protect the homesteads,
   their property, unguarded, is ravished,
Rustic goods of little value, a flock, squeaky wagons,
   the sort of wealth a poor farmer has.   60

Some are captured and herded off with their hands tied behind their
    backs,
  as they look back in vain on their fields and home.
Others die in agony, pierced by barbed arrows;
  for the winged steel is smeared with poison.
What the archers cannot carry with them, they destroy;   65
  innocent huts burn up in fires lit by the enemy.
Even when there is peace, people tremble in fear of an attack;
  no one takes up the plow to work the soil.
This peace either sees an enemy or fears one it doesn't see;
  the land, abandoned and left fallow, remains hard from neglect. 70
Not here do sweet clusters of grapes lie beneath shading vines,
  nor does fermenting must top the deep vats.
The area yields no fruits; Acontius would have nothing
  to write on for his lady to read his message.
You'd see fields stripped bare of leaves and trees: 75
  wastelands that a man would be fortunate to avoid.
So, this with the greatest expanse of the world open,
  yes, this was the land found to punish me.

3.11

Whoever you are, you bastard, who deride my misfortunes,
  and with no end to your bloodthirst accuse me,
You were born from rocks and weaned on the milk of a wild animal,
  and, I'll bet, you have a heart of flint.
To what farther level can you direct your anger?   5
  What do you think is missing in my troubles?
A barbaric land, the inhospitable shores of Pontus,
  the north wind, and the Great Bear look upon me.
I have no language to communicate with the wild native people;
  everywhere are dread and worry.   10
Just as a fleeing stag, caught by bears,
  or as a lamb, surrounded by mountain wolves, shakes in fear,
So I, hedged in on all sides by warlike tribes,
  am terrified; the enemy is almost touching my side.
Let's suppose that it is a slight punishment to deprive me   15
  of wife, country, and loved ones;
Let's say that I'm enduring no misfortune except the raw anger of
    Caesar,
  is Caesar's naked anger so trifling a matter?
Yet there is someone who is out to reopen raw wounds
  and to castigate my morals in clever speeches.   20
In an easy case anyone can be glib,
  to break what's already cracked requires minimum strength.

It takes courage to smash citadels and standing walls;
  cowards attack walls already breached.
I am not what once I was. Why do you trample on an empty
    shadow?   25
  Why are you attacking my ashes, my tomb?
Hector was Hector while he was in war: but the same man,
  tied to Achilles' horses, was no longer Hector.
And as for me, remember that I too am not the same person you once
    knew.
  Of that man only a phantom survives.   30
Why, you savage brute, do you assail a phantom with bitter words?
  I pray you, don't harass my shades.
Suppose all the charges against me are true, there's no substance in
    them
  to make you think they are more crime than mistake.
Glut your heart on this: banished, I am paying a heavy penalty,   35
  exile as well as the place of exile.
My fate could bring tears to an executioner,
and yet one judge deems it too shallow.
You are more barbaric than grim Busiris, more savage than the man
  who grilled a bogus bull by slow fire;   40
And they say he had given the bull to the Sicilian tyrant, Phalaris,°
  and recommended his artistry in these words:
"In this gift, O king, there is greater use than meets the eye;
  you should admire not just the beauty of my workmanship.
Do you see here, the right side of the bull that you can open?   45
  Shove in here any person you want to get rid of.
Shut him in and roast him over slow-burning coals:
  he will bellow; the sound will be like a bull's.
For this invention, to repay a service with a service,
  give me, please, a reward worthy of my talent."   50
But Phalaris replied to him: "You marvelous inventor of torture,
  you yourself in person inaugurate your invention."
Right away he was cruelly baked by the fires that he had
    demonstrated;
  he shrieked and bellowed doubled-voiced.
What are Sicilians to me when I'm here in the middle of Scythia and
    among Getae?
  I return my complaint against you, whoever you are.   56
So that you can sate your thirst on my blood,
  and fill your greedy heart with all the joys you desire,

3.11.41-42: the reference is to Perillus whose story follows in lines 43-54. Some
see an Ovidian hint of Augustus' cruelty.

In my banishment I have suffered so many misfortunes on land, so
     many on the sea
     that even you, I think, might lament to hear them.   60
Believe me, compare me with Ulysses:
     was Neptune's wrath less than Jupiter's?°
So whoever you are, don't renew those charges;
     lift your hard hands from my deep wound.
Allow oblivion to soothe the bad reputation of my offence,   65
     and allow a scar to form for what I did.
Be mindful of the lot of man that uplifts and humbles
     the same man, and respect and fear its uncertain vicissitudes.
And, since you display—something I never thought could happen—
     enormous interest in my affairs,   70
You have nothing to fear: my fate is most wretched;
     Caesar's wrath pulls along with it all other ills.
To put it more clearly, and lest I be thought to be making all this up,
     I'd like you yourself to experience this hell of mine.

3.14°

Patron and respected protector of men of letters,
     always a friend to my talent, what are your feelings?
As you once used to exalt me when I prospered, are you
     now hesitant to see to it that I not entirely disappear ?
Are you finishing my poems—with the sole exception, of course,   5
     of the *Art*, which did in its author?
Oh, please, do so, please, you fan of new bards,
     wherever you can, keep my body of work in the City.
Banishment was decreed against *me*, not against my books;
     they have not deserved the sentence of their author.   10
Quite often, when a banished father lives the life of an exile in a
     foreign land,
     his children can remain in the City.
My poems follow the precedent of Pallas; I created them without a
     mother;°
     they are my blood-line, my progeny,

3.11.61-62: Ovid had already compared himself to Ulysses in great detail (1.5.57-
84). In this passage the emphasis is on Jupiter's anger, equated with that of
Augustus.
3.14: the addressee in this poem is thought to be Gaius Iulius Hyginus, a friend
of Ovid, a patron of the arts, and curator of the libraries on the Palatine.
3.14.13: Athena (Minerva) was born fully grown and armed from the head of
Zeus.

That I entrust to you. Now that they have been orphaned without a
    parent,   15
  the heavier the burden imposed upon you to protect them.
I have three children who have caught my infection;
  but for the rest, make them your public care.
There are, too, my *"Transformations,"*° fifteen books of them,
  poems rescued from their author's final rites,   20
A work, had I not perished beforehand,
  that might have won a surer repute after some final touches.
But now it has reached the public's eyes uncorrected,
  if the public even reads any of my stuff anymore.
Add this little something to my corpus,   25
  which comes to you sent from a remote part of the world.
Whoever reads it, if there is a reader, should reflect beforehand
  where and when it was composed.
He will be fair in judging writings when he learns they were written
  in a time of exile and in a barbaric place: 30
He will be amazed that under so many adverse and depressing
    conditions
  I could sustain my hand to spin any poem.
My misfortunes have broken my talent,° a talent that even before
  sprang from an unfertile spring and small vein.
But such as it was, my lack of practice put it in exile,   35
  and, dried up, it perished from long disuse.
Not in this place do I have a library of books to stimulate and nourish
    me;
  instead of books I encounter the twangs of bows and the clang of
    weapons.
There's no one in this land, if I recite my poem,
  whose understanding ears I can appeal to.   40
I have no retreat. Guards on the walls
  and a bolted gate keep hostile Getae away.
Often I grasp for a word, a name, a place,
  but there is no one around who can prompt me.
Sometimes as I am trying to say something—it's a disgrace to admit
    it—   45
  words fail me, and I've unlearned how to speak.
Thracian and Scythian sounds echo around me,
  and I almost think that I can write Getic in verse.

3.14.19: the *Transformations*, in Latin *mutatae formae*, refers to the *Metamorphoses*,
  the usual Greek title.
3.14.33-36: as in 43-50, Ovid, no doubt, exaggerates his diminishing powers.

Believe me, I fear that I am mixing Latin with local speech,
    and you may read some "Black Sea" idioms in my verse.   50
So then, treat my little book, such as it is, with deserved pardon,
    and judge my fate, my circumstances, as an excuse.

4.1°

Whatever defects you may find—and there will be some—in my little
        books,
    dear reader, excuse them for the times when they were composed.
I was an exile; I was looking for peace, not renown,
    so my mind would not fret over my misfortunes.
For this very reason the ditch-digger, although shackled, sings   5
    in untrained melody to assuage his heavy work.
He sings too who strains in mud and sand
    to haul upriver against the current a slow-moving barge;
And likewise rowers, pulling as one the pliant oars toward their
        chests,
    stroke and strike the water in rhythm.   10
The weary shepherd, leaning upon his staff or sitting on a rock,
    plays his pipe to soothe the sheep.
A slave girl sings while she spins the yarn assigned to her
    in order to beguile and cheat her toil.
They say Achilles, unhappy that Briseis was taken from him,   15
    relieved his sorrow with a Thessalian lyre.
While Orpheus was moving forests and hard stones by his song,
    he was in grief over his wife twice lost.°
Me, too, the muse soothed, while I was on my way to the region of
        the Black Sea
    decreed for me. She stood as my only true comrade in my flight.   20
Only she feared no ambush, no sword of an uncivilized soldier,
    nor sea nor winds nor barbarity.
She knew, too, what error duped me at my fall,
    that what I did was a mistake, but not a crime.
Of course, she is fair to me now, whereas she opposed me before   25
    when she was charged along with me for abetting the crime.
And I would have never thought, since they were to hurt me,
    to have plied my hand to the sacred rites of the Muses.

4.1.1: this poem and 4.10 frame Book IV of the *Tristia*. 4.1 has a very pessimistic
    tone; it reiterates the numerous themes detailed in poems of the previous
    books. Despite the harshness of his physical surroundings and his emotional
    depression resulting from his lack of recall, Ovid continues to stress that
    the writing of poetry consoles his mind and soothes his spirit, even though
    writing becomes increasingly difficult.
4.1.17-18: for the story of Orpheus see Vergil, *Georgics* 4.454-457.

But now what am I to do? The creative power of their rites hooks me
    and, although ruined by poetry, I am crazy in love with verse.   30
When Ulysses' men savored the lotus, fruit new to their palate,
    they relished the taste that brought them harm.
A lover perceives his own doom, yet clings to it,
    pursues the very core of his ruin.
So I cherish my books, although they have hurt me,   35
    and I love the very weapons that inflicted my wounds.
It may be that this obsession of mine seems a madness,
    but this madness has some use:
It forbids the mind to brood on troubles,
    and makes it oblivious to the tragedy of the present.   40
As the wounded Bacchant does not feel her pain
    when she is in ecstasy, howling to the music on Mt. Ida,°
So my heart becomes excited and is healed by the green thyrsus;
    my spirit soars above the problems of humankind;
It feels no exile, nor the sea shores of Scythia,   45
    and does not perceive any anger the gods may have.
As though I were drinking goblets from soporific Lethe,
    I lack sense of the days against me.
Rightly I revere those goddesses who have relieved my misfortunes,
    comrades from Helicon in my worry and flight,   50
Who deemed it worthy to follow my tracks first on the sea,
    and now on land, either by ship or on foot.
I pray that they at least be easy on me. All the other gods
    have formed a cabal with mighty Caesar,
And have piled on me adversities as countless as grains of sand on a
    shore,   55
    as fish in the sea, and as eggs in a fish.
You will sooner count flowers in spring, wheat-ears in summer,
    fruits in the fall, and snowflakes in the cold of winter,
Than the troubles that I have endured, driven in misery all over
    creation
    on my way to the shores on the left of the Black Sea.   60
Nor was it my luck to have lighter distress after I arrived;
    here, too, Fate has tracked me.
Yes, here I recognize the threads of my natal day,
    threads spun for me from a black fleece.°
And I pass over the ambushes and perils to my life;   65
    true to be sure, but more serious than trustworthy truth.

4.1.41-42: the reference to Mt. Ida links the Bacchic ecstasy with the worship
    of Cybele.

4.1.63-64: an elaboration on the idea of the three Fates spinning out human
    life.

How miserable to live among the Bessi and Getae
    for him whose name was always on the lips of the people.
How dismal for him to protect his life by a gate and a wall
    in a place barely able to defend him.   70
As a youth I avoided the rigors of military training,
    I handled arms only in play;
But now, as an old man, I strap a sword to my side, clasp a shield in
    my left hand,
    and wear a helmet on my white head.
Whenever a sentry gives signals from the watch-tower of a raid,   75
    with trembling hand I don my armor.
The savage enemy, with bows and with arrows dipped in poison,
    on panting horses circle the walls.
Just as a wolf, that predator, carries off and drags through fields and
    forest
    a sheep that did not protect itself in the fold,   80
So a barbarian raider grabs anyone whom he discovers in the open
    plain,
    not yet safely welcomed within the gates:
Either he follows as a captive and shackled around the neck,
    or dies from the wound of a poisoned arrow.
Here I keep out of sight, a new colonist of a troubled outpost: 85
    too long are the years of my fate.
And yet the Muse, my guest in so many trials,
    withstands to return to her rhythms and her ancient sacred rites.
But, there is no one to whom I can read my poems, no one
    whose ears welcome the Latin language. No one.   90
I just write and read for myself—for what else can I do?
    as both writer and critic, my writing is safe.
I have often asked myself; "For whom do you devote this painstaking
    effort?
    Will Sarmatians or Getae read my poems?"
And often tears pour over me as I write,   95
    my weeping floods the pages.
My heart has felt the old wounds as if they were fresh,
    and into my lap cascades a shower of grief.
When I remind myself of my fortune's change, who I am and who I
    was,
    and recall where and whence chance has brought me,   100
Often my maddened hand, enraged at itself and its impassioned
    efforts,
    has hurled my poems into the fireplace to burn.
So, since out of many not many survive,
    treat them, my dear reader, whoever you are, with respect.

You too, Rome, city forbidden to me, consider kindly   105
   that my poetry is no better than my current fate.

4.10°

Who I was, whom you are reading, yes, I, that playful poet
   of tender loves, posterity, be ready to learn.
Sulmo is my native land, most rich in ice-cold waters,
   and ninety miles away from the City.
Here I was born, and so you may know the date—   5
   it was the year when both consuls met their deaths together—°
I, an heir, if that means anything, of ancient lineage, all the way back
   to great-grandfathers, not an equestrian exalted by recent good
      luck.
I was not the first offspring; I came after my brother's birth;
   he was born twelve months ahead of me;   10
The same morning star attended the day of birth for us both;
   one day is celebrated with two birthday cakes,
During the five-day holiday sacred to armed Minerva
   whose first day is bloodied by a traditional combat.°
We were educated at a tender age under the direction of our father; 15
   we went to attend teachers° in the City distinguished by their
      knowledge.
My brother from his green years applied himself to eloquence,
   born for the courageous combat of the wordy forum.
But as for me, from childhood I enjoyed sacred and heavenly
   connections,
   a Muse was subtly drawing me to her work.   20
My father often asked: "Why embark upon such a useless pursuit?
   Not even Homer bequeathed any wealth."
I was convinced by his words; I abandoned Helicon all together
   and strove to write prose—nothing in meter.
But poetry spontaneously kept coming, metrically perfect.   25
   whatever I tried to write cropped up verse.
Meanwhile the years glided by on silent step;
   my brother and I assumed a toga of a freer life;

4.10.1: the interest and charm of this poem lie not only in the wealth of auto-
   biographical detail it contains but in the implied contrast and comparison
   between Ovid and his poetic achievements, and Augustus. In a way it is an
   epitaph, and also a *res gestae* of Ovid's art and place in the literary canon.
4.10.6: in 43 the consuls Hirtius and Pansa lost their lives at the Battle of Mu-
   tina.
4.10.13-14: the holiday alluded to is the Quinquatrus, celebrated on 19-23
   March.
4.10.16: the teachers were Arellius Fuscus and Porcius Latro.

On our shoulders we donned the broad-striped toga,°
    our pursuits continued as before.   30
But my brother died just after he reached twenty,
    and I lost a part of myself.
I gained the first political office of a young career;
    I was a member of the Board of Three;°
The senate was next in line: but I narrowed my stripe;°   35
    the senate would have produced a burden beyond my strength.
For I lacked the endurance and the inclination for the task;
    I was an escapee from stressful ambition.
The sister Muses were urging me on to a life of leisure,
    the haven to which I'd always been inclined.   40
I cultivated and cherished the poets of that time,
    every bard I reckoned to be a god.
Time and again Macer of the older generation read to me his works
    on birds, the harmful snake, the healing herb;
Often Propertius would recite the poems about his fires;   45
    he was bound to me by a very close comradeship.
Ponticus, distinguished by heroic verse, Bassus by his iambics,
    were charming members of my coterie.
And Horace, versatile in meters, bewitched us
    with his sophisticated songs strummed to his native lyre.   50
Vergil I only saw, and greedy fate
    robbed me of time for a friendship with Tibullus.
He was Gallus' successor, as Propertius was his;
    I followed fourth in line after them.
As I had cultivated those elders, so the younger generation honored
    me;   55
    the reputation of my Muse was not slow to spread.
When I first read my youthful poems in public,
    my beard had only been trimmed once or twice.
Heralded in song throughout the City, a woman excited my genius;
    in my poems I gave her a phony name—Corinna.   60
I wrote a lot, but whatever I thought faulty,
    I myself consigned to the flames for revision.

4.10.29-30: the wearing of the toga with the broad stripe, restricted to the sons
    of senators and equestrians, indicated the pursuit of a political career
4.10.34: in Latin *tresviri*, either the board who oversaw the mint or the board that
    was in charge of prisons and executions. Ovid playfully alludes to *triumviri*,
    the triumvirate of which Octavius (Augustus) had been a member.
4.10.35: the elected office of quaestor qualified one for the senate whose members
    wore a toga with a broad stripe.

At the time that I was banished, I burned some verses that were
    bound to be popular,
  angered by my poems and by my obsession with poetry.
My heart was soft, not at all impregnable against Cupid's weapons, 65
  swayed by the slightest thing.
Yet, although it was in my nature that the tiniest spark would set me
    on fire,
  no scandal was ever attached to my name.
I was almost a boy still when I married a worthless and useless
  wife; only for a short period she was my bride.   70
There succeeded her a wife without blame,
  but yet was not long to share my bed.
And last, the woman who has stayed with me into my late years
  has endured to be the partner of an exiled husband.
My daughter, twice pregnant, but not by the same husband,   75
  though quite young, made me a grandfather.
But then my father had completed his destined days,
  he lived to be ninety, twice nine *lustra*.
I wept for him as he would have wept for me, if I had been
  the one taken. Next I carried out my mother's funeral.   80
Both of them were lucky and timely buried in the tomb,
  dying before the day of my punishment.
And lucky for me too that they are not still alive
  in my time of misery, and that they did not grieve on my account.
If something survives except a name after life is extinct,   85
  and if a flitting shade escapes the funeral pyre,
If some report about me, my parental spirits, has reached you,
  and if charges against me exist in the Stygian court,
Understand, I beg—it's not right for me to deceive you—
  that the cause of my exile was an error, not a crime.   90
Enough about the shades of the dead; I return to you, devoted hearts,
  who ask about the facts of my life.
With the passing of my best years whiteness came
  and blended with my aging hair.
Crowned with the olive of Olympia ten times°   95
  after my birth, the victorious jockey had carried off the prize,
When the wrath of the offended emperor decreed
  me to make my way to Tomis located on the left shore of the Black
    Sea.
The cause of my ruin, which is well-known to everybody,
  I have sworn under oath not to disclose.   100

4.10.95-96: an Olympiad was five years, if counted inclusively; hence, Ovid was
  in his fifties at the time.

Why should I revisit the wrong committed by associates and the hurt
    inflicted
    by household slaves? I have suffered wrongs not a bit less grievous
        than exile.
My mind disdained to succumb to misfortunes and proved itself,
    drawing on all its strength, to be invincible.
Forgetful of myself and the life of leisure that I had led,   105
    I took arms from the circumstances with inexperienced hand.
On land and sea I suffered as many trials as there are stars
    in the sky between the visible and unseen poles.
Driven though long wandering I reached the shore
    that links Sarmatians to quivered Getae.   110
Here, although the din of neighboring weapons resounds around me,
    I relieve my sad fate as best I can with verse;
And though there is no one whose ears hear it,
    in this way I while away and beguile the day.
Thus, that I am alive, that I confront my hardships,   115
    and that I am not worn stiff by the routine anxiety of my life,
I owe to you, my Muse: *you* bring me solace,
    you come bringing a respite from worry, a healing cure.
You are my leader, *you* are my comrade, *you* rescue me from the
    Danube,
    and *you* provide me a respected seat on Helicon;   120
You have granted me that rare commodity, a renowned name
    while still living, a fame that is usually given only after death.
Nor has envy, disparager of the present, with unjust tooth
    gnawed into any work of mine.
Although our times have produced great poets,   125
    my genius has not met a grudging fame;
I would rank many ahead of me, yet I am no less than they,
    cited and read in the whole world.
So, if the prophecies of poets contain any truth,
    even though I die today, I will not be yours, O earth.   130
Whether I've won this fame by favor or by poetry,
    to you, dear reader, rightly I pay thanks again and again.°

5.7

This letter you're reading comes to you from that region
    where the wide Danube flows into the waters of the sea.
If you are finding life sweet and you are in good health,
    then some part of my fate remains bright.

4.10.132: despite his numerous appeals to Augustus to be restored to Rome
    and rehabilitated to Roman life, in the end Ovid feels more beholden to his
    readers for judgment of his life and poetry.

Of course, as always, most dear friend, you ask what I'm up to,   5
 although you can know this even if I am silent.
I am wretched: that in brief is the sum of my misfortunes;
 anyone will be the same who is still alive after offending Caesar.
Do you want to learn who are the native folk of Tomis,
 and what are the customs where I am surviving?   10
This coastal area has a blend of Greeks and Getae,
 but the element of half-civilized Getae predominates.
A rather large horde of Sarmatians and Getaean tribes
 ride back and forth patrolling the roads on horses.
Among them there is not a single one who does not carry   15
 a quiver and bow, and ghastly arrows smeared with a viper's
  venom.
To each a wild voice, savage look, the epitome of Mars,
 with hair uncut and beard untrimmed by any hand,
And a right hand not slow to stab and run through with the dagger
 which every barbarian keeps strapped to his side.   20
Among them, forgetful of his "tender loves," your poet, my friend,
 lives now; them he sees and hears.
I wish he were alive, and dying among them;
 if only his shade could escape from this hateful place.
My songs are danced to a packed theater, you write,   25
 my friend, and my verses are applauded there.
You know very well that I have composed nothing for the theaters;
 my Muse is not ambitious for applause.°
Yet I am not ungrateful for anything that hinders forgetfulness of me
 and that revives the name of an exile to the public.   30
Sometimes, when I recall the harm they have caused me,
 I curse those poems and my Muses.
Although I have cursed them through and through, nevertheless I
  cannot be without them;
 still I pursue the gory weapons bloodied for my wounds.
So the Greek ship that was mangled by waves off Euboea   35
 still dares to run the waters around cape Caphareus.
Yet I do not spend wakeful nights in pursuit of praise nor act upon a
  concern
 for a future name which would have been better off unheralded.

5.7.25-28: no doubt that some of Ovid's poetry was adapted for the stage. As
a hit on Broadway attests, individual stories from the *Metamorphoses* would
be relatively easy to adapt.

I occupy my mind in study to beguile my pain,
    and I try to console my worried self.   40
What else can I do alone on these deserted coasts,
    what other help should I attempt to seek for my tragedy?
If I look at the place, it is a place unlovable,
    and nothing in the whole world can be more grim than it;
If I see men, they are scarcely men worthy of the name,   45
    they possess more wild savagery than wolves.
They don't fear laws, no, here might makes right,
    justice lies conquered beneath the pugnacious sword.
They ward off cold dressed in skins and baggy britches,
    their shaggy faces are covered with long hair.   50
Few retain traces of the Greek language,
    and even that is barbarized with a Getaean accent.
Not a single person exists in the population who can
    speak Latin using even a modicum of words.
I, that famous Roman bard—forgive me, Muses—   55
    am forced to speak mostly in Sarmatian.
And, —damn, I'm ashamed to admit it—because of long disuse
    I can barely remember Latin vocabulary.
Even this little book, I don't doubt, has some barbarisms,
    and that is the fault of the place, not the person.   60
To keep me from losing the use of the Latin language
    and my voice from becoming mute in my native speech,
I talk to myself and manipulate phrases long unused,
    and I retrace ill-omen signs of my pursuit.
Thus I drag out my life and time, thus I remove   65
    and disengage myself from the contemplation of my demise.
Through poetry I seek forgetfulness of my tragic state of affairs.
    If through my study I win such reward, that...is...enough.

GLOSSARY

This glossary identifies most of the names found in the poems. Unless otherwise indicated all dates are BCE.

ABYDUS: a harbor on the Asiatic side of the Hellespont.

ACCIUS, LUCIUS: (170-ca86) wrote primarily tragedies in a very florid style. He was appreciated and quoted by Cicero.

ACHERON: a river in the underworld whose name means "woeful."

ACONTIUS: suitor of a reluctant Cydippe. Acontius inscribed upon an apple: " I swear by Artemis to marry Acontius." When Cydippe picked the apple and read the inscription aloud, Artemis held the girl to the "oath."

ACROCERAUNIA: see CERAUNIA.

ACTIUM: a promontory in the Ambracian Gulf of western Greece. It gave its name to the naval battle in which Octavius/Agrippa defeated the combined forces of Antony and Cleopatra on 2 September, 31. The victory made Octavius the undisputed dynast of the Roman world and paved the way for his principate, the beginning of the Roman Empire.

ADMETUS: for the killing of a Cyclops, Apollo had to serve the mortal Admetus for one year. In a variant myth Apollo falls desperately in love with Admetus.

ADONIS: a beautiful youth beloved by Aphrodite. After he was killed by a wild boar during a hunt, the goddess resurrected him as an annual flower.

AEACUS: the grandfather of Achilles who became one of the judges of the underworld. He drew lots from an urn to determine the order in which cases were to be heard.

AEFULA: a small town in the hills of Latium.

AEGEUS: king of Athens, father of Theseus, who gave his name to the Aegean Sea. He jumped from a cliff believing that Theseus had failed to kill the Minotaur in Crete.

343

AEOLIC: one of the major dialects of Greek, used by Sappho and Alcaeus.

AEROPE: wife of Atreus, who had an affair with her husband's brother Thyestes.

AFRANIUS: Lucius Afranius; prolific writer of comedies based on Italian domestic life.

AGANIPPE: a fountain in Boeotia on Mt. Helicon, reputed haunt of the Muses, hence a source of poetic inspiration.

AGRIPPA, MARCUS VIPSANIUS: close friend, confidant, advisor, and very successful general of Octavius/Augustus. Until his death in 12 he was the second most powerful man in Rome after Augustus. He married Julia, Augustus' daughter, and had five children by her. He helped Augustus in his vast building program and was responsible for the Pantheon and a portico near it that was adorned with painting.

AJAX: son of Oileus who raped Cassandra in the temple of Pallas Athena, for which the goddess had him drowned at sea during his return home from the Trojan war.

AJAX: son of Telamon. When he was not awarded the arms of Achilles after the hero's death, he went temporarily insane; he slaughtered numerous sheep thinking them to be the Greek leaders who judged against him.

ALBA: a mountain range southeast of Rome, the site of Alba Longa. According to legend it was founded by Aeneas' son Ascanius (Iulus). Emigrants from there were the progenitors of the Romans. Near the site is a lake; the region also produced an excellent wine.

ALCAEUS: lyric poet from Lesbos at the end of the seventh century.

ALGIDUS: a mountain in the Alban district southeast of Rome.

ALLIA: a river in Latium circa twenty miles north of Rome where on 18 July, 390 the Romans suffered a defeat by Gauls.

ALLOBROGES: a Gallic tribe in the Rhone area who were enticed by Catiline to join his conspiracy of 63. They refused, but two years later revolted.

ALOIDAE: Otus and Ephialtes, the brothers who led a revolt of giants against Zeus and the Olympians. They tried to assault Olympus by piling the nearby peak of Mount Ossa onto Mount Pelion.

ALPHEUS: see ARETHUSA

AMPHIAREUS: the Argive seer in the Seven against Thebes who during the attack was swallowed up in the earth as he tried to escape.

AMPHION & ZETHUS: twin kings of Thebes who quarreled about the comparative value of music and the life of herding and hunting. Amphion's melodious playing of the lyre made stones leap into place to form the fortified walls and gates of the city.

ANCUS MARTIUS: the fourth king of Rome.

ANDROGEUS: son of Minos, king of Crete, brother of Ariadne.

ANDROMACHE: the wife of Hector.

ANDROMEDA: a princess of Ethiopia, daughter of Cepheus and Cassiopeia. She was chained to a rock in the sea to be devoured by a sea monster sent by Neptune. After striking a bargain with Cepheus to save his daughter, Perseus slew the monster, rescued Andromeda, and married her.

ANIO: a tributary of the Tiber flowing from the Apennines east of Rome through Tibur.

ANTENOR: old and wise counselor and friend of Priam, the king of Troy. He proposed returning Helen to the Greeks in order to stop the war.

ANTIMACHUS: an epic poet from Colophon who wrote a *Thebaid*; he is said to have fallen in love with his mistress Lyde, as Homer fell in love with Penelope.

ANTIOCHUS III: Seleucid king who was defeated by the Romans in 190.

ANTONIUS (IULUS): son of Marcus Antonius raised by his stepmother Octavia—sister of Octavius/Augustus. He was consul in 10 but was implicated in a scandal involving Augustus' daughter Julia in 2. He was then executed.

ANXUR: the Volscian name for Tarracina (Terracina). At the top of the hill overlooking the harbor was a large complex that included a temple to Jupiter built by Sulla.

AONIE (AONIA): ancient name of Boeotia.

APELLES: a famous Greek painter from Colophon who was known for his portraiture and realism. He was commissioned by Philip II and Alexander the Great of Macedon.

APIDANUS: a river in Thessaly.

AQUINUM: a small town in Latium.

ARATUS: third-century Greek poet from Soli in Cilicia who wrote a didactic poem on astronomy called *Phaenomena*, often translated and adapted by the Romans.

ARAXES: a river in Armenia flowing into the Caspian Sea.

ARCHELOUS: river-god in Aetolia who fought Hercules over Deianeira; he relinquished his claim to her after his defeat.

ARCHYTAS: a famous Pythagorean philosopher from Tarentum.

ARCTOS: Callisto, daughter of Lycaon, catasterized as Ursa Major, the Big Dipper.

ARCTURUS: the brightest star in the constellation Bootes.

ARETHUSA: river/fountain nymph of Syracuse, representing the muse of Sicily and pastoral song. In her myth the nymph Arethusa fled from the river-god Alpheus in the Western Peloponnesus, flowed under the sea, and emerged in Syracuse as a spring.

ARIADNE: the daughter of Minos, king of Crete. She gave Theseus a ball of yarn, a sword, and a wreath that lit up. These items helped him kill the Minotaur and escape the labyrinth where the Minotaur was housed. Ariadne wore the wreath on her flight with Theseus from Cnossus until she was deserted on the island of Naxos (Dia). There she was found and saved by Dionysus who set the wreath in the heavens where it became the constellation Corona.

ARICIA: a city southeast of Rome on the lower slope of the Alban Hills.

ARION: a) the wonder horse, offspring of Poseidon and Demeter, which could speak. Adrastus, the Argive king who led the storied expedition against Thebes (i.e. the Seven against Thebes), came to possess Arion and escaped the battle at Thebes on his back. b) a famous poet from Methymna on Lesbos who on his return to Corinth from Sicily was forced to jump into the sea by sailors. A dolphin, which had heard his music just before the sailors threw him overboard, rescued him and carried him safely to shore.

ASCRA: a site near Thebes which was the birthplace of Hesiod, author of *Theogony*, a work on the birth of the gods and universe, and of the pastoral-like and didactic *Works and Days*.

ATALANTA: a maiden from Arcadia, the daughter of Iasos. As a devotee of Artemis, she refused any suitor who could not best her in a footrace. Milanion was able to defeat her with the help of three golden apples from the Gardens of the Hesperides, given to him by Aphrodite. In a variant Milanion wooed Atalanta as she hunted in the woods of Arcadia. When he was wounded by a centaur, in pity she nursed him.

ATHOS: a mountain at the end of the peninsula of Chalcidice.

ATTA: Titus Quinctius Atta (died in 77); like Afranius he wrote comedies based on Italian domestic life.

ATTALUS: Attalus III, king of Pergamum, who willed his kingdom to Rome in 133.

AUFIDUS: a river in Apulia near Horace's hometown.

AUSONIA: the region of Italy deriving its name from the Ausones, the ancient name of the inhabitants of central and southern Italy.

AVERNUS: a lake near Cumae said to be an entrance to the underworld. It exuded a foul odor because of its sulfurous fumes.

BACTRA: the chief city of the vast region of BACTRIA which now comprises most of Afghanistan and Turkestan.

BAIAE: a fashionable resort town near Naples opposite Puteoli.

BASSUS: an iambic poet, friend of Propertius and Ovid.

BELLEROPHON: an exiled Corinthian hero who slew the Chimaera with the help of the divine winged horse Pegasus. When he tried to scale Olympus, Bellerophon was thrown from Pegasus' back to his death.

BELLONA: an old Italic goddess of war who assumed features of an Oriental orgiastic cult in which frenzied celebrants engaged in self-mutilation.

BESSI: a widely dispersed Thracian tribe occupying the southern range of the Haemus mountains from the Black Sea all the way to northern Macedonia.

BITHYNIA: the Roman province of Northern Turkey bordering on the Black Sea.

BRISEIS: the war "prize" awarded Achilles. When she was taken from him by Agamemnon, Achilles became so enraged that he withdrew from battle with the Trojans.

BRUNDISIUM: i.e. Brindisi, prominent Italian port at the "heel" on the Adriatic from which ships most conveniently departed to Greece and points eastward.

BRUTUS, a) LUCIUS IUNIUS: deposed Tarquin the Proud, the last king of Rome, and became the first consul of Rome. b) MARCUS IUNIUS: one of the assassins of Gaius Julius Caesar, who commanded, along with Gaius Cassius Longinus, forces at Philippi in Thessaly (42) against the combined armies of Mark Antony and Octavius Caesar. Antony and Octavius won a decisive victory.

BUSIRIS: pharaoh of Egypt who would sacrifice strangers to Jove to alleviate drought.

CADMUS: mythical founder of Thebes.

CAECILIUS STATIUS: highly acclaimed comic poet of the early second century.

CAICUS: a river in Lydia.

CAERE: Etruscan city ca. thirty miles north of Rome. It was one of the last communities whose citizens achieved full Roman status.

CALCHAS: the Greek prophet who revealed to Agamemnon at Aulis that his daughter Iphigeneia had to be sacrificed to procure favorable winds for the fleet to sail for Troy.

CALES: a city in Campania known for its wines.

CALLIMACHUS: the great poet of the third century from Cyrene who came to Alexandria to take charge of the Ptolemaic library there. He championed a new poetic program that heralded short, erudite, and highly polished poetry.

CALLIOPE: one of the Muses, often associated with epic poetry.

CALVUS, GAIUS LICINIUS: a friend of Catullus and writer of erotic poetry.

CAMILLUS, MARCUS FURIUS: conqueror of Veii, the Etruscan stronghold, in 394 and of the Gauls after their sack of Rome in 387.

CANACE: daughter of Aeolus, who fell in love with her brother Macareus and gave birth to a child by him. When Aeolus discovered the affair, he sent Canace a sword with which to kill herself; Macareus also committed suicide.

CANNAE: the site in Apulia of a disastrous Roman defeat by Hannibal.

CANOPUS: famed city on the western mouth of the Nile, ruled by the Ptolemies immediately after the conquest of Alexander the Great.

CAPANEUS: one of the leaders of the ill-fated Argive expedition against Thebes who was thunderbolted by Jupiter.

CAPHAREUS: a rocky promontory off southern Euboea where in myth much of the Greek fleet returning from Troy was lured to destruction by Nauplius.

CAPITO, FONTEIUS: friend and patron of Antony who represented Antony at the meeting of Brindisi. He was chosen consul in 33.

CAPUA: originally an Etruscan colony that became the recognized capital of Campania. Capua revolted against the Romans in the Second Punic War, joining Hannibal in 216. It was recaptured by Rome in 211.

CARPATHIAN SEA: the sea between Rhodes and Crete around the island of Carpathia.

CASSANDRA: daughter of Priam, unbelieved prophetess of Apollo; at the sack of Troy she was brutally raped in Athena's temple by Ajax of Locris.

CASTALIA: the spring at Delphi on Mt. Parnassos, sacred to Apollo and the Muses.

CATO, MARCUS PORCIUS: a) (235-147) known for his integrity and ascetic life style, as censor he tried to reform Roman morals. b) fought with Pompey against Julius Caesar and helped lead the Republican forces after Pompey's death. He committed suicide at Utica in North Africa in 46.

CATULLUS, GAIUS VALERIUS: (ca 84-54), writer of epigrams and lyric poetry, most famous for his love poems addressed to "Lesbia."

CAUDIUM: a Campanian town, site of an inglorious defeat of the Romans by Samnites in 321.

CAYSTER: a river in Lydia famous for its swans.

CELEUS: King of Eleusis who instituted the Mysteries honoring Demeter. He was the putative father of Triptolemus, the consort of the goddess.

CEOS: an island in the Cyclades near the mainland off Attica. It was the birth-place of the lyric poet Simonides.

CERAUNIA (ACROCERAUNIA): a mountain in northwest Epirus across the Adriatic.

CHALYBES: a people famous for working steel. They lived in Pontus, an area in northern Turkey along the Black Sea.

CHAONIA: the region around Dodona in Epirus so named from the Chaones, the people who inhabited the area.

CHIRON: a gentle centaur who was a teacher and healer.

CHRYSIPPUS: third century philosopher of Stoicism whose work became the orthodox standard of the school.

CIBYRA: a commercial city in Phrygia.

CLAUDIA: when the ship bearing the image of Cybele (Cybebe) ran aground in the Tiber, Quinta Claudia, in order to disprove a charge against her chastity and to prove her innocence, single-handedly pulled the ship free. A statue of her was erected in the temple to the goddess on the Palatine.

CLIO: one of the Muses, usually identified as patron of history.

CLITUMNUS: a river in Umbria, central Italy.

CLYTEMNESTRA: wife of Agamemnon who committed adultery with Aegisthus and murdered her husband on his arrival home from Troy.

COCCEIUS: Lucius Cocceius Nerva, an arbitrator who assisted in brokering the reconciliation of Antony and Octavius at Brindisi.

COCLES, HORATIUS: singled-handedly held a bridge across the Tiber against an Etruscan army attempting to capture Rome.

COCYTUS: a river of the underworld; the word means "lamentation."

COEUS: a titan, offspring of Uranus and Ge (Earth).

COLCHIS: famed area on the east coast of the Black Sea associated with Medea.

CONON: a mathematician/astronomer from Samos credited with the discovery of the constellation Coma Berenices.

CORYCUS: a city in Cilicia of Asia Minor.

CORVINUS: see MESSALLA.

COS: an island off the coast of Ionia known for its silk and woven garments.

CRASSUS, MARCUS LICINIUS: the triumvir who led a Roman army deep into Parthian territory where he was defeated and killed at Carrhae in 53.

CRATINUS: poet of Greek Old Comedy of fifth-century Athens who was a contemporary and rival of Aristophanes.

CREUSA: the daughter of Creon, king of Corinth, whom Jason married after he left Medea. Medea sent her a poisoned robe as a wedding gift, which caused her death.

CUMAE: the site of the first Greek settlement on the mainland of Italy founded by colonists from Pithecusae (Ischia). It was the home of the Sibyl, priestess of Apollo.

CURETES: young men of Crete who banged their shields to muffle the cries of the infant Jupiter. They became priests of Cybele.

CURES: a town near Rome that served as the capital of the Sabines.

CURIA: the Roman term for the senate building.

CURIUS: Manius Curius Dentatus; a prominent general against the Samnites and Pyrrhus in the early third century.

CURTIUS, METTIUS: a Roman hero during Rome's early wars with the Sabines. In response to an oracle, he leapt fully armed on horseback into a chasm which opened in the Roman Forum. An area called the Lake of Curtius commemorates this event.

CYBELE: The Great Earth Mother of Phrygia whose rituals included loud music and orgiastic dances.

CYDIPPE: see ACONTIUS.

CYRUS: known as the "Great", Persian king of the sixth century who founded the Persian Empire and from whom the Parthians claimed descent.

CYTHERA: an island just south of the Peloponnesus, reputed birthplace of Venus.

DACIANS: a people occupying the lower Danube who were to be defeated and incorporated into the Roman Empire by the Emperor Trajan.

DAEDALUS: famous scientist/inventor of Athens. He built the labyrinth at Cnossus to house the Minotaur. Later imprisoned in it, he escaped with his son Icarus by flying on wings fashioned from feathers and wax. After the wax melted in his flight, Icarus fell to his death.

DALMATIA: Roman province on the east coast of the Adriatic, north of Epirus.

DAMOCLES: Dionysius, tyrant of Syracuse, invited an obsequious Damocles to an exquisite dinner at which a sword suspended by a single thread hung precariously above his head.

DANAE: daughter of Acrisius of Argos, who was shut up in a tower by her father, but visited by Jupiter in the form of a shower of gold. Their son was Perseus.

DANAIDS/DANAUS: fifty daughters of Danaus who were forced to marry the fifty sons of Aegyptus, the brother of Danaus. Except for one, Hypermnestra, they all murdered their husbands on their wedding night. In the underworld they are eternally punished by having to fill leaky urns with water.

DAPHNIS: the quintessential shepherd reputed to be the inventor of pastoral song whose failed love affair was the subject of many poems.

DARDANUS: a son of Zeus who was the earliest king of Troy.

DAUNUS: mythic king of Apulia.

DECIUS: Publius Decius Mus, a Roman commander in the war against the Samnites who vowed himself to the gods of the underworld in a self-sacrificing charge against the enemy. His son and grandson performed the same act in subsequent wars.

DEIDAMIA: one of the daughters of Lycomedes, king of the island of Scyros, where Thetis hid Achilles dressed as girl to prevent his joining the expedition against Troy. He was recognized by Odysseus who tricked him with a fine set of armor. Achilles had a son, Neoptolemus, by Deidamia

DEMOCRITUS: fifth-century philosopher from Abdera in Thrace, adopter and proponent of the atomic theory of Leucippus. Supposedly he became so absorbed in his philosophical pursuits that he neglected his personal affairs.

DEUCALION: son of Prometheus, see PYRRHA.

DICTE: a mountain range in Crete.

DICTYNNA: a Cretan nymph whose cult was assimilated to the worship of Artemis.

DIDO: Phoenician queen of Carthage, also called Elissa, who loved Aeneas and committed suicide when he left her in order to complete his divine and historic mission.

DIGENTIA: a river flowing past Horace's estate into the Anio near Tibur.

DIOMEDES: in the Trojan War Pallas Athena endowed the Greek hero Diomedes with such prowess that he even attacked and wounded Aphrodite. After the Trojan War Diomedes came to southern Italy and founded several cities including Beneventum.

DIRCE: a spring near Thebes.

DIS: another name for the god of the underworld.

DODONA: isolated site in Epirus with a grove sacred to Jupiter. The doves at the site were believed to have prophetic powers.

DOG-STAR: Sirius, a star of Canis Major called by the Romans "Canicula," portended the hottest days of summer.

DRYAD: nymph of the woods.

EGERIA: a nymph of Latium who was the consort and advisor of King Numa of Rome.

ELEUSIS (ELEUSINIAN): refers to the site in Attica of the famous cult of Demeter.

ELIS: an area in northwest Peloponnesus where Olympia is.

ELYSIUM: a paradise in the underworld where purified souls reside.

EMATHIA: a district of Macedonia on the border with Thrace and the Haemus mountain range.

ENNIUS, QUINTUS: (239-169), one of the earliest poets of Rome who became known as the father of Latin Literature. He is particularly famous for his *Annales* that records in eighteen books the history of Rome.

EPICHARMUS: Greek comic playwright (540-450) from the island of Cos whose plays often burlesqued mythological figures.

ERIGONE: daughter of Icarius, who was catasterized as the constellation Virgo.

EUMENIDES: "the kindly ones," name of the transformed Erinyes (Furies). Their function in the underworld is to punish evil-doers.

EUPHORION: Greek scholar/poet from Calchis, Euboea.

EURYTION: see PIRITHOUS.

EVANDER: an Arcadian Greek migrant to the future site of Rome who founded Pallanteum on the Palatine Hill. According to Vergil he welcomed Aeneas and formed a military alliance with him.

FAUNUS: Italic god of forests and fields often associated by the Romans with Pan.

FAUSTA: daughter of the dictator Sulla (138-78), wife of Titus Annius Milo who was accused of murder in 52. She reportedly had numerous lovers.

FESCENNINE (VERSE): earliest form of drama of Etruscan origin that survived in bawdy songs sung at weddings and triumphs.

GABII: Latin city twelve miles east of Rome forced into a treaty favorable to Rome under king Tarquin the Proud.

GALATEA: Nereid (sea nymph) who inhabited the sea around Sicily and southern Italy.

GALLUS, GAIUS CORNELIUS: general, politician, and well-known elegiac poet. As the first prefect of Egypt he was recalled and disgraced by Augustus, after which he committed suicide (26). He was a personal friend of Vergil who dedicated *Eclogue* 10 to him, and he was an influential predecessor of Propertius.

GANGES: the storied river of India.

GARGANUS: lushly wooded mountain range in Apulia near the Adriatic.

GARGARA: the upper part of Mt. Ida near Troy with a city of the same name at its foot.

GELONI: a nomadic tribe in Scythia.

GENIUS: possessed by every human, this guardian spirit died with the death of the individual.

GERYON: a three-bodied giant who possessed a huge herd of cattle somewhere in the far west. Hercules took the cattle and killed Geryon in his tenth labor.

GLAUCUS: a sea god, son of Neptune.

GOOD GODDESS: Roman goddess of fertility, often identified with Italic Fauna. Men were strictly prohibited from her rites.

HAEDUS: a constellation, usually two stars (i.e. Haedi = the Kids), whose rising presaged the stormy season of autumn.

HAEMONIA: old name for Thessaly.

HEBRUS: principal river of Thrace flowing into the Aegean near the Hellespont.

HECATE: goddess of witchcraft and the occult.

HELICON: a mountain of Boeotia, reputed dwelling of the Muses. Below its summit is the spring Hippocrene.

HELLE: daughter of Athamas of Thebes. She and her brother, Phrixus, were persecuted by their resentful stepmother Ino. Rescued from impending doom by their natural mother, Nephele, they were placed on the back of a magical, flying golden ram. Helle, however, fell off the ram as it was passing the strait that bears her name: Hellespont.

HIPPODAMIA: see Pirithous.

HIPPOLYTA: queen of the Amazons, mother of Hippolytus by Theseus.

HIPPOLYTUS: son of Theseus. As a chaste worshipper of Diana, he rejected the advances of his stepmother Phaedra. She contrived his death.

HYDASPES: a river in India, tributary of the Indus.

HYMEN/HYMENAEUS: god of weddings.

HYPERBOREA: the land of a fabulous people living somewhere north of Greece.

IACCHUS: a deity associated with the cult of Demeter at Eleusis who is often identified with Bacchus.

ICARIUS: of Attica, he joyfully accepted and entertained Dionysus who in gracious return taught him the art of wine-making. Icarius gave some of his wine to his neighbors in his desire to help spread the cult of the god. When some of the locals over-indulged, they thought that they had been poisoned. As a result, they attacked and murdered Icarius, whom Dionysus catasterized as Bootes, the Plowman, to drive the Seven Plowing Oxen (Septentriones), otherwise know as Ursa Major (the Great Bear), the Big Dipper.

IDA: a) a mountain near Troy; b) a mountain range in Crete.

IDES: approximately mid-month, either the thirteenth or fifteenth day.

ILIA: another name for Rhea Silvia, a Vestal Virgin impregnated by Mars, and mother of Romulus and Remus.

ILYTHYIA: daughter of Jupiter and Juno, Greek goddess of childbirth in Latin identified as Lucina, i.e. either Diana or Juno in their role as protectors of childbirth.

IO: daughter of the river god Inachus, loved by Jupiter. To prevent Juno's discovering the affair, or when Juno found out about her husband's infidelity, Io was changed into a heifer and watched by a hundred-eyed monster Argus. Greeks and Romans identified her with the Egyptian goddess Isis because she wandered the earth before ultimately coming to Egypt where her natural form was restored and she was welcomed as a goddess.

IOLCUS: homeland of Jason and his father Aeson in Thessaly.

ISIS: the Egyptian goddess who had a cult at Rome; her worship involved a period of ten days during which strict sexual abstinence was observed.

ISMARUS: Ulysses put out the eye of the Cyclops Polyphemus while he was in a drunken stupor from guzzling the very strong wine that had been given to Ulysses by Maron, priest of Apollo, at Ismarus in Thrace.

IULUS: son of Aeneas, also called Ascanius, to whom the family of Julius Caesar traced its lineage.

JANUS: two-faced god of beginnings, new undertakings, and doorways. There was a temple to him in the Forum whose doors were kept closed when no wars were in progress.

JUBA: Juba II, king of Numidia.

JUGURTHA: king of Numidia, defeated and captured by Marius, and executed in Rome in 104.

KALENDS: the first day of the month.

LANUVIUM: a town twenty miles south of Rome with a famous temple to Juno Sospita.

LAOMEDON: king of Troy who reneged on paying Apollo and Neptune for building the walls of Troy. His perjury brought a curse upon the city.

LARES: household gods.

LAVINIUM: the supposed site in Latium settled by Aeneas.

LEANDER: a young man from Abydus on the narrows of the Dardanelles who would nightly swim across the channel to meet his lover Hero, who put out a light to guide him. One night a storm arose, extinguishing the light, and Leander was drowned. After she discovered his washed-up body, Hero drowned herself.

LEDA: wife of Tyndareus, king of Sparta, and lover of Zeus by whom she gave birth to the Gemini (Castor and Pollux), Helen, and Clytemnestra.

LETHE: the river of "forgetfulness" in the realm of the underworld.

LEUCAS: Apollo of Leucas, a temple to Apollo on the island of Leucas that overlooked the Bay of Actium.

LEUCOTHEA: a sea-goddess formerly Ino, a princess of Thebes who was transformed as she was chased by her maddened husband Athamas.

LIBO'S WELL: the *puteal*, a place in the Forum that had been struck by lightning; it was surrounded by a curbing (like a well) near which public and private business sometimes was conducted.

LICINIUS, AULUS TERENTIUS VARRO MURENA: brother of Maecenas' wife Terentia, consul in 23, executed in 22 for his part in a conspiracy against Augustus.

LINUS: putative son of Apollo and the muse Terpsichore; he was a master singer/poet and teacher of Orpheus and Hercules.

LIRIS: a river in southern Latium.

LIVIUS, ANDRONICUS: freedman, earliest known writer in Latin who produced a play in Rome (240); he is famous for his translation of the *Odyssey*.

LUCILIUS, GAIUS: (180-102), acknowledged founder of the genre and tradition of satire. In his poetry Lucilius openly attacked and lampooned famous contemporaries.

LUCINA: a cult name of Diana or Juno, referring to her attribute as a goddess of childbirth.

LUCRETIUS: Titus Lucretius Carus; early first century Latin poet who wrote *On the Nature of Things*, an Epicurean look at scientific realism.

LUCULLUS, LUCIUS LICINIUS: (ca.117-56), consul in 74, he had an eastern command against Mithradates of Pontus which he was forced to relinquish to Pompey the Great. After his return to Rome he lived a life of refined luxury.

LUPERCALIA: a celebration on 15 February honoring various woodland gods. Naked priests ran around the Palatine striking any and all women with thongs made from strips of goat-skin. The act was to inspire fertility.

LUSTRUM: a period of five years corresponding to the elections of censors every five years.

LYCAEUS: a mountain in Arcadia, a special haunt of the god Pan.

LYCMON: an alternate form of LUCUMO(N), eponymous hero of the Luceres, Etruscans who aided Romulus in his war against the Sabines led by Titus Tatius.

LYCOURGUS: a king of Thrace who violently opposed the cult of Bacchus. He was blinded, driven mad, and, in a common version of the myth, strangled by grape vines.

LYSIPPUS: famous Greek sculptor from Sicyon commissioned by Alexander the Great to be his "court" sculptor.

MACAREUS: see CANACE

MACER, AEMILIUS: a didactic poet who was a member of the circle of Messalla.

MAECENAS, GAIUS CILNIUS: close friend, advisor, and minister of culture of Octavius/Augustus; he was an equestrian of Etruscan blood from Arezzo who dabbled in poetry himself and became the literary patron of Vergil, Horace, and Propertius.

MAENALUS: a mountain range in Arcadia, sacred to Pan.

MAIA: one of the Pleiades, catasterized daughters of Atlas and Pleione, mother of Hermes; by metonymy her name refers to the constellation of the Pleiades.

MARCELLUS, MARCUS CLAUDIUS: a) a famous general in the Second Punic War who conquered Syracuse (212); b) Augustus' nephew, son-in-law, and adopted son.

MARIUS, GAIUS: military hero and "popular" leader, conqueror of Jugurtha, and victorious general over the Cimbri and Teutones, two Germanic tribes, in 102-101.

MARSI: an Italic hill people of central Italy known for their fierce soldiers who bitterly opposed the Romans in the Social War ca. 90-88.

MATINUS: a coastal mountain range in Apulia.

MEANDER: a river in Phrygia known for its winding course.

MEDES: the ancient people of the Middle East superceded by the Persians, often equated with the Parthians.

MELPOMENE: one of the Muses, usually associated with tragedy, but also lyric poetry.

MEMNON: king of Ethiopia, an ally of Troy in the Trojan War. He was the son of Tithonus and Dawn (Aurora).

MENANDER: famous Athenian writer of Greek New Comedy (342-ca.290), the most highly regarded of the Greek playwrights of "situation comedy."

MESSALLA: cognomen of the famous clan of the Valerii which included Marcus Valerius Messalla Corvinus, who had a distinguished military and political career; he was an orator and patron of the arts in whose literary coterie were Tibullus, Ovid, and his niece Sulpicia.

METHYMNA: a prominent city in Lesbos.

METTUS FUFETIUS: an Alban general who betrayed Rome in the reign of Tullus Hostilius, the third king of Rome. He was punished by being tied to two chariots that were driven in opposite directions.

MILANION: see ATALANTA.

MIMNERMUS: an elegiac poet of the late seventh century from Ionia.

MINOS: powerful mythic king of Crete who became a judge in the underworld.

MINTURNAE: a city on the coast of southern Latium that produced excellent wines.

MISENUM: seat of the harbor near Baiae, constructed by Agrippa for the imperial fleet.

MONAESES: a Parthian noble and general who defeated the army of Antony in 37.

MUTINA: a city west of Bologna besieged by Mark Antony in 43, relieved by the consuls of that year, Hirtius and Pansa, who were assisted by Octavius. Hirtius and Pansa were killed in the attack and Antony fled, leaving Octavius the victorious survivor.

MYRON: an Athenian sculptor of the fifth century, most famous for his naturalistic treatment of animals.

MYSIA: a country of Asia Minor between the Aegean and Hellespont Seas.

NAEVIUS, GNAEUS: early Roman poet who composed tragedies, comedies, and an epic called *The Punic War* in Saturnian verse, an early Latin form.

NAIADS: sea nymphs.

NAUPLIUS: king of Euboea who avenged his son Palamedes, falsely accused of treason by Ulysses; he lit false beacon fires for the returning fleet. See CAPHAREUS.

NEREUS: old man of the sea, father of fifty daughters, the Nereids.

NESTOR: the garrulous old man of the *Iliad*, king of Pylos, who tried to mediate quarrels among the Greek leaders at Troy.

NIOBE: daughter of Tantalus who foolishly asserted that she had more and better children than Latona, the mother of Apollo and Artemis. Apollo and Artemis shot down the children with arrows; Niobe herself was turned into stone as she wept mourning the fate of her children.

NISUS: king of Megara whose daughter Scylla betrayed him to Minos as he was besieging the city. She cut off a magical purple lock of hair on which his life depended. Both Nisus and Scylla were metamorphosed into birds, he the predatory sea-eagle.

NUMA POMPILIUS: the second king of Rome who is said to have built his house in the Forum, the so-called Regia, which became the headquarters of the Pontifex Maximus.

NYPHATES: a mountain in eastern Armenia.

OAXES: a river in Crete or referring to the Oxus which is in Asia Minor.

OCTOBER HORSE: every year on 15 October a horse was sacrificed to Mars after winning a race in the Forum. Its blood was kept in the Regia, headquarters of the Pontifex Maximus, and was used in rites of purification.

OEAGRUS: king of Thrace, father of Orpheus.

OENONE: daughter of the river-god Cebren, living on the slopes of Mt. Ida of the Troad. She married Paris who abandoned her in favor of Helen.

OETA: a mountain in Thessaly where Hercules died.

OMPHALE: queen of Lydia whom Hercules served for one year. She forced him to dress as a girl and perform womanly chores.

OPS: Roman goddess of plenty, wife of Saturn, identified with Cybele,

ORCUS: god of the underworld.

ORICOS: a port in Illyria.

ORION: the great hunter of mythology who was made a constellation and whose rising and descent were often associated with stormy weather.

ORITHYIA: daughter of Erechtheus, an early king of Athens. She was abducted by Boreas, the North Wind.

OSSA: see ALOIDAE.

PACORUS: son of Orodes, king of Parthia. In 40 he defeated a Roman army.

PACUVIUS, MARCUS: (220-130), famous writer of tragedies from southern Italy.

PAESTUM: a Romanized Greek colony in the Sele plain of Lucania.

PALES: an Italic deity of flocks and herds whose festival of the Parilia (Palilia) was celebrated on 21 April, the day of the foundation of Rome. See Ovid, *Fasti* 4.721.

PANCHAIA: a fabulous island on the Red Sea off the coast of Roman Arabia.

PANGAEA: a mountain range in Macedonia and Thrace.

PANSA, GAIUS VIBIUS: see MUTINA.

PARNASSUS: the mountain where Delphi is located, hence, of Apollo and the Muses.

PARTHENOPE: old name for Neapolis (Naples) where Vergil lived as a young man.

PASIPHAE: wife of king Minos of Crete, cursed with an unnatural passion for a bull. She forced Daedalus to build her a wooden cow in which she could be positioned in order to be mounted and penetrated by the bull. From her union with the bull came the Minotaur, half-man, half-bull.

PATARA: a site in Lycia, Asia Minor, where there was an oracle to Apollo.

PAULLUS, LUCIUS AEMILIUS LEPIDUS: consul of 34 and censor in 22.

PAULUS, LUCIUS AEMILIUS: a losing general against Hannibal at Cannae.

PAULUS, FABIUS MAXIMUS: a good friend of Augustus, consul in 11; he married Augustus' niece Marcia.

PELION: see ALOIDAE.

PELOPS: cut up and boiled by his father and served in a stew to the gods. The gods restored him to life, replacing with ivory the portion of his shoulder that had been eaten by Demeter. Pelops and his house, which included the figures of Thyestis and Atreus, and Agamemnon and Menelaus, were often the subject of tragedies because of the numerous crimes and sins committed by its members.

PELUSIUM: a town near the mouth of the Nile captured by Antony that capitulated to Octavius in 30.

PENEUS: the principal river of Thessaly arising in the Pindus mountain range.

PENTHESILEA: queen of the Amazons who warred with the Trojans against the Greeks. She was killed by Achilles.

PENTHEUS: king of Thebes who opposed the cult of Dionysus. He was killed by his mother and other Bacchants and his palace was destroyed by an earthquake.

PERGAMA: the name for the citadel of Troy.

PERILLUS: an Athenian inventor and craftsman who constructed for Phalaris, the king of Agrigentum, a bronze bull in which enclosed victims were to be roasted alive. Their screams were to reproduce the lifelike bellows of a bull. Unfortunately for Perillus he was the first victim of his own contraption.

PERMESSUS: a river arising from Mt. Helicon, home of the Muses.

PERSES (PERSEUS): king of Macedonia who was defeated by Lucius Aemilius Paullus at Pydna in 168. He claimed descent from Achilles.

PHAETHON: putative son of the Sun (Helios) who tried to drive this god's chariot across the dome of heaven but was blasted from the chariot by a thunderbolt hurled by Jupiter. His sisters wept for him until they were metamorphosed into alders.

PHEMIUS: a bard in the *Odyssey* who entertained Penelope's suitors.

PHERAE: Thessalian kingdom of Admetus, whom Apollo served.

PHILETAS: scholar/poet from the island of Cos whom Propertius often mentions as one of his models.

PHILIPPI: a city in eastern Macedonia near the site where the combined forces of Mark Antony and Gaius Octavius (the future Augustus) defeated the armies of Marcus Iunius Brutus and Gaius Cassius Longinus, the assassins of Julius Caesar.

PHILIPPICS: gold coins, so called because they bore the image of Philip II of Macedonia, father of Alexander the Great.

PHILOMELA: see TEREUS.

PHINEUS: was persuaded by his second wife, Idaea, to blind his son by his first wife. In a case of "poetic justice" he himself was later blinded but given prophetic powers.

PHLEGRA: a plain in Thessaly, reputed area of the gigantomachy, the battle of the Olympians with the Giants; or an area west of Naples where there are numerous sulfur geysers near Lake Avernus.

PHOCEA: an Ionian settlement on the coast of Asia Minor that abandoned the city being besieged by Persians (534) and emigrated to Elea on the Italian coast south of Rome.

PHOEBE: daughter of Leucippus, sister of Hilaira, both abducted by the Dioscouri.

PHOEBUS (PHOEBE): the name(s) meaning the "shining one", applied to Apollo and Diana after the name of their grandmother Phoebe.

PHOENIX: falsely accused of rape by his father's mistress, he was blinded by his father.

PHRAATES: Parthian king who restored the Roman standards captured from Crassus at his disastrous defeat near Carrhae in 53.

PHTHIA: a city in Thessaly, reputed birthplace of Achilles.

PIERIA: a reference to Mt. Pierus in Thessaly, sacred to the Muses.

PINDAR: (518-438), Greek lyric poet from Thebes, famous for his odes celebrating athletes victorious at the various quadrennial games in Greece.

PINDUS: large mountain range between Thessaly and Epirus.

PIRITHOUS: king of Lapiths. He hosted a great celebration of his wedding to Hippodamia and invited certain centaurs. When one of the centaurs, Eurytion, became drunk and assaulted the bride, a fight ensued in which Eurytion was killed. Pirithous was a good friend of Theseus. When these two friends tried to abduct Proserpina from the underworld, they were caught and held fast.

PLAUTUS, TITUS MACCIUS: comic playwright from Sarsina in Umbria; twenty-one of his plays survive dating from 205-184, mostly modeled on plays of Greek New Comedy, but injected with much exuberant Roman material.

PLEIADES: see MAIA.

PLOTIUS: Marcus Plotius Tucca, a good friend of both Horace and Vergil, who along with Lucius Varius Rufus edited the *Aeneid* soon after Vergil's death in 19.

PO: the major river that snakes its way across northern Italy south of the Alps.

POLLIO, GAIUS ASINIUS: consul of 40, an adherent of Julius Caesar, then of Antony; he was a patron of poets and writer of tragedies and of history. He celebrated a triumph for a victory over the Parthini, a tribe on the east coast of the Adriatic Sea.

POLYHYMNIA: the muse of sacred song.

POMPILIUS: see NUMA.

PONTICUS: poet, friend of both Propertius and Ovid, who wrote an epic on Thebes.

PONTUS: the district in northern Turkey along the Black Sea.

PORSENA, LARS: an Etruscan king of Clusium (Chiusi) who briefly captured Rome after the expulsion of Tarquin the Proud.

POULYDAMAS: a friend and counselor of Hector.

PRAENESTE: a town in the Apennines about twenty miles east of Rome.

PRIAPUS: a fertility god, particularly worshipped at Lampsacus on the Hellespont, whose statues were painted red. The god was represented with a phallus or ithyphallic pruning hook, and the statues were regularly placed in gardens as apotropaic devices.

PROCNE: see TEREUS.

PROCYON: the brightest star in the constellation Canis Minor.

PROETUS: a king of Argos whose daughters were punished with delusion, imagining themselves as cows.

PROMETHEUS: after stealing fire from heaven Prometheus was punished by Jupiter; he was chained to a rock in the Caucasus where an eagle (or vulture) daily ate his liver, which then regenerated during the night. He was eventually freed.

PROTESILAUS: the first Greek fated to be killed at Troy. His wife, Laodamia, grieved so deeply for him that the gods permitted her to visit with the resurrected Protesilaus for three hours; after the expiration of the time, she committed suicide.

PROTEUS: a prophetic sea deity in charge of the creatures of the sea, particularly seals.

PTOLEMIES: the dynasty of rulers who claimed lineage from Philip, the father of Alexander the Great.

PUTEAL: see LIBO.

PYLADES: good friend of Orestes, who married Orestes' sister Electra.

PYRRHA: wife of Deucalion. The couple survived the Great Flood and landed their boat at Delphi on Mt. Parnassus.

PYTHAGORAS: sixth-century thinker who emigrated from Samos to Croton in southern Italy, where he founded a religious community. He and his followers believed in the transmigration of souls and led an ascetic lifestyle that included abstention from meat.

PYTHIAN: a common epithet and cult title of Apollo at Delphi deriving from the name Pytho, the huge snake guarding the site which Apollo slew. Apollo's priestess of the site was called "Pythia."

QUIRINUS: usually identified as the deified Romulus, but originally a Sabine god of the Quirinal Hill with attributes of Mars.

REGULUS, MARCUS ATILIUS: Roman general in the First Punic War. He and much of his army were captured by the Carthaginians in 258. He was sent back to Rome to negotiate a truce, but he advised against any peace. After he returned to Carthage, he was executed.

RHEA SILVIA: see ILIA.

RHESUS: king of Thrace, ally of Troy; he was killed by Diomedes and Ulysses during their night raid to steal his prized horses.

RHIPAE: mountain range in northern Scythia where the source of the Don is located.

RHODOPE: a mountain range in Thrace

SABAEA: a town in Arabia Felix (Yemen) famous for its perfumes.

SACRED WAY: the main avenue of the Roman Forum.

SALII: twelve priests of Mars who celebrated a yearly sumptuous feast in honor of the god. They were known for their energetic dance.

SAPPHO: (ca.600), great lyric poet of Lesbos.

SARMATIA(N): Indo-European nomadic people closely related to the Scythians, generally occupying areas east of the Tanais (Don). Some infiltrated into the region of the lower Danube.

SARPEDON: king of Lydia, ally of Troy in the Trojan War.

SCAMANDER: a river in the Troad which Achilles fought.

SCAURI: a prominent Roman family one of whose members, Marcus Aemilius Scaurus, distinguished himself against the Cimbri (102).

SCIPIO, PUBLIUS CORNELIUS (AFRICANUS): a) the conqueror of Hannibal in the Second Punic War, b) the general in charge of the Third Punic War. Both invaded Africa.

SCIRON: a legendary highwayman who terrorized travelers on the road between Athens and Megara. He forced his victims to wash his feet . As they were doing so, he kicked them over the cliff that bears his name.

SCRIBONIA: mother of Cornelia, wife of Lucius Aemilius Paullus Lepidus, and the former wife of Octavius/Augustus; she was the mother of Julia, Augustus' only child, and divorced by him in 39 on the day of Julia's birth.

SCYLLA: see NISUS.

SCYTHIA: an area north of the Black Sea between the Don and Carpathia, roughly modern Ukraine and Bulgaria.

SERES: the "silk people" i.e. the Chinese.

SERVIUS TULLIUS: sixth king of Rome who reputedly had been a slave; he was assassinated in a plot that involved his daughter Tullia.

SIBYL: prophetess of Apollo of Cumae who came to Tarquin the Proud, the last king of Rome, and sold him a collection of prophetic verses. The books were stored and guarded by priests and consulted only in time of perplexity or disaster.

SICYON: a city on the Corinthian Gulf renowned for its olives.

SIGAEUM: a town in the vicinity of Troy.

SILVANUS: Italic god of woods and forests.

SILENUS: tutor and attendant of Dionysus with satyr-like qualities but with the power to prophesy.

SIMOIS: a river in the Troad which Achilles fought.

SISTRUM: a type of rattle used in the rituals of Isis.

SISYPHUS: a man who tried to cheat Death, for which he was punished in the underworld by forever rolling a boulder up a hill, only to have it roll back down once he reached the crest.

SORACTE: a mountain about twenty miles north of Rome visible from the city.

SPARTACUS: a trained gladiator who led a major revolt of slaves and malcontents (73-71). He was defeated by Marcus Licinius Crassus, the triumvir.

SPERCHEUS: a river in Thessaly.

STRYMON: a river in Thrace.

STYX: the main winding stream of the underworld. The divine oath to this river was held to be inviolable; only lovers were exempt.

SUBURA: unfashionable district of Rome between the Viminal and Esquiline Hills.

SULLA: LUCIUS CORNELIUS: ruthless winning general of the Civil War (83-81) against the Marians. Although Sulla instituted some positive political reforms, his proscriptions and confiscations during his dictatorship (81-80) earned him opprobrium. Poets of the Augustan age often decried the horror of the civil war between Marians and Sulla and its subsequent massacres.

SULMO: a town located in a plain among mountains of the Abruzzi; the area was occupied by Paelignians, an early Italic tribe.

SYGAMBRI: a Germanic tribe that invaded Gaul in 16 and defeated a Roman army. They withdrew and sued for peace shortly thereafter.

SYPHAX: a Numidian king defeated and captured by the Romans in 203.

TAENARUS: a promontory in the Peloponnesus (Laconia) wherein a cave was reputed to be an entry to the underworld.

TANTALUS: stole food from the gods and had it distributed to mortal friends. For his offence he was condemned in Hades to stand in a pool of water with fruit hanging above his head; his attempts to drink and eat, however, were frustrated by the disappearance of the water and food.

TARENTUM: modern Taranto, wealthy city on the inner "heel" of Italy.

TARPA, SPURIUS MAECIUS: appointed in 55 by Pompey the Great to decide what plays could be performed.

TARPEIA/TARPEIUS: A Vestal Virgin who betrayed Rome to the Sabines for the love of Titus Tatius, the Sabine king warring against Romulus and the Romans. She gave her name to a spur of the Capitoline Hill from which traitors were thrown. Sometimes the "Tarpeian Rock" stood for the Capitoline as a whole.

TARQUINIUS: Lucius Tarquinius Superbus (Tarquin the Proud), the last king of Rome deposed by Marcus Iunius Brutus.

TARTARUS: the deep recess of the underworld where "sinners" are punished.

TATIUS, TITUS: king of the Sabines who warred against Romulus and the Romans and for a brief period of time shared power with Romulus.

TAURUS, TITUS STATILIUS: Augustan marshal who shared the consulship of 26 with Augustus.

TAYGETOS: a mountain ridge west of Sparta.

TEGEA: a town in Arcadia.

TELEPHUS: during the Trojan War Telephus, the king of Mysia, was wounded by Achilles and healed by scrapings taken from the offending spear.

TEMPE: a valley in Thessaly washed by the Peneus river, celebrated for its beauty.

TENEDOS: an island in the Aegean near Troy behind which the Greek fleet "hid" before the final assault upon the city.

TERENCE: Publius Terentius Afer; a comic poet whose six plays survive. He was patronized by prominent Romans, particularly Publius Cornelius Scipio (Aemilianus).

TEREUS: married Procne, the daughter of Pandion, king of Attica. Tereus violated Philomela, Procne's sister, and cut out her tongue. When Procne discovered Tereus' crime, she avenged herself upon Tereus by murdering their son Itys and serving him up to Tereus. Eventually, Tereus was transformed into a hoopoe, Procne a nightingale, and Philomela a swallow. Among Latin authors Philomela becomes the nightingale.

TETHYS: a Titan, early goddess of the sea and sea creatures.

THAMYRAS: a Thracian poet who challenged the Muses to a singing contest. When he lost, he was deprived of his eyes.

THERMODON: a river in Pontus on the Black Sea.

THULE: an island in the extreme north of Europe, sometimes identified as Iceland.

THURII: a town in southern Italy, formerly Sybaris, known for its prosperity, extravagant lifestyles, and lasciviousness.

THYMBRA: a district near Troy that had a famous temple of Apollo.

TIBERIUS: Tiberius Claudius Nero; the son of Livia, wife of Augustus. Adopted by Augustus in 4CE, he became emperor upon Augustus' death in 14CE.

TIBUR: modern Tivoli about twenty miles northeast of Rome.

TIGELLIUS, HERMOGENES: a) a famous musician in the time of Julius Caesar and Cicero, b) a singer/poet, contemporary of Horace.

TIMAGENES: (fl. 55), a Greek rhetorician of Alexandria who came to Rome. He was famed for his eloquence and stinging wit.

TIMAVUS: a river in northeast Italy.

TIPHYS: the helmsman of the Argo, the ship that carried Jason and his crew (Argonauts) in quest of the Golden Fleece.

TITANS: offspring of Earth (Gaea) and Heaven (Uranus), pre-Olympian gods who fought Jupiter and his allies in a mighty war (Titanomachy) which Jupiter won.

TITHONUS: mortal lover of Aurora (Dawn) who was immortalized but without perpetual youth.

TITYOS: a giant killed by Apollo and Diana because he tried to rape their mother Latona. In Tartarus he is confined to suffer forever a vulture eating his liver.

TLEPOLEMUS: king of Rhodes killed in the Trojan War by Sarpedon.

TMAROS: a mountain range in Epirus.

TMOLUS: a mountain in Lydia.

TRITON: son of Neptune and Amphitrite who controls the waters of the sea by blowing a conch shell.

TROILUS: young son of Priam brutally raped and killed by Achilles.

TULLUS: a friend of Propertius whose uncle Lucius Volcacius Tullus was consul in 33 with Octavius and proconsular governor of Asia in 30-29.

TULLUS HOSTILIUS: the third king of Rome.

TYNDAREUS: king of Sparta, mortal father of Helen, Clytemnestra, Pollux, and Castor.

TYPHOEUS (TYPHON): a polymorphous monster, offspring of Gaea and Tartarus, who challenged Jupiter to hand-to-hand battle for the rule of the universe. Jupiter defeated him and hurled his wrecked carcass to Tartarus.

TYRE: city of Phoenicia known for its production of dyed textiles and garments.

VACUNA: a local Sabine goddess.

VALGIUS, Gaius Valgius Rufus; an elegiac poet and member of the circle of Maecenas.

VALERIUS: a distinguished clan in Republican Rome. One member, Publius Valerius Poplicola, was instrumental in deposing Lucius Tarquinius Superbus, the last king of Rome, in 509. He served as consul in that same year.

VARIUS: Lucius Varius Rufus, an epic and tragic poet, and a good friend of Vergil and Horace. He assisted Plotius Tucca in editing the *Aeneid* after Vergil's death.

VARRO: Publius Terentius Varro of Atax, translated the *Argonautica* of Apollonius of Rhodes into Latin, and then turned to love poetry.

VARUS: a) Quinctilius Varus; b) Alfenus Varus, an adherent of Octavius who helped Vergil retain his ancestral farm.

VENAFRUM: a region in the mountains of south-central Italy.

VIRGIN MOUNTAIN: Mount Parthenius in Arcadia; also a reference to the Greek poet Parthenius and his Roman follower C. Cornelius Gallus.

VULTUR: a mountain in Apulia, close to Venusia where Horace was born.

XANTHUS: a river in the vicinity of Troy often identified with the Scamander.

XERXES: the Persian king who invaded Greece in 480; he dug a channel through the isthmus in Chalcidice.

XETHUS: see Amphion.

ZEPHYRUS: god of the West Wind.

SUGGESTED FURTHER READING

General

Chisholm, Kitty, and Ferguson, John. *Rome: The Augustan Age* (New York: Oxford University Press) 1991.

Galinsky, Karl. *Augustan Rome: An Interpretive Introduction* (Princeton: Princeton University Press) 1996.

Gurval, Robert Alan. *Actium and Augustus: The Politics and Emotions of Civil War* (Ann Arbor: University of Michigan Press) 1995.

Lyne, R. O. A. M. *The Latin Love Poets: From Catullus to Horace* (Oxford: Oxford University Press) 1980.

Southern, Pat. *Augustus* (New York: Routledge) 1998.

Wallace-Hadrill, Andrew. *Augustan Rome* (London: Bristol Classical Press) 1993.

White, Peter. *Promised Verse: Poets in the Society of Augustan Rome* (Cambridge, Mass.: Harvard University Press) 1993.

Zanker, Paul. *The Power of Images in the Age of Augustus*, trans. by Alan Shapiro (Ann Arbor: University of Michigan Press) 1988.

Vergil

Alpers, Paul J. *The Singer of the* Eclogues: *A Study of Virgilian Pastoral* (Berkeley: University of California Press) 1979.

Gale, Monica R. *Virgil on the Nature of Things: The Georgics, Lucretius, and the Didactic Tradition* (Cambridge: Cambridge University Press) 2000.

Johnston, Patricia A. *Virgil's Agricultural Golden Age: A Study of the* Georgics (Leiden, E. J. Brill) 1980.

Lee, M. Owen. *Death and Rebirth in Virgil's Arcadia* (Albany: State University of New York Press) 1989.

Lee, M. Owen. *Virgil as Orpheus: A Study of the* Georgics (Albany: State University of New York Press) 1996.

Miles, Gary B. *Virgil's* Georgics: *A New Interpretation* (Berkeley: University of California Press) 1979.
Perkell, Christine G. *Poet's Truth: A Study of the Poet in Virgil's* Georgics (Berkeley, University of California Press) 1989.
Ross, David O. *Vergil's Elements: Physics and Poetry in the* Georgics (Princeton: Princeton University Press) 1987
Thomas, Richard F. *Virgil and the Augustan Reception* (Cambridge: Cambridge University Press) 2001.

Horace

Armstrong, David. *Horace* (New Haven: Yale University Press) 1989.
Bowditch, Phebe Lowell. *Horace and the Gift Economy of Patronage* (Berkeley: University of California Press) 2001.
Commager, Steele. *The Odes of Horace: A Critical Study* (New Haven: Yale University Press) 1962.
Fraenkel, Eduard. *Horace* (Oxford: Oxford Clarendon Press) 1957.
Johnson, W.R. *Horace and the Dialectic of Freedom: Readings in* Epistles I (Ithaca: Cornell University Press) 1993.
Kiernan, V. G. *Horace: Poetics and Politics* (New York: St. Martin's Press) 1999.
McNeill, Randall L. B. *Horace: Image, Identity, and Audience* (Baltimore: The Johns Hopkins University Press) 2001
Oliensis, Ellen. *Horace and the Rhetoric of Authority* (New York: Cambridge Univeristy Press) 1998
Rudd, Niall. *The* Satires *of Horace* (Berkeley: University of California Press) 1982.

Propertius

Benidiktson, D. Thomas. *Propertius: A Modernist Poet of Antiquity* (Carbondale, Ill.: Southern Illinois University Press) 1989.
Hubbard, Margaret. *Propertius* (London: Duckworth) 1974.
Janan, Micaela. *The Politics of Desire: Propertius IV* (Berkeley: University of California Press) 2001.
Papanghelis, Theodore. *Propertius: A Hellenistic Poet on Life and Death* (Cambridge: Cambridge University Press) 1987.
Stahl, Hans-Peter. *Propertius: Love and War: Individual and State under Augustus* (Berkeley: University of California Press) 1985.
Sullivan, J. P. *Propertius: A Critical Introduction* (New York: Cambridge University Press) 1976.

Tibullus

Ball, Robert J. *Tibullus the Elegist: A Critical Survey. HYPOMNEMATA* 17 (Gottingen: Vandenboeck and Ruprecht) 1983.
Cairns, Francis. *Tibullus, a Hellenistic Poet at Rome* (New York: Cambridge University Press) 1979.
Lee-Stecum, Parshia. *Powerplay in Tibullus* (Cambridge: Cambridge University Press) 1998.

Ovid

Barchiesi, Alessandro. *The Poet and the Prince: Ovid and Augustan Discourse* (Berkeley: University of California Press) 1997.

Boyd, Barbara Weiden. *Ovid's Literary Loves: Influence and Innovation in the* Amores (Ann Arbor: University of Michigan Press) 1997.

Jacobson, Howard. *Ovid's* Heroides (Princeton: Princeton University Press) 1974.

Mack, Sara. *Ovid* (New Haven: Yale University Press) 1988.

Williams, Gareth D. *Banished Voices: Readings in Ovid's Exile Poetry* (Cambridge: Cambridge University Press) 1994.